# INTRODUCTION

## TO

## MASS COMMUNICATIONS

**FOURTH EDITION**

# INTRODUCTION
# TO
# MASS

DODD, MEAD & COMPANY
New York   1975

# COMMUNICATIONS

## FOURTH EDITION

**Edwin Emery**  *Professor of Journalism*
*University of Minnesota*

**Phillip H. Ault**  *Associate Editor*
*South Bend Tribune, Indiana*

**Warren K. Agee**  *Dean, Henry W. Grady School of Journalism*
*The University of Georgia*

ISBN: 0–396–06753–0

LIBRARY OF CONGRESS CATALOG CARD NUMBER: 72–12028

Fifth Printing

PRINTED IN THE UNITED STATES OF AMERICA

# Foreword to the Fourth Edition

The Fourth Edition of this book, like the earlier ones, is designed to give the reader a full description of the mass communications industries, to introduce him to all the areas of professional work in journalism and mass communications, and to illuminate for him the importance of the communicator in modern society. It thus seeks to give every reader a comprehensive picture of the mass media upon which he depends so heavily as a citizen, and for those who are considering careers in mass communications it offers detailed analyses of the communications agencies which seek their talents, updated to the 1970's.

Part I, "The Role of Mass Communications," is an introductory essay which describes briefly and simply the communication process and the role of the mass media in developing the political, social, and economic fabrics of a modern democratic society. In it, and throughout the book, the authors' aim is to answer in a positive, yet realistic, way the question: Is mass communications a desirable profession, important to society? One of the best replies to this question was given by the famous editor-publisher Joseph Pulitzer in 1904:

> Our republic and its press will rise or fall together. An able, disinterested, public-spirited press, with trained intelligence to know the right and courage to do it, can preserve that public virtue without which popular government is a sham and a mockery. A cynical, mercenary, demagogic press will produce in time a people as base as itself. The power to mould the future of the republic will be in the hands of the journalists of future generations.

The story of how the mass media came to occupy such a crucial role is told in Part II, "The Historical Perspective." One chapter reviews the unending battle to win and preserve the rights to print, to criticize, and to report the news. Another offers a comprehensive synthesis of the history of the print media, in terms of journalistic trends and the contributions of men who helped to shape the American newspaper and magazine. Added to this edition are sections dealing with the "New Journalism" and the black press. A third chapter traces in detail the relatively brief histories of radio, television, and film, focusing on the news and opinion roles of these essentially entertainment media.

The upsurge in criticisms of the mass media which characterized the late 1960's and early 1970's has caused the authors greatly to expand Part III, "Current Problems and Criticisms." The new or expanded materials in this section include such subjects as the following:

The credibility duel between the government and the media in the aftermath of Vice President Spiro Agnew's criticisms, including the "Pentagon Papers" case, "The Selling of the Pentagon" confrontation, and the subpoenaing of reporters by grand juries.

The public credibility of the media.

Pressures on the media occasioned by the powerful consumer movement, including proposals for "counter-advertising" on television and other restrictions on advertising.

The pressures brought by minority groups for fuller access to the airwaves, including broadcast license renewal challenges and attempts to influence program content.

Increases in minority employment by both print and broadcast media.

Anti-Establishment press trends, including the growth of the underground press, journals published by working newsmen criticizing media practices, advocacy journalism, and the new "reporter power" concept.

The growth of public broadcasting.

The problems of violence and good taste on the airwaves.

The coverage of demonstrations and political campaigns, including the McGovern-Nixon confrontation and the 1972 elections.

In this section also are found research findings and analyses of media performance, as well as internal and external efforts to improve the quality of the media.

The major section of the book is Part IV, "The Mass Communications Industries and Professions." Eleven chapters describe in detail how the mass media and related agencies are organized, their current sizes and roles, and opportunities and qualifications for those contemplating professional careers in them. The authors' aim is to present in each chapter a unified picture of a major area of communications work, and to note the interrelationships among the various media and among editorial, advertising, and management functions.

The descriptive materials and figures contained in these chapters have been brought up to date. The chapters introduce the reader to the various media and professional areas: the newspaper, at the weekly, small daily, suburban daily, and metropolitan levels; the magazine, including general and specialized periodicals, industrial editing, and free-lance writing; television and radio, including cable television and video-casette TV; press associations and feature syndicates; photographic communication; the film, including entertainment, documentary, industrial, and educational films, and film criticism; book publishing; advertising, including the media, agency, and company department fields; public relations and information writing; and the growing fields of mass communications research and education.

A selected, annotated bibliography is offered those readers who wish to explore further some of the many facets of mass communications.

Also available is a revised and greatly expanded instructor's manual, which contains study questions and projects printed in the first two editions of the text, as well as suggested lesson plans and examination questions. The manual incorporates a number of successful approaches to the study of mass communications provided by instructors who have taught the introductory course during the past decade or more and whose adoption of the book have made it the most widely used textbook in its field.

The book throughout represents a pooling of the professional media experience and scholarly interests of its authors, who wish to thank a number of individuals for their aid and interest in the project. Professor R. Smith Schuneman of the University of Minnesota wrote the chapter on photographic communication in consultation with the authors, and Professor Barbara McKenzie of the University of Georgia wrote the chapter on the film. Joining Professor Jack B. Haskins of the University of Tennessee in assisting the authors with the chapter on mass communications research was Professor Emery L. Sasser of the University of Georgia. Professor Leslie G. Moeller of the University of Iowa reviewed the entire manuscript for the first edition and made many valuable suggestions and criticisms; Professor Joseph A. Del Porto of Bowling

Green State University read galley proofs and made helpful comments. Dean I. W. Cole of the Medill School of Journalism, Northwestern University, contributed to the planning of the book in its earliest stages. Professors John T. McNelly of the University of Wisconsin and Hugh E. Curtis of Drake University supplied criticisms in preparation for the second edition. More than 100 journalism and communications professors offered suggestions and criticisms for the Third and Fourth Editions.

Among professionals in the mass media with whom the authors consulted were James A. Byron, general manager and news director, WBAP and WBAP-TV, Fort Worth; Andrew Stewart, president, Denhard and Stewart, advertising agency, New York; David F. Barbour, copy chief, Batten, Barton, Durstine & Osborn, Inc., Pittsburgh office; Chandler Grannis, editor-at-large, *Publishers' Weekly;* Earl J. Johnson, vice president, United Press International; William C. Payette, president, United Feature Syndicate, New York; K. P. Wood, vice president, American Telephone & Telegraph Company; and William Oman, vice president, Dodd, Mead & Company, Inc.

Professors of journalism or communications who proved helpful in contributing to or reviewing chapters of the book during the past decade were Milton E. Gross, University of Missouri; Max Wales and Warren C. Price, University of Oregon; R. C. Norris, Texas Christian University; James R. Young and William Robert Summers, Jr., West Virginia University; Baskett Mosse, Northwestern University; Scott M. Cutlip, University of Wisconsin; Henry Ladd Smith, University of Washington; Sam Kuczun, University of Colorado; Robert Lindsay, Harold W. Wilson, and Roy E. Carter, Jr., University of Minnesota; Dean John R. Wilhelm, Ohio University College of Communication; Michael C. Emery, San Fernando Valley State College; Emma Auer, Florida State University; Mel Adams, James E. Dykes, and Lee F. Young, University of Kansas; and James L. Aldridge, William S. Baxter, Worth McDougald, Ronald Lane, and Frazier Moore, University of Georgia.

The authors wish to thank all of these individuals, and others who have expressed their interest in the book since it first appeared 13 years ago. They hope that the many changes they have incorporated in this Fourth Edition will meet with the approval of all who read it.

EDWIN EMERY
PHILLIP H. AULT
WARREN K. AGEE

# Contents

## Part III   CURRENT PROBLEMS AND CRITICISMS

## Part IV   THE MASS COMMUNICATIONS INDUSTRIES AND PROFESSIONS

# INTRODUCTION
## TO
## MASS COMMUNICATIONS

# PART I

THE

ROLE

OF

MASS

COMMUNICATIONS

# Chapter 1

# Communication and the Mass Media

## THE IMPACT OF MASS COMMUNICATIONS

Men today learn almost everything they know through some medium of mass communications—television, radio, newspapers, magazines, books, and film. The classroom, the pulpit, and person-to-person contacts have lessened in importance as means of effecting either social stability or social change.

Instantaneously learning, men react with equal celerity. Wars, riots, changes of governmental policies—these and other actions of great import stem from the impact of news transmitted by the mass media.

Our environment, for better or for worse, is mass-media oriented. Television and radio programs are viewed and heard by almost everyone in the United States and by an increasing number in many foreign countries. Newspapers and magazines are read by the millions of issues. Books alter the goals of society, especially as they affect opinion leaders. Film speaks a universal language.

The challenge is clear: Mass communicators must be among our best educated, most responsible citizens. And every person must learn how to read, listen, and watch—critically and intelligently—so as to order his life most efficiently and satisfyingly.

Those who choose to report, interpret, and perform in the mass media can expect meaningful, often exciting, lives. As mass communicators, they will help shape our destiny.

Mass communicators, for example:

Bounce television signals and other information data off satellites whirling through space.

Report the achievements, and the transgressions, of men in public office.

Interpret the aspirations of all peoples, including minorities, for a better way of life.

Design a newspaper, magazine, book, film, or broadcast program so as to make people read, watch, and listen . . . and think and act.

Speed a press association report to millions within a matter of minutes.

Turn a public spotlight upon the activities of antisocial groups and individuals.

Persuade a community, state, or the nation to improve its educational programs, control air and water pollution, and build more efficient and safe transportation systems.

Advertise products and services, aimed at improving our standard of living and keeping our economy sound.

Entertain with movies, accounts of sports events, comics, stories of fact and fiction, and dramatic and musical programs of every sort.

In short, mass communications provides the very fabric with which our lives are ordered. Were mass communications suddenly to cease, our civilization would collapse. That is why this book was written: (1) To promote a better understanding of our world of mass communications, and (2) to inspire the brightest young men and women to seek socially useful and rewarding careers in a field whose importance is second to none.


## WHAT COMMUNICATION MEANS

Man has another fundamental need beyond the physical requirements of food and shelter: the need to communicate with his fellow human beings. This urge for communication is a primal one and, in our contemporary civilization, a necessity for survival.

Simply defined, communication is the art of transmitting information, ideas, and attitudes from one person to another.

Upon this foundation modern men have built intricate, many-faceted machinery for delivering their messages. The unfolding achievements of science are making this communication machinery more and more fantastic in its ability to conquer the physical barriers of our world. Our minds and our electronic devices are reaching into areas not considered even remotely possible by our grandfathers.

Men hurtling through space send back radio and color television reports of what they experience. Cameras mounted on space vehicles give us closeup televised photographs of the moon and the planet Mars and of men walking on the moon itself. Television programs are transmitted from one side of the world to another by bouncing their signals off a satellite in orbit. Each year brings additional wonders in the craft of communicating our messages. With computers and instantaneous transmission systems we are bending time and space to our will.

Yet all this costly structure is a meaningless toy unless its users have something significant to say. The study of communication thus involves two aspects—a broad comprehension of the mechanical means and, more important, an understanding of how men use these tools in their daily round of informing, influencing, inspiring, convincing, frightening, and entertaining each other.

Each of us communicates with another individual by directing a message to one or more of his senses—sight, sound, touch, taste, or smell. When we smile, we communicate a desire for friendliness; the tone in which we say "good morning" can indicate feelings all the way from surliness to warm pleasure, and the words we choose in speaking or writing convey a message we want to "put across" to the other person. The more effectively we select and deliver those words, the better our communication with him.

Contemporary society is far too complex to function only through direct communication between one individual and another. Our important messages, to be effective, must reach many people at one time. A housewife who is angry at high meat prices may talk to a half-dozen neighbors about organizing a boycott, but if the editor of the local newspaper publishes a letter she writes, she communicates her idea to hundreds of women in a fraction of the time it would take her to visit them individually. The politician running for the Senate spends much of his campaign time visiting factories and meetings, shaking hands with the citizens in the hope of winning their votes. He knows, however, that he can reach only a small percentage of the voters this way, so he buys time on television and radio to deliver his message to thousands of voters simultaneously. This is mass communication—delivering information, ideas, and attitudes to a sizable and diversified audience through use of the media developed for that purpose.

The art of mass communication is much more difficult than that of face-to-face discussion. The communicator who is addressing thousands of different personalities at the same time cannot adjust his appeal to meet their individual reactions. An approach that convinces part of his audience may alienate another group. The successful mass communicator is one who finds the right method of expression to establish empathy with the largest possible number of individuals in his audience. Although this audience may number in the millions, the contact fundamentally is between two individuals: the mind of the communicator must be in touch with the mind of each recipient. Successful mass communication is person-to-person contact, repeated thousands of times simultaneously.

The politician reaches many more individuals with a single television speech than he does through his handshaking tours, but his use of mass communication may be a failure if he is unable to project over the air the same feeling of sincerity and ability that he conveys through his handshake and smile.

Thus the mass communicator's task breaks down into two parts, knowing *what* he wants to communicate and knowing *how* he should deliver his message to give it the deepest penetration possible into the minds of his audience. A message of poor content, poorly told to millions of people, may have less total effective impact than a well-presented message placed before a small audience.

Every day each of us receives thousands of impressions. Many of these pass unnoticed or are quickly forgotten. The effectiveness of the impression is influenced in part by the individual's circumstances. A news story from Washington about plans by Congress to increase unemployment benefits raises hopes in the mind of the person who fears he is about to be laid off his job; the same dispatch may disturb the struggling small businessman who sees in it the possibility of higher taxes. The communicator's message has had differing effects upon these two members of the audience; it may have none at all upon another reader who is distracted somehow while scanning the newspaper or listening to a newscast.

Obviously the mass communicator cannot know the mental outlook and physical circumstances of everyone to whom his message goes. There are many principles and techniques he can use, however, to assure that his message has an effective impact upon the greatest possible number of individuals in the largest possible audience. Some of these he learns by mastering the basic techniques of journalistic communication (writing, editing, newscasting, graphic presentation, etc.); others he learns by studying the mass communication process and by examining the character of the mass media.

## THE COMMUNICATION PROCESS

Research men call our attention to four aspects of the communication process: the *communicator,* the *message,* the *channel,* and the *audience.* (In research language, the communicator is also known as the *encoder;* the message—whether words, pictures, or signs—becomes *symbols;* the channel, in the case of mass communication, is one of the mass *media;* the person in the audience is known as the *decoder.*) A properly trained communicator understands the social importance of the role he has undertaken and also knows what he wants to communicate as his message. He understands the characteristics of the channels (media) to be used and studies the varying interest and understanding levels of groups of people who make up the total audience. He molds his message to the style requirements of each channel he uses and to the capabilities of the audiences he is trying to reach. He knows about the limitations and problems which communication researchers have studied.

The communication process: Communicator (C) places his message in selected channel to reach audience (A) but is subject to "noise" interferences.

One of these is *channel noise,* a term used to describe anything which interferes with the fidelity of the physical transmission of the message (such as static on radio or type too small to be read easily); but broadly speaking, channel noise may be conceived of as including all distractions between source and audience. The professional communicator helps overcome its effects by attention-getting devices and by careful use of the principle of *redundancy* (repetition of the main idea of the message to make sure it gets through even if part of the message is lost).

A second kind of interference, called *semantic noise,* occurs when a message is misunderstood even though it is received exactly as it was transmitted. The communicator, for example, might use words too difficult for an audience member to understand or names unknown to him

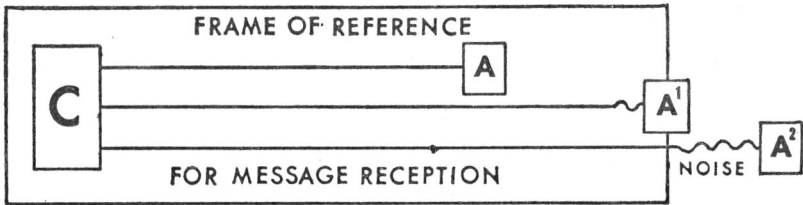

Communicator and audience member A have the same frame of reference; $A^1$ is only partially receptive; $A^2$ is unable to understand.

(material outside his *frame of reference*). Or the words used may have one meaning for the communicator and another for the listener or reader (the common or dictionary meaning is called *denotative,* the emotional or evaluative meaning is called *connotative*—a word like "socialist" has widely differing connotations). Semantic noise can be reduced if the communicator will take pains to define his terms and adjust his vocabulary to the interests and needs of the audience he wishes to reach. Sometimes, difficult or strange words are understood by the reader because he grasps the *context* in which they appear, but it is also possible for a poorly defined word to be misunderstood this way. And if the material presented is too complex, the reader either will be forced to *regress* and restudy the message or, more likely, will turn to some other more rewarding and pleasant material.

Even if the communicator has surmounted all these hurdles, he still has other problems in message reception. The receiver interprets the message in terms of his frame of reference, we have said. Each person has a *stored experience,* consisting in part of his individual, ego-related beliefs and values and in part of the beliefs and values of the groups to which he belongs (family, job, social, and other groups). A message which challenges these beliefs and values may be rejected, distorted, or misinterpreted. Conversely, a person whose beliefs on a given subject are under pressure may go out of his way to seek messages bolstering his viewpoint. In cases where beliefs are firmly fixed, the communicator finds it is often more effective to try to redirect existing attitudes slightly than it is to meet them head on. Another audience problem is called *dissonance.* This occurs when a person takes an action which is inconsistent with what he knows or has previously believed, or else acts after considering two or more attractive alternatives. He is uncomfortable until he achieves some dissonance-reduction by seeking out messages which help adjust his beliefs to his action (a familiar example is the man who, having bought one make of car from among several attractive ones, continues to read advertisements for the car he bought—if he has switched makes, he needs even more reassurance).

The communicator is aided in his work by what are called *feedback effects*. These are reactions which take place along the communication process and which are transmitted backward: by the communicator (reporter) to his original news source; by another media worker (editor) to the reporter; by members of the audience to the editor, the reporter, or the news source; and by different persons in the audience to each other. Obviously there is much more discernible feedback in person-to-person communication than in mass media communication, and thus a better opportunity to deliver a convincing message face to face. But the communicator who has knowledge of feedback reactions in mass communication and who solicits them may enhance the acceptance of his messages.

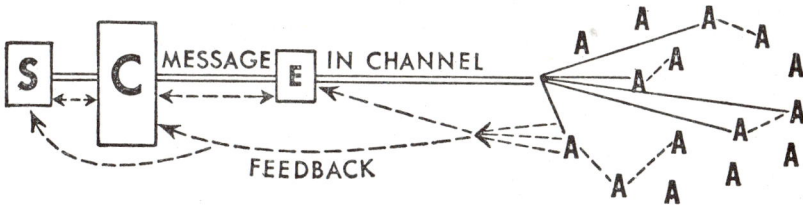

Mass communication for a given message at one moment in time is illustrated here: Source (S) has his message reported by communicator (C) in channel controlled by editor (E); some audience members (A) receive the message directly, others indirectly, but some are inattentive; feedback interactions may occur along the communication route.

All this is summed up in Professor Harold D. Lasswell's question: "Who, says what, in which channel, to whom, with what effect?" Chapter 18 on "Mass Communications Research" examines the different types of studies carried on by the mass media and by individual scholars to aid in more effective communication. The first steps for the would-be communicator, however, are to gain an understanding of the role of the communicator in our contemporary society and to examine the mass media through which audiences are reached. To take him through these steps is the purpose of this book.

## WHAT ARE THE MASS MEDIA?

A message can be communicated to a mass audience by many means: hardly an American lives through a day without feeling the impact of at least one of the mass media. The oldest media are those of the printed word and picture which carry their message through the sense of sight: the weekly and daily newspapers, magazines, books, pamphlets, direct mail circulars, and billboards. Radio is the mass communications medium aimed at the sense of sound, whereas television and motion pictures appeal both to the visual and auditory senses.

The reader turns to his newspaper for news and opinion, entertainment, and the advertising it publishes. In the weekly the focus is upon the reader's own community; in the daily the focus is upon the nation and the world as well. Magazines give him background information, entertainment, opinion, and advertising; books offer a longer range and more detailed examination of subjects, as well as entertainment; pamphlets, direct mail pieces, and billboards bring the views of commercial and civic organizations. Films may inform and persuade as well as entertain. Television and radio offer entertainment, news and opinion, and advertising messages and can bring direct coverage of public events into the listener's home.

There are important agencies of communication which are adjuncts of the mass media. These are (1) the press associations, which collect and distribute news and pictures to the newspapers, television and radio stations, and news magazines; (2) the syndicates, which offer background news and pictures, commentary, and entertainment features to newspapers, television and radio, and magazines; (3) the advertising agencies, which serve their business clients, on the one hand, and the mass media, on the other; (4) the advertising departments of companies and institutions, which serve in merchandising roles, and the public relations departments, which serve in information roles; (5) the public relations counseling firms and publicity organizations, which offer information in behalf of their clients, and (6) research individuals and groups, who help gauge the impact of the message and guide mass communicators to more effective paths.

Who are the communicators who work for and with these mass media? We think of the core as being the reporters, writers, editors, announcers, and commentators for newspapers, news magazines, television and radio, press associations, and syndicates. But there are many others: news photographers; book and publications editors and creative personnel in the graphic arts industry; advertising personnel of all types; public relations practitioners and information writers; business management personnel for the mass media; radio-television script and continuity writers; film producers and writers; magazine writers and editors; trade and business publication writers and editors; industrial publication editors; technical writers in such fields as science, agriculture, and home economics; specialists in mass communications research; and teachers of journalism. Actors in television and motion pictures also are communicators in a special sense, adding emotional impact to the written script.

## WHAT IS JOURNALISM?

A somewhat narrower definition is traditionally applied to the use of the mass media in order to identify the role of the journalist. In journalism there is an element of timeliness not usually present in the more leisurely types of writing, such as the writing of books. Journalism is a report of things as they appear at the moment of writing, not a definitive study of a situation. Historically the journalist has been identified by society as carrying out two main functions: reporting the news and offering interpretation and opinion based on news. A journalist may write an account that is entertaining as well as newsworthy; but a person who writes for sheer entertainment only, such as some television script writers, is not a journalist.

Periodical journalism constitutes the oldest and most widely identified area. Periodicals are printed at regular and stated intervals. To be considered newspapers, periodicals must appear at least weekly in recognized newspaper format and have general public interest and appeal. Commonly identified as "journalists" are the reporters, writers, editors, and columnists who work for newspapers, press associations and syndicates, news magazines, and other magazines devoted largely to public affairs. The print media they serve have been known collectively as " the press," although many newspapermen reserve that term for their medium.

News reporting and commentaries delivered by television and radio are equally a form of journalism, as are public affairs documentaries, direct broadcasts of news events, and filmed and videotaped documentaries. The reporters, writers, editors, and photographers in the television-radio-film area point out that the general descriptive term "the press" applies to them as well as to the print media men when they are dealing with news and opinion. But they tend more often to identify themselves with the name of their medium than with the collective word "journalist." So do others in the list of communicators given above—photographers, book editors, advertising men, industrial editors, and so on.

The ephemeral nature of journalistic writing does not mean that it is poor and careless writing, as is sometimes assumed. Quite the contrary is true in many cases. Journalistic writing is a contemporary report of the changing scene, intended to inform readers of what is happening around them. The impact of journalism can and often does influence the course of events being reported, because it brings public opinion into focus and sometimes creates it. Thus the newspaper and broadcast reports of a street or campus demonstration can touch off heavy unfavorable reaction among the citizenry and force a shift in local, state, or national policy.

The journalist deals in immediacy; he enjoys the stimulation of being close to events and the knowledge that his efforts can help shape the future. He is *communicating* the developments of the day to an audience whose lives are affected by the events he discusses. The sum total of articles printed in the continuing issues of a periodical constitutes a big slice of history as it is being made. Many of the facts reported in any issue soon are outdated by later developments; yet they are true at the moment of writing.

The television and radio journalist communicates news of contemporary events by means of electronic devices rather than with paper and ink. Although this makes the transitory nature of airwave journalism even more pronounced than that of the written word, it is not necessarily less effective and may often be more so. Events with strong elements of sound or sight, such as a forest fire, a football game, or a political convention, are especially well communicated by television and radio.

Dramatic evidence of how electronic and newspaper reporting can dominate the life of the world during a great crisis is found in the reporting of the assassination of President John F. Kennedy and Senator Robert

F. Kennedy and the astronauts' journey to the moon. Television, radio, and newspapers provided a massive portrayal of events and held the world tightly in the grip of intense emotion.

## ALL MEDIA ARE INTERRELATED

Trying to separate the various mass media into tight compartments is a futile task, and pointless, too. They are closely interrelated, both in functions and in personnel. Employees shift from one medium to another with comparative ease. Certain details of technique are different and must be learned by the newcomer, no matter how much experience he may have in other fields, but the principles of mass communication among humans are remarkably similar in all media.

The newspaper reporter who happens to have a good voice may become a radio commentator. He must learn to write his copy in a more narrative style to please the ear rather than the eye, but the precepts of objectivity, fair play, and persistent digging for facts he learned on his newspaper beat still apply. Press associations supply the same daily budget of world and national news to radio and television stations as to newspapers, although the reports are prepared in slightly different form to meet the technical requirements of the various media. The broadcaster may desire to see his viewpoint preserved in more durable form, so he writes a magazine article or a book. An author whose novel becomes a best seller may soon find himself in a Hollywood studio writing screen plays at a salary that startles him.

A hard line of demarcation between motion pictures and television was maintained by the film industry during television's early years immediately after World War II. The film makers feared the commercial competition of TV. Inevitably this separation broke down because the two media are linked so closely in their appeal and techniques. Hollywood studios which once put clauses in their stars' contracts forbidding them to appear on television now film dozens of TV shows on their sound stages and outdoor sets. Numerous prominent motion picture actors "break in" on television, then move into films. Scripts first shown to the public as TV shows have been successfully expanded into feature-length motion pictures. Newspaper publishers also own almost one-fourth of our television stations and almost one-tenth of our radio stations.

The mass media have a common need for men and women with creative minds, who can use words and pictures effectively to transmit information and ideas. This is true whether the communication is intended to enlarge the recipient's knowledge, entertain him, or convince him through advertising that he should purchase a commercial product or service.

Advertising is an essential part of the major media and constitutes an additional service to persons seeking that type of information. In newspapers and magazines, stories and advertisements appear side by side and are absorbed by the reader's mind almost simultaneously. On radio and television, presentation of the commercial has been developed into an intricate art, often closely integrated with the entertainment portion of the program which the advertiser also controls. At times, unfortunately, more ingenuity and effort go into the commercial than into the program itself. Large national advertisers conduct sales campaigns for their products in the press and on the air at the same time, spending huge sums to make certain that their messages reach a mass audience as frequently as possible. They are employing the proved technique of repetition. Without advertising revenue, newspapers and magazines could not be sold at their present prices and radio and TV programs could not be provided without charge.

Also, advertising has an important function in attracting an audience for the various media. The film studios, theatres, and television producers are heavy advertisers in newspapers and magazines, and newspapers take commercial time on radio and television to publicize their features in an effort to build circulation. Public relations men and women provide a steady stream of stories, photographs, and motion picture film for use by the mass media.

Thus it is evident that the mass media are heavily dependent upon each other. They turn to common sources for talent, for news, for ideas, and even for ownership. In the early days of radio, newspapers feared that the competition of this swift news-dispensing medium would ruin them; when television came along, newspapers, magazines, and motion pictures all were frightened of it at first. Gradually they learned that there is room and a need for all and that no medium need ruin another. The older media had to develop fresh techniques to meet the newcomer's challenge, and they improved themselves in doing so.

In the United States the mass media are commercial ventures, without government subsidy, and survive only if they make money. This is in the best tradition of the free enterprise system. They compete with each other for the audience's time and the advertiser's dollar. Yet all realize that basically they are serving the same purpose—to provide a transmission belt for the free flow of ideas.

# Chapter 2

# *The Social Importance*

# *of Communicators*

## THE COMMUNICATOR'S TASK

Recording history as it happens is an exciting assignment. In this day of almost instantaneous mass communications, members of the mass media are doing even more than recording history; they are helping to shape it. The responsibility is stimulating. From its practitioners, mass communications work demands broad knowledge, sound judgment, quick decisions, and the realization that the words they write or speak may influence the lives of many millions of people.

This sense of influence and responsibility extends to others in mass communications work than those dealing with breaking news. Their opportunities to reach wide audiences and to affect attitudes may be as great. Perhaps all this sounds overwhelming, and in some ways it is. But an intelligent, college-educated man or woman who approaches the job with a proper sense of ethical responsibility and adequate knowledge of the basic techniques will find the work satisfying, mentally and financially, and at times truly exciting.

There is the excitement of creative accomplishment: writing a series of stories exploring the successes and failures of a ghetto youth club project; helping to entertain a nation with a television program and having millions adopt a line like "sock it to me" as their own; writing a story for *Esquire* interpreting the personality of a noted musician; helping to solve a marketing problem for a great industry through an advertising campaign, or coming up with the magic of a slogan like "We try

16

harder"; shooting a photo series that catches the hopes and feelings of the participants in an "Upward Bound" program.

There is the additional sense of participation felt by those handling the flow of the day's news. Their reporting and commenting take many forms: it may be a television reporter's on-the-scene description of a forest fire as massive flames illuminate the sky behind him, a newspaper writer's word-for-word account as the jury delivers the verdict in a murder trial, a radio newsman's summary of the world's main news developments packed tightly into a five-minute period, or an editorial writer's analysis of the forces shaping a foreign policy decision by the President of the United States. Just as important, it may be a conference by the little-publicized men behind the news, the editors. They must decide which stories in the day's flow of events deserve the most prominent place in print or on the air. Or it may be a political news writer patiently checking the advance text of a prominent political leader's speech against its actual delivery to see whether he has inserted an unscheduled piece of major news. That is exactly the way President Lyndon Johnson unexpectedly informed the world that he would not run for reelection in 1968 at the height of the Vietnam conflict.

Mass communications work is not always exciting. To pretend that it is would be misleading and unrealistic. As in any business, there are hours of routine, often repetitive work. A solid, disciplined routine and a well-defined set of operating principles underlie everything. What makes news work so intriguing, however, is that exciting events may break loose at the most unexpected moment. Then, in an instant, the newsman's training, experience, and judgment are called into action. The instantaneous quality of radio and television has added even greater challenges for all those seeking to provide fair and objective presentation of news.

Throughout the mass media of communication, the challenge of social responsibility is felt by those at work. Frequently their judgment is tested under pressure in matters of taste, social restraint, and fairness, with few absolute rules to guide them. The jobs they perform make possible the general diffusion of knowledge about life in today's world and, more than that, influence many aspects of our social, political, and economic patterns. By the way they select and present information, they help in sometimes small, sometimes unintentional, ways to shape our society.

Our mass media illuminate the social fabric of the nation. They are essential to the continued development of the economic fabric in a modern industrial state. And they continue to fulfill their historic role in protecting and improving the political fabric of a democracy. Among the many opportunities enjoyed by the communicator, none is more important than the opportunity to help shape public opinion.

## COMMUNICATION, PUBLIC OPINION, AND DEMOCRACY

Public opinion is the engine that keeps the wheels of democracy turning. Although we elect public officials to conduct our government's business and give them power to make decisions controlling our lives, we do not let them exercise arbitrary power as leaders do in a dictatorship. They are restrained by the influence of public opinion, the very instrument that put them into office. This public opinion is expressed primarily through the news media. If the official strays too far from the desires of the mass of the public, counterforces go to work. The most potent and obvious of these is the threat of defeat at the next election, a fact always near the surface of a professional officeholder's mind. More subtle forms of pressure also may be applied by adverse public opinion, such as moves to restrict his power, damage his prestige, or discredit him in public.

Those mass media which do not deal in the urgency of spot news— books, most magazines, and films, and a large portion of radio and television programs—also are vital in the formation of public opinion. They examine vital contemporary issues in a reflective manner that is possible because their writers and editors have more time to consider the ramifications of events. Social attitudes and political viewpoints can be examined with telling impact through fictional narrative as well as by factual reporting.

Sometimes an excessive amount of time is required to correct a flagrant misuse of governmental authority, but ultimately it is almost always accomplished. In the long run, a democracy gets the kind of government that the majority of its people desires. To be successful, a political leader must convince the voters (1) that he represents the viewpoint of the majority, or (2) that his policies are wise and should be endorsed by the voters.

How is public opinion brought to bear in political affairs, above and beyond the impact of events themselves? This is a complicated process insofar as arrival at a decision on an issue or an election contest is concerned. The average person is likely to be affected more strongly by social pressures, group associations, and the attitudes of "opinion leaders" he knows than by direct use of the mass media. Since the social group and the opinion leader also reflect information and opinions gained from the mass media, there is a close interrelationship among the three—the mass media, opinion leaders, and the social group—in the decision-making process.

But whatever other forces come into action, it is clear that the mass media of communication have a key role in the building of the political fabric of a democracy. They are the widely available channels through which political leaders express their views and seek to rally public backing for their policies. The President of the United States makes a statement in a press conference, and within minutes the news is sped around the world by the press associations and broadcasters. President Franklin D. Roosevelt found his famous "fireside chats" on radio during the 1930's to be an effective tool in winning support for his economic reforms and later in alerting the American people to the dangers of fascist aggression. Development of television gave later presidents even greater access to the American mind. President John F. Kennedy used live televised news conferences with exceptionally good effect because of his easy delivery and quick wit. On the other hand, President Lyndon Johnson failed to develop an empathy with millions of Americans in his television appearances. His personality was not conveyed well by the cameras, coming into many homes as cold, calculated, and less than candid. This intangible weakness on television contributed to charges of a "credibility gap" that undermined his power in the later years of his term.

The media also work in the reverse direction to bring the officials news of what the people think and desire. Newspapers publish stories reporting the viewpoints of political opponents and the actions taken in public meetings concerning government policy; on their editorial pages they express their own reactions to developments and make suggestions; frequently newspapers publish the interpretative comments of well-known columnists. In the columns of letters to the editor the readers express their views. Still another form of expression appearing in the press is the public opinion poll, such as the Gallup poll or the Roper survey, in which carefully selected samples of the population are invited to give their views on timely issues.

Television and radio help to publicize this interplay of opinion through news reports similar to those appearing in the newspapers, interviews, and panel discussions. An especially effective television technique is found in programs such as "Meet the Press," in which a public official submits to intensive and sometimes belligerent questioning by a group of newsmen.

Weekly news magazines have become a significant factor in the two-way transmission of political policy and reaction. With more leisurely deadlines than the daily newspapers have, these periodicals provide background for the news developments and seek to put them into context. Magazines of opinion examine the news critically and express their views on its meaning, much as newspaper editorials do; whereas scholarly periodicals published at intervals of a month or longer delve more deeply into specialized aspects of the contemporary scene.

Books, particularly the heavy-selling paperbacks, convey facts and opinion about public candidates and officeholders. In many respects the paperback, often heavily subsidized and promoted by political factions, has replaced the political tract, such as Thomas Paine's *Common Sense* (1776), which was widely circulated in an effort to influence public opinion.

The political education role of the mass media reaches into the local scene, as well. If, for example, a municipal government decides to put into effect a new system of one-way streets, it turns to the newspapers, television, and radio for help in publicizing the plan. The newspapers publish charts of the new traffic routing and explanations of the streets along which cars are to move. The mayor broadcasts an explanation of the changes, and the stations repeat the instructions in their newscasts. TV viewers are shown pictures of the new routes, perhaps with cartoon figures being depicted following them. By the day the traffic plan goes into effect, a large majority of the motorists who customarily drive in the area are aware of the enforced change in their motoring habits. Without such publicity, there would have been a chaotic traffic tie-up of bewildered, angry motorists.

The publicity process is of tremendous importance to public officials. Many of them owe their success in winning office to well-organized and cleverly conducted publicity campaigns. Some officials try to control the opinions of the citizens by manipulating and restricting the release of government information, with the hope that they can create a carefully calculated public image of a problem. If this image can be made to appear authentic, their own political solutions for the problem will seem more desirable; but if all the facts are made available to the voters, quite a different solution may seem best. Too many public officials are special pleaders for their own causes.

If political leaders attempt this approach, and many of them do, how does the public obtain the rest of the essential facts? It must depend largely upon the investigative work of the news media, which should be—and usually are—dedicated to the cause of putting the complete story before the public.

The fight for free access to the news, from the national level in Washington down to the city hall in a small municipality, has become a major concern of the mass media. They are aware of the tendency among officials to make themselves "look good" by releasing and emphasizing facts favorable to their cause—the paper curtain of official mimeographed handouts which often stands between the public and the entire story. Diligent editors and commentators work on the principle that the public is entitled to all the facts in a political situation and that, on the basis of these facts, it can make its own decisions.

The news media also have the vital role of "watchdog" over the government, searching out instances of malfunctioning and corruption. Without the searching eyes and probing questions of reporters, the public would have far less control over the affairs of city, state, and national governments than it does. Many significant congressional investigations have been started as the result of revelations in the press. High government officials have been forced to resign because a reporter has uncovered evidence of unethical and sometimes illegal conduct by them.

Once a bad situation is exposed, public opinion can quickly be brought to bear for reform; but without the watchful eyes of newsmen to disclose the misbehavior, the situation might remain uncorrected indefinitely. Generally, the news media have been less zealous in observing the misdeeds of shady business enterprises, even when these have affected the general public welfare, than they have been in watching over the government.

Plainly, then, in a democracy the press is the "market place" of political thought. The policies and aims of government are made known through the channels of the press and are examined exhaustively by opposition political figures, and by commentators, editors, and the public at large. Stories from the newspapers and newscasts are used as the basis for discussions in classroom and clubs. When a high government official wants to test the public reaction to a policy idea, he often sends up a "trial balloon" in the form of a guarded newspaper interview suggesting the possible advantages of such a step, or he has a friendly columnist discuss the advisability of the move. Other editors and commentators pick up the proposal and examine it in print or on the air. Soon millions of Americans are aware of the tentative plan and are expressing either favorable or negative opinions. The official and his staff keep close watch on this reaction. If the plan encounters heavy opposition, perhaps stirred up by an antagonistic pressure group, the official quietly abandons it; but if it receives popular support, he takes positive steps to put it into operation, either by legislation or executive order. It is in such ways that public opinion shapes governmental policy in a democracy. Note the contrast in a dictatorship, where the ruling clique issues decrees arbitrarily and enforces them regardless of the public's feelings.

## COMMUNICATIONS AND THE ECONOMIC FABRIC

Without an extensive and swift system of mass communications, the economic life of a major industrial country cannot function properly.

When we think how large the continental United States is—more than 3000 miles in width and covering many kinds of terrain, population, and living conditions—the degree of economic cohesion is remarkably high. People in the deserts of Arizona drive the same kinds of automobiles, wear the same makes of shoes, and eat the same brands of breakfast food as their fellow Americans in chilly New England. They are able to do so because of two major factors in contemporary American life—good transportation for moving the goods from the factory and a highly developed system of advertising and marketing.

Students of mass communications should be very conscious of the role and influence of advertising. It informs readers and listeners about the products the manufacturer and merchant offer for sale; it influences them by stimulating their desire for those commodities; and, if it is successful, it convinces them that they should purchase the goods as soon as possible or as soon as they are needed.

Ever since this country was founded, Americans have lived in an expanding economy, except for a few temporary periods of depression. As the population grew and pushed westward, it automatically created a need for goods and services. But, if Americans had not learned to want the products of factories, population growth itself would not be sufficient to keep the nation's industrial plants growing and its economy expanding. Americans' desire for new products and their demonstrated willingness to purchase them encourage producers to develop attractive new commodities. With few exceptions, companies which spend money to advertise their goods become larger and more profitable than their competitors who do not. This lesson has been driven home so firmly that modern business practice leads most successful companies to expend fixed percentages of their income upon advertising. The advertising budget has become as essential in a company's financial operations as money designated for salaries, factory operating expenses, and distribution of the products.

It is no exaggerated claim for advertising to state that it has played a major role in the steady rise of the American standard of living, which has now risen to the highest point of any country in history. The existence of a free enterprise economy such as ours without advertising is inconceivable.

From the consumer's standpoint, the rival advertising of competing companies increases his range of choice and actually saves him time and money. From reading or viewing the advertising for new automobiles he learns what new features each line of cars offers and sees photographs in color of the body designs. If his personal inclinations and the influences of his social group have given him a casual, indefinite idea of trading in his old car for a new one this year, the advertising brings him into action. He visits the showrooms of the cars which attract him most, and the chances are good that he will come home with a purchase contract in his pocket.

On a smaller scale, the dollars-and-cents importance of advertising in everyday living is evident if we watch a housewife read the grocery ads in her newspaper. She builds her weekend shopping list from these announcements. One market offers a special price on soap, another nearby market lists a bargain on pork roast. She decides to shop first at the market offering the pork roast, but may also visit the store featuring a special price on soap. Without advertising the housewife might have found these bargains by a prolonged search among the shelves, if she had the time. Or she might have missed them and paid full price for the roast at still another market. By checking the advertisements, she can shop more rapidly and effectively, and with an actual saving of money.

How does the food store benefit if it spends money on advertising to attract a shopper who buys goods at special low prices, thus reducing the shop's profit margin on those items? The answer to that question contains the secret of price advertising. The housewife saves money on the advertised items but having been attracted to the store by them, she is beguiled by point-of-purchase displays of additional items she hadn't realized she desired, and she buys these, too. The advertisement creates foot traffic in the market, and it is an axiom of merchandising that the more traffic that goes through a store, the more goods are sold. These additional purchases beyond actual realized needs help build our expanding economy.

Advertising in the United States is divided into two broad categories, national and local. National advertising is used by manufacturers to inform a nationwide audience, or perhaps a large regional one, about the advantages of their products. Sometimes a company devotes its advertising space to creating an image of itself in the public mind, emphasizing its reliability, friendliness, or public service, rather than concentrating upon a direct selling message for its products. This is institutional advertising, whose results cannot be measured directly upon a sales chart. Large corporations also use institutional advertising to influence public opinion on matters of national economic policy which are important to them. National advertisers use television, magazines, newspapers, and radio for the bulk of their advertising. Placement of the advertising campaigns is done through large advertising agencies, many of which have their head offices along Madison Avenue in New York City; these agencies earn their money principally by receiving a percentage of the price charged by the media for their space and time.

Local advertising is placed by merchants in their community newspapers and on their television and radio stations. It is directed to a well-defined, easily comprehended audience. Rarely does local advertising appear in magazines, because few periodicals have sufficient circulation concentrated in a single community. Chain-store merchandisers also use direct mail to distribute hundreds of thousands of advertising pieces called "mailers" at bulk rates. Sometimes these multiple-page advertisements are published simultaneously in newspapers. Whereas the main function of national advertising is to present products to a huge audience and to stimulate buying interest in them, local advertising is largely concerned with direct sales, making the cash register ring. Emphasis upon price is much greater in local advertising copy, because an attractive price is often the stimulus that converts the potential customer from intention to action.

The automobile manufacturer introduces his new models in the autumn with an elaborate national network television program featuring famous entertainment personalities and glamorous shots of the automobiles surrounded by beautiful girls. That is the national approach. A few days later the community auto dealer purchases time on his home-town television station. He appears on the screen, fondly patting the fender of a new model, and tells each viewer, "You can have this beautiful car for only $500 down. Come in and see it tonight; we are open until 9 p.m." That is the local follow-up.

A department store may take a half-page advertisement in a local newspaper just to publicize a bargain price for nylon hose. It knows that the expenditure will be profitable if the advertisement is attractive enough to draw a throng of women into the store. The item chosen is a low-cost one, regarded by most women as a necessity, with a frequent replacement need. Thus, if it is sufficiently attractive, thousands of feminine readers almost automatically are potential customers for such a sale.

At the end of the day the department manager can tell exactly how many pairs of stockings have been sold and compare this with a normal day's total. Thus he can measure the pulling power of his advertisement. However, the item may have been priced so low that, with the cost of the advertising added, the store may have lost money on the nylon hose sale. The venture would still be regarded as highly successful, however, if a large percentage of the sale shoppers bought additional unadvertised merchandise while they were in the store.

The mass media, then, play key roles in the business life of the country, at both the national and local levels of production and sales, by providing channels for advertising messages. They also help in other ways to shape the economic fabric of the country. They bring people, from industrial leaders to laborers, the necessary information upon which their business and personal decisions are based. They help the public to crystallize its attitudes on matters of national economic policy. They serve as sounding boards of public opinion for business, labor, agriculture, and other segments of society. Deprived of rapid and effective mass communications, a country whose sections and people have become as closely interdependent as ours would quickly tumble into economic and social chaos.

## THE MASS MEDIA AS SOCIAL INSTRUMENTS

So far we have looked briefly at the mass communicator's role as a transmitter of political opinions in a democracy and in promoting the country's economic growth. Equally vital is his work in reporting the swiftly changing American social customs and opinions.

The upheaval that struck many aspects of American life during the past decade was abundantly reported and analyzed in the news media. Indeed, television, radio, newspapers, magazines, and books were responsible for publicizing such phenomena as the miniskirt, leading to its adoption even by women whose desire to be fashionable was stronger than the warnings they saw in the mirror. The outburst of college protests and violence could be traced from campus to campus by televised and printed news stories. Within a few hours methods used by protestors in one part of the country were adopted on other campuses thousands of miles away. The techniques of racial protest could be traced from city to city in much the same manner.

Even the increase in public use of language previously considered indecent and the growing interest in displays of public nudity have been reflected in the news media. Notably, however, newspapers are far more cautious in their use of increasingly uninhibited visual and spoken material than magazines, books, motion pictures, and the stage.

Virtually no aspect of our habits, desires, and relationships escapes examination in our public media. As the years have passed, discussion has become increasingly frank; for better or worse, the evasions have all but disappeared. Some portions of the mass media have forced this trend while others have followed reluctantly.

Our curiosity about each other as individuals is intense. We want to know how the other man lives. We chuckle at the ludicrous situations in which fellow humans involve themselves, and we read with sympathy of their tragedies. No matter how sternly he may deny it, every person has a little of the back-fence gossip in his soul. He likes to peek into the lives of others, whether for mere satisfaction of his curiosity or for the higher purposes of social research. As we absorb our daily quota of stories, abundantly provided by the media, we are, without fully realizing it, receiving a multicolored picture of the contemporary social scene. The news media are the recorders of day-by-day history on a broader scale than ever before. Historians who try to reconstruct life in the centuries before there were newspapers would give much to have similar material available about those days.

Always in news coverage there is the underlying pressure of the necessity for speed. Few mass media workers enjoy the luxury of philosophical reflection in tranquility. Theirs is a "now" business. Decisions must be made quickly, often when all the facts are not yet available. The deadline is ever-present—most urgently for press association, daily newspaper, and television newsmen, but to a lesser degree for others, too. Mass communications work is for men and women who can think rapidly, act decisively, and report the world with clarity and compassion.

# PART II

# THE
# HISTORICAL
# PERSPECTIVE

# Chapter 3

# *Theories and Realities*
# *of Press Freedom*

## SOCIETY'S CRUCIAL FREEDOMS

The history of journalism and of the development of the mass media begins with the story of man's long struggle for personal liberty and political freedom, upon which the freedom to write and speak depends. Without that freedom, the magic of print and electronic technologies is of no value to free minds. One basic tenet of Anglo-American society has been freedom to print without prior restraint. How fragile such concepts are became apparent in 1971 when, for the first time in the history of the American republic, a President sought to impose prior restraint upon his country's newspapers. He succeeded for 15 days. And while then overruled, he clouded the future of press freedom. The roots of this 1971 Pentagon Papers case are found in the historic duel between the people's press and the people's governors.

Five centuries ago the printing press began to revolutionize man's ability to communicate information and ideas. But almost from the moment Johann Gutenberg introduced movable type to the western world, around 1440 in Germany, barriers were erected against its use to influence public opinion through the free flow of news and opinion. In the English-speaking world printers and writers struggled until 1700 to win the mere right to print. They fought for another century to protect that liberty and to win a second basic right: the right to criticize. Addition of a third right—the right to report—came equally slowly and with less success. Today's journalist knows that there remains a constant challenge to the freedoms to print, to criticize, and to report and that therefore the people's right to know is in constant challenge. This is true in the democratic western world where freedom of the press is a recognized tenet as well as in the larger portion of the world where it is denied. And it is true of the twentieth-century additions to the printing press: film, radio, and television.

Freedom of the press is intertwined with other basic freedoms. These are freedom of speech, freedom of assembly, and freedom of petition. Upon these freedoms rest freedom of religious expression, freedom of political thought and action, and freedom of intellectual growth and communication of information and ideas. A society possessing and using these freedoms will advance and change as it exercises democratic processes. Very naturally, then, these freedoms will come under attack from those opposed to any change which might diminish their own power or position in society—today as in past eras. The press, occupying a key role in the battle for these basic freedoms, is a particular target. To the closed mind, the press always has been a dangerous weapon to be kept as far as possible under the control of adherents of the status quo; to the inquiring mind, it has been a means of arousing interest and emotion among the public in order to effect change.

The social and political environments of the past five centuries have produced two basic theories of the press. The older we call the Authoritarian theory. The controlled society of the Renaissance era, into which the printing press was introduced, functioned from the top down; a small and presumably wise ruling class decided what all of society should know and believe. This authoritarian concept of the relationship between man and the state could brook no challenge from those who thought the rulers were reflecting error, not truth. Publishing therefore existed under a license from those in power to selected printers who supported the rulers and the existing social and political structure. The authoritarian press theory still exists today in those parts of the world where similar controlled societies are dominated by small ruling classes. A variant of this theory, called the Soviet Communist theory of the press by the authors of *Four Theories of the Press* (Fred S. Siebert, Theodore Peterson, and Wilbur Schramm; University of Illinois Press, 1956), arose with the twentieth-century dictatorship. Whether fascist or communist, it exalts the state at the expense of individuals and its government-owned and party-directed press is dedicated to furthering the dictatorship and its social system.

As the western world advanced through the Renaissance and Reformation into the democratic modern era, the second basic theory of the press developed. This we call the Libertarian theory. Its roots extend back into the seventeenth century but it did not become dominant in the English-speaking world until the nineteenth century. In libertarian theory, the press is not an instrument of government nor a spokesman for an elite ruling class. The mass of people are presumed able themselves to discern between truth and falsehood, and having been exposed to a press operating as a "free market place" of ideas and information, will themselves help determine public policy. It is essential that minorities as well as majorities, the weak as well as the strong, have free access to public expression in the press of a libertarian society.

In the battle against authoritarianism, the printer gradually became an ally of thinkers and writers who struggled for religious, political, and intellectual freedom and of the rising commercially based middle class which demanded economic freedom and political power in its contest with feudalism. Slowly the journalist evolved as one with dual functions to exercise: the opinion function and the news function. His media were the printed broadside and the pamphlet before he developed regularly issued newspapers in an established format. These appeared on the European continent before 1600, in England after 1622, and in the American colonies after 1704. In the eighteenth century they were joined by the early magazines. By our standards early newspapers were poorly printed, haphazard in content, and limited in circulation. But their influence can be measured by the amount of effort expended by those in authority to erect barriers against them and the stimuli to thought and action they contained. The traditions of freedom their printers and editors won by breaking down the barriers in the seventeenth and eighteenth centuries are the heritage of the modern newspapers and magazines developed in the nineteenth and twentieth centuries and of the film and electronic media of our times.

It was John Milton in his *Areopagitica* of 1644 who argued against repression of freedom of expression by advocating reliance upon truth: "Let her and Falsehood grapple: who ever knew Truth put to the worse in a free and open encounter?" Those who are afraid of truth will of course seek to prevent its entrance into a "free market place of thought," but those who believe in the public liberty should realize that its existence depends upon liberty of the press. Thomas Jefferson put it well in a letter to his friend, Carrington, in 1787:

> I am persuaded that the good sense of the people will always be found to be the best army. They may be led astray for a moment, but will soon correct themselves. The people are the only censors of their governors; and even their errors will tend to keep these to the true principles of their institution. To punish these errors too severely would be to suppress the only safeguard of the public liberty. The way to prevent these irregular interpositions of the people, is to give them full information of their affairs through the channel of the public papers, and to contrive that those papers should penetrate to the whole mass of the people. The basis of our government being the opinion of the people, the very first object should be to keep that right; and were it left to me to decide whether we should have a government without newspapers, or newspapers without a government, I should not hesitate a moment to prefer the latter.

Jefferson qualified his final statement, however, by adding: "But I should mean that every man should receive those papers, and be capable of reading them." Jefferson used the word "reading" because the problem of absolute illiteracy still was a major one in his day; he meant also "understanding" in the sense of intellectual literacy. In these words of Milton and Jefferson are found the libertarian arguments for freedom of printing and other forms of communication, for freedom to criticize, and for freedom to report. They also argue for public support of the kind of mass media which carry out their responsibilities to provide free flow of news and opinion and to speak for the people as "censors of their governors." The ability of journalists to discharge their responsibilities to society is conditioned, as Jefferson warned, by the level of public education and understanding; there is a public responsibility in this regard implied in this philosophic statement of the role of press liberty in supporting all of society's crucial freedoms.

There is also a public responsibility, and a journalistic one, to maintain the libertarian theory that everyone can be freely heard in the press, through a variant concept called the Social Responsibility theory of the press. Today it is no longer economically feasible for anyone so minded to start printing or airing his views. Concentration of much of the mass media in the hands of a relatively few owners imposes an obligation on them to be socially responsible, to see that all sides of social and political issues are fairly and fully presented so that the public may decide. The social responsibility theory contends that should the mass media fail in this respect, it may be necessary for some other agency of the public to enforce the "market place of ideas" concept.

## THE RIGHT TO PRINT

William Caxton set up the first press in England in 1476. It was more than 200 years later, in 1694, before freedom to print without prior restraint became a recognized liberty of the English people and their printer-journalists.

Prior restraint means licensing or censorship before a printer has a chance to roll his press. Unauthorized printing in itself becomes a crime. Under our modern concept anyone is free to have his say, although he stands subject to punishment if what he prints offends society (obscenity, sedition) or harms another individual (libel). Authoritarian government does not care to grant this much freedom; it wishes to control communication from the start and to select the communicators.

Caxton printed the first books in the English language and otherwise aided in bringing the culture of the Continent to England. He enjoyed royal support and needed subsidizing by the ruling class since his market was so limited by illiteracy. He and his successors improved the quality and volume of printing during the next half-century, which saw the rise of the Tudor dynasty. Henry VIII, in his efforts to grasp absolute power, issued a proclamation in 1534 requiring printers to have royal permission before setting up their shops. This was a licensing measure, imposing prior restraint. Except for short periods, the theory of prior restraint remained in effect in England until 1694.

Henry VIII took other measures to control the press, including banning foreign books, issuing lists of forbidden books, and punishing ballad printers who offended Henry and his powerful Privy Council. But neither he nor Queen Elizabeth I was able to frighten all the printers and writers into compliance. After 1557 the Stationers Company, an organization of the licensed publishers and dealers, was given power to regulate printing and to search out bootleg jobs which had not been registered with it. Severe penalties for unauthorized printing were imposed in 1566 and 1586, in the latter year by the authority of the infamous Court of the

Star Chamber. But despite arrests and smashing of presses of unlucky printers, some defiance always remained.

The struggle between the rising commercial class and the crown, which broke out into revolution in 1640 and brought the establishment of the Commonwealth in 1649 by Oliver Cromwell, gave printers some temporary freedom. James I and succeeding Stuart kings found that Puritan opposition was increasingly difficult to contain, and the journalists were more alert to their opportunities. Public interest in the Thirty Years' War on the Continent and in other political and economic affairs inevitably brought increased publication. Nathaniel Butter, Thomas Archer, and Nicholas Bourne produced the first regularly issued news book in 1621, on a weekly basis. Containing translated news from European news sheets, it was called a coranto. Diurnals, or reports of domestic events, appeared first as handwritten newsletters and later, after the Long Parliament raised the crown's ban on printing in 1641, in print.

But freedom was short-lived. By 1644 Milton was protesting against new licensing laws. After the execution of Charles I in 1649, Cromwell and his Puritan regime permitted only a few administration publications, censored by none other than Milton. The return of the Stuarts under Charles II in 1660 merely brought a switch in the licenser and censor to the royal party and more strict repression of unauthorized printing. Noteworthy, however, was the founding of the court newspaper, the London *Gazette,* in 1665. It remains today the oldest English newspaper.

The decline of the Stuarts, preceding the Revolution of 1688 which brought William and Mary to the throne, restored freedom to printers. Parliament allowed the licensing act to lapse in 1679. It was revived temporarily but finally died in 1694. Though severe seditious libel laws remained, and taxes on print paper and advertising were to be instituted beginning in 1712, the theory of prior restraint was dead. Newspapers by the score appeared in London, among them the first daily, the *Daily Courant,* in 1702. The early eighteenth century saw a flowering of newspapers and popular "essay" papers, edited by such figures as Daniel Defoe, Richard Steele and Joseph Addison, and Samuel Johnson.

Licensing and the theory of prior restraint did not die immediately in the American colonies. The Puritans imported the first press to New England in 1638 to print materials for their schools and Harvard College. Commercial presses followed, and some news broadsides and pamphlets appeared. In 1690 a refugee editor from London, Benjamin Harris, issued the first number of a Boston newspaper, *Publick Occurrences,* but his frank reporting nettled the colonial governor and council, which promptly ruled him out for not having a license. When the postmaster, John Campbell, brought out the first regular weekly paper, the Boston *News-Letter,* in 1704, he voluntarily trotted to the authorities for advance censorship and put "Published by Authority" at the top of his columns. It was not until 1721, when James Franklin began publishing his famed *New England Courant,* that a colonial editor printed in defiance of authority.

Freedom to print became an accepted principle in America; nine colonies had already provided such constitutional protection by 1787, when the Constitutional Convention met in Philadelphia. Many felt it was a state matter, but when the Bill of Rights was added to the Constitution, the First Amendment included freedom of the press among the basic liberties which Congress could not violate. Under British Common Law and American judicial interpretation, prior restraint violates press freedom. Suppression of publications in anticipation of wrongful printing, or licensing measures to control those who would publish, cannot be authorized by the Congress. In 1931 the Supreme Court for the first time applied the press guarantees of the First Amendment to the states, through the due process clause of the Fourteenth Amendment. The ruling came on an appeal against suppression of a Minneapolis news sheet under the Minnesota "gag law" of 1925 permitting suppression of malicious and scandalous publications. The court held the Minnesota law unconstitutional because it permitted prior restraint and said that those damaged by the newspaper had proper recourse through libel action.

There was a flaw in the courts' protection of the press, however. Was the prohibition of prior restraint absolute? When the New York *Times* in 1971 began publication of a summary of the secret Pentagon Papers laying bare U.S. decisions to escalate the Vietnam War, the government won a temporary restraining order prohibiting more stories. Shaken, the newspaper attorneys retreated, arguing only that the government had failed to show a danger to national security. The Supreme Court agreed, 6–3, but legal scholars warned that the ban on prior restraint could not be considered absolute. Part III will examine reasons for this setback.

The Post Office Department, with its power to exclude publications from the mails under certain conditions, has given publishers the most censorship troubles. Matters came to a head in 1946 after the department sought to withdraw use of the second-class mailing rate from *Esquire* magazine on the grounds that the rate was a privilege intended only for those making a "special contribution to the public welfare." *Esquire,* faced with an additional half-million dollars a year postal bill, appealed to the Supreme Court, which ruled in its favor. The court commented, "But to withdraw the second-class rate from this publication today because its content seemed to one official not good for the public would sanction withdrawal of the second-class rate tomorrow from another periodical whose social or economic views seemed harmful to another official." The decision put the Post Office back to judging specific issues on the basis of obscenity or inclusion of illegal news of lotteries.

The motion picture industry instituted its own regulatory code in 1922, as a form of self-censorship, through the Motion Picture Association of America. Even before that date, state and city censorship boards were exercising precensorship functions by viewing and clipping films in advance of movie showings, or banning them, a practice still continuing even though increasingly challenged as unconstitutional by the courts. Extralegal pressures have been brought by such unofficial groups as the former Legion of Decency. The same informal pressures have affected book publication and book purchases by public libraries and school systems. In addition, book publishers run the risk of having specific volumes barred from the mails as obscene. By drawing a line between material merely objectionable and that violating the courts' tests for obscenity, court decisions since the 1950's have tended to clip the powers of those seeking to restrict films and books. But the guidelines and the outer limits of the courts' thinking are still obscure. As the 1970's opened, scholars in the area felt there were virtually no restrictions against material presented to adult audiences but that the courts would draw a line protecting minors—a conclusion that a welter of "adult" movies, books, and magazines seemed to prove.

Radio and television, like the printed media, are not subject to precensorship. But more charges of "censorship" are raised in their cases, with the objection being to self-censorship or control of content in anticipation of adverse reaction. The broadcast media are more sensitive on this score because their managers realize that violations of what is considered to be "good taste" might cause difficulties for an individual station with the Federal Communications Commission under broadcasting licensing provisions.

If history has proved licensing to be a dangerous practice inimical to press freedom, why did the American public agree to licensing of radio and television stations? The answer is that by common consent we have recognized that broadcast channels are in the public domain. Congress in 1912 first legislated that the Department of Commerce should issue licenses to private broadcasters and assign them wave lengths so that they would not interfere with government wave lengths. During World War I all wireless operations were put under government control, but by 1919 private broadcasters were again experimenting. Numbers of stations increased rapidly and chaos developed on the air waves. The radio industry, the National Association of Broadcasters, the American Newspaper Publishers Association, and other groups petitioned the government for relief.

This came from Congress through the Radio Act of 1927 which established a five-man commission to regulate all forms of radio communication. The government retained control of all channels, granting three-year licenses to broadcasters "in the public interest, convenience, or necessity" to provide "fair, efficient, and equitable service" throughout the country. Federal authority was broadened in 1934, with establishment of the seven-man Federal Communications Commission to exercise jurisdiction over all telecommunications. The responsibility of the license holder to operate his station in the public interest was more clearly spelled out. The commission was given the power to refuse renewal of a license in cases of flagrant disregard of broadcasting responsibility, but the FCC rarely has used this power. The law forbids any attempt at censorship by the commission; no station can be directed to put a particular program on or off the air. But the FCC undeniably is able to exercise indirect pressure upon license holders, who are understandably wary of its ultimate powers. FCC insistence upon stations building some record for broadcasting in the public interest has led to attention to news and public affairs programs; on the other hand, the licensing problem has led to broadcasters dragging their feet in airing controversial issues.

American radio and television are as free as American newspapers and magazines to provide whatever news their news editors see fit. Radio and television have also widely broadcast the opinion programs of individual commentators. But they have been reluctant until recently to broadcast opinion as that of the station itself. The FCC in 1941 issued a ruling that "the broadcaster cannot be advocate"; then in 1949 the commission decided that stations could "editorialize with fairness" and urged them to do so. Many broadcasters felt they did not have the trained manpower to do effective editorializing or did not wish to identify the station management as an advocate in controversial situations, and 20 years later only a little more than half of the stations were broadcasting editorial opinions (see Chapter 10).

## THE RIGHT TO CRITICIZE

Winning the liberty to print without prior restraint did not free the press from the heavy hand of government. In eighteenth-century England, and in the American colonies, the laws of seditious libel ran counter to the philosophical theory that the press should act as "censor of the government." To the authoritarian mind, the mere act of criticism of officials was in itself a crime, and "the greater the truth, the greater the libel" was an established tenet. This meant that publishing a story about a corrupt official was all the more seditious if the official indeed was corrupt.

The journalist's problem was to establish the principle of truth as a defense against charges of sedition or criminal libel. Mere fact of publication then would not be sufficient to determine guilt, and the accused printer or editor would be able to present his case in open court, preferably before a jury. Once the principle of truth as a defense could be won, governments would be less likely to press sedition charges, and laws defining what constitutes sedition could be revised.

The landmark case in what is now the United States was that of John Peter Zenger, who was tried in New York colony in 1735 for seditious libel. Zenger was an immigrant printer who lent the columns of his weekly paper, the *Journal,* to the cause of a political faction opposed to the royal governor. Some of the leading citizens of the colony were aligned with Zenger in the struggle against the governor, whom they accused of various arbitrary actions in the *Journal's* columns. Zenger was jailed and brought to trial in a hostile court. At this juncture a remarkable 80-year-old lawyer from Philadelphia, Andrew Hamilton, entered the case as Zenger's attorney.

The crown prosecutor reviewed the laws of seditious libel and argued that since Zenger had admitted publishing the newspaper issues in question, the trial was as good as over. His aged opponent skillfully tilted with the presiding justice and the prosecutor and insisted that truth should be permitted to be offered as a defense, with the jury to decide upon the truth of Zenger's publications. These arguments were denied by the court, but Hamilton ignored the ruling and delivered a stirring oration to the jury. He ended with a plea for the jury to take matters into its own hands; "The question before the court . . . is not just the cause of the poor printer. . . . No! It may in its consequence affect every freeman . . . on the main of America. It is the best cause; it is the cause of Liberty . . . the liberty both of exposing and opposing arbitrary power . . . by speaking and writing Truth."

Zenger was acquitted, and the court did not challenge the jury's verdict, even though it ignored existing law. A similar court victory on the issue of admission of truth as evidence was not won in England itself until the 1770's. The threat of trials for seditious libel remained until the end of the century, although in the colonies no further court trials of editors were held. Some editors were harassed by governors and their privy councils, but in general the colonial press was free to criticize the English authorities and to promote the cause of American independence (the reverse was not true, however, and Tory editors were suppressed by colonial radicals). By the early 1770's such papers as the Boston *Gazette* were openly seditious in their attacks upon constituted authority, but they continued to appear and to fan the fires of revolution.

Once the revolution was won, there was sharp cleavage along political and economic lines in the new nation. The newspapers continued to take pronounced partisan stands, accompanied by abuse and vituperation. The two political factions, the Federalists headed by Alexander Hamilton and the Republicans headed by Thomas Jefferson, split on many domestic issues and particularly over the country's emotional reaction to the French Revolution. Most of the weeklies and the few dailies which had started after 1783 were published in seaboard towns for the commercial classes and tended to be Federalist in sympathy. Hamilton sponsored some party organs in addition: John Fenno's *Gazette of the United States,* Noah Webster's *American Minerva,* and William Coleman's New York *Evening Post.* Topping the Federalist editors in partisan criticism was William Cobbett with his *Porcupine's Gazette.*

Jefferson countered with Philip Freneau's *National Gazette* and also had other Republican supporters, including William Duane and Benjamin Franklin Bache at the *Aurora.* The impulsive Bache, grandson of Benjamin Franklin, more than matched Cobbett in vituperative criticism. When it appeared that war with France was imminent in 1798, the Federalists decided to crack down on their tormentors.

The Alien and Sedition Acts they passed in 1798 were aimed at deportation of undesirable aliens and at curbing criticism of the government. Undesirable aliens in Federalist eyes were those who supported Vice-President Jefferson; some were déported and others were harassed. The Sedition Act by its terms restricted prosecutions to those who "write, utter, or publish . . . false, scandalous and malicious writing" against the federal government, its officials and legislators, or its laws (including the Sedition Act itself). It provided for admission of truth as a defense. In theory, only false criticism was to be punished; but in practice, Federalist politicians and judges set out to punish anti-Federalist editors. One, for example, was jailed and fined for printing a letter to the editor which accused President John Adams of "ridiculous pomp, foolish adulation, and selfish avarice."

Vice-President Jefferson, fearful for his own safety, retired to Monticello, where he and his supporters drafted the Virginia and Kentucky Resolutions, advocating the theory of nullification by the states of unconstitutional acts of the Congress. But the issue did not need to be joined; Federalist excesses in administering the Alien and Sedition Acts contributed to a popular revulsion and to Jefferson's election as President in 1800. The dangerous Alien and Sedition Acts expired the same year. Jefferson insisted that his administration permit partisan journalism, "to demonstrate the falsehood of the pretext that freedom of the press is incompatible with orderly government." He urged that individuals protect themselves against journalistic excesses by filing civil suits for libel. The calm course Jefferson took was vindicated when his party retained control of the government for a generation. Party newspapers, with one-sided news and fiercely partisan opinion, continued to flourish, but after the great crisis of 1798 no federal administration attempted to repress criticism. Soon after 1800 the libertarian theory of the press had eclipsed the authoritarian theory by common consent.

During wartime, national safety requirements and emotional feelings bring some restriction of criticism. The Civil War saw suppression of a few newspapers in the North, but considering the violence of many editors' criticisms, retaliation by Lincoln and his generals was almost negligible. During World War I, the Espionage Act of 1917 widened the authority of the Post Office Department to bar periodicals from the mails, and the Sedition Act of 1918 made it a crime to write or publish "any disloyal, profane, scurrilous or abusive language" about the federal government. The axe fell heavily upon German-language newspapers, in many cases unfairly. It also fell upon Socialist magazines and newspapers, because they opposed the war, and upon pacifist publications. Max Eastman's brilliant magazine, *The Masses,* was barred from the mails, as were two leading Socialist dailies, the New York *Call* and the Milwaukee *Leader.* Socialist party leader Eugene Debs went to prison for criticizing America's allies as "out for plunder." Clearly the theory of liberty to criticize was disregarded in these violations of minority opinion rights. During World War II only a few pro-Nazi and Fascist publications were banned—and they had few friends to plead their cause.

The right to criticize needs constant protection, as was demonstrated when Louisiana political boss Huey Long attempted to punish newspaper opponents through taxation. Long and his political machine imposed a special tax on the advertising income of larger Louisiana dailies, virtually all opposed to him. The Supreme Court held the punitive tax unconstitutional in 1936. In the early 1950's courageous newspapers and magazines which spoke out against Senator Joseph McCarthy of Wisconsin, and what became known as McCarthyism, were harassed and denounced. But neither McCarthy nor his followers could bring about actual legislation restricting criticism, much as they might have liked to do so.

Contempt-of-court citations bring about another kind of clash over the right to criticize. A series of Supreme Court decisions in the 1940's widened the freedom of newspapers to comment upon pending court cases and actions of judges. This was done by applying the "clear and present danger" theory to a judge's contention that administration of justice was being impeded by newspaper comment. But judges have great power in contempt-of-court matters, and editors remain wary of criticizing their acts without pressing need to do so.

## THE RIGHT TO REPORT

The right to report is not nearly as much a right safeguarded by law and legal precedent as the right to print and the right to criticize. Rather, it is based on a philosophical argument. What would be gained through the right to print and to criticize if no news were forthcoming? What good would a free press be for the reader if editors and reporters had no way to find out what government was doing? Denial of the right of access to news is a denial of the people's right to know, the journalist maintains.

Yet, no person can be compelled to talk to a reporter; no government official need grant an interview or hold a press conference; courts and legislatures admit the press through historical tradition and have the power to eject the press (unless specific statutes have been passed requiring open legislative sessions). There is another side to the coin: no newspaper can be compelled to print any material it does not wish to use, including paid advertising.

While the laws of seditious libel were in vogue, no right to report was recognized. The mere reporting of a government official's action, or of a debate in Parliament, was likely to be construed as seditious (unfavorable) by some person in authority. William Bradford in Pennsylvania, James Franklin in Massachusetts, and other colonial editors were haled before authorities for reporting a disputed action of government. In England, reporting of the proceedings of Parliament was banned until 1771, when the satirical writings of Dr. Samuel Johnson and the open defiance of newspaper publisher John Wilkes crumpled the opposition.

The House of Representatives of the American Congress opened its doors to reporters in 1789, two days after it was organized as a legislative body. The Senate, however, excluded reporters until 1795. Congress came to depend upon newsmen, particularly the editors of the Jeffersonian party organ, the *National Intelligencer,* to publish a record of debates and proceedings. Not until 1834 did the government publish its own records.

Today there is little likelihood that the Washington correspondents will be denied access to the congressional press galleries, except when the legislators are meeting in emergency executive session (a rare event). But reporters are admitted to sessions of legislative committees only upon the willingness of the committee chairman and members. Some 40 per cent of congressional committee sessions were closed to the press in the 1960's. The situation in state capitals is similar. Television and radio reporters and photographers have won access to legislative sessions only by persistent effort, and their ability to use all their equipment is often circumscribed.

Reporters similarly are admitted to court sessions only by the agreement of the presiding judge. They may be excluded, with other members of the public, if the court deems it necessary. Juvenile courts, for example, operate without reportorial coverage in most cases. Ordinarily reporters are free to attend court sessions, since public trials are the rule, but they have no automatic right of attendance. Photographers and TV-radio men have had only spotty success in covering trials with cameras and microphones, due to restrictions applied to them by Section 35 of the Canons of Judicial Ethics of the American Bar Association. A long campaign by the National Press Photographers Association, the Radio-Television News Directors Association, and the American Society of Newspaper Editors to persuade the bar association to revise its Canon 35 failed when that group reaffirmed its stand in 1963. In 1972 the association approved and submitted for endorsement a replacement for Canon 35 in a form (Canon 3A7) that was equally as restrictive. The objections centered on the grounds of distracting participants, impairing the court's dignity, and influencing proceedings by concurrent media use.

An important doctrine which has grown up is the doctrine of qualified privilege. This provides that a news medium in reporting the actions of a legislative body or a court is free of the threat of libel suits provided its report is accurate and fair. This doctrine carries with it the implication that the media have an obligation to report legislative and judicial sessions so that the public may know what government and courts are doing. Defamatory statements affecting the reputations of individuals made in legislative sessions and courts may therefore be reported without fear of damage suits.

The right to report is denied more often at the "grass roots" level of government than at the national level, insofar as legislative bodies are concerned. Boards of education, water commissions, city councils, county boards, and other similar groups often seek to meet in private and conduct the public's business in virtual secrecy. Newsmen wage an unending battle against this practice, without much avail, unless the public demands its right to know. Some newsmen accept the practice and forfeit their right to report the news firsthand, thereby forfeiting their most important right as journalists. Passage of "open meetings" laws in an increasing number of states during the 1950's, at the insistence of various news groups, somewhat improved the access to news at the local level. These laws provide that actions taken in closed sessions are invalid; but they do not force a reluctant legislative group to open the doors wide. By 1972 there were 42 states with "open meetings" laws and 43 with laws guaranteeing opening of public records to reporters needing access to them.

Perhaps the most publicized denial of access to news has been in the national executive departments. This increasing trend—stemming from the necessity for secrecy in limited areas of the national defense establishment and atomic energy research—has alarmed responsible editors and newsmen. The American Society of Newspaper Editors and the professional journalistic society, Sigma Delta Chi, have well-organized campaigns demanding free access to news so that the people may know the facts necessary to make intelligent decisions.

Appointment of a House subcommittee headed by Representative John Moss of California, in 1955, to study the information policies of the government brought some relief. The Moss committee has acted as the champion of the people's right to know and the reporter's right of access to news. By publicizing executive department refusals to make information available on public matters, the Moss committee has forced some reforms, including passage of the Freedom of Information Act of 1966 giving the citizen legal recourse against arbitrary withholding of information by a federal agency. But Washington correspondents say they are fighting a losing battle against administrative orders which forbid federal employees from talking to newsmen and employ other devices to keep an executive department's actions secret unless the administrator deems it desirable to make them public. In this battle, as in others involving the right to report, the newsman's best weapon is the power of the press, which is in turn based on the pressure of public opinion. Reporters who are determined to find out the facts can usually prevail over reluctant public officials.

# Chapter 4

# *Growth of the*
# *Print Media*

## THE BASIC EDITORIAL FUNCTIONS

Newspapers, despite their impact on society, have a relatively brief historical tradition. Two hundred and fifty years ago there was but one struggling weekly in the colonial outpost of Europe which was to become the United States. It was only about 125 years ago, in the 1830's and 1840's, that the "penny press" dailies ushered in America's first era of popular journalism, made famous by James Gordon Bennett and his New York *Herald,* Horace Greeley and his New York *Tribune,* and Henry J. Raymond and his New York *Times.* Bennett taught others how to search out and report the news; Greeley fashioned an editorial page; Raymond put his emphasis upon news interpretation. With their contemporaries and successors they laid the foundations for present-day American journalism.

The basic journalistic principles thus espoused were further advanced before the nineteenth century had ended by such noted publishers as Joseph Pulitzer, Edward Wyllis Scripps, and Adolph S. Ochs. The goals were two in number. The primary goal was ever-increasing concentration of effort on impartial gathering and reporting of the news and its comprehensive display. The other was demonstration of responsible opinion leadership, provided both through an intelligently written editorial page and integrity and zealousness in telling the news.

As even the colonial editor knew, however, there is a third editorial function of the press and that is to entertain the reader, as well as to inform and instruct him. What is called "human interest" news—stories with appeal based on writing skill rather than necessarily upon news value—has always been in great reader demand. Sensational news—stories involving the human passions, crime, and violence and spicy accounts of the doings of the famous—is likewise age-old in its appeal. The newspaper has also always contained a budget of nonnews material: short stories and other literary content (more prevalent a century ago than today), comics and Sunday feature sections (favorites since the 1890's), advice to the lovelorn (highly popular for early eighteenth-century readers), and a host of varying entertainment items.

The responsibility of any of the mass media has been to strike a balance among the functions of informing, instructing, and entertaining. The newspaper, as it reached out for mass circulation, sought to fulfill the first two functions in more popularized ways: a more readable writing style, skillful use of human interest elements in news, better makeup and headline display, effective pictures, color. Such popularizing, in the interests of appealing to the entertainment desire, need not detract from the newspaper's social usefulness. There is no reason why the "hard news" of political and economic importance should not be presented as interestingly as possible and in company with other less important, but more attractive, ingredients. But there is a line to be drawn. Overemphasis on sensationalism at the expense of news and a lavish dressing up of purely entertainment features are merely cheapening, not popularizing.

How well American newspapers have responded to these basic principles over the decades is a matter of judgment. One thing is certain; they responded differently, for there is no such thing as a "typical newspaper" to analyze any more than there is a typical magazine, television or radio station, or book publishing house. What can be measured is the response made by the leaders in different historical periods, as they reshaped their journalistic products to fit the demands of their times and the desires of their audiences. As the sociologist Robert E. Park put it: "The newspaper has a history; but it has, likewise, a natural history. The press, as it exists, is not, as our moralists sometimes seem to assume, the willful product of any little group of living men. On the contrary, it is the outcome of a historic process in which many individuals participated without foreseeing what the ultimate product of their labors was to be. The newspaper, like the modern city, is not wholly a rational product. . . . it has continued to grow and change in its own incalculable ways."

## THE COLONIAL PRESS

**Early concepts of news.** Reporting, as defined today, means gathering information of interest to other people and presenting it to them accurately in a way which makes them understand and remember it. This definition is broad enough to fit all media of information and comprehensive enough to provide a measuring stick for present and past performance.

The first newspaper publishers were primarily printers, not editors. The majority had a sense of what interested people, but only a few had real reportorial instincts. Only a few, too, were good enough writers to tell their stories in an interesting way. Since their access to news was severely limited, and inadequate transportation and communication facilities made the collecting of news a very haphazard business, they scarcely could be expected to be either complete or accurate in their reports. But even so, very few made any move to go out and find the news; they ran what came over their doorsteps or what could be gleaned from other newspapers and periodicals, particularly those coming from London. None had local news reporters as we know them today. Nevertheless, what meager news and entertainment they offered were eagerly devoured by their readers, who had little other choice.

James and Benjamin Franklin were early publisher-printers who were also journalists. James, in his *New England Courant*, gave Boston readers of the 1720's the first readable and exciting American newspaper. He printed news, despite the opposition of Puritan political and religious authorities, and covered local issues in a dramatic and crusading fashion. He and his contributors, including his younger brother Ben, wrote well and the paper had high literary qualities, modeled on the successful "essay" papers of Joseph Addison and Richard Steele in England. Personality sketches, feature stories, and human interest material lightened the pages. Benjamin Franklin carried on the traditions in his *Pennsylvania Gazette*, editing his meager scraps of news more cleverly than did his rivals and offering more substance.

During the Revolutionary War period, publishers such as Benjamin Franklin and Isaiah Thomas of the *Massachusetts Spy* were alert to forward the patriot cause, but even as well-to-do a publisher as Thomas did not attempt to have his own correspondent with Washington's army. The paper nearest to the scene of an event covered it; other papers copied the report or relied upon official announcements, messages sent to their local authorities from military and governmental headquarters, and reports of travelers.

**The political pamphleteers.**    Throughout the eighteenth century the political pamphleteer was more important than the editor-printer. Three examples from the years preceding the Revolution are John Dickinson, Samuel Adams, and Thomas Paine—all well-known in the pages of American history, and all of whom used the newspaper of their day as a vehicle to reach the public.

John Dickinson of Pennsylvania, an articulate spokesman of the colonial Whigs, wrote his series of "Letters from a Farmer in Pennsylvania" for the *Pennsylvania Chronicle* of 1767–1768. Dickinson was opposed to revolution and was actually a spokesman for the business class and its Whig philosophy rather than for the agrarian class. But he and the colonial Whigs could not afford to let the British Whigs impose commercial restrictions that were harmful to American interests. The mercantile system, preventing development of colonial industry and trade, and taxation measures imposed by a Parliament in which the colonial Whigs were not directly represented were threats which Dickinson could not ignore. His forceful arguments for home rule helped swing Americans of his economic group to the revolutionary cause after it became apparent that compromise was no longer possible.

Samuel Adams, the great propagandist of the Revolution, belonged to the Radical party. Only briefly an editor himself, he worked with the group of Boston patriots assembled in the office of the Boston *Gazette* including the publishers, Benjamin Edes and John Gill, and the engraver, Paul Revere. Sam Adams was called the "master of the puppets" and the "assassin of reputations" by his enemies, and undoubtedly he was both. He wrote tirelessly for the columns of the *Gazette*, twisting every possible incident or administrative action of the British into an argument for revolution. When the news was dull and the fires of dissatisfaction needed fanning, he "blew up" minor scrapes into events of seemingly major import. When a crisis arose, such as the passage of the Stamp Act or the imposition of the tax on tea, Adams worked with others to fire up resistance throughout the colonies. His Committees of Correspondence, organized in 1772, kept the word moving among Patriot editors. When British rifles fired in Boston to restrain a street crowd, the *Gazette* called the affair the Boston Massacre. But a year later the *Gazette* was reporting on a memorial service held for the massacre victims, consisting of a propagandistic display in the windows of Paul Revere's house. Such touches as this were the work of Sam Adams, who knew how to stir the popular emotions.

Tom Paine, the political philosopher, arrived in the colonies from England in time to make two great pamphleteering contributions to the patriot cause. His *Common Sense,* which sold 120,000 copies in three months in the spring of 1776, was a hard-headed, down-to-earth argument for independence that the common man could understand. That December, when Washington's discouraged army was camped on the Delaware river across from Trenton, Paine was drafted to write the first of his *Crisis* papers for a Philadelphia weekly:

These are the times that try men's souls. The summer soldier and the sunshine patriot will, in this crisis, shrink from the service of their country; but he that stands it NOW, deserves the love and thanks of man and woman. Tyranny, like hell, is not easily conquered; yet we have this consolation with us, that the harder the conflict the more glorious the triumph. What we obtain too cheap, we esteem too lightly; it is dearness only that gives every thing its value. Heaven knows how to put a proper price upon its goods; and it would be strange indeed if so celestial an article as *FREEDOM* should not be highly rated.

Paine's words lived to be broadcast to occupied Europe during World War II; at the time they helped to spur the first American victory of the war.

## PRESS OF THE NEW REPUBLIC

In the early years of the new nation, two types of newspapers were developing. One was the mercantile paper, published in the seaboard towns, primarily for the trading and shipping classes interested in commercial and political news. Its well-filled advertising columns reflected the essentially business interest of its limited clientele of subscribers— 2000 was a good number. The other type was the political paper, partisan in its appeal, and relying for reader support on acceptance of its views, rather than upon the quality and completeness of its news. Most editors of the period put views first and news second; the political paper deliberately shaped the news to fit its views. In the struggle over the adoption of the Constitution and the establishment of the new federal government, these party papers played a key role.

The *Federalist Papers*, written for the newspapers of New York state and reprinted throughout the country, were largely the work of Alexander Hamilton, brilliant leader of the pro-Constitution party which received its name from the series of 85 articles. Written for mass consumption, they still rank as one of the best expositions of political doctrine ever conceived. When Hamilton's party assumed control of the new federal government, Hamilton directed the editorial opinion of the Federalist party papers he helped to establish. He dictated his ideas to his editors, who, with their Jeffersonian opponents, developed a briefer, one-argument form of editorial writing.

Ranged on the anti-Federalist side with Thomas Jefferson were his personally sponsored poet-editor, Philip Freneau of the *National Gazette,* and other masters of partisanship like Benjamin Franklin Bache of the *Aurora*. Editors on both sides attacked each other with biting sarcasm and bitter invective. Their political sponsors were also viciously treated; the climax came when Bache accused Washington of being a "front man" for the Federalists and said, "If ever a nation was debauched by a man, the American nation has been debauched by Washington." William Cobbett, most fiery of the Federalist editors, retaliated in his *Porcupine's Gazette* with a classical character sketch of Bache in which the kindest word was "liar."

The American press survived the excesses of the 1790's and the dangerous effort at repression of press freedom through the Alien and Sedition Acts. But the traditions of partisan journalism lived on in the political party press of the nineteenth century. Particularly was this true of the frontier papers which supported Andrew Jackson and the Democratic party. The *Argus of Western America* of Frankfort, Kentucky, was one of these grubby but virile sheets which helped to spark the Jacksonian revolution. Amos Kendall and Francis P. Blair, two of its editors, graduated to Jackson's "kitchen cabinet," where Kendall served as Postmaster General and journalistic adviser to the President and Blair as editor of the hard-hitting administration paper, the Washington *Globe*. The tradition of an administration organ in Washington had begun with the *National*

*Intelligencer* of Jefferson's day; but none was edited with more single-minded driving purpose than Blair's *Globe.* "Give it to Bla-ar," Jackson would say, and Blair would pass the word along to the party faithful. The Whigs had their strong editors, too, like Thurlow Weed of the Albany *Evening Journal.* The attitude of the political paper was well expressed by the pro-Jackson New York *Evening Post,* which advised its readers to buy a Whig paper if they wanted the other side of the argument of the moment. This was the spirit of the pamphleteer rather than that of the true journalist.

The political papers were much more important in the story of the development of the opinion function. The mercantile papers, however, played a role in the development of the news function concept. Even though their primary interest was in shipping news and digests of foreign news taken from European newspapers arriving by boat in the American ports, the leading mercantile papers took pride in excelling in their specialties. And as the struggle between the Federalists and the Republicans for control of the national government intensified, news of Hamilton's fiscal policies and Jefferson's moves became important to the business community. Competition was tough, too; in 1800 there were six dailies in Philadelphia (twice as many as in 1970) and five in New York. The weekly publishers had been forced into the daily field to meet the competition of the coffee houses, where the London papers were filed as soon as ships arrived with the latest issues and where news was freely exchanged.

So the individual papers began to go out after the news. Correspondents covered sessions of the Congress in Washington as early as 1808 and were well established by the late 1820's. Seaport dailies hired boats to meet the incoming ships out in the harbor so their editors would have a headstart on digesting the foreign news. The leading New York mercantile papers, the *Courier and Enquirer* and the *Journal of Commerce,* set up rival pony express services between Washington and New York to get presidential messages and congressional news faster.

What the mercantile papers did not do, however, was widen the appeal of their news columns to satisfy the demands of a new reading audience which was emerging from what is now called the Jacksonian revolution. More widespread education, extension of the right to vote, increased interest in politics by a growing laboring class, and other socioeconomic factors were operating to pave the way for a more popular and responsive journalism which was destined to overwhelm the older types of newspapers.

## THE PENNY PRESS

Between 1833 and 1837 the publishers of a new "penny press" proved that a low-priced paper, edited to interest ordinary people, could win what amounted to a mass circulation for the times and thereby attract an advertising volume which would make it independent. These were papers for the "common man" and were not tied to the interests of the business community, like the mercantile press, or dependent for financial support upon political party allegiance. It did not necessarily follow that all the penny papers would be superior in their handling of the news and opinion functions. But the door was open for some to make important journalistic advances.

The first offerings of a penny paper tended to be highly sensational; human interest news overshadowed important news, and crime and sex stories were written in full detail. But as the penny paper attracted readers from various social and economic brackets, its sensationalism was modified. The "common man" reader came to want a better product, too. Popularized style of writing and presentation of news remained, but the penny paper became a respectable publication, offering significant information and editorial leadership. Once the first of the successful penny papers had shown the way, later ventures could enter the competition at the higher level of journalistic responsibility the pioneering papers had reached.

This was the pattern of American newspapers in the years following the founding of the New York *Sun* in 1833. The *Sun,* published by Benjamin Day, entered the lists against 11 other dailies. It was tiny in comparison; but it was bright and readable, and it preferred human interest features to important but dull political speech reports. It had a police reporter writing squibs of crime news in the style already proven successful by London papers. And, most important, it sold for a penny whereas its competitors sold for six cents. By 1837 the *Sun* was printing 30,000 copies a day, which was more than the total of all 11 New York daily newspapers combined on the day the *Sun* first appeared four years earlier. In those same four years, James Gordon Bennett brought out his New York *Herald* (1835) and a trio of New York printers who were imitating

Day's success founded the Philadelphia *Public Ledger* (1836) and the Baltimore *Sun* (1837). The four penny sheets all became famed newspapers.

**Bennett and news enterprise.** James Gordon Bennett can serve as the symbol of the penny press news enterprisers. He had been a Washington correspondent, reporter, and editor for other dailies before he launched the *Herald* in 1835. Disillusioned by a previous venture with a political paper, he kept the *Herald* relatively free of political ties. He more than matched the *Sun* with sensational coverage of crime and court news, on the one hand, and challenged the more sober journals with detailed coverage of Wall Street affairs, political campaigns, and foreign news, on the other. As profits from his big circulation and extensive advertising piled up, he spent money on news coverage. He matched his rivals in establishing pony express services to carry the news from Washington and other points. One *Herald* courier service stretched all the way from Newfoundland, carrying European news by pony rider, boat, and train to the first telegraph point. Bennett was among the first to use each of the new means of communication as they burst upon the scene in the 1830's and 1840's, hiring locomotives to race presidential messages from Washington and utilizing the telegraph as soon as Samuel F. B. Morse's invention proved itself in 1844 and wires were strung from city to city. He personally toured the country with presidential candidates and sailed to London on the newest steamship to arrange for better coverage of foreign news. By the 1850's he had made the *Herald* the leading newsgathering paper and the richest in advertising.

Bennett's competitors were not being left in the dust. The New York *Sun*, Philadelphia *Public Ledger*, and Baltimore *Sun* were all in the race for news. So were such older New York papers as the *Courier and Enquirer, Journal of Commerce,* and *Evening Post.* So were two new competitors, Horace Greeley's New York *Tribune,* founded in 1841, and Henry J. Raymond's New York *Times,* founded in 1851. Greeley shunned the sensationalism which had helped the *Sun* and *Herald* to their initial circulation successes and concentrated instead on building up an editorial page and offering news interpretation, but he also covered the running news. His managing editor, Charles A. Dana, directed a reportorial staff of high quality, although perhaps not as slambang as the *Herald's* growing group of newsmen. By the time Raymond entered the New York field with the *Times,* the lines of staff organization were fairly well defined. The owner might still be editor-in-chief, but he had a news executive and a business manager operating the day-to-day business. Raymond concentrated on the *Times'* foreign coverage and editorial policy, seeking to give his reports more depth and meaning in the pattern of the *Times* of London.

The coming of the telegraph speeded the gathering of news, but it also increased the cost. In 1848 six New York morning papers formed the Associated Press of New York, forerunner of the modern press association of the same name. They did so to share the costs of telegraphing digests of foreign news from Boston and of routine news from Washington. Soon other papers asked to share in this common news report and the New York papers began selling it. Papers in the interior of the country could now, with the telegraph, get the news as rapidly as their eastern metropolitan competitors. The excitement of the Mexican War and of the political crises leading up to the Civil War spurred attention to the need for better mass communications.

The Civil War called for great efforts in news enterprise. The *Herald* sent its own small army of correspondents into the field; other leading papers followed suit. Printing advances of the previous two decades —the flat-bed cylinder press, the type-revolving press, and stereotyping— were needed to handle increased circulations. Sunday editions of daily papers came into being. The illustrated periodicals, *Harper's Weekly* and *Frank Leslie's Illustrated Newspaper,* led the way in using woodcut illustrations and maps, and newspapers followed suit as best they could. By the time the guns finally ceased firing, the traditions of news enterprise and emphasis upon the news function had been well established.

**Greeley and the editorial page.**   Horace Greeley is recognized as one of the most influential editors in the history of American journalism. His New York *Tribune,* which he founded in 1841, was the first American newspaper to develop an editorial page which was the product of the thinking of a group of individuals. Not that it was a well-tailored, coherently organized page, such as many newspapers publish today. Orderly departmentalization had not yet come to newspapers in Greeley's day, and in any event methodicalness and consistency were not part of the Greeley temperament. But what the *Tribune* printed represented a dramatic change from the tradition of the pamphleteer.

Greeley was deeply conscious of his responsibility to the reader. He knew the *Tribune* had to be enterprising in reporting the news if it were to compete successfully for readers. But he felt it his responsibility to be just as enterprising in seeking to influence public opinion by devoting much space to serious discussion, editorial argument, and interpretation of events. The *Tribune* examined issues and debated ideas; it did not follow a set party line or insist that there was only one solution to a problem. True, it advocated some of its opinions as vehemently as did the pamphleteer, but in sum total it illuminated the social and economic issues of the day, from differing viewpoints, far more than any other paper had.

Unlike Bennett's *Herald,* which minimized the opinion function while concentrating on news enterprise, Greeley's *Tribune* made the opinion function the key to its popular acceptance. And popular it was. His weekly edition, in which the best of the daily news and opinion was reprinted for mail circulation (a practice of some bigger papers of the period), had the largest circulation of any contemporary publication. It was called the "Bible of the Middlewest," where many of the 200,000 copies went. "Uncle Horace," as Greeley was called, was as well known as any American of his time—only Lincoln, of the men of the period, has had more books written about him. Greeley lived through a period of momentous events and of great social change and, like Lincoln, was able to give expression to the aspirations and hopes of less articulate countrymen.

To many, the activities of Greeley and the *Tribune* must have appeared strangely inconsistent. The editor was greatly concerned with the impact of the industrial revolution upon society and the social ills which unrestricted capitalism produced. He was willing to examine and debate any seemingly reasonable experimentation in social reform or economic theory, in the hope that it would give workers and farmers a more equitable share in the accumulating wealth. So the *Tribune,* ostensibly a Whig newspaper, advocated a form of collective living called "associationism" and ran many columns of material written by the Socialist Albert Brisbane and the Communist Karl Marx. Few of Greeley's readers were won over to socialism, but they enjoyed the debate. Greeley's fight for free land in the West to which people in the slums could emigrate was more popular—but that stand was inconsistent with Whig political principles. Eventually his stand on the slavery issue led him into the Republican party, and he ended his career by running unsuccessfully for the presidency in 1872 as the candidate of the Liberal Republicans and the Democrats against General Grant, candidate of the Whig-minded Republicans.

Greeley was not always the great editor; he pressed his demands for immediate emancipation of the slaves upon Lincoln with such emotionalism that Lincoln was hard-pressed not to abandon his carefully worked-out strategy for keeping the northern and border states united in the common purpose of preserving the Union. But over a generation's time Greeley won the right to be known as the "Yankee radical"; he was responsive to the problems of his times and a purveyor of stimulating ideas. He brought together an admirable staff, including Charles A. Dana as his chief assistant and such thinking writers as Margaret Fuller, George Ripley, and Solon Robinson, to help produce the editorial page for which the *Tribune* was noted. They did much to teach others a fuller concept of the newspaper's opinion function.

**The personal editors.**    Greeley belonged to the group of editors of the middle nineteenth century called the "personal editors," men who were as well known to their readers as were their newspapers, in contrast to the much more anonymous editors of modern corporate journalism. Some of Greeley's farmer readers were surprised to keep getting the *Tribune* after his death; they assumed the paper would quit publishing, so much did he seem to be the newspaper itself.

William Cullen Bryant, who joined the New York *Post* staff in 1825 and remained to edit it for a half-century, also fell into this category of the personal editor. His journalism was much more reserved than Greeley's and his thinking more logical, but through Bryant's personal editorial opinion, the *Post* exercised considerable influence. He supported Jacksonian democracy and, like Greeley, he showed sympathy for the workingman. During the Civil War, he was one of the most effective interpreters of Lincoln's policies. Henry J. Raymond, founder of the New York *Times,* played a personal role outside the newspaper office, as a leader in the Republican party, although he tried to make the *Times'* editorial columns calmly interpretative in character.

There were editors outside New York City who made their influence felt during the Civil War period. One was Samuel Bowles III, publisher of the Springfield *Republican* in Massachusetts, a daily of just 6000 circulation. Bowles' editorial ability was so great that his weekly edition of 12,000 copies rivaled Greeley's 200,000-circulation in reputation and did much to unify the North and Middlewest in the pre-Civil War years.

Another was Joseph Medill, builder of the Chicago *Tribune,* who was one of Lincoln's firmest supporters. The abolitionist editors, William Lloyd Garrison of the *Liberator* and the martyred Elijah Lovejoy, should be noted too, although they were agitator-pamphleteers.

In the post-Civil War years, the name of Edwin Lawrence Godkin stands out. Godkin founded the *Nation* magazine in 1865 and succeeded Bryant as the driving force of the New York *Post* in 1881. British-born, Godkin decided the United States needed a high-grade weekly journal of opinion and literary criticism, similar to those in England. His distinctive style of writing and skill in ironic analysis made the *Nation* a favorite of other intellectuals. William James, the philosopher, said of him: "To my generation his was certainly the towering influence in all thought concerning public affairs, and indirectly his influence has assuredly been more pervasive than that of any other writer of the generation, for he influenced other writers who never quoted him, and determined the whole current of discussion." This was high accomplishment for the editor of a weekly magazine with no more than 10,000 circulation.

## THE "NEW JOURNALISM" ERA

Between 1865 and 1900 the dynamic capitalism of an expanding America, utilizing vast natural resources and the new machines of the industrial revolution, transformed the national economy. Industrialization, mechanization, and urbanization brought extensive social, cultural, and political changes: the "rise of the city," improved transportation and communication, educational advances, political unrest, and the rise of an extensive labor movement. The mass media could not fail to go through great changes along with the society they served. In the world of newspapers, the era is known as that of the "New Journalism," a designation used by the men who lived through that time to describe the activities of the master editor of the period, Joseph Pulitzer.

In the 35 years between the close of the Civil War and the turn of the century the population of the country doubled, the national wealth quadrupled, and manufacturing production increased sevenfold. It was the period of the coming of the age of steel, the harnessing of electricity for light and power, and the mechanizing of production processes. National growth and increased wealth meant cultural progress in literature, science, and the social sciences; a great stirring in scholarship and a rapid rise in the universities; and sharp increases in public school attendance and adult interest in popularized knowledge. Growing social and economic interdependence could be measured by two statistics for the year 1900: a third of the population was urban and 62 per cent of the labor force was engaged in nonagricultural work.

Communication facilities expanded in this period of the nationalization of the United States. Telegraph lines and railroad tracks reached near-saturation points; the telephone, coming into use in the 1870's, provided direct communication through intercity lines which covered the country by 1900. The federal postal service greatly extended free carrier service in the cities and instituted free rural delivery in 1897. The low postal rate for newspapers and magazines of 1885 opened the way for cheap delivery of publications. By 1900 there were 3500 magazines with a combined circulation of 65,000,000 an issue. Weekly newspapers tripled in number between 1870 and 1900, reaching a total of more than 12,000. During the same 30 years the number of daily newspapers quadrupled and their total circulation increased almost sixfold; the figures for 1900 were 1967 general circulation dailies, selling nearly 15,000,000 copies each day. It was this tremendous increase in the circulation of the printed mass media which was the impetus for inventions such as the rotary press, the typesetting machine, photoengraving, and color printing, which transformed the newspaper into its modern form.

Obviously a "New Journalism" would emerge for this new society. Again, as in the penny press period, there was a new audience: More people were interested in reading; the labor class increased rapidly; and there was a heavy concentration of immigrant population in the rapidly growing eastern cities (New York City residents, who increased 50 per cent between 1880 and 1890, were 80 per cent foreign-born or of foreign parentage). Such readers, stirred by political and social unrest in a period when reform movements sought to readjust the economic balance to bring relief to the worker and farmer, looked for aggressive editorial leadership and opinion-forming crusading in their newspapers and magazines. But they also wanted impartial and thorough coverage of the news. The newspaper which appealed to them was also low-priced, easily read, popularized in content, and bright in appearance. Particularly in the big cities, the entertainment ingredient had to be high, and for the really new readers a new cycle of sensationalism was the major attraction.

**Pulitzer and the news.**   Joseph Pulitzer serves as the symbol of the New Journalism era. An immigrant himself, he served his apprenticeship as a reporter before founding the St. Louis *Post-Dispatch* in 1878. In the next five years, Pulitzer built it into the city's leading paper by giving his readers what they wanted. He developed a liberal, aggressive editorial page and gave both the editorial and news columns a fierce crusading spirit. He insisted on accuracy, digging deep for facts, thoroughness of local news coverage, and good writing. One of his famous commands to his staff was "Accuracy! Accuracy!! Accuracy!!!" Another was "Terseness! Intelligent, not stupid, condensation." Still another showed his concern for the lighter side of the news; he reminded reporters to look for both the significant news and the "original, distinctive, dramatic, romantic, thrilling, unique, curious, quaint, humorous, odd, apt to be talked about" news.

In 1883 Pulitzer left the *Post-Dispatch* as his monument in St. Louis and invaded New York City by buying the run-down *World*. Within four years the paper had reached a record-breaking 250,000 circulation, had eclipsed the *Herald* as the leader in advertising volume, and had become the country's most talked-about newspaper.

Pulitzer's success lay in the fact that he had not forgotten the basic news function while he was wooing new readers with entertaining and sensational material. He gave his audience its money's worth in the quality and extent of significant news coverage and presented it in an enlivened style. He plowed money into the building of a competent staff of newsmen and he kept pace with mechanical innovations which permitted them to fashion a better product. He combined a popular editorial aggressiveness and crusading spirit with a great promotional skill to make the mass of readers feel the *World* was their friend. To attract them to its solid news stories and editorial column, the *World* offered big headlines, human interest stories, illustrations, and other sensationalized approaches. With the advent of color printing in the early 1890's, the *World* added popular Sunday supplements and the comic strip.

Some of Pulitzer's competitors did not sense the total character of his journalistic product and mistakenly assumed that sensationalism alone had made the *World* successful. One of these was William Randolph Hearst, who took over the San Francisco *Examiner* in 1887 and then invaded New York in 1895 by buying the *Journal*. The circulation war between Pulitzer's *World* and Hearst's *Journal* brought the cycle of sensationalism to a new height. Critics who eyed one of the comic strip characters of the times, the "Yellow Kid," dubbed the papers "yellow journals." The yellow journal prided itself on being the crusading friend of the "common man," but it underestimated his interest in significant news and overestimated his capacity for absorbing gaudy, oversensationalized news. The result was a degrading of the news function, which reached its climax during the period of the Spanish-American War. After a few years the *World* and other serious-minded papers withdrew from the competition, leaving the techniques of yellow journalism to Hearst and his imitators. While the yellow journals cannot be held solely responsible for causing the war, their news policies certainly contributed to the war fever of 1898.

There were other notable leaders in the New Journalism era. The master teacher of the art of human interest writing was Charles A. Dana's New York *Sun,* which developed many a great reporter or editor for other papers. Dana, however, resisted change, and the *Sun* set its face against the general trend of the times. Edward Wyllis Scripps began developing his group of papers, headed by the Cleveland *Press.* They were low-priced, small in size, well-written and tightly edited, and hard-hitting in both news and editorial columns. Melville Stone's Chicago *Daily News* and William Rockhill Nelson's Kansas City *Star* were two more distinctive new papers fashioned in the New Journalism pattern. In the South, Henry W. Grady became known as a master news executive for his work with the Atlanta *Constitution,* and because of his own reporting skill.

## THE PEOPLE'S CHAMPIONS: PULITZER, HEARST, SCRIPPS

The rise of the architects of the New Journalism, in the 1870's and 1880's, brought a heightening of attention to the exercise of the opinion function. Joseph Pulitzer, the leading exponent of the New Journalism, has been named by his colleagues of this century as the leading American editor of modern times. A memo written by Pulitzer to an editor of his St. Louis *Post-Dispatch* summarizes his idealistic goal for the editorial page:

. . . every issue of the paper presents an opportunity and a duty to say something courageous and true; to rise above the mediocre and conventional; to say something that will command the respect of the intelligent, the educated, the independent part of the community; to rise above fear of partisanship and fear of popular prejudice.

No finer statement of the responsibility imposed upon those who exercise the newspaper's opinion function has ever been written. Those who even occasionally can meet such a challenge win the respect of both the newspaper craft and their readers.

Pulitzer and his contemporaries of the New Journalism era developed a growing independence of editorial opinion from partisan pressures. They did not hesitate to support political candidates, but they did not do this automatically as part of a political machine, as did the political press. Most of the leaders were champions of the "common man"—people's champions, doing battle against the trusts and monopolies that characterized big business, the crooked politicians who were "the shame of the cities," the money lenders and the speculators, and the opponents of reform. The majority supported the political leaders of the Democratic party—Grover Cleveland, William Jennings Bryan, Woodrow Wilson— but they also gave aid to such progressive Republicans as Theodore Roosevelt and Robert M. La Follette. Pulitzer himself believed that the Democratic party best carried out the principles he espoused, but he bolted from the radical Bryan candidacy and gave aid and comfort to such New York Republicans as Charles Evans Hughes in the battles with Tammany Hall. His great editor, Frank I. Cobb, who carried on the traditions of the New York *World* after Pulitzer's death in 1911, was a close adviser to Woodrow Wilson and his solid champion. Cobb, however, insisted that it was part of his job to criticize the administration as well as to defend it. This is part of what is meant by "independence of editorial opinion from partisan pressures."

A distinctive feature of the New Journalism paper was its eagerness to crusade in behalf of the community welfare. Pulitzer developed the coordinated crusade, using both the news and editorial columns, at the *Post-Dispatch,* and that paper remained famous for its tenacious attacks on wrongdoers in public or business life. These words written by Pulitzer in 1907, which became the *Post-Dispatch* editorial platform, sum up the crusading spirit:

I know that my retirement will make no difference in its cardinal principles; that it will always fight for progress and reform, never tolerate injustice or corruption, always fight demagogues of all parties, never belong to any party, always oppose privileged classes and public plunderers, never lack sympathy with the poor, always remain devoted to the public welfare, never be satisfied with merely printing news, always be drastically independent, never be afraid to attack wrong, whether by predatory plutocracy or predatory poverty.

William Randolph Hearst, in his New York *Journal* and other newspapers, likewise was a crusading champion of the people. His editorial platform at the turn of the century called for nationalization of the coal mines, railroads, and telegraph lines; public ownership of public franchises; the "destruction of the criminal trusts"; a graduated income tax; election of United States senators by popular vote rather than by state legislatures which could be influenced by big business; and extensive new financial support for the public schools. To this he added an active support of labor unions that made them regard his papers as their champions.

One would suppose the liberals of the time would have clasped Hearst to their bosoms. But they did not. They distrusted Hearst's own political ambitions, which extended to the White House; they disliked the bitterness of his editorial attacks upon his opponents; repelled by the sensationalism and near-cynicism of his news policies, they rejected his editorial page as shallow and insincere. But undoubtedly Hearst had great influence upon the "common man" reader of the pre-World War I generation. By the 1920's, however, the Hearst papers were much less progressive in outlook, and by the 1930's their position was almost reversed from the one they had held in 1900. Always strongly nationalistic, in contrast to Pulitzer's support of international cooperation, the Hearst papers became bitterly isolationist by the time of World War I, and remained so even past their founder's death in 1951.

Edward Wyllis Scripps was the third of the great "people's champions" of the New Journalism era. Scripps set his circulation sights on the working people of the smaller but growing industrial cities of the country, as he developed his chain of newspapers from his headquarters at the Cleveland *Press*. His social goal was to improve the position of the mass of people through better education, labor union organization and collective bargaining, and a resulting reasonable redistribution of wealth. In this way, he reasoned, a peaceful and productive pattern of society could emerge in an industrialized America.

Scripps viewed himself as the only real friend of the "poor and ill-informed." He said his newspapers were the only schoolroom the workingman had; the public school system did not serve him adequately, and other newspapers were either capitalistic in outlook or too intellectual in their appeal. He pictured himself as a "damned old crank" who was instinctively rebellious against the status quo in any field of human activity. He made a point of running small, tightly edited papers which could assert their independence of the business community and resist any attempted influence by advertisers. But he was businessman enough to make a profit on his journalistic ventures, and his employees found him to be cautious in wage policies. Politically, the Scripps papers were strongly liberal; they supported the third party candidacies of Theodore Roosevelt in 1912 and Robert M. La Follette in 1924, Woodrow Wilson's "New Freedom," the right of workers to organize, and public ownership. This liberal pattern continued after Scripps' death in 1926 and until the late 1930's when, under the influence of the late Roy W. Howard, the Scripps-Howard papers became substantially more conservative.

## THE OPINION MAGAZINES

Highly important among the "people's champions" of the reform era at the opening of the twentieth century were the magazines. Dismayed by the bitterness of some of their attacks, Theodore Roosevelt called their work "muckraking," comparing the more sensational writers to the Man with the Muckrake in *Pilgrim's Progress,* who did not look up to see the celestial crown but continued to rake the filth. The magazine men and women, however, considered the appellation as a badge of honor.

Magazines had been published since colonial times. Surviving in 1900 were such leaders as the *North American Review,* which began its long career in 1815; *Harper's Monthly,* which appeared in 1850; and the *Atlantic Monthly,* which began in 1857. These highly literary periodicals were joined by the *Century* in 1881 and *Scribner's* in 1886.

More influential in public affairs were *Harper's Weekly,* edited by George William Curtis and famous for the political cartoons of Thomas Nast; Godkin's *Nation;* the *Independent,* founded in 1848; and the following new arrivals of the 1880's and 1890's: Albert Shaw's *Review of Reviews,* Lyman Abbott's *Outlook,* the *Literary Digest,* and the *Forum.* Three new magazines of the same period which depended upon humor, cartoon, and satire were *Puck, Judge,* and *Life* (the original *Life* featuring the famed Gibson girl drawings).

Entered in the mass circulation field during the 1880's and 1890's were Cyrus H. K. Curtis' *Ladies' Home Journal* and *Saturday Evening Post,* Robert J. Collier's *Collier's,* Frank Munsey's *Munsey's,* S. S. McClure's *McClure's,* and *Cosmopolitan,* which became a Hearst property. Low-priced and popular in appeal, they carried both fiction and nonfiction.

This was an impressive battery of magazines to turn loose during the reform era of the Theodore Roosevelt administrations (all of the public affairs and mass circulation magazines except *Munsey's* and the *Saturday Evening Post* joined in the chase). *McClure's* touched off the major muckraking movement in late 1902 when it offered almost simultaneously Ida M. Tarbell's "History of the Standard Oil Company" and Lincoln Steffens' "Shame of the Cities" series. *Cosmopolitan* countered with "Treason in the Senate," an attack upon conservative spokesmen of "the interests" written by David Graham Phillips, a Pulitzer editorial writer. Samuel Hopkins Adams and Mark Sullivan exposed the patent medicines in *Collier's.*

The cream of the writers moved to John S. Phillips' *American Magazine* in 1906, after a break with McClure. In the crowd were Miss Tarbell, Steffens, Ray Stannard Baker, Finley Peter Dunne ("Mr. Dooley"), and a somewhat gingerly progressive named William Allen White, who achieved primary fame as the highly personal editor of the Emporia *Gazette* in Kansas. They continued to lead the muckraking movement until it dwindled away by the time of World War I.

Coming on the scene in 1914 was the *New Republic,* featuring the writing of Herbert Croly and Walter Lippmann. Shocking American complacency in the 1920's was H. L. Mencken's *American Mercury.* But by and large American interest in magazines of opinion has declined. Of all the magazines listed in this account only the *Nation* and *New Republic* survived as magazines of dissent. *Harper's* and *Atlantic* were the only survivors among the public affairs and literary periodicals listed; joining them in the quality magazine field which plays a role in opinion formulation were the *New Yorker* and *Saturday Review*. Among all the more general magazines mentioned, only the *Ladies' Home Journal* and *Cosmopolitan* are still published. Showing interest in public affairs is the current leader in the general magazine field, the *Reader's Digest*. The news magazines—*Time, Newsweek,* and *U.S. News & World Report*—also exercise the opinion function.

## TWENTIETH-CENTURY NEWS TRENDS

Impartial gathering and reporting of the news was generally recognized to be the basic obligation of newspapers by the early 1900's. Some did the job in a much more comprehensive and intelligent fashion than others. But the editor who put views ahead of news, and who tied his newspaper to a political machine, had pretty well gone out of style. Slanting of news to fit the prejudices or political preferences of a publisher was also recognized as a detriment, although some newspapers continued to persist in the practice. The "Canons of Journalism" adopted by the American Society of Newspaper Editors in 1923 contain these two paragraphs which summarize the aspirations of modern journalistic leaders:

The right of a newspaper to attract and hold readers is restricted by nothing but considerations of public welfare. The use a newspaper makes of the share of public attention it gains serves to determine its sense of responsibility, which it shares with every member of its staff. A journalist who uses his power for any selfish or otherwise unworthy purpose is faithless to a high trust.

Partisanship, in editorial comment which knowingly departs from the truth, does violence to the best spirit of American journalism; in the news columns it is subversive of a fundamental principle of the profession.

No matter how impartial and well intentioned a newspaper's editors might be, they had to expend an increasing effort on comprehensive coverage and display of the news, and its intelligent interpretation, if they were to meet their full responsibilities. Great events of this century made the business of reporting the news far more complex, decade by decade. In the first decade, the story was one of economic and political reform in the United States. In the second decade, it was World War I.

In the third decade, it was the world's effort at postwar readjustment. The fourth decade brought the Great Depression and a collapse of world order. The fifth and sixth brought World War II, the atomic era, and the cold war, which rose to the climactic crises of Korea and Vietnam.

The mass media made a reasonable effort to fulfill their increased responsibilities for interpreting the news of events which all but overwhelmed the world. Professional standards had to be raised to meet the challenge. Better trained and more knowledgeable men and women came to occupy key reportorial assignments and news desk posts. The range of subject matter with which a Washington correspondent had to be familiar in the 1920's was narrow indeed compared to the complexities of Washington news in the 1960's. And since all news tended to become "local" in its impact with the narrowing of geographical barriers in the atomic age, every general assignment reporter had to know far more about such areas as international affairs, science, and economic trends than did his predecessors. The modern press associations, particularly, were put under heavy pressures. Newspapers were stimulated by the appearance of new competitors: radio, television, and the news magazine. Radio and television challenged the newspaper both in providing spot news coverage and in news analysis. The news magazines competed with the newspapers by giving the reader background information and point-of-view interpretation. Together, the print and electronic media offered a persistent reader-listener-viewer a sizable amount of information about the swirl of events which virtually engulfed even the most conscientious citizen.

**Ochs and the Times.** The editors of the New York *Times* built what is generally conceded to be the greatest single news machine of this century, publishing what was called by its admiring competitors a "newspaper of record." The story of the growth of the *Times* since Adolph S. Ochs rescued it from bankruptcy in 1896 illustrates the trend in acceptance of the news function responsibility, even though it is the story of a nontypical journalistic leader. For what the *Times* did in its methodical completeness was done at least in part, and in some respects as successfully, by other responsible newspapers.

Ochs told his readers in 1896: "It will be my aim . . . to give the news impartially, without fear or favor . . ." He also promised them all the news, in concise and attractive form, and a paper which would be "a forum for the consideration of all questions of public importance, and to that end to invite intelligent discussion from all shades of opinion."

He made no attempt to match the sensationalism of the yellow journals of the time, and he shunned many of the popularized entertainment features of most newspapers, including the comic strip. His Sunday magazine featured articles of current news significance and became, with its more than 1,000,000 circulation of today, an important fixture in the magazine world. His book review section became the best known in the country. His coverage of financial and business news soon matched that of any older competitor. His editorial page, if quieter and more cautious than that of Pulitzer, was intelligently directed.

What made the *Times* great, however, was not so much these accomplishments as its persistence in gathering and printing the news in all its varied aspects. One of the great managing editors, Carr V. Van Anda, was given control of the *Times* newsroom in 1904 with the understanding that he should do whatever it took to do a comprehensive job with the news. Ochs was willing to spend money to get the news; Van Anda was willing to do the spending, and he knew how to get the news. It was an ideal association for a quarter of a century, during which time the *Times* rose to its position of news leadership. Van Anda rode the news, 12 hours a day, seven days a week, giving as much attention to the entire flow of the news as to the major story breaks. He loved to match his wits against a deadline, to exploit an undeveloped but important story, and to beat his competitors on such a colorful story as the sinking of the "Titanic" or such a significant story as the first announcement of the Einstein theory of relativity. With the coming of wireless communication, the *Times* began to present two or three pages of wireless news from Europe each Sunday, and it eventually built its own trans-Atlantic wireless receiving station, which in turn gave way to a radio facility.

World War I gave Van Anda an opportunity to show his full ability. Using the cables and wireless almost with abandon, the *Times* added the reports of its own correspondents to those of the press associations and syndicates. It reported in detail not only on military operations but on political and economic developments in the European capitals. War pictures were carried in a rotogravure section added in 1914. Most importantly, the paper began to publish the texts of documents and speeches, beginning with the British White Paper of August, 1914, which covered six full pages, and including the Treaty of Versailles, which filled eight pages—more than any other American paper was willing to give that important document. This policy, combined with the publication of the annual *New York Times Index,* made the *Times* the leading newspaper for librarians, scholars, government officials, and other newspaper editors.

If there was any complaint to be registered against the *Times* of the Van Anda period, it was that the paper presented a voluminous amount of news without sufficient interpretation or screening for the average reader. The "dead pan" objective fashion of reporting was considered the best, if impartiality was to be achieved, as late as the 1920's. But Van Anda did a goodly share of interpreting the news, and the editors who followed him did more. The Washington and foreign staffs built by the paper ranked with the best, and during the following decades they came to offer interpretative analysis along with factual reporting. The *Times* developed experts in the fields of science reporting and labor news in the early 1920's, far ahead of the general trend toward specialized reporting. It followed with authoritative reporters in virtually every field of news activity. Its Sunday news in review section, offering a weekend analysis of major news events, became outstanding. No institution is perfect, and the *Times* suffers from some faults—perhaps because it became almost unwieldy in staff size and in the number of pages it printed —but it continues to stand as a shining example of a newspaper dedicated to carrying out the news function as completely as a group of men can manage to do.

**The Daily News.**    One more wave of sensationalism was to precede the "era of interpretation," however. The 1920's were know as the "Jazz Age," and the papers which catered to a new group of readers won the dubious honor of being identified as "Jazz Journalism." Their sensationalism was accompanied by the two identifying techniques of the period: the tabloid format and great emphasis upon photography.

Leading the sensational tabloids was the New York *Illustrated Daily News,* founded in 1919 by Joseph Medill Patterson, cousin of Robert R. McCormick and partner with him in the publishing of the Chicago *Tribune.* Patterson, unlike his ultraconservative Chicago cousin, was unconventional in his socioeconomic beliefs—socialistic, his wealthy friends said. He wanted to reach and influence the lowest literate class of Americans and was attracted to the tabloid format by the success Lord Northcliffe was enjoying with it in England. The *Daily News* appeared with a photograph spread across its front half-page and was well stuffed with pictures, human interest stories, and entertaining features. By 1924 it had the largest circulation of any newspaper in the country, a position it continued to hold by a wide margin from that time on.

The tabloid format, it should be noted, did not have to be equated with sensationalism. It was used by other papers that were similar to the dailies of conventional size in all respects save that of the half-fold style.

**Interpretative reporting.** This type of more skillful, yet impartial, handling of the news was not unknown before the 1930's. But by then the socioeconomic revolution known politically as the New Deal, coupled with the impact of international crises, forced editors to emphasize "why" along with "who did what." Old-style objectivity, which called for the reporter to stick to a factual account of what had been said or done, did not give the reader the full meaning of the news. The new concept of objectivity was based upon the premise that the reader needed to have a given event placed in its proper perspective if truth really was to be served. Also discarded were older assumptions that such subjects as science and economics could not be made interesting to a mass readership. Reporter-specialists who could talk both to their news subjects and to a popular reading audience appeared to cover politics, foreign affairs, business, science, labor, agriculture, and urban affairs.

E. W. Scripps' Science Service began blazing one trail in 1921, along with such reporters as William L. Laurence of the New York *Times* and Howard W. Blakeslee of the Associated Press. In labor news, two pioneers were Louis Stark of the *Times* and Edwin A. Lahey of the Chicago *Daily News*. The 1960's saw the rise of urban and architectural specialists like Ada Louise Huxtable of the New York *Times* and Wolf Von Eckardt of the Washington *Post*. Examples of successful interpretative writers in Washington are David Kraslow, former Los Angeles *Times* bureau chief; Stewart Hensley, United Press International's state department specialist; and syndicated columnist Mary McGrory of the Washington *Star*.

## ANOTHER "NEW JOURNALISM"

In the late 1960's the literature of the mass media began to herald a "New Journalism" which at least borrowed the title of the innovations of the 1880's. Its reportorial and writing techniques were variously described as tell-it-as-you-see-it, impressionistic, saturation, humanistic, investigative—and even interpretative. Its second and more controversial characteristic was described as advocacy, activist, or participatory. The latter trend merely reflected the widespread frustration of the era and the demand that the conservative Establishment give heed and power to others—youth, minorities, women. The mass media should be used, the argument ran, to further such reforms.

Perhaps the leading spirit of this "New Journalism" was Tom Wolfe, although he viewed his efforts as a revolt against old-fashioned book writing rather than news writing. Other major figures were Truman Capote, Norman Mailer, Gay Talese, and Jimmy Breslin. Their work appeared in *Esquire,* the *New Yorker, Harper's,* and the fast-rising *New York.* Those magazines, the old New York *Herald Tribune,* and such underground papers as the *Village Voice* served as vehicles for the new style of reporting, perhaps best described as "saturation." Capote's *In Cold Blood,* although a novel, demonstrated intense journalistic research; Mailer's description of the march on the Pentagon was powerfully impressionistic; Talese utilized incredible detail in his account of life at the New York *Times* in *The Kingdom and the Power;* Breslin made his readers feel the crunch of police clubs on their skulls as he wrote of the 1968 Chicago convention riots.

Out of. that 1968 crisis came the best known example of "advocacy" journalism. The *Chicago Journalism Review* was founded in October, 1968, in the wake of disillusionment among young Chicago news men and women over management and public reaction to the role of the press in the riots. Edited by Ron Dorfman, the monthly aggressively criticized the city's press and offered a forum for general media criticism and self-improvement. Across the country similar publications appeared, among them the New York review called [*MORE*]. In many city rooms "reporter power" movements developed among young staff members who sought to make their professional contributions more meaningful but also challenged the established system of command. Among the advocacy journalists were Gloria Steinem, Jack Anderson, Seymour Hersh, and Sander Vanocur.

First of the underground papers spawned by the sex revolution and the credibility gap was *Village Voice,* founded in 1955 and boasting such names as Norman Mailer, Jules Feiffer, and Jack Newfield. Art Kunkin's *Los Angeles Free Press* proved more radical and anti-Establishment. Best known of the campus-based papers was the *Berkeley Barb,* founded by Max Scherr as spokesman for the "free speech" movement and a passionate opponent of the older educational order. Among other underground papers which enjoyed at least brief fame were Chicago's *Seed*, Boston's *Avatar*, San Francisco's *Rolling Stone*, and New York's *East Village Other*.

Combining radical dissent and underground qualities were such pungent political journals as *I.F. Stone's Weekly* (1953–71), the *Guardian* of New York City, the *Texas Observer*, and Bruce Brugmann's *San Francisco Bay Guardian*, a crusading opponent of that city's orthodox press.

## THE BLACK PRESS

Only recently have the American mass media exhibited an understanding interest in the black 10 percent of citizens; even so, the capacity to be sensitive to blacks as readers or viewers was severely limited. There has always been a clear need for a black press.

And more than 3000 Negro newspapers—owned and edited by blacks for black readers—have appeared since the first, *Freedom's Journal*, in 1827. But the black community has had few socioeconomic resources to support a press. Historically, the average life span of a Negro newspaper has been nine years. Henry G. La Brie III, of the University of Iowa, a research specialist on the black press, found 203 black newspapers were being published in 1972, of which only 11 had founding dates before 1900, as compared to 86 founded since 1960. Total circulation was 4,000,000; only three were dailies; only 37 had their own printing equipment. But collectively this struggling press had made its impact on the country.

"We wish to plead our own cause. Too long have others spoken for us," said the editors of *Freedom's Journal*, John B. Russwurm and Samuel Cornish, in 1827. The first black journalist to do that effectively was Frederick Douglass, the remarkable ex-slave who founded *The North Star* in 1847 and became the symbol of hope for blacks both of his generation and of today. Douglass helped rally public opinion against slavery and through his writing and speaking helped white men and women to see the degradation of slavery through black eyes.

Ranking in fame with Douglass is W. E. B. Du Bois, who founded *The Crisis* in 1910 as the militant protest voice of the National Association for the Advancement of Colored People. "Mentally the Negro is inferior to the white," said the 1911 *Britannica;* to Du Bois this belief was the "crisis" which had to be destroyed before discrimination in education, housing, and social status could be overcome.

Just as the standard daily press grew in numbers, circulation, and stature during the New Journalism era between 1880 and World War I, so did the black press. Important papers today founded in that period include the largest, New York's *Amsterdam News* (1909); the leading papers in the two most important publishing groups, Baltimore's *Afro-American* (1892) and the Chicago *Defender* (1905); the Pittsburgh *Courier* (1910), Philadelphia *Tribune* (1884), and Norfolk's *Journal and Guide* (1909). Among the major figures in Negro publishing ranks to 1910 were Robert S. Abbott of the Chicago *Defender,* John H. Murphy, Sr., of the *Afro-American,* Robert L. Vann of the Pittsburgh *Courier,* T. Thomas Fortune of the New York *Age,* and William Monroe Trotter of the Boston *Guardian.*

In 1970, Abbott's nephew, John H. Sengstacke, was elected to the board of the American Society of Newspaper Editors, the first black to be so honored. Sengstacke was head of the Chicago *Defender* group, which included the Pittsburgh *Courier* and the *Michigan Chronicle* of Detroit. John H. Murphy III headed the *Afro-American* papers.

Out of 45 efforts to publish dailies in the United States for blacks, as recorded by Professor Armistead Scott Pride of Lincoln University, only the Chicago *Defender* and the Atlanta *Daily World,* have prevailed, the latter since 1932. Its founder, William A. Scott, was assassinated in 1934; his successor, Cornelius A. Scott, produced an essentially conservative newspaper. Most of the leading black papers have been moderate in tone, heavily local in news coverage, strong in sports and social news, and occasionally crusading.

Largest in audited circulation in 1972 was the *Amsterdam News* with 83,000 copies. Second was the Los Angeles *Sentinel,* founded in 1934 and edited by Leon H. Washington as a mildly sensational and liberal paper. By far the largest in unaudited circulation was *Muhammad Speaks,* voice of the Nation of Islam, reportedly rolling 625,000 copies weekly out of its ultra-modern Chicago plant. The *Central News-Wave* group of free circulation weeklies in Los Angeles totaled 233,000 for seven editions. The *Black Panther,* radical voice of the left, claimed 100,000 copies. The *Defender* group had circulation claims exceeding 200,000; the *Afro-American* group some 135,000. Historically, black newspaper circulations peaked during the World War II period, when the Pittsburgh *Courier* achieved a national circulation of 286,000. As the regular press better covered stories involving racial issues, Negro paper readership declined, and community-based weeklies replaced the bigger nationally circulating papers.

If there was a single major voice in black journalism in the 1970's, it was *Ebony,* the picture magazine founded by John H. Johnson in 1945 as a monthly version of *Life.* By 1972 it had a circulation of 1,250,000 copies and was far more economically secure than its model. Johnson also published *Jet, Tan,* and *Black World,* the latter an outlet for black authors. *Tuesday,* a magazine supplement edited by blacks to appear in regular dailies, achieved 2,500,000 circulation in the five years after its 1965 founding.

## THE NEWS MAGAZINES

The news magazines offered a relatively small segment of the population another means of keeping abreast of events. The biggest, *Time,* has built a 4,000,000 circulation; *Newsweek* and *U.S. News & World Report* have circulations of about half that number. Although some issues go to subscribers who use them to bulwark inadequate news coverage by small local newspapers, many go to relatively well-informed citizens who read one or more daily newspapers, listen to television and radio news, subscribe to public affairs magazines, read books, and take one to three news magazines.

Henry R. Luce's formula for *Time* was to organize and departmentalize the news of the week in a style "written as if by one man for one man," whom *Time* described as too busy to spend all the time necessary to peruse the other media. Coverage of national affairs, foreign affairs, science, religion, education, business, and other areas was to be written for this "busy man," not for experts in each of the fields. The magazine developed a big research and library staff, as well as its own good-sized newsgathering organization, to supplement press association services. Begun in 1923, *Time* helped to drive the older *Literary Digest* out of business with this approach. *Newsweek* appeared in 1933, with an almost identical format. *U.S. News & World Report* grew out of a combination of two of David Lawrence's publications in Washington, hitting its stride in the late 1940's. Two picture news magazines, Luce's *Life* (1936) and Gardner Cowles' *Look* (1937), offered additional news coverage and interpretative articles.

It should be noted that the news magazines offered both news and opinion to their readers. *Time* made no attempt to distinguish between the two functions, intermingling opinion and editorial hypotheses with the straight news. Its use of narrative and human interest techniques, and overuse of adjectives, added to its editorial bias. *Time* said it wanted to be "fair," not objective or even impartial. The trouble was, some readers mistook *Time*'s "fairness" (opinion-giving) for factual reporting. *Newsweek* injected less opinion into its columns and offered separate editorial opinions written by commentators.

## THE PRESS ASSOCIATIONS

The major job of newsgathering beyond the local level is done not by the mass media themselves, but by the two big associations, Associated Press and United Press International. Newspapers, of course, cover their own local communities (although sometimes they even use press association reports about events taking place in their own cities). Some newspapers maintain area or state coverage through strings of correspondents who filter in news to a state desk; this practice varies from one part of the country to another, and many a large paper depends on the press associations for news of events as close as 50 miles from the city room, staffing only major news developments in its area. Only a small percentage of American dailies have their own Washington coverage, and the bulk of this is directed toward stories of regional or local interest, rather than the major news stories of the day. And only a handful of newspapers have their own correspondents abroad. The situation is much the same in television and radio, where the press associations supply virtually all the news for smaller stations, all but local news for many larger stations, and even the bulk of the news for the network-affiliated stations. The news magazines, too, use the press association reports for the basis of their work.

Cooperative newsgathering in this country began, as we have seen, in 1848 with the Associated Press of New York. The telegraph enabled the New York papers which controlled this early AP to sell its news to a gradually expanding group of papers. Opening of the Atlantic cable in 1866 gave the agency better access to European news, which it obtained under exchange agreements with Reuters of Great Britain, Havas of France, and other press services. Regional AP groups formed, the most powerful of which was the Western Associated Press. The dailies outside New York City resented the tight-fisted control of the AP by the

New York morning dailies which had founded it; the new evening dailies of the Midwest felt they were being ignored in the supplying of news on the two differing time cycles for morning and evening publication.

A bitter battle broke out among the newspapers in the 1880's. Control of the AP fell to the Western AP members, headed by Melville E. Stone, founder of the Chicago *Daily News.* Stone drafted exclusive news exchange contracts with the European agencies, cutting off the New York papers from their traditional supply of foreign news, and broke his rivals by 1897. An adverse court ruling in Illinois threatened the membership status of the AP at this same moment, so its headquarters were returned to New York in 1900.

The basis of the AP was its cooperative exchange of news. The members found it necessary to finance a larger and larger staff, however, which took over direction of the flow of news and eventually much of the newsgathering. Its organizational structure was not entirely democratic; the older and larger newspaper members kept control of the board of directors by giving themselves extra voting rights during the 1900 reorganization. Until an adverse Supreme Court decision in 1945, an AP member could prevent the entry of a direct competitor into the group by exercising a protest right which could be overridden only by a four-fifths vote of the entire membership.

Newspapers which could not gain entry to the AP, or which disliked its control by the older morning papers of the East, needed press association service from another source. Edward Wyllis Scripps, possessing both a string of evening dailies and an individualistic temperament which made him dislike monopoly, founded the United Press Associations in 1907 from earlier regional agencies. William Randolph Hearst, whose newly founded papers were denied AP memberships, started the International News Service in 1909. Other agencies came and went, but the AP, UP, and INS survived until 1958, when the Hearst interests liquidated a losing business by merging the INS into the UP to form the United Press International.

The strong men in the AP over the years were Stone, the first general manager, and Kent Cooper, general manager from 1925 to 1948. Builders of the UP were Roy W. Howard, who later became a partner in the Scripps-Howard newspaper group, and presidents Karl A. Bickel and Hugh Baillie. Since 1962 Wes Gallagher has been general manager of AP and Mims Thomason president of UPI.

Unlike the AP plan of organization, the UP and INS had a service to sell to clients. Howard set out to do this job for the young and struggling UP by building up a foreign service, first in Latin America and then in Europe. He embarrassed his agency by sending a premature flash announcing the end of World War I, but both Howard and the UP survived the incident. The enthusiasm and aggressiveness of the "shoestring" UP operation brought it into competitive position with the AP by the 1930's. In 1934 Kent Cooper brought an end to the restrictive news exchange agreements between the AP and foreign news agencies, and the AP joined in the foreign service race more determinedly. The AP also capitulated in supplying news to radio stations, five years after UP and INS entered that field in 1935, and made the radio and television stations associate members, without voting rights. The INS, smallest of the three agencies, did not attempt to supply news at the state level except in a few states; it concentrated instead on out-reporting and out-writing the other two on major news breaks and features. The UP-INS merger put the United Press International in a position of competitive equality with its older rival and assured the mass media that there would be intense rivalry between two well-managed press associations which serve both in this country and abroad.

## SOME CURRENT NEWSPAPER LEADERS

Opinions differ about the quality of individual newspapers; any "list of ten" compiled by one authority would differ to some degree from the listing made by a second competent observer. But newsmen generally agree that a top-flight newspaper must offer both impartial and comprehensive coverage of the news, as a first prerequisite for national recognition. The second prerequisite for recognition by the craft is a superior demonstration of responsibility in providing community opinion leadership and of integrity and zealousness in protecting basic human liberties. The second prerequisite is much harder to judge than the first.

The United States, unlike many other countries, has no truly national newspapers. It has two dailies without "home communities," however, which have won widespread respect and which circulate nationally with their regionally edited editions. These are the *Christian Science Monitor* and the *Wall Street Journal* (neither of which carries a nameplate which seems to indicate the general-interest character of the paper). The *Mon-*

*itor,* founded in 1908 by the Church of Christ, Scientist, built a high reputation for its Washington and foreign correspondence and its interpretative articles. Edited by Erwin D. Canham since 1945, it serves more than 175,000 readers across the country from its offices in Boston. The *Wall Street Journal's* staff, led by Bernard Kilgore from 1941 to his death in 1967, has seen its readership rise from 30,000 to 1,250,000 to make the paper one of the country's top ten in size. The paper is produced in eight printing plants across the country, connected by electric typesetting devices to its New York office. It won its position on the basis of its excellent writing, clear-cut reporting of important news, and its specialized business and financial information. The firm in 1962 established an affiliated national weekly newspaper of more general appeal, the *National Observer,* edited in Washington.

The New York *Times,* generally recognized as the country's leading daily and "newspaper of record," also has a sizable national circulation, particularly for its Sunday edition. It clearly has been the leader over a period of time in developing its own Washington and foreign staffs, whose stories are also sold to other papers. Publisher-owner Arthur Hays Sulzberger ably carried on the duties of his father-in-law, Adolph S. Ochs, after Ochs' death in 1935 and maintained a remarkable news institution to which many staff members—editors and reporters—contributed leadership. His son, Arthur Ochs Sulzberger, succeeded to power in the late 1960's and favored the judgments of reporter-columnist James Reston.

Across the continent, the Los Angeles *Times* surged forward in the 1960's to reach the top levels of American newspaper journalism. Young publisher Otis Chandler and a competent staff turned the paper to a more progressive editorial outlook than it had exhibited in earlier years, plunged vigorously into civic affairs, and vastly improved the news content. Chandler joined with the Washington *Post's* owners in establishing a spectacularly successful news syndicate covering the nation's capital and worldwide news centers. The *Times'* editorial page showed intellectual depth.

When one turns to newspapers which have won top recognition for their editorial leadership and for their aggressiveness in defense of basic liberal principles of a progressive democracy, the names of four are readily apparent: the St. Louis *Post-Dispatch,* the Washington *Post,* the Milwaukee *Journal,* and the Louisville *Courier-Journal.*

The St. Louis *Post-Dispatch,* published by a third generation of the Pulitzer family, continued to offer American journalism a highest type of example in the exercise of the opinion function—excelling the standard set by Joseph Pulitzer's New York *World,* which ceased publishing in 1931. A talented *Post-Dispatch* editorial page staff, writing superbly and with a depth of understanding on a wide variety of subjects, made the editorial columns outstanding. The paper continued to win recognition for its crusading zeal and its outstanding Washington bureau.

Rising to prominence since the 1930's has been the editorial page of the Washington *Post.* Financier Eugene Meyer and his son-in-law, Philip L. Graham, the paper's publishers, had as their major aim the molding of a vigorous, intelligent, and informative editorial page for capital readers. This they accomplished, with the help of an able staff who could tap Washington news sources for background and interpretation and the provocative cartoons of Herbert L. Block. Meyer's daughter, Katharine Graham, maintained the *Post*'s quality after the deaths of her father and husband.

Known as "Milwaukee's Dutch Uncle," the staff-owned Milwaukee *Journal* has demonstrated editorial page excellence since the days of founder Lucius W. Nieman. The *Journal* has paid close attention to city and state affairs and has cultivated both good writing and a wide grasp of political and human affairs on the part of its good-sized group of editorial writers. The same characteristics have been exhibited by the Louisville *Courier-Journal,* owned and edited by Barry Bingham. Both these papers exhibited local and regional news reporting of excellent quality.

Among other newspapers of highest quality, the Chicago *Daily News,* the Baltimore *Sun,* and the Minneapolis *Star* and *Tribune* maintain both strong Washington bureaus and limited foreign staffs. Respected for their news play are such other leading papers as the Kansas City *Star,* Cleveland *Press,* Toledo *Blade,* and Chicago *Sun-Times* in the Midwest; the Washington *Star,* Long Island *Newsday,* and Hartford *Courant* in the East; the Miami *Herald,* Atlanta *Constitution,* and Charlotte *Observer* in the South; and the Denver *Post* in the West. Another dozen could be named with almost equal justice to such a list of current leaders in exercising the news function.

While all these newspapers have capable editorial pages, some have won particular attention. Examples of effective conservative opinion are found in the editorial columns of the Los Angeles *Times,* the *Christian*

*Science Monitor,* and the *Wall Street Journal.* Rising in quality and in aggressive independent opinion have been the pages of the Minneapolis *Tribune* and Toledo *Blade.* The Baltimore *Sun,* Chicago *Daily News,* and Providence *Journal* constitute another trio whose editorial pages have won substantial respect over a period of time. At the liberal left, the New York *Post* has admirers of its opinion pages (particularly of its columnists) and of the intellectual level of its political discussion (a level not matched, however, in its general news play). A paper of smaller circulation which has won attention for its vigorous editorial comment on political affairs and independent-mindedness, is the Mc-Clatchy family's Sacramento *Bee* in California.

As Gerald Johnson once said, "The greatest newspaper is as difficult to identify as the greatest man—it all depends upon what you require." Certainly an intelligent, honest, and public-spirited editorial page is as much an essential of an effective newspaper as is comprehensive and honest reporting and display of the news.

# Chapter 5

# Growth of Radio, Television, and Film

Public interest in news made it natural for men to use any new medium of communication—the telegraph, the telephone, the underseas cable, the wireless, the motion picture film, radio broadcasting, telecasting, and the communications satellite—to hurry the news to waiting eyes and ears, or to bring news events directly to distant audiences.

The telegraph, the telephone, the cable, and the wireless were nineteenth-century inventions that could speed the transmission of messages to waiting newspaper editors and printing presses. The motion picture film became a competitor that could bring to audiences in theaters a visual portrayal of such an exciting event as the Corbett-Fitzsimmons heavyweight prize fight of 1897—the first news event so shown. Soon excerpts of films of news events were put together into newsreels, which were a part of the standard fare of the movie palace of the 1920's. But the time lag before a newsreel could be shown kept it from being more than an incidental competitor for the newspaper. Interpretative films like Time Inc.'s *The March of Time* of the 1930's and the development in that decade of the techniques of the documentary film—*The Plow that Broke the Plain* and *The River* were notable examples—foreshadowed the impact film would have on other news media once it had the direct way to reach the public that television provided. In the meantime news took to the air through the magic of radio.

80

The first news broadcast in the United States is generally credited to Dr. Lee De Forest, the man who in 1906 invented the vacuum tube that made voice broadcasting possible as the next step beyond Marconi's wireless telegraphy of the 1890's. On November 7, 1916, the New York *American* ran a wire to De Forest's experimental station at High Bridge, New York, so that the "father of radio" could broadcast to a few amateur radio enthusiasts the returns from the Wilson-Hughes presidential election. Like the *American* and other newspapers misled by the early returns from that closely contested election, De Forest signed off with the statement that "Charles Evans Hughes will be the next president of the United States."

The inventive and engineering resources of wireless and radio were needed for military purposes during World War I, and private broadcasting was banned until 1919. Even then few saw the possibilities of mass radio listening. One who did was David Sarnoff, son of a Russian immigrant family who got his start as a Marconi wireless operator. When three big companies of the communications and electric manufacturing industries—Westinghouse, General Electric, and American Telephone & Telegraph—pooled their patent rights interests in 1919 and formed the Radio Corporation of America, Sarnoff became RCA's sparkplug and the eventual head of both it and its subsidiary, the National Broadcasting Company. His active career was to extend to 1970.

It was a Westinghouse engineer, Dr. Frank Conrad, who offered the first proof of Sarnoff's contentions that people would listen to radio. His broadcasts of music in Pittsburgh in 1919 stimulated sales of crystal sets and led Westinghouse to open KDKA on November 2, 1920, as the first fully licensed commercial broadcasting station. The featured program consisted of returns from the Harding-Cox presidential election, one whose outcome was more easily predictable. The station got its vote results from the obliging Pittsburgh *Post.*

Other newspapers were more directly involved in broadcasting. One, the Detroit *News,* broadcast news regularly beginning August 31, 1920, over an experimental station that was to become a regular commercial station in 1921, WWJ. Others quick to establish stations were the Kansas City *Star,* Milwaukee *Journal,* Chicago *Tribune,* Los Angeles *Times,* Louisville *Courier-Journal,* Atlanta *Journal,* Fort Worth *Star-Telegram,* Dallas *News,* and Chicago *Daily News.* By 1927 there were 48 newspaper-owned stations, and 97 papers presented news over the air. The publishers thought radio newscasts stimulated sales of newspapers—and subsequent events proved them correct.

But despite these evidences of concern for news, radio's pioneers were more intent on capturing the public's interest by entertaining it than by informing it. Dramatic news events and on-the-spot sports coverage combined both objectives. News summaries themselves remained infrequent in the 1920's because they excited little advertiser interest, because radio itself did not collect news, and because news merely read from the newspaper sounded awkward and dull on the air. Meanwhile, KDKA broadcast accounts of prize fights and major league baseball games in 1921. The next year American Telephone & Telegraph's New York station, WEAF (now WNBC), used phone lines to bring its listeners the Chicago-Princeton football game from Stagg Field. By 1924 an estimated 10,000,000 Americans heard presidential election returns; there were 3,000,000 sets that year and the number of stations had grown from 30 in 1921 to 530. Twenty-one stations from New York to California joined in a March, 1925, hookup to broadcast President Coolidge's inauguration.

Development of networks was vital for radio news progress. In early 1924 the Eveready Battery Company bought time on a dozen stations for its Eveready Hour performers—the first use of national radio advertising. By 1925 AT&T had organized a chain headed by WEAF with 26 outlets stretching as far west as Kansas City. RCA, Westinghouse, and General Electric had a competitive chain led by WJZ, New York, and WGY, Schenectady. In 1926 the big companies reached an agreement under which AT&T would retire from the broadcasting business in favor of RCA, and in return would control all forms of network relays. RCA, Westinghouse, and General Electric bought WEAF for $1,000,000. They then formed the National Broadcasting Company as an RCA subsidiary. The station chain organized by AT&T and headed by WEAF became the NBC Red network at the start of 1927, while the chain headed by WJZ became the NBC Blue network. Regular coast-to-coast network operations began that year. Sarnoff emerged in full control of RCA and NBC in 1930 when Westinghouse and General Electric withdrew under pressure of an antitrust suit.

Only 7 per cent of the 733 stations operating in early 1927 were affiliated with NBC. Some rivals organized a network service with the support of the Columbia Phonograph Record Company in 1927; financially reorganized the next year under the control of William S. Paley, it became the Columbia Broadcasting System. CBS bought WABC (now WCBS) in New York as its key station and by 1929 was showing a profit. In 1934 it had 97 station affiliates compared to 65 for NBC Red and 62 for NBC Blue.

Passage of the Radio Act of 1927 strengthened the two big networks, since the number of stations on the air was reduced by the new Federal Radio Commission to avoid interference in receiving stations' programs, and a group of some 50 powerful "clear channel" stations was authorized. By 1938 all but two of the clear channel stations were either network-owned or affiliated. And while only 40 per cent of the 660 stations then in operation were network-affiliated, they included virtually all of those licensed for nighttime broadcasting. The two independent clear channel stations, the Chicago *Tribune's* WGN, and WOR, New York, formed the loosely organized Mutual Broadcasting System in 1934 but found competition difficult. Mutual's complaints to the Federal Communications Commission (the regulatory body was renamed in the Communications Act of 1934) brought about the sale by NBC in 1943 of its weaker Blue network to Edward J. Noble, who renamed it the American Broadcasting Company in 1945.

The growth of the networks after 1927, and their success in winning advertising revenues, made radio a more disturbing challenger to the newspaper industry. So did radio's increasing interest in broadcasting news and public affairs. In 1928, Republican Herbert Hoover and Democrat Alfred E. Smith took to the air, spending a million dollars on campaign talks over NBC and CBS networks reaching many of the nation's 8,000,000 receiving sets. That year the press associations—Associated Press, United Press, and International News Service—supplied complete election returns to the 677 radio stations. Radio's success in covering that bitter presidential election whetted listeners' appetites for more news broadcasts. In December, KFAB in Lincoln, Nebraska, responded by hiring the city editor of the Lincoln *Star* to put on two broadcasts daily of what it called a "radio newspaper." Other stations developed similar programs, and as the great depression deepened after October, 1929, the public became even more interested in news. By 1930, KMPC in Beverly Hills, California, had put 10 reporters on the Los Angeles news runs.

A bitter war now broke out between radio and newspapers over broadcasting of news. Newspaper advertising revenues were sharply contracting as the depression years proceeded toward the 1933 national crisis. Radio, however, as a new medium was winning an increasing, if yet small, advertising investment. Why let radio attract with news broadcasts listeners who will become the audience for advertisers' commercials, asked some publishers. This argument gave more weight to public interest in news than it deserved, considering the demonstrated public interest in listening to such entertainers as Amos 'n Andy, Jack Benny, Walter Winchell, the Boswell sisters, Rudy Vallee, Kate Smith, and the stars of the radio dramas. But after both 1932 political conventions were aired on coast-to-coast networks, and after the Associated Press furnished 1932 election returns to the networks to forestall the sale of United Press returns, the American Newspaper Publishers Association cracked down. The press associations should stop furnishing news to radio; broadcasting of news should be confined to brief bulletins which would stimulate newspaper reading; radio program logs should be treated as paid advertising. There were dissenters to this approach, but after a majority of AP members voted in 1933 for such restrictions, all three press associations stopped selling news to stations. Radio now had to gather its own news.

Columbia Broadcasting System set up the leading network news service with former newspaperman Paul White as director. He opened bureaus in leading U.S. cities and in London and developed a string of correspondents. Hans Von Kaltenborn and Boake Carter, already CBS commentators, did daily news broadcasts. Kaltenborn, a former Brooklyn *Eagle* managing editor, had started broadcasting in 1922 and had joined CBS in 1930 to become the first of a long line of radio commentators. NBC organized a less extensive news service. Local stations got their news from the early editions of newspapers, despite AP court suits to stop the practice.

A compromise was soon proposed. This was the Press-Radio Bureau, which would present two five-minute newscasts daily on the networks from news supplied by the press associations. Bulletin coverage of extraordinary events also would be provided. In return, the networks would stop gathering news. The bureau began operating in March, 1934, but was doomed to quick failure. Stations wanting more news bought it from five new agencies which jumped into the field, led by Transradio Press Service. A year later UP and INS obtained releases from the Press-

Radio Bureau agreement and began selling full news reports to stations. UP began a wire report written especially for radio delivery, which AP matched when it began to sell radio news in 1940. The Press-Radio Bureau suspended in 1940; Transradio succumbed in 1951.

Radio meantime was developing a blend of entertainment and news. The trial of Bruno Hauptmann in 1934 for the kidnap-murder of the Lindbergh baby attracted more than 300 reporters, including many with microphones. Listeners were bombarded with more than 2000 Press-Radio Bureau bulletins. President Roosevelt's famed "fireside chats" and the presidential nominating conventions and campaigns were major events. In December, 1936, the entire world listened by shortwave broadcast as Edward VIII explained why he was giving up the British throne for "the woman I love." Kaltenborn hid a CBS portable transmitter in a haystack between the loyalist and rebel lines in Spain to give his American audience an eyewitness account of the Spanish Civil War. Kaltenborn, Boake Carter, Lowell Thomas, Edwin C. Hill, and Gabriel Heatter were the public's favorite news commentators. Ted Husing and Clem McCarthy were the leading sports announcers. America's top radio entertainment favorites in 1938 were Edgar Bergen and his dummy Charlie McCarthy, Jack Benny, Guy Lombardo and his orchestra, Kate Smith, the Lux Radio Theatre and "One Man's Family" dramatic shows, Burns and Allen, Eddie Cantor, Don Ameche, Nelson Eddy, Bing Crosby, and announcer Don Wilson. But before the end of the year it was Kaltenborn who stole the laurels as the world stopped all else to listen to news of the Munich crisis, which brought Europe to the brink of war.

## RADIO NEWS COMES OF AGE

Radio fully met the challenge of diplomatic crisis and worldwide war which began with Adolf Hitler's annexation of Austria and ultimatum to Czechoslovakia in 1938. Beginning with a patched-together but impact-producing coverage of the Munich crisis, the radio networks expanded their news reporting and technical facilities tremendously during World War II. At the station level, newscasts took a place of prime importance.

Network news staffs had continued to develop on a modest scale after the 1933 cut-off of press association news. NBC's Abe Schechter placed staff men in London and Paris, in Geneva for the disarmament conference, and in Shanghai for the Japanese invasion of China. G. W. Johnstone of Mutual was financially handicapped but had reporters in the major news centers. CBS news director Paul White had developed the largest organization for both U.S. and foreign coverage, but its staff was stretched thin.

In 1937 CBS sent a then-unknown Edward R. Murrow to Europe as news chief. For an assistant he hired William L. Shirer, who had been working for the just-closed Universal Service, a Hearst-owned press association. Like the others, they did human interest stories and cultural programs for shortwave broadcasts which were rebroadcast by U.S. stations. Then came Hitler's invasion of Austria and the *Anschluss.* Murrow hustled to Vienna. On March 12, 1938, the first multiple pickup news broadcast in history went on the air. Shirer spoke from London, Murrow from Vienna, and newspapermen CBS had hired gave their impressions from Berlin, Paris, and Rome. The pattern was set for radio's coverage of the fateful 20 days in September beginning with Hitler's demand that the Czechs cede him the Sudetenland and ending with the Munich Pact. Key staffers like Murrow (who went on to become television's best-known commentator and director of the United States Information Agency) and Shirer (author of *Berlin Diary* and *Rise and Fall of the Third Reich*) bore the brunt of the effort, reinforced by the cream of the U.S. newspaper and press association correspondents.

American radio listeners heard news broadcasts from 14 European cities during the 20-day Munich crisis period. Beginning with the plea for support made by President Eduard Beneš of Czechoslovakia on September 10 and Adolf Hitler's challenge to the world two days later from Nuremberg, listeners heard the voices of Chamberlain, Goebbels, Mussolini, Litvinoff, and Pope Pius XI. Such broadcasts were not new, but the intensity of coverage was. CBS devoted 471 broadcasts to the crisis, nearly 48 hours of air time; of these, 135 were bulletin interruptions, including 98 from European staffers. NBC's two networks aired 443 programs during 59 hours of air time. On climactic days, these efforts kept the air alive with direct broadcasts, news summaries, and commentaries by the news analysts.

In his "Studio Nine" in New York City Kaltenborn spent the 20 days catnapping on a cot, analyzing the news reports, and backstopping the CBS European correspondents with hours of analysis and commentary. It was Kaltenborn who provided the translations of Hitler's fiery oratory before the Nazi rallies, and who later predicted what diplomatic steps would follow. He was heard 85 times, many of them lengthy commentaries, during the three weeks. A few times he carried on two-way conversations with Murrow, Shirer, and other European correspondents. The CBS "European News Roundup," usually a 30-minute show from three or four points, was matched by NBC after two weeks. Aiding Murrow and Shirer were Maurice Hindus from Prague, Pierre Huss of INS from Berlin, John Whitaker of the Chicago *Daily News* from Paris, and Sir Fredric Whyte from London. Hindus scored a beat on the Czech backdown.

Heading NBC's European effort was Max Jordan, who had a 46-minute beat on the text of the Munich Pact, which he broadcast from Hitler's radio station. He relied especially on M. W. Fodor of the Chicago *Daily News* and Walter Kerr of the New York *Herald Tribune* in Prague, Alistair Cooke in London, and such leading press association men as Karl von Wiegand and William Hillman of INS and Webb Miller, Edward Beattie, and Ralph Heinzen of UP. Mutual had only John Steele in London and Louis Huot in Paris, and used their occasional broadcasts, cabled news, and shortwave pickups to augment the regular press association news flow.

American listeners felt the brutal impact of Hitler's demands when Jordan and Shirer spoke from microphones inside the Berlin Sportpalast against a background of hysterical oratory and frenzied Nazi crowd reaction. They were grave when they heard Murrow describe war preparations in London, relieved when Kaltenborn predicted that Chamberlain, Daladier, Mussolini, and Hitler would find a peaceful solution at Munich. While they devoured columns of type, it was radio that brought them a sense of personal participation in what they realized was the world's crisis, not merely Europe's.

By the summer of 1939 Murrow had a four-man staff: himself, Shirer, Thomas Grandin, and Eric Sevareid, a young newsman who also was to become a leading television commentator for CBS. When German troops marched into Poland, Americans tuned in their radios to hear Prime Minister Chamberlain announce that Great Britain was at war. Bill Henry of CBS and Arthur Mann of Mutual became the first front-line radio reporters. Radio news staffs expanded, and eyewitness broadcasts made history. James Bowen of NBC described the scuttling of the German battleship *Graf Spee* off Buenos Aires. Shirer of CBS and William C. Kerker of NBC reported the surrender of the French to a strutting Hitler in the railroad car at Compiègne. Radio brought news of Dunkirk, of the fall of Paris, Winston Churchill's stirring oratory. And in August, 1940, Murrow's "This Is London" broadcasts made the Battle of Britain come alive for his American audience. His graphic descriptions of bomb-torn and burning London, in a quiet but compelling manner, did much to awaken a still neutral United States to the nature of the world's danger.

The first news of Pearl Harbor reached Americans by radio bulletins which shattered the Sunday quiet of December 7, 1941. A record audience listened next day to President Roosevelt's war message to Congress. Radio newsmen, using mobile units and tape recordings, joined the coverage of American forces in the Pacific and Europe. There were many memorable broadcasts: Cecil Brown of CBS reporting the fall of Singapore; Murrow riding a plane in the great 1943 Berlin air raid and describing it the next night; George Hicks of ABC recording a D-Day broadcast from a landing barge under German fire. Network reporters made broadcasts and recordings, filed cables, and competed on equal terms with press association and newspaper correspondents.

The demand for news seemed inexhaustible. In 1937, NBC had devoted 2.8 percent of its total program hours to news; in 1944 the figure was 26.4 percent. CBS in 1945 spent 26.9 percent of its network time on news and sports. Variety shows still ranked highest in audience size— Jack Benny, Fibber McGee and Molly, Bob Hope, Edgar Bergen and Charlie McCarthy, and Fred Allen. Dramatic shows and popular music were next. But four of the leading programs in listenership in 1944 and 1945 were news shows: CBS commentator Lowell Thomas, the "March of Time," Mutual's emotional Gabriel Heatter with his human interest commentaries, and the irrepressible Walter Winchell. As the war drew to a close, radio expressed the sorrow of the people by devoting three days of programing to solemn music and tributes to a dead President Roosevelt.

## RADIO'S POSTWAR EXPANSION

The war years were exceedingly prosperous ones for radio. Total annual revenue more than doubled between 1937 and 1945, and income on revenues increased from 20 percent to 33 percent. When the FCC returned to peacetime licensing procedures in October, 1945, there were 909 licensed commercial standard (AM) radio stations. Sixteen months later there were approximately 600 new stations either on the air or under construction, and the FCC had 700 more applications pending. These mainly were for smaller stations; the number of communities having radio stations nearly doubled in those 16 months. By 1950 there were 2086 AM radio stations on the air and 80,000,000 receiving sets.

Frequency modulation (FM) broadcasting, done experimentally beginning in 1936, was represented by 30 stations on the air in 1942 when wartime necessity brought a freeze in new construction and licensing. In the postwar years many AM stations took out FM licenses and the number of FM stations on the air in 1950 reached 743, a figure which proved to be a high for the ensuing decade. Few of the FM stations were operating independently and giving audiences the selective programing which later was to characterize FM broadcasting.

Radio newsmen, somewhat to their surprise, found listener interest in news sustained during the postwar years. Sponsors, who by 1944 had pushed news and commentaries into third place behind dramatic and variety shows in sponsored evening network time, kept up their interest in news at both network and local levels. The established stations had in many cases developed their own newsrooms during the war, with personnel to prepare both general news summaries and local and regional news shows. The newly licensed stations, often without network affiliation, found news one area in which they could compete. Indicative of the trend was the founding in 1946 of an association of radio news directors, now known as the Radio-Television News Directors Association. Among its early leaders were John Hogan, WCSH, Portland, Maine; John Murphy, WCKY, Cincinnati; Sig Mickelson, WCCO, Minneapolis; Jack Shelley, WHO, Des Moines; and Edward Wallace, WTAM, Cleveland. Part of the stimulus for local station activity was the 1946 FCC "Blue Book," making it clear stations should log public service records, including news and public affairs broadcasts.

Among the network commentators, Edward R. Murrow began his "Hear It Now" program for CBS, where he was joined by his wartime associate Eric Sevareid. H. V. Kaltenborn, who left CBS in 1940, became NBC's leading commentator. Radio listeners who sat glued to their sets all night in 1948, wondering whether President Harry Truman had upset

Thomas E. Dewey in the presidential voting, found Kaltenborn one of the first to realize that Truman's popular vote lead would hold up in electoral college totals. ABC had Raymond Gram Swing, one of the finest of the war era commentators. It also obtained Elmer Davis, who had replaced Kaltenborn at CBS before becoming director of the Office of War Information. Davis won high praise for his postwar reporting, his dry humor and telling barbs, and his ability to get at the heart of complex and confusing issues. NBC scored with public affairs programs from the United Nations during 1946 and 1947. The networks and some local stations also offered documentary programs, analyzing important social issues in a semidramatic format.

But television was casting its shadow over radio. Television's "breakthrough" year was 1948, the one in which the value of time sales for the national radio networks reached an all-time high. Competition among the four networks already was intense, and the vogue for program popularity ratings as a means of snaring sponsors led to such devices as the "giveaway" program featured by 1948 radio. The smaller stations found plenty of local advertising revenues in newly exploited markets, fortunately, and after 1947 radio had more revenue from local advertisers than from network advertisers. The networks already in 1948 were shifting their attention to television, and station owners were seeking television licenses until the FCC instituted a four-year "freeze" so that comprehensive plans for television broadcasting could be worked out. In the meantime, CBS forecast the fate of network radio when it made its famed 1948 "talent raid" on NBC to capture such stars as Amos 'n Andy, Jack Benny, Burns and Allen, Edgar Bergen, and Bing Crosby for future television shows.

### TELEVISION ARRIVES

Experimental television broadcasting in the United States began in the 1920's. The scientific advances which preceded actual broadcasting stretched back over a century in the fields of electricity, photography, wire transmission, and radio. Early television experimenters used a mechanical scanning disk which failed to scan a picture rapidly enough. The turning point came in 1923 with Dr. Vladimir Zworykin's patenting of the iconoscope, an all-electric television tube. Zworykin, then a Westinghouse scientist, soon joined RCA, where he developed the kinescope, or picture tube. Other leading contributors were Philo Farnsworth, developer of the electronic camera, and Allen B. Dumont, developer of receiving tubes and the first home television receivers.

There were experiments in wire transmission of pictures during the 1920's, which were to lead to the founding of AP Wirephoto in 1935. One of the researchers, H. E. Ives of AT&T, sent a closed-circuit television picture from Washington to New York in 1927. The next year General Electric's WGY began experimental telecasting. In 1930 NBC began operating W2XBS in New York; in 1939 it became the first station to offer regular telecasting schedules. Large numbers of people first saw television that year at the New York World's Fair. Commercial broadcasting was authorized by the FCC in 1941, but the wartime "freeze" left only six pioneer stations on the air. Among them were the first commercially licensed station, NBC's WNBT in New York, and WCBS-TV in the same city. The two big radio networks thus had their entries in television broadcasting.

Because of postwar equipment shortages and industry uncertainties, it was 1948 before television could achieve a significant place among the media. In the meantime RCA's image-orthicon camera tube had appeared to enhance the possibilities of live pick-ups, and AT&T was busily extending the coaxial cables which preceded the microwave relay for transcontinental broadcasting. During 1948 the number of stations on the air increased from 17 to 41, and the number of sets in use neared half a million. Cities with television increased from 8 to 23, and the arrival of the coaxial cable and network programing stirred a city's excitement much like the arrival of the telegraph a century before. Cities along the Atlantic coast from Boston to Richmond saw and heard the 1948 political conventions and the Metropolitan Opera. Television's first great star, Milton Berle, stepped before the cameras for NBC in 1948, as did Ed Sullivan at CBS.

Then, in the fall of 1948, came the FCC's "freeze" on additional station authorizations, which lasted until June, 1952. During that time the FCC worked out a comprehensive policy for telecasting designed to give all areas of the country equitable service. In the interval only 108 stations were eligible for broadcasting. A few failed, but many became firmly established. The number of sets in use rose to 15,000,000. The transcontinental microwave relay was completed in 1951, and on September 4 the first coast-to-coast audience saw the Japanese peace treaty conference in San Francisco. NBC also offered the first telecast of a World Series and the first regular coast-to-coast sponsored program, the "NBC Comedy Hour."

The FCC's 1952 plan which ended the "freeze" called for more than 2000 channel assignments to nearly 1300 communities. To do this, the FCC extended telecasting from the established Very High Frequency channels (numbered 2 through 13) to 70 more Ultra High Frequency channels (numbered 14 through 83). There were more than twice as many UHF as VHF assignments, and in addition 242 channels were reserved for educational television stations. But different equipment was needed to tune a set to the UHF and VHF stations, and the established pattern of set making and broadcasting was VHF. The FCC did not require set makers to include both UHF and VHF tuning until 1964; in the meantime UHF languished. In a 1953 decision, the FCC ended a long controversy over color telecasting in favor of the RCA compatible system permitting reception in either black-and-white or color.

Television's great "gold rush" came in 1952–53 with the end of the "freeze." Among the networks, NBC and CBS were well along in their transition from emphasis on radio to emphasis on television. ABC merged with Paramount Theatres in 1953 and took a third-ranking position in television. Mutual did not attempt to enter television; a Dumont network gave up the attempt to compete nationally in 1955. That year there were 439 stations on the air and 33,000,000 receivers. By 1960 there were 533 stations and 55,000,000 receivers. In 1970 there were 690 commercial stations on the air (182 of them UHF), plus 182 educational stations. There were 85,000,000 sets covering 96 percent of U.S. homes. Television surpassed radio and magazines by 1955 in total advertising revenues and a year later passed newspapers as the number one national advertising medium, although newspapers continued to lead in total advertising thanks to their top-heavy position in the field of local advertising.

## TELEVISION AND THE NEWS

Television's first efforts at news shows too often consisted of newsreels supplied by the United Press and Acme Newspictures and still pictures shown while the on-camera announcer read the news script. But television newsmen, equipped with mobile units and magnetic tape, gradually overcame the problems of developing news shows with live film and sound. During the first decade of telecasting, they did far better with on-the-spot broadcasts of major news events, public affairs programing, and documentaries.

In 1951 Edward R. Murrow turned from "Hear It Now" to "See It Now" for CBS. NBC's early morning "Today" show with Dave Garroway, a mixture of news and entertainment, opened in January, 1952. That year network viewers saw an atomic blast at Yucca Flats, the political conventions, and a heavyweight championship prize fight. An estimated 60,000,000 Americans saw President Eisenhower inaugurated in 1953. Television audiences next followed live broadcasts of the McCarthy-Army hearings, which resulted in the Senate's censure of the Wisconsin senator, and watched a parade of gangsters before Senator Kefauver's crime subcommittee. Crucial United Nations sessions went on camera. At least 85,000,000 Americans saw one of the "Great Debates" between John F. Kennedy and Richard M. Nixon in 1960, with the presidency at stake. President Kennedy opened some of his news conferences to live telecasting in 1961, and used television extensively at the height of the Cuban crisis in October, 1962. An estimated 135,000,000 saw some part of television's coverage of John Glenn's 1962 first manned orbital flight.

If proof were needed of television's ability to report great events, it came on November 22, 1963, when President Kennedy was assassinated in Dallas, Texas. Within minutes the networks began a four-day vigil ending with the burial at Arlington. Many heard the first bulletins on radio, then rushed to watch the unfolding drama and hear news summaries on television. An audience study for New York City homes showed that TV viewing rose from 25 percent to 70 percent on Friday after the assassination reports became known. Viewers saw the new President, Mrs. Kennedy, and the casket returning to Washington. They went with the cameras into the White House, saw the Sunday ceremonies at the Capitol. Sunday viewers on NBC (the only network "live" at the precise moment) saw Jack Ruby lunge forward in a Dallas police station to shoot fatally the alleged assassin, Lee Harvey Oswald, and heard reporter Tom Pettit describe the incredible event. Viewership in New York homes jumped to 80 percent as all the networks ran and reran their film. On Monday the funeral of President Kennedy drew a 93 percent viewership figure, the highest known level in television history. The nation agreed that both television and radio had reported the four days magnificently.

With full involvement of American troops in Vietnam after 1965, the ugliness of the indecisive war there was brought into American living rooms by television news crews. Public reaction against the war led to President Lyndon Johnson's decision to retire from the 1968 election race—an announcement made "live" to a Sunday evening television audience. There were even greater public shocks in 1968: the assassinations of the Rev. Martin Luther King and Senator Robert F. Kennedy, and the turmoil and rioting accompanying the Democratic convention in Chicago. In each event television played a major news coverage role.

Happier was the role played in July, 1969, by television when it brought to a worldwide audience the flight of Apollo 11 and direct transmission of pictures of man's first steps on the moon. Viewers saw black and white pictures originating from the moon for five hours, including two hours with the astronauts on the moon's surface. Some 125,000,000 Americans saw the climactic night-time broadcast, and a satellite network carried the pictures to an eventual audience estimated at 500,000,000. Truly a "See It Now" triumph of immediacy, the pictures from the moon gave all men a sense of participation in a great feat of exploration.

After Murrow left the CBS screen in 1958, Walter Cronkite became that network's leading personality. A United Press war correspondent, Cronkite joined CBS in 1950 and became the star of many of its documentaries, including "Eyewitness to History," "The Twentieth Century," and "CBS Reports." He took over the major CBS news program from Douglas Edwards and transformed it into a 30-minute dinnertime show in the fall of 1963. Mike Wallace joined CBS News in 1963 to do its morning show. Other leading CBS newsmen included Eric Sevareid, Charles Collingwood, Harry Reasoner, Roger Mudd, Charles Kuralt, Marvin Kalb, Bill Henry, Martin Agronsky, Winston Burdett, Robert Trout, Daniel Schorr, Dan Rather, and Heywood Hale Broun. Lowell Thomas held forth on radio.

NBC's top stars were two seasoned newspapermen, Chet Huntley and David Brinkley, whose mixture of news and comments between 1956 and 1970 made them a top-ranking television team. When Huntley retired in 1970, John Chancellor emerged as the chief NBC newscaster and Frank McGee as the "Today" show chief. Brinkley continued to contribute his editorial opinions on the evening news program. For many years Morgan Beatty and Merrill Mueller had leading newscasts. Other NBC newsmen included Joseph C. Harsch, Irving R. Levine, and Elie Abel in Europe; Pauline Frederick at the UN; Hugh Downs, Ray Scherer, Tom Pettit, Aline Saarinen, Sander Vanocur, Edwin Newman, Herbert Kaplow, Robert Goralski, Peter Hackes, and commentator Garrick Utley. The "NBC White Paper" was the network's major documentary effort, along with "First Tuesday."

With less resources, ABC has kept pace with such commentators as Frank Reynolds, Harry Reasoner, and Howard K. Smith. James C. Hagerty, President Dwight D. Eisenhower's press secretary, became news chief after he left the White House and pumped new blood into the operation. Leading correspondents were Edward P. Morgan, William H. Lawrence, John Scali, Robert Clark, Peter Jennings, Peter Clapper, and Lisa Howard. "ABC Close-Ups" and "ABC News Reports" are major documentary efforts for the network, which has scored with such programs as "The Making of the President" and "The Soviet Woman." John Daly long conducted the network's top television news show.

Westinghouse's Group W (11 television and radio stations headed by KDKA, Pittsburgh; WBZ, Boston; and WJZ, Baltimore) had its own news organization with Jim Snyder as national news director. Mutual radio had Stephen J. McCormick as news director.

Singling out local station operations for mention is difficult, and a list can serve only as an example. Some award winners for news or public service excellence in recent years have been, among television stations: WNBC, WRCA, and WCBS, New York; WBZ and WGBH, Boston; WFIL, Philadelphia; WTVJ and WCKT, Miami; WHAS, Louisville; WGN and WBBM, Chicago; WCCO and KSTP, Minneapolis-St. Paul; WMT, Cedar Rapids; WIBW, Topeka; KLZ, Denver; KSL, Salt Lake; KHOU, Houston; WBAP, Fort Worth; KNXT, Los Angeles; KPIX, San Francisco; and KING, Seattle. Among radio stations: WNEW, New York; WJR, Detroit; WAVZ, New Haven; WCAU, Philadelphia; WBZ and WEEI, Boston; WMAQ, Chicago; WCCO, Minneapolis; WOOD, Grand Rapids; WSB, Atlanta; WBT, Charlotte; KPHO, Phoenix; KIRO, Seattle; and KNX and KPFK-FM, Los Angeles.

News by satellites became television's most sensational achievement of the 1960's. The successful launching of AT&T's Telstar on July 10, 1962, permitted the first live transmissions between the United States and

Europe. These were "staged" shows of a few minutes' duration while the signals could be bounced off the satellite, but they thrilled TV audiences. RCA's Relay carried pictures of events surrounding the Kennedy assassination to 23 nations. Howard Hughes' efforts to launch a satellite that would achieve a fully synchronous orbit (an orbit and speed that keep the craft directly over one point on earth) met success with Syncom III in 1964. Four such satellites, equally spaced around the world, could provide television coverage to all inhabited portions of the planet. The Communications Satellite Corporation, formed by Congress in 1962 to unify the U.S. effort, put Early Bird into synchronous orbit in 1965, then followed with the Intelsat II series in 1966 and 1967 and the larger Intelsat III series in 1968 and 1969. By the time Intelsat IV satellites followed in 1971–73, no fewer than 78 ground facilities in 53 countries would be connected to a greatly expanded television facility whose social-political use remained to be determined.

## TELEVISION AND ENTERTAINMENT

The period from the end of World War II to the present has been one of turmoil and indeed revolution in the world of visual entertainment. Television's sudden emergence as a major home entertainment medium affected all other media, but particularly radio and motion picture. In the years after 1948 the aerial became a fixture atop almost every roof; inside the living room the TV screen grew from 7 inches in width to 12, to 17, to 21, and in some cases to 24 inches. During the first years of television's popularity, at least, the presence of such free entertainment had a profound effect upon American social habits. Some families planned their day's activities so that they could be at home for favorite programs; that gastronomical phenomenon, the TV dinner, was marketed to be eaten by families sitting in partially darkened rooms with eyes focused on the screen. Gradually audiences became more selective, but the average set still remained on for more than six hours each day.

Having captured a very large portion of the entertainment-seeking audience, television too found many serious problems. Program directors discovered that, operating as they did many hours a day, the television stations devoured good program material faster than it could be created. The writing and producing talent drawn into the television industry simply could not conceive enough fresh material of broad general appeal to fill the stations' program time.

As a result the mass of television programing offered to the public was uneven in quality. Much of it was trite, inane, and repetitious. The critics denounced it vehemently, with good cause. Yet every week, at least during the winter months, a selective viewer could find many hours of literate, provocative, informative, and frequently very entertaining programs. Some of the best were the "spectaculars" or "specials" originated by Sylvester (Pat) Weaver for NBC to break the monotony of regularly scheduled series. The cost of these lengthy and star-studded productions also could be spread to several sponsors.

Television programing suffered from two major difficulties: (1) the tendency of many program directors and sponsors to underestimate the intelligence of the audience and (2) a severe case of overexposure— too many hours of program time in relation to the amount of good-quality program material, even when old Hollywood movies were added to the fare.

New program ideas quickly attracted imitators. The public was subjected to cycles of entertainment, a number of programs similar in nature. For two or three seasons in the late 1950's quiz programs were extremely popular; these gave away fantastic amounts of money to contestants who made the correct replies to many kinds of questions. But the public began to grow weary of these giveaways, and when revelations of unethical assistance to some contestants were made, most of the quiz programs disappeared from the air. Western programs, a modification of the Western movie or "horse opera" that long was a standard item in the motion picture industry, came into vogue. Soon the obvious tales of the Old West were exhausted, and producers took to exploring many ramifications of life, translated into a Western setting. In some cases they took classic fiction plots and reworked them as Westerns. At the peak of the Western craze, so many of these "oaters" (as the industry called such horse pictures) were being shot around the overcrowded Hollywood outdoor locations that the casts of competing shows had to wait in line for turns to perform their heroics before the camera.

Milton Berle was television's first great star, going on the air for NBC in 1948. During the medium's first decade the top audience ratings went to variety shows and comedies. Holding steady places for several years each were Berle, Groucho Marx, Ed Sullivan, and Arthur Godfrey. "I Love Lucy," starring Lucille Ball, held first-place rating for five years. Then, in 1958, came the Westerns, led by "Gunsmoke," and in 1959 half the "top ten" were action-filled, bullet-punctuated tales. "Wagon Train" took top honors for four years, then gave way to "Bonanza." A public outcry against violence contributed to a decline of the westerns in the late 1960's and the rise to number one ratings of the "Smothers Brothers Comedy Hour" and "Laugh-In." Situation comedies like "Gomer Pyle," "The Andy Griffith Show," and "Julia" ranked high. Perennials like Bob Hope, Dean Martin, and Lucille Ball kept their ratings.

But not all of television entertainment was keyed to the audience ratings. The educational program "Omnibus" was a rewarding contribution of the 1950's; so was "Playhouse 90." There were such artistic productions as "Peter Pan" and "Victoria Regina." Leonard Bernstein and the New York Philharmonic orchestra played for appreciative television audiences. The National Educational Television network contributed "NET Playhouse" and "NET Festival." Walt Disney's "Wonderful World of Color" even made the "top ten" lists of the 1960's. Such shows, combined with the news and documentary programs, gave television some claim to a role more socially useful than the casual entertainment role identified by critics as a "vast wasteland."

### RADIO'S NEW PATTERN

Within the few years between 1948 and 1955, virtually all radio network drama, comedy, musical, and suspense shows were dropped, as the sponsors switched to similar programs on television for larger audiences at much higher cost and with a presumption of stronger impact on the viewer. The radio networks declined sharply in importance, and many local stations adopted the "music, news, and sports" format which kept costs in line with decreased revenues. But far from fading away in the face of television's popularity, radio expanded. The number of AM stations increased from 2086 in 1950 to 4269 by 1970. FM broadcasting found sharply increased audience favor in the 1960's and by 1970 there were 2471 FM stations on the air. Radio sets were everywhere—an estimated 303,400,000 of them in homes, cars, and coat pockets.

Radio found it could best sell brief time slots and spot announcements to sponsors. The result was the rise of the disc jockey, a glib fellow who could project a vocal personality on the air and through his chatter give a semblance of unity to a melange of popular recordings, commercials, and news summaries. Many stations became more profitable for their owners with this new style of programing.

Network radio news programs conformed to the new pattern. NBC in 1957 began offering news on the hour for 18 hours of the day, in five-minute segments. Stations added local news, weather, and sports coverage. Bigger stations maintained more comprehensive news shows for morning, noon, and evening audiences, but many smaller stations failed to get beyond the headlines. In the mid-1950's CBS offered a news analysis in depth, "The World Tonight," and NBC introduced its weekend "Monitor" show with a substantial news-and-comment base. Each of the networks developed a four-minute information program fitting the news sponsors' time desires—"Dimension" on CBS, "Emphasis" on NBC, and "Flair" on ABC

With mobile units, beeper phones, and tape recorders, radio can go where the news is with little difficulty. Radio has continued to offer coverage of major news events as they happen. Enterprising stations cover hometown meetings, air interviews, and conduct "open mike" opinion shows. With its widespread listening availability, radio continues to be an important news medium.

## CHANGES IN THE MOTION PICTURE

The motion picture preceded radio as a medium. The genius inventor Thomas A. Edison used some of George Eastman's earliest Kodak film in inventing the Kinetoscope in 1889, but Edison was more interested in his phonograph and let the motion picture project lag. One of his assistants projected the highly popular *The Great Train Robbery* for the Nickelodeon era viewers of 1903, the first motion picture to tell a story. The first great milestone in motion picture art was David Wark Griffith's *The Birth of a Nation,* completed during 1914–1915.

Early motion pictures had to depend upon sight and occasional printed titles; the arrival of the sound motion picture in 1926 put the industry on its modern basis. The electronic sound recording and reproduction process, developed by Warner Brothers, was a by-product of telephone and radio technology. The first synchronized music was heard in *Don Juan* in 1926; the first dialogue, in *The Jazz Singer* in 1927. Technicolor was the next step forward in making motion pictures; the first three-color feature appeared in 1935. Cinerama, hailed as the most important development since the introduction of sound in 1926, ushered in the wide-screen vogue in 1952. Magnetic sound arrived with Cinemascope in 1953; magnetic strippings were used to put the sound on the same film with the pictures. The wide-screen development was exploited by the motion picture industry to help offset the inroads of television.

The changes in Hollywood's film output were equally drastic. The theme for the major producers became "fewer and bigger pictures," many of them filmed in Europe because of tax considerations and a favorable labor market. The producers found their market for the routine Class B drawing room drama and adventure tale taken over by the televised half-hour show, which the home audience could watch free. So the major studios turned to producing pictures of epic proportions in color, shown on gigantic screens. Here was sweep and grandeur the TV screen could not match, qualities sufficiently alluring to draw the viewer away from his easy chair and the admission fees out of his pocket.

A segment of the film industry went off in another, less desirable direction in pursuit of ways to draw the viewer from television. These film makers tried to achieve shock value with material that was too grotesque, socially daring, or close to obscenity for the home TV screen.

One result of the film industry's struggle for survival was a breakdown in the self-imposed censorship code by which the producers policed themselves. This had been adopted in reply to outcries by organized religious and social groups against a too-liberal treatment of sex in some films. For years some producers grumbled that the code was unrealistic in many respects, but generally it was respected and obeyed. Then, in the late 1950's, certain producers intentionally violated its strictures. Sensing a more liberal attitude among the citizenry, and arguing that they were dealing with socially significant subjects which had been forbidden unwisely, these film makers plunged ahead. One of these "breakthrough" efforts was Otto Preminger's picture on the previously banned topic of narcotics, *The Man with the Golden Arm.*

In the 1960's, numerous films were being released by European and Hollywood producers and accepted by the public which would have been taboo a decade earlier. Some of these rightfully could be credited to a more adult and open attitude toward social problems and were sponsored by men willing to fight against censorship barriers they believed to be outdated and unreasonable. Certain legal decisions hitting at film censorship practices in some states, such as that permitting the showing of the controversial British film, *Lady Chatterley's Lover*, broke down the barriers even further. These developments created a more friendly atmosphere for such films as the British *A Taste of Honey*, the American *The Graduate* and *Lolita*, and Ingmar Bergman's Swedish-produced psychological studies like *Through a Glass Darkly* and *Wild Strawberries*. Unfortunately they also opened the way for pictures which had no social purpose but which blatantly exploited the market for lustful crime and sex films. The history of photography is related in Chapter 12, and detailed film developments may be found in Chapter 13.

# PART III

CURRENT
PROBLEMS
AND
CRITICISMS

# Chapter 6

# *Criticisms and Challenges:*
# *Television, Radio, and Film*

## BROADCAST MEDIA: SOME BASIC QUESTIONS

Violence and sex, riots and demonstrations, poverty and plenty, "mass" man and the "forgotten" man—these were some of the social problem areas confronting the broadcast world and the American public during the 1970's.

Since virtually every American home had television and radio, and the average family spent almost nine hours daily watching and listening, the broadcasting media were unavoidably involved in the nation's search for solutions—and often accused of accelerating its problems. Broadcasters, then, had to analyze their own roles in the problems of American society. The broad questions had been asked earlier:

1. What should be offered to the American public over the public airwaves?
2. Who decides what shall be aired?
3. What factors inside and outside the industry affect programing decisions?

With the 1970's well under way, the public and the broadcasters put the questions in more blunt terms:

1. Are the seeds of violence being nurtured through the public airwaves?
2. Does the coverage of riots and demonstrations contribute to more violence and disorder?

3. Should militants and minority groups be granted access to the airwaves and "consumer" opinions heard?
4. Should investigations of vital social problems be curtailed or censored?
5. Can public broadcasting provide uncensored alternative programing of high merit?
6. Does permissiveness in broadcast programs and films degrade standards of good taste?

Seeking answers to these and other relevant questions were White House offices and commissions, Congress, the Federal Communications Commission and other governmental agencies, the networks and individual stations, businesses, universities, foundations, social agencies, and many other segments of the American public.

## VIOLENCE AND THE STEINFELD REPORT

Man's history has been filled with violence, including wars, conquests, and individual crimes. American history itself is riddled with socially and economically caused violence, as well as eight wars or other major conflicts. Since the 1920's, violence has been a central theme of countless American novels, plays, movies, newspaper comics, comic books, radio and television scripts, and other art forms. The assassinations of President John F. Kennedy, Senator Robert Kennedy, and Dr. Martin Luther King, and the attempted assassination of Governor George Wallace of Alabama, combined with recent civil disturbances and the disorder in the universities, all have focused attention on the violent behavior of Americans, forcing them to ask what kind of people they are.

In 1972 a 12-member Scientific Committee on Television and Social Behavior, appointed by U. S. Surgeon General Jesse L. Steinfeld, completed a two-year, $1,000,000 study to determine whether there is a causal relationship between television programs that depict violence and aggressive behavior by children.

Summarizing its five volumes of research encompassing 23 projects, the committee reported that the study "does not warrant the conclusion that televised violence has a uniformly adverse effect nor the conclusion that it has an adverse effect on the majority of children." However, continued the report, "the evidence does indicate that televised violence may lead to increased aggressive behavior in certain subgroups of children, who might constitute a small portion or a substantial portion of the total population of young television viewers." The difficulty of finding evidence, the group reported, "suggests that the effect is small compared with many other possible causes, such as parental attitudes or knowledge of and experience with the real violence in our society." In addition, "the sheer amount of television violence may be unimportant compared with such subtle matters as what the medium says about it: Is it approved or disapproved, committed by sympathetic or unsympathetic characters, shown to be effective or not, punished or unpunished?"

The committee reported that the general prevalence of violence on television remained constant between 1967 and 1969, but that a smaller proportion of characters was involved and the violence was far less lethal near the end of that period. Violence in cartoons and comedies, however, increased.

The Senate Subcommittee on Communications, headed by Senator John O. Pastore, at whose request the study was made, conducted hearings on the report. Surgeon General Steinfeld, declaring that the causal relationship between televised violence and antisocial behavior was sufficient to warrant "appropriate and immediate remedial action," suggested a violence rating system to guide parents and aid the government in determining whether to renew station licenses. He said the problem should be solved by voluntary action by networks and stations and not by censorship.

The networks, meanwhile, had committed more than $1,000,000 to violence research studies by independent social scientists, and the Department of Health, Education, and Welfare had authorized grants for study of the problem. The networks increased their requests to producers to avoid gratuitous violent acts, and efforts were made to reduce drastically the Saturday morning children's TV diet of "mayhem and monsters."

At the same time, television officials made it clear that news programing would not be affected except that every effort would be made to avoid overplaying and sensationalizing news of violence both at home and abroad. Some critics had complained that television was bringing the horrors of the Vietnam war too vividly into the American home and that many of the facts reported were too painful for the public to know. Officials replied that the public *had* to be informed since the responsibility for the decisions made in Washington and culminating on a battlefield 10,000 miles away begin and end in the living room. Because that final responsibility rests with the people, they must have the facts— the bad news as well as the good, the unpleasant as well as the pleasant.

## SEX AND GOOD TASTE

Lesbianism and other sexual deviations, nudity, explicitly portrayed seductions, daring feminine fashions, innuendoes, and gutter-language— all, and more, have become all too common in the mass media and American society in general during recent years. The result is what sociologist and columnist Max Lerner has described as a sort of "Babylonian society," where almost anything goes.

Whereas magazines and books are directed to select audiences, mostly adult, and the audiences viewing motion pictures and plays in theaters may largely be controlled, television enters practically every home and is viewed by young and old alike. Accordingly, the television industry has developed its own Television Code of Good Practice and seeks, with only mixed success, to follow its tenets. Adhering to the code, on a voluntary basis, has been the prime responsibility of individual stations and networks. The networks, however, both because they own and operate numerous stations and because they feed to affiliated stations programs which they do not wish cancelled or edited, have closely supervised their own programing, in concert with other private producers. Consequently, programs are scripted, rehearsed, recorded, and edited before broadcast, to insure that "daring" décolletage by feminine performers is covered and unsavory dialogue is "blooped" before the program is aired.

On the other hand, since sex, violence, and daring language have often brought higher ratings to shows than those of a more wholesome variety, the tendency has been to push the restrictions of the code to the limit. Rowan and Martin's "Laugh-In" is a prime example of the public appeal of shows that combine sex, satire, and borderline innuendoes.

When CBS canceled the Smothers Brothers' comedy show on grounds that the taped programs were not submitted to the network soon enough before broadcast time for adequate editing, a public outcry of censorship arose. CBS executives replied that they saw no reason "to allow any performer who, by his talent, has earned exposure to a microphone or camera to voice his own personal political views at any opportunity he chooses," adding that someone had to be the judge of the difference between entertainment and propaganda. Involved in the dispute was the previous censoring of segments of the show by CBS on grounds of poor taste. The Smothers' "taste test," in fact, led Richard W. Jencks, at that time CBS' broadcast group president, to ask a more disturbing question: "In today's society, is taste obsolete?"

The Senate Subcommittee on Communications, long disturbed by television programing, asked the networks to grant to the Code Authority of the NAB the right to prescreen any television entertainment program at will and to determine prior to broadcast whether the program violated the NAB Television Code. NBC and ABC accepted, but CBS declined on the grounds that the responsibility for evaluating and judging programs cannot be centralized. CBS, and the other networks as well, vowed to increase the policing of programs, to consult with the Code Authority, and to continue their practice of providing closed-circuit prescreening for affiliated stations, which bear ultimate responsibility as licensees.

## RIOTS AND THE KERNER REPORT

Television has been considered by many observers to be a primary cause of the so-called Revolution of Rising Expectations among America's disadvantaged peoples. Both the programs and the commercials aired on television held out a better way of life for minority groups without changing their own real worlds. Unfulfilled expectations built up angry frustrations that erupted into the ghetto riots of Los Angeles, Newark, Detroit, and other cities. America's affluence, of course, was also reflected in movies, radio, newspapers, and other media; undoubtedly, too, there were other factors contributing to the social unrest. But television, the medium most often seen by minority groups, had made an impact that could not be denied. Before big-city riots, television had covered the suppression of civil discontent in the South, principally at Little Rock; Selma, Alabama; and Oxford, Mississippi, and a new level of awareness and indignation had spread throughout the rest of the country.

Many public officials criticized television for its thorough coverage of the disturbances and threatened the network news services with new investigations. Critics maintained that black leaders Rap Brown and Stokely Carmichael had no real followings until television and radio provided almost daily platforms. It was alleged that the mere arrival of a

TV camera crew on the scene of a demonstration often set off crowd action that had not occurred before. Moreover, public opinion polls disclosed a widespread feeling that the news media incite the violence they report merely by being present during riots and reporting on them.

The National Advisory Commission on Civil Disorders, with Governor Otto Kerner of Illinois as chairman, criticized the news media, including television, for incidents in which it felt bad judgment had been displayed and material treated sensationally. But on the whole, the commission found, the media had tried hard to present a balanced factual account of the riots in Newark and Detroit in 1967. Errors in many cases were attributed to false police reports. This was also true in 1971 when false official statements were made that the prison guards at Attica in New York state had had their throats slashed. Actually they had been shot by their would-be rescuers. A coroner and persevering media reporters forced a prompt retraction of the false statements in fairness to the black convicts.

The Kerner Commission indicted the mass media for failing to communicate to their predominantly white audience "a sense of the degradation, misery, and hopelessness of living in the ghetto" as well as "a sense of Negro culture, thought, or history," thus feeding black alienation and intensifying white prejudices. With few black reporters and fewer race experts, the report charged, the media had not seriously reported the problems of the black community. Pointing out that fear and apprehension of racial unrest and violence are deeply rooted in American society, coloring and intensifying reactions to news of racial trouble and threats of racial conflict, the commission asserted that those who report and disseminate news must be conscious of the background of anxieties and apprehension against which their stories are projected.

The news media soon developed guidelines and expertise with the aim of reporting demonstrations as faithfully as possible. It was generally admitted that the media had not properly prepared the American people for an understanding of social unrest. Through television documentaries, radio and TV "talk" programs and interviews, in-depth newspaper and magazine articles, and the like, the media explored the issues thoroughly and sought solutions. Efforts were intensified to recruit black and other minority reporters.

## STUDENT DEMONSTRATIONS

As student unrest spread across the nation with disruptions at the University of California at Berkeley, Columbia University, and elsewhere, coverage of the disorders by the mass media was criticized both by proponents of "law and order" and by the protesters themselves. A large segment of the public, greatly disturbed by what they saw and read, complained that television was being "used" by the demonstrators for purposes of propaganda. Furthermore, it was alleged, news coverage of the occupancy and burning of buildings and especially of counter-action by both civil and campus authorities provoked similar disturbances on other campuses.

On the other hand, student militants and their supporters complained that the mass media, as part of the Establishment which they hated, failed to focus on the root problems of the disorders and thus to help the public understand the issues involved. They saw scant evidence that the media were bringing before the public such matters as the universities' tie-ins with the military, their heavy involvement in real estate and other extraneous enterprises, the role of ROTC on campus, the vesting of control of some institutions in boards composed of such "remote" groups as wealthy businessmen and lawyers, the alleged depersonalization of campus life, and the often blocked channels of communications between college administrations and student bodies.

Student militants had observed the unprecedented media attention given to the problem of Negro employment and representation of blacks on the screen as a result of the civil rights protest movement and the later riots. Many now sought to direct nationwide attention to what they considered the ills of society as reflected in the universities. A hard core of militants obviously sought to tear down the entire structure, while most students merely desired changes in some patterns of university life.

The mass media, as communicators and interpreters of such emotionally upsetting events and issues, were caught in the middle. Never before, in this and the other disrupting social issues of the times, had such heavy demands been placed upon the media to illuminate and thus help solve the problems which threatened permanent damage to the health of American society.

## ~ NATIONAL POLITICAL CAMPAIGNS

Newspapers were the primary targets of complaints of press coverage of the Johnson-Goldwater election campaign of 1964, largely because of the newspapers' overwhelming editorial support of Johnson. In 1968, however, most of the complaints were leveled at television. Supporters and nonsupporters of Governor George Wallace of Alabama felt that he had been treated unfairly on television. Objections were raised to the almost daily TV reporting of the heckling that disrupted speeches by Wallace and Vice-President Hubert Humphrey. Some suspected that the legacy of frigid relations between Richard Nixon and the press, coupled with the alleged "Eastern Establishment" orientation of television newscasters and commentators, led to occasional uncomplimentary and subjective judgments relating to the Nixon campaign.

Charges of bias and distortion were leveled at the television networks over coverage of the Democratic National Convention in Chicago. Proponents of "law and order" declared that the film coverage showing police assaults in the streets and parks upon youthful dissenters, largely anti-Vietnam war supporters of Senator Eugene McCarthy in his presidential bid, failed to include provocations which led to many of the beatings and that too much attention was paid to the demonstrators. Network news executives replied that restrictions imposed upon the movement of camera crews prevented a more balanced coverage. They pointed out that only about 1 percent of network time was devoted to violence during the week.

Strong-arm tactics employed against some TV newsmen at the convention site itself, coupled with reports of assaults upon reporters in downtown Chicago and a conviction that convention proceedings were unduly controlled, led to strongly voiced expressions of resentment by TV news anchormen. In the words of one observer, "TV lost its cool."

Democratic Party officials objected to what they considered a disruption of proceedings and biased reporting caused by constant interviewing by TV camera crews on the convention floor.

Altogether, it was an almost unbelievable, tension-filled four days of events without precedent, as one TV network described them, "either in the history of American politics or in the experience of American journalism." Thousands of viewers wrote and sent telegrams to network and Congressional offices. A federal grand jury, the Department of Justice, the Senate Subcommittee on Communications, and the House Interstate and Foreign Commerce Committee investigated television's convention coverage. The Federal Communications Commission ruled, over strong protests, that the coverage was indeed protected by the Constitution's freedom of the press clause.

**The Walker Report.** The National Commission on the Causes and Prevention of Violence asked Chicago attorney Daniel Walker to study the convention disturbances. Walker's staff took statements from 1410 eye-witnesses and participants and had access to more than 2000 interviews conducted by the FBI. The report described both provocation and retaliation. The provocation "took the form of obscene epithets, of rocks, sticks, bathroom tiles, and even human feces hurled at police by demonstrators," some planned, some spontaneous, and some provoked by police action. The retaliation was "unrestrained and indiscriminate police violence on many occasions, particularly at night," with newsmen and photographers singled out for assault, and their equipment deliberately damaged. The final report of the commission in December 1969 said the Chicago police used "excessive force not only against the provocateurs but also against the peaceful demonstrators and passive bystanders. Their conduct, while it won the support of the majority, polarized substantial and previously neutral segments of the population against the authorities and in favor of the demonstrators."

Although the Walker Report disclosed that no fewer than 70 broadcast and print reporters and cameramen suffered injuries at the hands of the police, scant attention was paid to this fact by a disturbed public. In the words of TV news executive William Small, the public, rather than accept reality, will prefer "to kill a messenger." (Small wrote a book with that phrase as its title.) CBS anchorman Walter Cronkite, angered when he and the TV audience saw floor guards slug CBS correspondent Dan Rather to the floor, later found himself virtually apologizing to Chicago Mayor Richard J. Daley.

CBS correspondent Eric Sevareid found the public's reaction obvious: "Over the years the pressure of public resentment against screaming militants, foul-mouthed demonstrators, arsonists, and looters had built up in the national boiler. With Chicago it exploded. The feelings that millions of people released were formed long before Chicago. Enough was enough: the police *must* be right. Therefore, the reporting *must* be wrong."

**The 1972 presidential campaigns.** Four years later, however, the atmosphere had changed. Dissident groups demonstrated in Miami Beach during the Democratic and Republican conventions, but had little effect upon either. The networks covered the demonstrations as thoroughly as in 1968, but little reaction ensued from the public. For one thing, the disturbances were marked by much less violence than those of 1968. In covering the demonstrations at the Republican convention, CBS for the first time used its new electronic television camera capable of broadcasting live black-and-white pictures without artificial light. CBS also used a film camera equipped with a color light amplifier said to permit filming in almost total darkness. Altogether, the networks spent about $20,000,000 covering the two conventions.

Seeking national television debates with President Nixon, renominated by his party, Sen. George S. McGovern, the Democratic presidential candidate, urged the passage of legislation to repeal the equal-time provision of Section 315 of the Communications Act, so that debates between the major presidential and vice-presidential candidates might take place. The Senate approved the measure, but Nixon refused to lend support, and the House thereupon took no action. In 1960 Nixon had appeared in the first and last series of such debates, and it was generally agreed that his opponent, John F. Kennedy, won the election largely as a result of his performance in the debates. Political incumbents generally see no advantage in debating their challengers. In 1964, with both the White House and Congress under Democratic control, no serious effort had been made to obtain legislation to make possible debates between Republican Sen. Barry Goldwater and President Lyndon Johnson.

It also was not possible, during the 1972 campaigns, to obtain disclosure by both parties of the source of the money that bought television time nor to rule out what New York *Times* columnist James Reston termed, "the vicious 30-second TV political advertisements that appeal to fear and prejudice and mislead the voters."

Under the Federal Election Campaign Act, presidential and vice presidential candidates in 1972 were permitted to spend up to 10 cents per eligible voter, or $14,250,509 each, for all communications media. Of this amount, 60 percent could be spent for broadcast media services and the remainder with newspapers, magazines and periodicals, billboards, and telephone companies.

## ✗ THE FAIRNESS DOCTRINE

For many of the nation's broadcasters, one specific legal requirement —the "fairness doctrine"—had the effect of discouraging, rather than implementing, coverage of many important social issues. Since 1949, broadcasters had been obligated to offer reasonable opportunity for opposing sides to respond to the coverage of controversial public issues. This statutory requirement to be "fair" was based on two legal philosophies not relevant to print media: (1) the airwaves are public property; and (2) broadcasters are licensed to operate in the "public interest, convenience, and necessity." Public interest is served, the Congress and the FCC have ruled, if the airwaves are made accessible to many differing viewpoints.

Most broadcasting leaders took issue with the "fairness" principles, charging that the doctrine abridged freedom of speech and press traditionally applied to electronic media, by forcing the presentation of various sides of an issue, even when the views may be unfounded, untrue, or hard to identify in a local community. Even more annoying to broadcasters was the "personal attack" clause of the fairness doctrine. This clause said that if an individual is attacked in an editorial or program, a script or tape of the attack had to be sent to him, with an offer of a reasonable opportunity to reply. Furthermore, if the licensee endorsed or opposed legal candidates for office in an editorial statement, the same notice and offer of time had to be made within 24 hours after the program was aired.

The industry considered the clause unconstitutional, as a violation of freedom of the press. Its effect would be to curtail meaningful discussion of issues, spokesmen said, because of the expense involved in offering time for reply and because the licensee would avoid controversial issues if he were uncertain about his freedom to comment.

The Supreme Court did not agree with the broadcasters; in 1969 it held the personal attack rules constitutional, noting that "it is the right of the viewers and listeners, not the right of the broadcasters, which is paramount" in such instances. If broadcasters were not willing to present representative community views on controversial issues, Justice Byron White of the court wrote, the granting or renewal of a license might be challenged. To make this "threat" of a license loss, he continued, "is consistent with the ends and purposes of those constitutional provisions forbidding the abridgement of freedom of speech and freedom of the press." In law circles, this became known as the "Red Lion" decision (*Red Lion Broadcasting Co.* v. *Federal Communications Commission*).

"Counter-commercials." This reinterpretation of the First Amendment, establishing the right of access to the airwaves by viewers and listeners, resulted in a movement to require the running of "counter-commercials," presenting points of view opposing those expressed by advertisers. The groundwork had been laid when the FCC in 1967 decided that cigarette advertising came under the fairness doctrine and stations had to carry enough anti-smoking messages to counter-balance cigarette commercials. Congress banned all cigarette commercials, effective January 2, 1971, but the anti-smoking messages continued because the FCC had announced that continuing to run them would be regarded as a public service.

The ecology-oriented Friends of the Earth and other consumer groups then reasoned that, if cigarette commercials could be banned, why not also extend the fairness doctrine to include commercials for other products which they considered deleterious to society? The networks replied that commercials for cigarettes were a special case since they had been determined by the Surgeon General to be dangerous to health, linked by numerous studies to such diseases as lung cancer and heart damage. To extend the fairness doctrine to include advertising of products ranging from detergents to gasoline would mean, the networks said, branding most areas of commercial selling as qualifying for debate as public issues. Advertisers would withdraw their advertising and, if a number of counter-advertisements had to be provided free of charge, the networks and individual stations could not survive financially.

Nevertheless, the Federal Trade Commission asked the FCC to force radio and TV stations to offer time—even free time—to almost anyone who wanted to challenge the contents of commercials. Consumer groups asked the FCC to require stations to run "right to reply" messages countering commercials that touched on controversial "public issues," such as pollution. In addition, it was argued, counter-commercials should be aired in reply to commercials which, while not involving public issues, are subject to allegations of factual inaccuracy. Advertisers, moreover, should be required to substantiate all factual claims before the commercials could be aired. These views found support in a U. S. Court of Appeals decision in 1971 ordering the FCC to reconsider an earlier ruling that the fairness doctrine does not apply to spot television commercials for cars and gasoline products that allegedly pollute the atmosphere.

Declaring that the compulsory allocation of broadcast time for "counter-advertising" would destroy one of the mainsprings of the country's economy and very likely broadcasting itself, the networks and stations mounted a major campaign to defeat the proposals. Although well-intentioned, argued Dr. Frank Stanton, these proposals and other such restrictions were "insidiously erosive." He quoted Justice Louis Brandeis: "The greatest dangers to liberty lurk in insidious encroachment by men of zeal, but without understanding."

Julian Goodman, president of NBC, said that compelling the airing of such attacks on advertising would destroy both television's economic base and the programing built on that base, with the public having no voice in the matter. Pointing out that the regulatory process has created a conflict between the specific provisions of the Communications Act that bar censorship and the provision that requires broadcasters to operate in the public interest, Goodman proposed a solution. "Congress," he said, "can resolve this conflict by making it clear that the anti-censorship provision means just what it says—that the commission may not require broadcasters to put anything on the air or take anything off the air, subject to existing laws on profanity and obscenity."

## PUBLIC BROADCASTING

Public broadcasting has emerged only recently as a major force in television and radio. In seeking to provide alternative programing for the American public, the noncommercial medium offered *The Great American Dream Machine, Sesame Street, The Electric Company,* news and public affairs programs, and other contributions of merit. An integrated system of national direction, program production and distribution, and local station influence evolved. But its chief problems were how to determine the right mixture of central and federated control, how to determine the appropriate audience, and how to obtain enough no-strings-attached funding. Since politics is public broadcasting's marketplace, strong political winds whirled about the system, seeking to determine its direction. Only permanent financing, most public broadcasting advocates argued, could substantially insulate the system from the vagaries of political life and insure its long-range stability.

The Corporation for Public Broadcasting was established by Congress in 1967, acting largely upon a Carnegie Commission report which declared that, "A well financed and well-directed system, substantially larger and far more pervasive and effective than that which now exists in the United States, must be brought into being if the full needs of the American public are to be served." The commission was referring to National Educational Television, which supplied programs for noncommercial stations licensed almost exclusively to educational institutions, state school systems, and public school boards. Some critics viewed NET educational and public programing as "pedantic, impoverished, noble, and often deadly dull," with negligible audiences, minimizing its many years of notable educational accomplishments.

In 1970 the newly authorized CPB established the Public Broadcasting Service to manage programing production and distribution and station interconnection. Production centers were designated at seven noncommercial stations across the country. In addition, the Children's Television Workshop, producer of *Sesame Street* and *The Electric Company,* became, in effect, an eighth center, although it was a nonprofit corporation with ties to no one except that it was funded by CPB, the U. S. Office of Education, and the Ford Foundation. National Public Radio, a noncommercial radio interconnection largely exchanging locally produced programs, was created in 1971.

PBS was unlike any other national broadcasting network. With a board of directors dominated by local station managers, it was far more federated and far more loosely organized. The programs it distributed were produced by the major centers and funneled through the network, but final responsibility for clearance and scheduling rested with the local stations, which could screen programs before airing. NET continued to produce most prime-time evening programing but was no longer the heart of the national system.

The National Public Affairs Center for Television was organized in Washington, D.C., in 1971 to provide public affairs coverage, including news. When the center hired liberal former network commentators Sander Vanocur and Robert MacNeil, Congressional and White House criticism followed. President Nixon in 1970 had established an Office for Telecommunications Policy in the White House and named Clay T. (Tom) Whitehead its director. Whitehead's first effort was to negotiate a compromise agreement among cable television, commercial television, and copyright owners (see page 233). Turning to public television, his office expressed the view that news and public affairs programing was not a wise use of public television money and proposed that more federal funds expended by PBS should go to local stations, thus reducing the amount allocated to the regional production centers.

At the heart of administration and some Congressional displeasure apparently were such programs as comedian Woody Allen's satire of the President, which was not aired; a broadcast documentary entitled, "Banks and the Poor"; Ralph Nader's reports on consumer issues; and a 12-minute segment of *The Great American Dream Machine,* in which the FBI was accused of encouraging or instigating violence within radical organizations. The employment of Vanocur, MacNeil, and Bill D. Moyers, at high salaries, was another apparent factor.

President Nixon in 1972 vetoed a bill that would have provided $65,000,000 for CPB in 1973 and $90,000,000 in 1974. Instead of a two-year measure, the President indicated that he would approve appropriations only one year at a time until changes were effected that met administration approval.

## × LICENSE RENEWAL THREATS

A decision of the U. S. Court of Appeals for the District of Columbia Circuit in June 1971 sent shock waves through the broadcasting industry. In the case of *Citizens Communications Center et al. v. Federal Communications Commission,* the court reversed and declared illegal an FCC policy statement issued in January 1970. That statement had declared that if, in a license renewal contest, the licensee could demonstrate "substantial" past performance without serious deficiencies, all other applications would be dismissed without a hearing on their merits.

Indicating that the FCC must choose the applicant who would provide the best service to the public and who would insure the maximum diffusion of control of the mass media, the court ruled that the Federal Communications Act places the licensee on renewal in the same position as an initial applicant. Each must make the best case possible on the basis of program offering, integration, diversification, past performance, and any other matters the parties might ask the FCC to consider as pertaining to licensee fitness.

Although at one time *average,* and later *substantial,* performance by the station has been sufficient to maintain its license, now, the court ruled, only *superior* performance should be considered a plus of major significance in renewal proceedings. The court suggested that anyone involved in *superior* programing would (1) eliminate excessive and loud advertising, (2) deliver quality programs, and (3) reinvest to a great extent the profits on his license to the service of the viewing and listening public. The court pointed out that this decision would permit new interest groups and hitherto "silent minorities," as they emerge in our society, to be given some stake in and chance to broadcast on radio and television frequencies. The court concluded that its decision restored healthy competition by repudiating an FCC policy unreasonably weighted in favor of the licensees it regulates, to the great detriment of the listening and viewing public.

Chairman Dean Burch of the FCC, informed of the decision, declared, "If this decision stands, it is the end of multiple ownership." *Broadcasting* magazine previously had editorialized, "Nothing less than survival is at issue." Broadcasters viewed the decision as designed to restructure the broadcasting industry so as to eliminate all absentee ownership and all multiple ownership. Few broadcast licensees, it was contended, could meet the test of a carefully contrived application; those who could would not be able to buy a second station because then, under these criteria, both would be lost. The value of broadcast facilities would be diminished if not destroyed, it was contended, and all stations sooner or later would be confronted with an expensive, time-consuming renewal hearing and the possible loss of their licenses to groups assembled for the purpose of obtaining a valuable franchise at a low price.

The decision affected all stations including those owned by the networks (although not the networks themselves).

Broadcasters had been virtually secure from challenge as a result of the WBAL, Baltimore, decision in 1951 and the Wabash Valley verdict in 1963, wherein programing performance was weighted heavily against the uncertainty that the challenger could carry out his proposals. Only WLBT-TV Jackson, Mississippi, had lost its license, on grounds of discrimination against blacks. In 1969, however, the FCC denied renewal of the license of station WHDH-TV, Boston, and awarded it to a competing applicant. The unprecedented decision rocked the broadcasting industry since it seemed to signal a new FCC policy under which renewal applicants with other media holdings, like WHDH-TV (which was owned by the Boston *Herald-Traveler*), were vulnerable to challenges by applicants that had no other media interests. The commission endeavored to establish that this was a unique case, but broadcasters remained apprehensive. The *Herald-Traveler,* which had been supported financially by the TV station, ceased publication in 1972.

The Boston decision encouraged the immediate filing of eight applications against major television licenses, none by minority groups. Broadcasters sought relief from Congress, where Senator John O. Pastore introduced legislation that would require the FCC to find a licensee disqualified to continue operation before it accepted other applications for the franchise. Moving to ease the fears of broadcasters, especially those with other media holdings, the FCC in January 1970 adopted a policy statement asserting that it would favor an incumbent broadcaster over rival applicants if he could show in a comparative hearing that his programing "has been substantially attuned to the needs and interests" of his area. The statement also made clear that the FCC would not deny renewal to a licensee simply because he had other media interests.

Senator Pastore thereupon dropped his bill and no further renewal challenges were filed. However, two community interest groups and two previous renewal challengers filed an appeal to the policy statement which resulted in the court's 1971 reversal of the FCC policy. Pastore, who was subjected during his 1970 re-election campaign to charges of racism because of his sponsorship of the bill, declined to resume the fight. Other Congressmen, however, endorsed legislation that would prevent the FCC from considering any competing application until, and unless, it determined that the renewal would not be in the public interest, convenience, and necessity. Largely because of allegations in the earlier Pastore bill hearings that the measure would insulate broadcasters from challenges by minority groups ("back-door racism" it was termed), the legislation gained only limited support. By 1973 more than 100 renewal applications faced challenge.

## MINORITIES PRESSURES

Blacks, Chicanos, and other minority groups have brought strong pressures to bear against the media in recent years. They allege that racism has been rampant in employment, news coverage, and programing practices. They charge that the media have been engaged in a conspiracy—

conscious or unconscious—to prevent the public from learning that blacks and the poor are exploited by media advertisers. They maintain that some commercials and dramatic programs on television and radio depict false, stereotyped images of minority individuals, particularly Mexican-Americans and American Indians.

Actual or threatened challenges to broadcast license renewals have been the principal means of breaking down the barriers. The first assault, on grounds of racial discrimination, cost the operators of WLBT-TV, Jackson, Mississippi, their license in 1969. Next, KTAL-TV in Texarkana, Texas, succumbed to black demands. The station agreed to employ two black reporters to appear on camera, to consult with substantial community groups to determine area needs, and not to preempt network programs of interest to any substantial community group without prior consultation. In Atlanta, 28 area stations agreed to black demands in areas of programing, employment and service to minorities. Numerous other stations acceded to similar demands.

The Time-Life, Inc.-McGraw-Hill agreement in 1972 set a precedent in the buying and selling of television stations in blocs by multi-station owners. When McGraw-Hill proposed to buy five stations from Time-Life, Inc., Chicano groups in each city protested the sale on grounds of violation of the FCC policy prohibiting a single licensee from acquiring more than two VHF and one UHF stations in the 50 largest television markets without making a compelling public interest showing. Although the FCC approved the sale, threatened court action resulted in McGraw-Hill's decision not to buy WOOD-TV in Grand Rapids, Michigan. In addition, the company agreed to the establishment of a minority advisory council to act as consultants in program planning and production and in the recruitment and training of minorities for station employment. A national coordinating council was established to review these actions. Moreover, provision was made for one-minute public-access, public-service announcements; the appointment of a national minority-affairs coordinator; the goal of 15 percent employment of minorities within three years; assistance to minority businessmen; substantial minorities programing; and a continuous program of ascertainment of community needs.

Legal and financial support for minority groups' challenges to the media have been provided by national coordinating organizations. They include the Office of Communications of the United Church of Christ, the

Citizens Communications Center, the Stern Community Law Firm, the National Citizens Committee for Better Broadcasting, and the National Mexican-American Anti-Defamation Committee, Inc.

The movement greatly accelerated the hiring and programing practices which numerous broadcasters had adopted voluntarily during the past decade in recognition of minority needs. Even so, the demands mounted. A Congressional black caucus in 1972 called for establishment of a national task force to aid local organizations in eliminating media discrimination through license-renewal challenges and litigation. The caucus urged the appointment of a qualified black to the FCC. (Benjamin L. Hooks was later named to the commission by President Nixon.) It called on the FCC to "stop excluding service to the (minority) community when it reviews license-renewal applications" and laid plans seeking authorization of an Office for Community Affairs within the FCC to process citizens complaints. The media, the caucus declared, should promote more blacks into decision-making positions and give black reporters assignments handled almost exclusively by whites. A study of television's effects on black children also was urged.

## PRIME-TIME ACCESS

For more than a decade the Federal Communications Commission has expressed concern about the networks' dominance of the air waves. Diversity in programing, as well as in ownership, has been its goal. In late 1971 the FCC reduced network time from three and a half to three hours a night during so-called prime viewing time, 7–11 P.M. EST. The commission reasoned that this action would force local stations to originate at least half an hour of programing every evening, thus providing "a healthy impetus to the development of independent program sources" and inevitably leading to "diversity of program ideas."

Involved in the commission's ruling were TV stations in any of the top-50 markets in which three or more commercial stations were operating.

The testing of the effectiveness of the ruling was delayed a full year when the FCC told local stations that they would not be expected to provide fresh program fare until October 1, 1972. The reason: Independent program sources would need time to produce new programs and the stations would be hard-pressed to provide original shows quickly.

The results of the order were varied. Some stations increased their local news time. A few tried newly produced programs; some imported shows from Canada and England. Most, however, turned to reruns of old favorites such as *Jeannie* and *Dragnet*. Syndicators failed to begin production of new shows on the grounds, among others, that station-by-station distribution of prime-time programs competitive with network offerings was impracticable and not economically feasible.

A Screen Gems survey revealed that more than 75 percent of the television executives in major markets were opposed to the rule. In general, they felt that the order would not encourage more original and diversified programing and could well lead to the lowering of overall quality of television programing available to the public.

The FCC refused to grant a waiver of the rule to permit ABC to broadcast the 1972 Summer Olympics during three and a half hours of prime time for 10 evenings. Instead, the network, which had paid $6,500,000 for TV rights three years previously, was forced to reduce its coverage by five hours. The requirement had been waived for such telecasts as the "Miss America" contest, the Oscar awards program, and over-length movies, but the commission apparently decided to draw the line—and hold it.

Nevertheless, prospects that the ruling would accomplish its laudable purpose seemed dim, and its early repeal was anticipated.

### "THE SELLING OF THE PENTAGON"

A landmark case over broadcasters' rights under freedom of the press vs. Congress' right to legislative inquiry was sidelined in July 1971 when the House of Representatives returned to committee a proposed contempt citation against the Columbia Broadcasting System and its president (now vice chairman), Dr. Frank Stanton.

The citation was recommended by the House Commerce Committee when the network refused to supply all of its "out-takes," or unused pieces of film and tape, used in the production of the controversial documentary, "The Selling of the Pentagon." The award-winning investigative report contended that the Department of Defense spends millions of dollars promoting both its activities and political points of view and that, moreover, it had stopped none of its promotions despite a presidential directive to executive agencies to end "inappropriate promotional activities" and curtail "broadcasting, advertising, exhibits, and films."

Critics, including Vice President Spiro Agnew and high-ranking Congressmen, assailed the report, one terming it a "professional hatchet job." It was charged that CBS News edited some answers selectively and out of sequence and in one disputed case made it appear that a Marine colonel was expressing his own views when, for two sentences, he may have been quoting someone else. Other allegations of error and distortion also were made.

In reply to a subpoena Stanton testified before the House Special Subcommittee on Investigations, but declined to produce the "out-takes" of the program—those edited from the finished product. Pointing to the "chilling effect" not only of the subpoena but of the investigation itself, Stanton stated: "If newsmen are told that their notes, films, and tapes will be subject to compulsory process so that the government can determine whether the news has been satisfactorily edited, the scope, nature, and vigor of their newsgathering and reporting activities will inevitably be curtailed." He said the vital question was whether news and editing judgments shall continue to be made independently by a free press—and whether the letter and spirit of the Constitution could possibly contemplate distinctions between print and broadcast journalism.

On the contrary, contended Committee Chairman Harley Staggers. "Fraud and deception in the presentation of purportedly bona fide news events," he said, "is no more protected by the First Amendment than is the presentation of fraud and deception in the context of commercial advertising or quiz programs." He said the committee needed the out-takes to determine whether the network was "giving viewers an erroneous impression that what they were seeing has really happened, or that it happened in the way and under the circumstances in which it is shown."

The FCC studied the issues and concluded that the CBS editing decisions were a matter of journalistic judgment into which it should not inquire. The FCC also ruled that the network had fulfilled its responsibilities under the fairness doctrine by providing significant opportunities for contrasting viewpoints to be heard.

The House, by a vote of 226 to 181, declined to cite Stanton and the network for contempt. The dean of the Congress, Emanuel Celler, chairman of the Judiciary Committee, reflected the sense of the majority: "The First Amendment," he said, "towers over these proceedings like a colossus and no *esprit de corps* and no tenderness of one member for another should force us to topple over this monument to our liberties; that is, the First Amendment . . . There may be no distinction between the right of a press reporter and a broadcaster. Otherwise, the stream of news may be dried up."

Thus the question of press freedom did not come up before the Supreme Court, as anticipated. CBS, however, issued a new statement of standards of news and documentary production designed to correct questionable editing practices. The Pentagon initiated a review and promised "corrective action" concerning its promotional activities.

The celebrated case came on the heels of an FCC examiner's finding that WBBM-TV, a Chicago station owned by CBS, "prearranged" a marijuana party; Secretary of Agriculture Orville Freeman's charges of news-slanting in a controversial CBS report on "Hunger in America," a complaint found groundless by the FCC; an FCC ban on cigarette advertising on broadcast media; and a drive by the Federal Trade Commission to uncover "false and misleading" advertising.

Network officials declared their intention of continuing their investigations of such social problems as marijuana and dope addiction, hunger, and poverty. Many observers, however, believed that the threat of Congressional and federal agency action requiring costly and time-consuming defensive activities, coupled with the unpopularity of such documentaries with most advertisers and much of the public, would indeed have a "chilling effect" that would greatly reduce the production of such reports.

## CRITICISM OF THE FILM

For many years criticism of commercial motion pictures focused on the artificial world they created. The vision of life presented in Hollywood films was far from everyday reality. It had excitement, glamour, romance, and comedy, but rarely paid attention to the squalid, perplexing problems of life. The film makers were selling noncontroversial entertainment featuring stars who had been blown up bigger than life by astute publicity. The major Hollywood studios, which dominated the market, had developed a successful formula and rarely deviated from it. Before television, they had no important rivals in presenting visual entertainment.

A limiting factor against realism on the screen was the highly restrictive censorship code, conceived and enforced by the producers' association as a result of scandals that besmirched some silent film stars in the

1920's. Pressure from the Catholic Legion of Decency and other policing groups strengthened enforcement of the code.

The taboos went to such extremes that a husband and his wife could not be shown together in the same bed. Mention of narcotics was forbidden. Criminals could not emerge as victors, although Hollywood made millions of dollars with gangster pictures full of violence by having the criminal lose at the last moment. A frequently heard claim that movies were aimed at the mentality of a 12-year-old had much evidence to support it.

Shortly after World War II, Hollywood's attitude began changing. The postwar world wanted more realism. Television's rapidly developing lure was keeping potential moviegoers at home. Film makers realized that they needed to alter their approach. More daring producers started making films that dealt with narcotics and contained suggestive sex scenes. They placed their products in theaters without the supposedly essential code seal of approval and drew large audiences.

Eventually enforcement of the code broke down completely. The growing permissiveness of American society emboldened the film makers; the increasingly frank films they released in turn contributed to the trend. Several U.S. Supreme Court decisions greatly broadening the interpretation of what was permissible under the obscenity laws speeded up the process. So did the success of uninhibited films imported to this country, especially from Sweden. While they were shown mostly in metropolitan "art" theaters, their impact on American film making was intense.

The second half of the 1960's saw swift acceleration of boldness on the screen. Nude scenes became commonplace. Sexual situations which had been only hinted at a few years earlier were shown explicitly. An imported Swedish film, "I Am Curious (Yellow)," broke a barrier by showing actual scenes of sexual intercourse. Actresses and actors casually used language in films that was taboo in polite conversation a decade earlier. Films dealt with such themes as homosexuality, lesbianism, sadism, and other deviations from accepted norms. Greater liberality in these fields brought no reduction in the amount of violence shown, a major source of complaint by Europeans against American films.

The complaints against motion pictures were reversed: instead of being accused of sugar-coated blandness, they were charged with undue frankness. But with all its boldness, was American film making being realistic? Many critics said no. They contended that, while obviously such problems as homosexuality existed, film producers were putting too much stress on them in order to cash in on shock value at the box office, and still were not coming to grips with the broader social problems of the country. They accused Hollywood of forcing moral looseness upon its audience, often to the embarrassment of theater patrons.

Anxious to preserve their profits from this new freedom, and to prevent any government censorship moves, the Motion Picture Association of America adopted a new rating plan. Starting in November, 1968, each new Hollywood film was released bearing a code letter. This was to inform potential viewers what kind of picture to expect. The letter ratings were: G—for general audiences; M—for adults and mature young people; parents should decide if their children should attend; R—restricted; those under 16 must be accompanied by a parent or adult guardian; X—those under 16 not admitted.

Quickly many producers found that it was profitable to make films that barely stopped short of the "X" label, getting an "R" so the pictures could be shown to youth under 16 when chaperoned. Some producers welcomed an "X" rating, to reach an audience they found to exist for such material. Theater operators reported difficulty at times in finding an adequate supply of good quality "G" films.

Largely because of misunderstanding as to the meaning of the word, "mature," the "M" rating was changed in 1970 to "PG"—all ages admitted; parental guidance suggested. In addition, the age limit for the "R" category was raised from 16 to 17, and the same change was made for the "X" category. In some areas, the age limit may vary, according to choice of theater owners.

By using the new code, the film makers placed the responsibility of censorship upon the audience, rather than upon themselves. By the early 1970's they seemed to have discovered a profitable solution to the competition from television, which because of its home audience was more cautious in selection of material than theater operators were. Many newspapers, however, either refused to print advertisements for "X"-rated movies or placed severe restrictions upon their content.

Undoubtedly the revolution in American films had made them better related to the realities of life, more experimental and stimulating, and more influential in shaping the country's social patterns, especially among people under 30. Independent producers now were better able to get their films, often uncommercial by the old standards, before the public. Whether the latent resistance among many Americans would curb the extremes to which some film makers were going was still uncertain.

# Chapter 7

# Criticisms and Challenges:
# The Print Media

## SOME BASIC QUESTIONS

American newspapers and magazines are under severe scrutiny and pressure for change today. Already stirred by drastic changes of the past decade in methods of production and to a slightly less degree in subject matter, the print media are in the midst of a revolution that will see further major alterations during the remainder of the 1970's. As parts of the power structure, they are caught up in the reexamination of values that is sweeping American society. Newspapers are free enterprise businesses, but they approach the status of "common carriers" of essential information and interpretation, and, with the broadcast media, they largely determine the community's agenda of discussion of current issues each day. Since they exist by soliciting public support in the form of paid readership, they are more exposed to criticism and challenge than many other institutions.

This criticism in its simplest stage takes the form of second-guessing the editor. He gave one story too much space, he omitted important details in another, his front page picture was too daring, he put the main headline on the wrong story: these are typical routine criticisms. Most of them are subjective, reflecting the individual reader's prejudices.

The significant criticisms of the print media run much deeper. Some are overstated or outdated. Others have merit and deserve more corrective action than they have received from the nation's press.

Basic questions confronting the newspaper industry and the public during the 1970's include the following:

1. Is the press, early enough and well enough, informing the American public about the causes of serious social disturbances?

2. Are portions of the nation's press guilty of sensationalism, and of overemphasizing trivial happenings, in their treatment of the news?

3. Is it possible to inform the public about suspected criminal activities and the processes of law without violating the right of the individual to a fair trial?

4. Is the press fair in its treatment of candidates for political office and, protected by recent court rulings, in its criticism of office-holders themselves?

5. Is the absence of newspaper competition harmful to a community?

6. Do regular newspapers deal adequately with issues of war, drugs, and living styles, which the "underground" press stresses?

These and other issues, such as the very credibility of the print media themselves, require constant examination if the press is adequately to fulfill the roles for which it has been granted First Amendment protection. Some of the most frequently discussed areas of criticism follow.

## SENSATIONALISM AND VIOLENCE

Groups of college students, asked for their opinions of newspapers when they are receiving their first exposure to mass communications study, frequently reply, "They are too sensational." Pressed for specific evidence, many of them are unable to supply it. Sensationalism is an emotional, abstract word, not easily defined, but meaning essentially an exaggerated or lurid presentation of news and feature stories. Some students are speaking of a newspaper's physical appearance; others refer to the kinds of stories published.

Despite this difficulty in documenting the charge, the fact is that many do have the conviction that newspapers are guilty of sensationalism. They believe that the newspapers inflate the news, deal in trivialities, create conflict to build readership, and give too much attention to pseudo-events and insignificant "personalities."

Newspapers as a whole are less guilty of headline sensationalism with crime and sex stories than they were a generation ago. They have a valid answer to the easy charge, "You are playing up that story to sell papers." Since the arrival of instantaneous television and radio news, single copy street sales are only a relatively minor part of most newspapers' circulation. Most copies are delivered to homes by subscription; the headlines on a single day's edition have little effect on these sales. It is true, of course, that editors include crime and sex stories because they help maintain basic reader interest in the medium.

A frequently heard criticism is that newspapers give too much attention to violence, both traditional crime and racial disturbances. Considering the amount of violence there is in today's society, and the newspapers' obligation to report all aspects of life, criticism of contemporary newspapers on this point has been overstated at times. Reporting of racial violence became a difficult problem for newspapers in the late 1960's. After the first shock of the outbreaks came the realization that the tone of news handling could influence the course of the rioting. Many editors became cautious and played down later disturbances, even beyond the dictates of normal news judgment. Correspondingly, the better newspapers belatedly began to give more attention to the causes of the violence. Demonstrations on the campuses and in the cities against the Vietnam War added a further source of violence, of which the fatal shooting of four Kent State University students by National Guard troops was the most tragic example.

✶ A study of "Sex and Violence on the American Newsstand" by a sociologist, Herbert A. Otto (summarized in *Journalism Quarterly,* Winter 1963), provides a comparison among different segments of the print media. The researchers analyzed issues of 55 representative magazines and found a total of 2524 incidents of violence and 1261 incidents dealing with sexual themes. Police and detective magazines contained an average of 77 incidents of violence per issue and 15 involving sex; men's magazines, 63 involving violence and 19 involving sex; romance magazines, 33 involving violence and 50 concerned with sex. The highest quality magazines—*Atlantic, Harper's,* and *New Yorker*—averaged 15 incidents of violence and 5 involving sex. Family magazines scored 12 and 4, respectively. Of a sample of 300 paperback books found on a representative newsstand, 44 percent had covers or illustrations with a seductive, sadistic, or violent theme.

Turning to issues of 10 representative metropolitan newspapers, the researchers found that on the average they devoted 5 percent of their news space to stories dealing with incidents of violence, including accidents and war as well as crime. One, the New York *Daily News,* used a third of its news space for such stories; the other nine used from 2 to 8 percent. The *Daily News* devoted 3.3 percent of its space to subjects dealing with sex, the other nine less than 1 percent. These figures should surprise many critics of the newspaper press.

## THE PRESS AND THE INDIVIDUAL

Newspaper reporting of arrests and trials, especially in crimes of a sensational nature, came under attack from the American Bar Association and certain civil rights groups during the 1960's. This development coincided with an increasing concern by the United States Supreme Court about the rights of defendants. The editors were accused by their critics of "trying the case in the newspapers" and printing material prejudicial to the defendant.

The American Bar Association's house of delegates in 1968 adopted guidelines intended to restrict the reporting of crime news. This is known as the Reardon report, for Associate Judge Paul C. Reardon of the Supreme Judicial Court of Massachusetts, chairman of the committee that wrote it. Newspaper spokesmen protested vehemently, asserting that the attorneys had overstepped their role and were trying to sabotage freedom of the press. Eventually a press-bar committee, set up through the American Society of Newspaper Editors, resolved much of the conflict. Under court and ABA pressures, the newspapers grew more cautious about what they printed concerning a crime and the suspects in it, before the matter reached trial. Also, the police became reluctant to disclose the facts of a crime to reporters—the kind of facts they had usually given freely in the past. Responsible editors admitted that there had been excesses; their primary concern was that restrictions on crime reporting, in the interest of a fair trial, did not become a wedge toward restriction of press freedom in other fields. Almost 25 states adopted voluntary free press-fair trial guidelines.

The general tightening of restrictions on coverage of trials included orders by federal judges in several judicial districts forbidding news photographers from bringing cameras onto the building floors where federal courts are situated. Photographers also were forbidden to operate in certain other areas near the courtrooms through which the prisoners moved. Previously, the ban had been only against photographs in the actual courtrooms.

One constant challenge facing editors of the print media is to cover controversial news vigorously without violating the laws of libel. These laws, designed to protect the individual from unfair and damaging attacks in print, create well-defined limits as to what a publication can print without risking legal action and possibly a heavy fine.

Libel laws are complex, but the fundamental principles are relatively simple. They are well summarized in this statement by the Appellate Court of New York in the suit *Dall* v. *Time Inc.* ·

> Any written or printed article published of and concerning a person without lawful justification or excuse and tending to expose him to public contempt, scorn, obloquy, ridicule, shame or disgrace, or tending to induce an evil opinion of him in the minds of right-thinking persons, or injure him in his profession, occupation or trade, is libelous and actionable, whatever the intention of the writer may have been. The words need not necessarily impute actual disgraceful conduct to the plaintiff; it is sufficient if they render him contemptible and ridiculous.

The words "lawful justification" include material that is *privileged;* that is, statements made on the official record during court trials and public meetings of governmental bodies, such as city councils or Congress. For example, Councilman Jones may call Councilman Smith "a liar and a thief" during a council session, and a newspaper can publish the allegation safely, because it is privileged. However, if Jones made the same statement about Smith in the corridor after the meeting adjourned, the newspaper that printed it would risk a libel suit from Smith unless it could prove that the Jones charges were true.

The basic defenses in a libel action are: truth, proof of privilege, that the statement was fair comment and criticism, that the publication was innocently made and without malice, and publication of a retraction. A retraction actually is an admission of guilt, but its publication generally lessens the amount of any award of money as damages to the plaintiff.

Historically, the libel law has protected individuals, or small groups of easily identified persons, but not large, amorphous groups. Agitation is developing to enlarge its protection to cover broader groups, such as ethnic minorities, but the difficulty in writing such laws has discouraged their adoption.

A landmark case in broadening the print media's right to comment was the Supreme Court's ruling in *New York Times* v. *Sullivan,* in 1964. The court held that a public official cannot recover damages for a defamatory falsehood relating to his official conduct unless he proves that the statement was made with actual malice. This and related rulings have broadened the interpretation of "public official" to include relatively minor public employes and even "public figures" such as former office-holders and prominent personalities in the news. Because of these rulings, the pressure of libel laws on editors has eased a little.

Many of the court suits involving the laws of libel and the right to privacy have involved magazines. One large segment of the magazine press has depended heavily for circulation upon the well-known pro-clivity of human beings for reading the "true story" and the "dirt" on other human beings. These types of stories sometimes extend beyond the movie, true confessions, and exposé types of magazines into the pages of the widely circulating general magazines, women's magazines, and Sunday supplements. Some are based merely on human interest and entertainment elements—for example, the endless articles about Jacqueline Kennedy Onassis. Some appear as crusading efforts. The unhappiest example was the story "exposing" a Georgia football coach run by the *Saturday Evening Post,* which cost that magazine a heavy sum for damage and contributed to its demise.

### POLITICAL BIAS

Charges popular a few years ago that newspapers slanted their coverage of election campaigns to help the candidates they favored are heard less frequently today. That is because far fewer newspapers are guilty of the charge now than in the past. With certain glaring exceptions, American newspapers generally try diligently to provide balanced political reporting. Some keep exact measurements of their stories, to be sure that by election day the rivals in each race have had approximately an equal number of news column inches and photographs, as well as equal front-page treatment. Responsible editors are careful to remove prejudicial adjectives, verbs, and descriptions from the news copy.

Even so, the goal of total objectivity is difficult to achieve, particularly since editors are placing more emphasis on interpretative reporting in order to give their readers better understanding of the news background. Unless done with skill, interpretation in news columns can involve injection of the writer's personal feelings, or those of his publisher.

The support given by newspapers on their editorial pages to presidential candidates has been another source for charges of political bias. Figures compiled by *Editor & Publisher* magazine explain why. Historically, the majority of daily newspapers giving support to a presidential candidate has been on the side of the Republican party.

While Vice-President Agnew waged a running oratorical campaign against what he called the news-slanting and anti-Nixon bias of the "Eastern establishment press," Nixon's elaborate communications department wooed the rest of the American daily and weekly press with direct contacts and frequent mailings of pro-administration material. Nixon reduced the frequency of press conferences and sought impact on the voters through nationally televised speeches, in situations where he was not subject to questioning by reporters. Nixon had the endorsement of 753 daily newspapers in his one-sided 1972 reelection victory while 53 supported Sen. George McGovern, *Editor and Publisher* reported.

In 1960 Vice-President Richard M. Nixon was supported by newspapers with 70.9 percent of the polled circulation in his unsuccessful race against John F. Kennedy, who had 15.8 percent.

A dramatic reversal occurred in 1964. President Lyndon B. Johnson, who succeeded to the White House after Kennedy's assassination, faced a right-wing conservative Republican, Barry Goldwater. Johnson had the support of dailies representing 61.5 percent of the polled circulation, Goldwater 21.5 percent.

The trend swung back to the Republican side four years later, when Nixon faced Vice-President Hubert Humphrey, the Democratic nominee. Nixon had the support of newspapers representing 56 percent of total U.S. circulation, to Humphrey's 15 percent. A few papers supported George C. Wallace, the conservative third-party candidate, and the remainder either did not reply to the questionnaire or remained uncommitted.

Some leading magazines have taken an editorial stand on presidential elections, as well as other issues of the day. They include the *Reader's Digest,* among the giants. *Saturday Review, Harper's,* and the magazines of opinion regularly take stands on public issues, including candidates. Generally, the magazines have followed the consensus established in the newspaper press, except for the small group of politically oriented opinion journals.

Critics have pointed to the interpretations and analysis interjected into *Time*'s reporting as "political bias"—*Time* replies it never meant to be merely objective. *Newsweek* sought to separate news and interpretation by the use of columnists, but often ran into the same difficulties as those encountered by the newspaper press. Readers are quick to charge "bias" when presented news adverse to their candidate.

## BREADTH OF COVERAGE

A valuable guide to measuring the balance and depth of a newspaper's coverage is found in the 1947 report of the Commission on Freedom of the Press, chaired by Robert Maynard Hutchins, at that time chancellor of the University of Chicago. Although written a quarter-century ago, the commission's list of society's five requirements of the mass media remains pertinent today. They are: (1) a truthful, comprehensive, and intelligent account of the day's events in a context which gives them meaning; (2) a forum for the exchange of comment and criticism; (3) the projection of a representative picture of the constituent groups in the society; (4) the presentation and clarification of the goals and values of the society; and (5) full access to the day's intelligence.

This philosophical statement viewed the agencies of mass communication as "an educational instrument, perhaps the most powerful there is." The images created by the mass media can be helpful or detrimental in the making of public decisions and in the maintenance of social goals and values. The obligation to inform, the commission emphasized, extends beyond mere relating of current news, or mere entertainment in the cases of magazines, books, film, radio, and television. Entertainment can also be informative in nature, but that type of approach does not meet the full obligation of the mass media to reflect educational leadership.

In a statement about sensationalism, the commission commented:

> To attract the maximum audience, the press emphasizes the exceptional rather than the representative, the sensational rather than the significant. Many activities of the utmost social consequence lie below the surface of what are conventionally regarded as reportable incidents: more power machinery; fewer men tending machines; more hours of leisure; more schooling per child; decrease of intolerance; successful negotiation of labor contracts; increase of participation in music through the schools; increase in the sale of books of biography and history.

In most news media such matters are crowded out by stories of night-club murders, race riots, strike violence, and quarrels among public officials. The Commission does not object to the reporting of these incidents but to the preoccupation of the press with them. The press is preoccupied with them to such an extent that the citizen is not supplied with the information and discussion he needs to discharge his responsibilities to the community.

The manner in which our national values change is evident in the way the commission, writing a quarter-century ago, listed "race riots" in the same category with "night-club murders." Today we consider the riots significant news to be covered with great care, reflecting as they do deep dissension among segments of the American people.

## MONOPOLY

The disappearance of competing newspapers from many large cities has raised concern about news monopolies. Critics fear that the sole publisher in a "one-paper city" will print only the news that he wants his readers to see, leaving out or de-emphasizing stories that are embarrassing to him, his friends, or his advertisers, or that, on other grounds, he does not wish to have published. There are enough instances when this has happened to give a sound basis for this worry. On the other side, there are frequent cases where a monopoly publisher, sensitive to his vulnerability to the charge, has made extra effort to provide his city with more extensive, deeper news coverage than he did previously in a competitive situation. Competitive pressure from other news media in the area, especially television, encourages him in this positive attitude.

Closely connected is the charge that advertisers dictate a newspaper's coverage, or at least exercise veto power over certain kinds of stories that might damage their trade. This charge is especially important in cities with only a single newspaper. Again, there are numerous episodes to document this complaint. Stories have gone unreported because an advertiser requested them to be killed. Yet there are many cases in which newspapers have defied such pressures. Usually the readers do not hear of the latter.

An example of rejected pressure occurred in a middle-sized city when its only newspaper published a series of stories advising teenagers how to buy a used car. The writer explained the tricks used by "fast buck" dealers to cheat the purchasers. After the first article appeared, the local automobile dealers angrily demanded that the publisher stop the series. He refused. The series was published in full. In retaliation the dealers cancelled all their advertising in the newspaper, costing it thousands of dollars in revenue. Eventually, because they needed the newspaper's columns to sell their cars, the dealers resumed advertising.

Publication of columns called Action Line or some similar name, in which the newspaper acts as its readers' problem-solving agent in their dealings with commercial firms and government agencies, often causes it to print facts that show its advertisers in a poor light.

The completeness of a newspaper's coverage of controversial issues and sensitive stories depends largely upon the moral courage and journalistic integrity of the men running it.

The newspaper failures and consolidations of the 1950's and 1960's, frequent in metropolitan areas, were due primarily to rising costs. Some competing publishers sought to maintain a semblance of independence by putting out separate newspapers, but for economy combining their mechanical departments and even such front-office departments as advertising. This raised protests of restraint of trade. In other cities, one newspaper bought out the other completely.

After dubiously watching the merger trend, the federal government moved into the situation. It filed antitrust charges against the Los Angeles *Times* when that powerful newspaper purchased the San Bernardino *Sun-Telegram,* a successful daily newspaper within the *Times'* circulation zone. The government was victorious in the trial, and the *Times* was ordered to sell the San Bernardino newspaper; also it was forbidden to purchase other newspapers that might help it obtain unfair dominance in Southern California.

A measure called the "Newspaper Preservation Act" was passed by Congress and signed into law by President Nixon in 1970, after lively controversy within the newspaper industry. The law created exemptions to the antitrust law, so that a financially troubled newspaper may join forces with a healthy publication in the same city. The newspapers are allowed not only to operate joint production facilities, but to combine business departments and have joint advertising and circulation rates. Their editorial departments remain separate. An argument for the measure is that it will preserve a second "voice" in the city. Publishers who testified against it, especially those from aggressive suburban newspapers, asserted that it would increase the monopoly trend.

The federal antitrust prosecutors also have taken action against the syndicates that sell features to newspapers, such as comic strips and political columnists. These suits have sought to break up the practice by some syndicates of selling exclusive territory. It works this way: a metropolitan newspaper which circulates through a large area purchases a popular feature from a syndicate for a high price. The syndicate grants the newspaper exclusive rights to publish the feature in a broad territory. This prevents other newspapers in the territory from buying the feature, and gives the large paper a monopoly on it. Once widely practiced, the sale of exclusive territory has dwindled because of government pressure.

No magazine may have a "monopoly" in the sense of the newspaper published as the single daily in a community, but the disappearance of many prominent magazines in recent years has restricted the reading choice of citizens. The deaths of *Look* in 1971 and *Life* in 1972 were preceded by those of the two weekly general interest magazines, *Collier's* and the *Saturday Evening Post.* The disappearance of these organs of popular readership left a void that could be filled only partially by the *Reader's Digest.*

Generally speaking, the magazine world offers "pairs" to the reading audience: *Time* or *Newsweek, Harper's* or *Atlantic, Nation* or *New Republic, McCall's* or *Ladies' Home Journal.* There are some notable "singles": *Reader's Digest, National Geographic, Playboy, Esquire, National Review,* and the *New Yorker.* Thoughtful critics say only a handful of the magazines named live up to their potential.

## TREATMENT OF SOCIAL PROBLEMS

Newspapers can be criticized more pertinently for what they fail to do than for what they do. They have been too slow to recognize the extent of social and economic problems in their cities and to report them frankly. They have allowed their concern with the daily routine to blind them to the social changes going on around them. Editors were as shocked as their readers by the racial riots in the Watts area of Los Angeles, Detroit, and other cities. Many admitted that they had virtually ignored the underlying causes of the urban explosion until it occurred. They realized that they had been too complacent about accepting official views.

By the nature of their work, publishers and editors mingle professionally and socially with financial leaders, major businessmen, public officials, and other decision makers. Among these people there usually is a
reluctance to rock the boat, a tendency to protect the status quo. They are
persuasive in their approach. Unless the newspaper's makers of policy
are careful, they can be unduly influenced by these associations. Newsmen
need to talk also with the leaders of labor unions, minority groups, youth
organizations, and others whose viewpoints often are poorly represented
in the press. Many contemporary editors and publishers make an effort
to develop these contacts.

A daily newspaper must please widely divergent tastes in order to have
a strong cirulation. Should its approach become completely political and
sociological, readers would lose interest. Many newspapers are quicker
to print stories about neighborhood automobile accidents, crimes, emotional crises, and popular personalities than stories about a tax debate in
Congress. Readers look to a newspaper for entertainment and for the
small change of everyday life, as well as for intellectual uplift. For the
men who make a newspaper, the challenge is to give readers a balanced
menu of the news they need and the news they enjoy. The two are not
always identical.

## ENTERTAINMENT

Much of the criticism of the mass media revolves around their entertainment content: overemphasis on entertaining rather than informing,
and lack of diversity of offerings for audience segments of different cultural levels. It is necessary, while examining these criticisms, to recognize
the nature of the entertainment function.

Historically the mass media through which news and opinion are
circulated also have entertained their readers, viewers, and listeners.
Some media, in fact, devote the bulk of their time and space to entertainment, assigning only a relatively small portion to the dissemination of
news and opinion. In newspapers, the news and opinion functions dominate. The degree and quality of what we call entertainment vary widely,
even within a single medium, according to the character of the offering
and the intent of the media producers.

In some cases the goal is primarily a fulfillment of aesthetic pleasure—
the audience receives a sense of enjoyment as a dominant reaction. Ex-

amples would be reading good fiction or poetry in books and magazines, viewing some motion pictures, hearing radio music or viewing television drama of quality, seeing some types of photographs. In other cases a simpler definition of entertainment prevails: "to amuse, interest, divert." This is true of much of the offerings of the print media, films, radio, and television, including those in which an entertainment quotient is sought to accompany news and opinion.

Indeed, the more deeply we probe the relationship between entertainment and news-opinion, the thinner the line of separation appears. Material which the recipient believes to be solely for his entertainment may in fact carry a social or political message and be closely linked to the news of the day. In reverse, the purveyors of news often use the techniques of the entertainers—such as suspense, change of pace in delivery, conflict, and incongruity—to dramatize their information. Thus they strengthen its impact on many of their readers and listeners.

## ANTI-ESTABLISHMENT PRESS TRENDS

**The underground press.** Supplementing orthodox newspapers and magazines, and influencing them to some degree, is a body of publications that differ sharply in purpose and method from the traditional.

One group of these are the underground press—tabloid size publications, usually weekly, that reject normal standards of objectivity, balance, and restraint in language. This polemic journalism makes no attempt to separate editorial comment from reporting; these are run together to project the views of the youthful counter-culture. The art work of these papers is psychedelic, the writing free in style and personalized. Underground papers were vehement against the American role in Vietnam, and the military establishment, and they condemn police methods. They cover the drug scene in detail, often but not always promoting the use of drugs; give extensive space to contemporary music, elevating to hero status rock stars and groups in the same exaggerated way they accuse the regular press of doing with Hollywood and political figures; write favorably about homosexuality, and laud black militancy. Their advertising is sex-ridden, their use of four-letter words casual and frequent. They are vituperative against their enemies, sometimes libelous, and intentionally crude in illustrations and language.

Out of the welter of underground newspapers in the late 1960's and early 1970's, a few such as the Los Angeles *Free Press,* the Berkeley *Barb,* and Chicago's *Seed* became nationally known. So did the *Village Voice* in New York, which became so successful that it took on some aspects of the Establishment it once scorned. Many others died of financial anemia. Through the discarding of inhibitions and writing, often quite well, about the concerns of young people that the regular press largely ignored or treated gingerly, the underground press has had a significant impact on youthful American thinking.

Although the orthodox press as a whole still rejects the publication of "dirty" words, the frequency of their use in the underground press, books, and magazines is resulting in a softening of standards. These words are beginning to slip into metropolitan newspapers when used in the context of trial testimony, speeches, and placards.

Recent years have seen a pronounced liberalization in the printing of photographic nudity in magazines and books, as well as underground papers, but not in general circulation newspapers. *Playboy* and other magazines of that type publish full frontal nude photographs of women as a matter of course; to have such pictures on sale on neighborhood market shelves is a radical departure from the restrictions of only a few years ago. Similar revealing photographs of nude males were not published in general circulation magazines in the early 1970's, although *Cosmopolitan* came close to breaking the barrier by publishing a centerfold photograph of actor Burt Reynolds nude but in a carefully posed position that was a spoof of *Playboy.* Supported by liberal court interpretations of obscenity laws, the trend was toward greater permissiveness.

**The concept of "reporter power."** The widespread questioning of the *status quo* and challenging of the Establishment which characterized intellectual American social movements beginning in the mid-1960's resulted in a movement known as "reporter power." It reflected the desire of young, professionally-trained journalists to make the most effective contribution to society and to help meet some of the urgent problems of the 1970's. They expected the media, as institutions, to reflect a similar sense of urgency, to exhibit the highest professional standards, and to put service ahead of profits.

When the Newspaper Guild first was organized in the 1930's, various units proposed reporters' councils which would advise newspaper editors and owners on policy matters. Publisher skepticism led to dropping the idea in favor of wages-and-hours campaigns. But by the early 1970's Guild contracts from Providence to Denver were carrying clauses calling for a committee of journalists to meet regularly with management for informal conversations. At other newspapers "reporter power" groups sprang up, predominantly among young staffs, to seek improvements in their professional contributions. Some which attracted attention were those at the Minneapolis *Tribune,* the Chicago *Sun-Times,* and even the closely-organized *Wall Street Journal.*

At times these groups did no more than reflect localized dissatisfactions with management policies, unpopular news executives, or restrictive rules. But underneath ran some themes of discontent. Reporters, it was said, should not be arbitrarily overruled by city desks on matters concerning reporters' news beats. Staff members should have strong voices in selection of assistant city editors, city editors, and even managing and executive editors (an argument paralleling student insistence in universities that they have a voice in selection of faculty and administration members). "Reporter power" also reflected the reinvigorated movement toward investigative, personalized reporting in the style of the "New Journalism." Use of teams of reporters to dig deeply into issues involving the environment, pollution, health, education, poverty, and consumer protection became popular. Conversely, reporters sought freedom to muckrake, to attack corruption, special privilege, and Establishment insensitivity. The trouble was, who was to judge the boundaries of action—the reporters or their editors?

Giving impetus to "reporter power" concepts were the journalism reviews, spearheaded by the *Chicago Journalism Review,* founded by Ron Dorfman and his young associates in the wake of the disastrous 1968 Democratic national convention. The *Review,* soon locked in combat with the Chicago newspaper managements, attracted a national following and by 1972 was a well-printed 16-page journal. Other self-criticism sheets appeared in St. Louis, Providence, Honolulu, Denver, Cleveland, the Twin Cities, Albuquerque, and other cities. One of the most ambitious was the journal named [*MORE*], launched in 1971 in New York City by Richard Pollak.

As a part of [*MORE*] promotional efforts, the editors called for a "Counter-Convention" to meet in New York City in April 1972 at the time of the American Newspaper Publishers Association annual meeting. Several thousand people attended sessions in a union hall across town from the ANPA's Waldorf-Astoria headquarters, listening to panels of speakers drawn from the leadership of the New Journalism, women's liberation, and "reporter power" movements. The convention was dedicated to the memory of A. J. Liebling, long a critic of the Establishment press in his writings in the *New Yorker*. Out of its sometimes pungent, often meandering sessions, came a declaration of "fundamental requirements of any serious reform in American journalism" from a 50-person steering committee. Among the points:

1. Journalists must be free to do their best work.

2. Editors must be free to edit but not to censor, and journalists must be as free from censorship and arbitrary interference by management as management is free from censorship and interference by government.

3. The only proper standards of journalism are accuracy, excellence, newsworthiness, and taste, the first two to be interpreted strictly, the last two freely. ·

4. Because all journalists are degraded when one is shelved or blacklisted, and all are censored when one is censored, arbitrary discrimination against one's colleagues will not be tolerated.

There was one thing certain. As in nearly every facet of society, the so-called Establishment was going to share some of its power in media offices. The degree of "serious reform" remained to be determined.

Related to the "reporter power" concept was the action by the executive board of the American Newspaper Guild endorsing Sen. George McGovern for President in the 1972 election, the first time the Guild had made a presidental endorsement. Many Guild members protested, charging that the endorsement compromised their role as objective reporters of political news.

The entire issue of objectivity in newspapers has become a matter of controversy, after long acceptance of the belief that objectivity was a basic tenet of journalism. One group of editors and writers contends that objectivity is undesirable; that in their preoccupation with objectivity and the traditional forms of reporting, newspapers and magazines touch only the surface of the story. These are proponents of "advocacy" journalism, sometimes called "participatory" journalism, in which the writer injects his personality and opinions into his coverage, especially of political affairs. The underground or "alternative" press uses this approach, making no pretense of neutrality. While recognizing the need for greater flexibility of style and interpretation, the majority of newspaper editors reject advocacy journalism except in some cases by bylined special writers.

# Chapter 8

# Criticisms and Challenges:
# Intermedia

## McLUHAN'S "HOT" AND "COOL" MEDIA

A new level of confrontation between print and electronic media developed in the 1960's as the theories of Marshall McLuhan, a professor of English and director of the Center for Culture and Technology at the University of Toronto, evoked widespread attention and controversy. His books, *The Gutenberg Galaxy* (1962), *Understanding Media* (1964), and *The Medium Is the Massage* (1967), coupled with extensive lecture and television appearances, projected McLuhan as the prophet of a new age of electronics in which the medium, in his opinion, is more important than the message and conventional values less relevant than "depth involvement."

In his work McLuhan has carried forward explorations of various earlier observers. Among them was the late Harold Innis, whose *Empire and Communications* (1950) and *The Bias of Communication* (1951) analyzed the relationship of media to power structures, beginning with those of ancient times.

McLuhan declares that each new medium alters our psychic environmen, imposing on us a particular pattern of perceiving and thinking that controls us to an extent we scarcely suspect. For example, the written language, mass-produced by print, became the main cultural transmission belt for many generations. Knowledge and ideas were necessarily processed into a linear, one-step-at-a-time form required by the medium. Man was thus pushed into sequential habits of thinking, quite unlike the complexity and richness and all-at-onceness of face-to-face communication, and without the resonance of the human voice.

Today, however, the electronic media have restored the resonance (radio) and reintroduced the complexity and all-at-onceness (film, television), and have done it on a scale that gives the world potentially a tribal unity. McLuhan sees modern man in a state of shock, unable to adjust to the rapidly changing state of communication, clinging to linear habits in an all-at-once world.

Given to puns and a measure of flippancy unlike most philosophers, McLuhan insists not only that "the medium is the *message*" (that is, more important in itself than what is transmitted) but also that "the medium is the *massage*" (that is, it "roughs up and massages" our senses, altering the environment of our preelectronic world).

Two key terms in McLuhanese are "hot" and "cool." The cooler the medium, the more information must be supplied by the audience, and that is why wide-screen movies are "hot" and a fuzzy television picture is "cool." The more information the audience supplies, the more involved it becomes, and television has given its audience a sense of "depth involvement" more far-reaching than any previous medium, McLuhan believes. "When you go to the movies," he states, "you are the camera, but when you watch TV, you are the screen. The image is not projected from you, but charges at you. The movies were an extrovert orgy, but television is a depth experience." Movies were hot when Humphrey Bogart made them, but television cools them down into an art form, he insists.

Since television demands involvement, children carry the habit of participation away from the TV set and into the classroom, McLuhan states. Accustomed to incomplete, even chaotic images on television, children are quick at making connections on the basis of partly sensed patterns. They are busy "data processing," and may be the hardest-worked generation in history. In watching TV, they formed the habit of looking for the reaction, not the action, and they find the step-by-step method of classroom teaching a bore. "Today's children are reluctant to interrupt their education by going to school," McLuhan declares, picking up an observation attributed to the late George Bernard Shaw.

McLuhan's disciples believe that his theories explain the insistence of much of today's youth on becoming involved in solving social problems rather than merely preparing for jobs and traditional life roles; on actively seeking to alter customary methods of education, such as the lecture; and on refusing (or being unable) to categorize individuals by race, religion, economic and social condition, and the like (since all peoples are bound together by instant communication, the family circle has widened, and we have extreme concern about everyone else's lives).

Critics charge that his theories are confusing, illogical, mystical, and lacking in documentation. They deplore his "pop-art intellectualism" and his puns, and his seeming call for a return to the jungle, away from print-based civilization as we have known it. McLuhan retorts that he is merely an investigator and an explorer of ideas, trying to persuade us to think about the changes in our environment caused by successive mass media, and that he sees no need to offer logical explanations.

By the 1970's the excitement generated by McLuhan's far-reaching theories had died down somewhat, but his ideas were still being reviewed in mass communications classrooms and in scholarly circles in many countries.

## GOVERNMENT AND PRESS: A CREDIBILITY DUEL

The mass media during the past decade have come under the most severe attacks from the public and the federal government since the days of the Revolution and the Civil War, when patriots eliminated the newspapers they did not like by destroying the printing offices where they were published.

The public, frustrated and bewildered by rapidly changing social and technological conditions, an unpopular war, and the emotional bombardment caused by near-total and near-instant mass communication, tended to blame the mass media for many of their problems.

The federal government, always an adversary because of the constitutional role of the press in a democratic society, capitalized on the growing feeling of disenchantment toward the media and engaged in a credibility duel characterized by both frontal and indirect assaults.

**The Agnew criticisms.**   The spark for a steadily growing conflagration of debates, pressures against the media, and proposed and actual regulatory action by numerous agencies of government, as discussed in this and previous chapters, was touched off by Vice President Spiro Agnew in 1969. In two speeches, he declared that the networks and newspapers with multiple media holdings exercised such powerful influence over public opinion that they should vigorously endeavor to be impartial and fair in reporting and commenting on national affairs. Specifically, Agnew criticized network managements for employing commentators with a preponderant Eastern Establishment bias and for failing to provide a "wall of separation" between news and comment. A similar liberal bias, he inferred, affected the policies of the Washington *Post* and its other media holdings, and the New York *Times*. Because Agnew referred to the dependence of broadcast stations upon government licensing, although disclaiming any thought of censorship, some observers saw in his remarks an implied threat to the freedom of broadcasters to report and comment freely on public affairs.

Never before had such a high federal official made such direct attacks upon those reporting and commenting on the news. A research study by Dennis T. Lowry comparing random samples of newscast items reporting administration activities for one-week periods in 1969 and 1970 bore out the contention that the Agnew-generated criticisms had significantly affected the newscasts in the direction of "safe" handling.

**The Pentagon Papers.**   When the New York *Times* began to publish in June 1971 a series of news articles summarizing the contents of a 47-volume study of the origins of the Vietnam War, the "Pentagon Papers case" erupted. The study had been ordered by Defense Secretary McNamara as a "History of the U.S. Decision-Making Process on Vietnam Policy" and had been made by a group from the RAND Corporation and other researchers.

The study was historical and revealed no military secrets or strategy, but it was highly explosive in terms of political and diplomatic interest. As a Supreme Court justice put it, the Pentagon Papers were also highly embarrassing (to Kennedy, Johnson, and Nixon administrations alike).

Executives of the *Times* decided it was in the national interest to report the documentary evidence which had come to their hands, even though it was stamped "top secret," as was the widespread custom in the government. A team of *Times* staff members led by managing editor Abe Rosenthal and reporter Neil Sheehan labored for three months to prepare the series.

When the first story appeared, Attorney General John Mitchell asked the *Times* to stop the series. The newspaper refused, and the Nixon administration went to court to seek a prior restraint order forbidding further publication. The government obtained a temporary restraining order;

was refused a permanent one; engaged in a second duel in the courts with the Washington *Post* and met increasing resistance from the Boston *Globe* and other newspapers dismayed that prior restraint had been invoked.

The case finally reached the Supreme Court, which by a 5–4 order continued the temporary prior restraint order, a shocking setback to the free press concept. The newspaper lawyers then avoided a historic showdown on the absolute nature of the constitutional ban on prior restraint, and argued only that the government could not prove any involvement of national security in the banned publication. To this, the Supreme Court agreed, 6–3. Its members disagreed widely, however, on the ethics of the newspapers in printing documents stamped "secret" and on the nature of the prior restraint concept.

Subsequent alterations in the composition of the court, including the death of free press champion Justice Hugo Black, made it appear likely that the court would rule in a future case that it would be possible for the government to show a justification for the imposition of prior restraint, even though the court said, "Any system of prior restraints of expression comes to this court bearing a heavy presumption against its constitutional validity."

The political sensitivities of the case made the Nixon administration pause in seeking criminal indictments against any newspaper editors or reporters involved in the Pentagon Papers disclosures, although it moved against Daniel Ellsberg, accused of taking the secret papers from the files.

It was hoped that, as with the John Peter Zenger case, the Pentagon Papers case would not be repeated. That is, no president would again seek to impose a prior restraint upon the press, as had been done in 1971 for the first time in the history of the Republic.

**Classification of public documents.** The Pentagon Papers case produced widespread realization that democratic principles are incompatible with the present sweep of executive privilege and its corollary—the executive practice of classification and withholding information from both the people and Congress. The knowledge that the government had classified the entire history of a foreign policy-making era, during which secret debate decided not only how but whether to conduct a war, resulted in the most concerted attack ever launched by the press and Congress on the classification system.

*New Republic* magazine reported that, since World War II, bureaucrats wielding classified labels had consigned 20,000,000 documents to the government's "subterranean empire of buried information." Most of these documents had been classified under the authority of President Eisenhower's 1953 Executive Order 10501, which ruled that official secrecy would be limited to defense matters, under three categories: top secret, secret, and confidential. President Kennedy set up guidelines for declassification in 1961, but for several reasons very little declassification has since taken place.

After 11 years of wrestling with the problem of the people's right to know the facts of government, Congress passed the Freedom of Information Act in 1966. The law states basically that any person can go to court to gain access to public records, and the burden of proof that secrecy is necessary is upon the government.

In 1972 the House of Representatives and the Supreme Court began separate inquiries into the effectiveness of the FOI law. Samuel J. Archibald of the University of Missouri Freedom of Information Center was commissioned to plot the trend of court interpretation of the act by studying significant cases. His analysis concluded that court judgments have leaned toward the people's right to know. The courts, however, generally have protected "investigatory files compiled for law enforcement purposes" and they have been wary of second-guessing executive decisions about matters that are kept secret "in the interest of national defense and foreign policy."

Declaring that his action was intended to challenge the government's security system, syndicated columnist Jack Anderson in January 1972 released secret and sensitive documents revealing that Dr. Henry Kissinger, the President's adviser on foreign policy, had directed administration spokesmen to support Pakistan against India in the war between those two countries. The fact that the anti-India policy had not been revealed even to Congress aroused further outcries against White House secrecy.

President Nixon in March 1972 established a new system for classification and declassification. Among other things the system reduced the number of authorized "top secret" classifiers and made declassification, except for particularly sensitive information, automatic after 6–10 years. Media response was modest in its praise, and qualified. Noting that the Pentagon Papers would have been ineligible for release under the time period, one newspaper editorialized that, "If the Congress is to have a voice in war and nuclear testing, it must have quicker access."

Congress continued its move toward the enactment of legislation designed to insure maximum flow of information while protecting truly vital defense interests. Meanwhile, the credibility gap between government and the press, and Congress and the White House, showed little sign of diminishing.

## PUBLIC CREDIBILITY OF THE MEDIA

While many Americans in the last decade viewed the mass media as "too liberal," despite their predominantly conservative ownerships, liberals and young activists saw the media as unresponsive, obtuse, and largely irredeemable as instruments for illuminating the root issues of social unrest. As a result, they turned to underground newspapers, discovered ways in which to "use" the media for their own ends, and increasingly sought government intervention with which to gain access.

Many intellectuals viewed the mass media with disdain for catering to mass tastes. Public officials generally resented the press' role of "watchdog" for the public's interests. Specialists in most fields complained that reporting of their activities often was over-simplified or erroneously stated. Many persons felt that the media conspired with other elements of the Establishment in withholding the truth of events. And many newsmen themselves dissented through publication of at least 20 critical journalism reviews. These and other criticisms of the media are reflected through Chapters 6–8 of this book. In addition, the media were caught in the public mood of distrust for almost all institutions, including business corporations, the church, educational institutions, and government.

A number of groups and individuals took up Vice President Agnew's assault against what was considered to be biased and often inaccurate reporting of national issues and events, primarily by the Washington press corps, the New York *Times,* the Washington *Post, Newsweek, Time,* CBS, NBC, and, to a lesser extent, ABC.

Among them were two "nonpartisan, nonprofit" organizations, Accuracy in Media, Inc., and the American Institute for Political Communication. AIM investigated complaints of serious error in news reporting, such as those alleged in the CBS documentary, "The Selling of the

Pentagon" (see page 122), statements on defense spending made by NBC newsman David Brinkley, and New York *Times* articles about the Vietnam war. Congressmen inserted a number of AIM's studies in the *Congressional Record,* prefaced with highly complimentary remarks. The American Institute for Political Communication in 1971 began a series of studies on the relationship of the Nixon administration and the media. One survey, it reported, revealed "a significant degree of bias" in television news coverage of the 1972 Democratic presidential primary ("pro-McGovern") and the Vietnam war ("anti-Nixon").

In addition to numerous magazine articles and newspaper columns, a spate of books appeared with similar contentions of "media pollution." They included Edith Efron's *The News Twisters;* Arnold Beichman's *Nine Lies About America;* and James Keogh's *President Nixon and the Press.*

In reaction to the criticisms, the networks commissioned extensive studies of their own news practices and specifically examined the programs which were the subjects of the Efron and AIPC charges. Independent scholars in each instance questioned the methodology and the objectivity of those studies.

A Freedom of Information Center report in May 1972 analyzed the major attitudes toward the media by their most avid critics in comparison with those of media workers. Under scientific scrutiny, the attitudes of this group fell under six categories: The Revolutionary, espousing minority rights and opposing "corporate tyranny and media irresponsibility"; the Pro-Media Critic, defending the media while pointing to its failures; the Silent Majority, distrusting the media's liberal tendencies; the Critical Intellectual, wanting the press kept free but favoring some government regulation; the Traditional Journalist, defending newspapers but skeptical of broadcasting; and the Staunch Defender, desiring both newspapers and broadcasting to be kept free of governmental control. Overall, the study found that the seeds had been planted for an era of stricter governmental control of the media.

A *Newsweek*-Gallup poll found little support for a public inquisition of American journalism. A *Time* Magazine-Louis Harris poll discovered that, although Americans are quick to criticize the way news is handled, underlying trust in the nation's press and its constitutional safeguards remained strong. Another Gallup poll disclosed that the public was fairly closely divided on the question of the fairness of news coverage by the nation's newspapers, although a slightly greater proportion of people said newspapers "favor one side" than held this opinion about television networks.

Summarizing these surveys, and others, the American Newspaper Publishers Association concluded: "Most Americans believe that newspapers are doing a good job of balanced, objective, and informative reporting. This is particularly true for local news coverage . . . . There is, however, a suspicious minority who claim that the press is guilty of partiality, distortion, and inaccuracy—and some believe that there is a strong imbalance between the coverage of undesirable and sensational type events and the good things that should be reported."

A survey conducted for the National Association of Broadcasters by the National Opinion Research Center in 1970 found that all media were drawing increasingly critical appraisals from the public. In comparison with a similar study in 1966, the survey revealed a decline in public acceptance of the established practices of radio and television. Generally, people were more dissatisfied with commercials than with programs. A significant increase was shown in public sentiment for governmental controls for all media. The percentage of respondents calling for more controls on TV rose from 20 to 26 percent; on radio, from 9 to 11 percent; on newspapers, from 14 to 22 percent; and on magazines, from 19 to 23 percent.

Clearly, the mass media were in trouble—a condition exacerbated by the sweeping indictments which government officials continued to express. How the media are seeking to improve their operating standards and practices is discussed in the "Efforts to Improve" section of this chapter, beginning on page 166.

## THE NEWSMAN AND HIS SOURCES

Two recent developments—a decision by the Supreme Court and the questionable practice of the impersonation of newsmen by police agents —have increased the difficulties experienced by newsmen in gathering and reporting information for the American public.

**Subpoenas and confidentiality.** The Supreme Court in 1972, by a 5-to-4 vote, decided that news reporters have no special immunity under the First Amendment not to respond to grand jury subpoenas and provide information in criminal investigations, even at the risk of "drying up" their sources.

Two newspaper reporters and one broadcast newsman, in separate appeals, urged the court to make it clear that the First Amendment guarantee of a free flow of information gives reporters at least some degree of immunity to government subpoena powers. The appeals from contempt citations were made by Paul M. Branzburg, a Louisville *Courier-Journal* reporter, who had investigated the use of illegal drugs; Earl Caldwell, New York *Times* reporter; and Paul Pappas, newsman employed by television station WTEV, New Bedford, Massachusetts, both of whom had investigated Black Panther Party activities.

Justice Byron R. White, writing the decision with the support of four Nixon administration appointees to the court, said: "The Constitution does not, as it never has, exempt the newsman from performing the citizen's normal duty of appearing and furnishing information relevant to the grand jury's task."

Justice Potter Stewart, in an opinion in which he was joined by Justices William J. Brennan and Thurgood Marshall, said the decision "invites state and federal authorities to undermine the historic independence of the press by attempting to annex the journalistic profession as an investigative arm of government." He added: "The full flow of information to the public protected by the free press guarantee would be severely curtailed if no protection whatever were afforded to the process by which news is assembled and disseminated . . . for without freedom to acquire information the right to publish would be impermissibly compromised."

In his own dissent Justice William O. Douglas wrote: "If [a reporter] can be summoned to testify in secret before a grand jury, his source will dry up and the attempted exposure, the effort to enlighten the public, will be ended. If what the court sanctions today becomes settled law, then the reporter's main function in American society will be to pass on to the public the press releases which the various departments of government issue."

The five justices in the majority, however, did leave open some avenues for relief:

1. They acknowledged, for the first time, that the process of news-gathering qualifies for some First Amendment protection. According to Justice White, the First Amendment might come into play to protect a newsman if he could show "a bad faith attempt by a prosecutor to harass a reporter and disrupt his relationship with his news sources" (a fact not in evidence in the three cases before the court). Justice White

declared that if a newsman does not believe a grand jury investigation is being conducted in good faith, he could seek relief from the courts. That eventuality might occur, he said, if the reporter is called upon to give information "bearing only a remote and tenuous relationship to the subject of the investigation" or if he has "some other reason to believe that his testimony implicates confidential source relationships without a legitimate need of law enforcement."

2. The court left the door open for Congress to enact legislation binding on federal courts and grand juries. (Spurred by the incarceration of reporters Peter Bridge in New Jersey and William Farr in California on contempt charges, major journalism groups in the fall of 1972 urged Congress and the states to enact strong "shield" laws.)

3. The court left state legislatures free to fashion their own standards. (Such laws already are in effect in 17 states, affording protection on a statutory basis that the court rejected on a constitutional basis. Newsmen in those states, however, are required to testify before federal grand juries and courts.)

4. The court conceded itself "powerless" to bar state courts from construing state constitutions so as to recognize a newsman's privilege of some type.

Newspaper and broadcast reaction to the decision was typified by a Los Angeles *Times* editorial which declared: "The Supreme Court of the United States has struck a heavy blow at the independence of the press of this nation." Enumerating seven investigations of its own since 1967 which disclosed corruption and mismanagement by governmental agencies, the *Times* asserted: "These revelations, like similar revelations by other newspapers, were conducted in the interest of the public, and they were successful, in great part, because of the trust imposed in *Times* reporters by their news sources. Such investigations are always difficult, but they will be doubly so now under the Supreme Court's grand jury decision."

**Impersonation of newsmen.** Another threat to the integrity of the news-gathering process has occurred in recent years when law enforcement agents have masqueraded as news reporters and cameramen in order to obtain information.

The Twentieth Century Fund Task Force on the Government and the Press reported in 1972 that Army agents both in the United States and in Vietnam, as well as intelligence units of local police agencies throughout the country, have posed as newsmen since at least 1967. Fourteen instances were cited. The militant antiwar movement was the subject of many of the investigations; others involved surveillance of black militants. The tactic appears to have been used almost exclusively to gather information about dissident groups, that is, in "political" as opposed to "criminal" investigations.

As disclosures of police masquerading as newsmen increased, barriers of suspicion began to rise between radical elements and the newsmen who wanted to report on their internal as well as external affairs. Journalists were assaulted by militants and excluded from their meetings.

In almost every instance of disclosure, promises were made that the practice would be forbidden. However, the prohibitions were not strongly worded, no masquerader is known to have been punished, and no government has publicly condemned the tactic.

The FBI reportedly has not allowed its agents to pose as newsmen, but has placed journalists on the payroll when they initiated the move. A news photographer and a television reporter-cameraman testified in court that they had been paid as FBI informants, a practice which most newsmen regard as a betrayal of a reporter's duty as well as his profession.

Fred P. Graham, in a background paper prepared for the Task Force, pointed out that government may need strategms to determine the intentions of some militant organizations and prevent or anticipate acts of violence such as bombings.

"The penetration of such groups by undercover agents is nothing new," Graham said, "but the use of newsmen as agents is relatively new—and hazardous. By making journalists suspect, the practice threatens to cut off the flow of information needed to enable the public to make sensible judgments about dissident groups. Conversely, a free press that can be trusted to report on dissident groups fairly may well defuse extreme militancy. The press is a safety valve for dissent that protects both the public interest and the right of legitimate social criticism."

### OWNERSHIP ACROSS THE MEDIA

One of the major challenges to the mass media in recent years has been sharp criticism of the trend toward their control by relatively small groups of individuals. Newspapers have drawn the heaviest fire on the issue of ownership concentration and lack of local competition. But similar trends have occurred in all the mass communications industries, as they developed in a society whose economic atmosphere encouraged mass production, bigness of business enterprises, and diversification of corporate investments.

More detailed examinations of the present-day positions of each of the mass media will be presented in later chapters dealing with each medium individually. But a summary of historical trends in the rise of intermedia competition, and of the growth of ownership groups cutting across the media, can be noted now so that the criticisms can be evaluated.

The twentieth century has seen a steady lessening of competition between daily newspapers within a single city. It has also seen the rise of competition between radio and television stations within that same city. This has meant, then, the substitution of intermedia competition for internewspaper competition in all but a handful of American cities and towns.

Two graphs show the trends in internewspaper competition and intermedia competition since 1880. They summarize analyses of the problem made by Professor Raymond B. Nixon, using data from *Editor & Publisher International Year Book, Broadcasting Yearbook,* and other sources. In Figure 1, the number of dailies published in the United States rises from 850 in 1880 to a peak of 2200 in 1910, then declines to a plateau figure of 1750 after 1945, plus or minus a few as stops and starts of dailies fluctuated.

Figure 1 also shows the steady increase in single-daily cities from 509 (42 percent) in 1910 to 1284 (85 percent) by 1969. Another 171 cities were being served by 342 dailies published in morning-evening combination ownership situations or joint-printing operations. That left 123 dailies in 45 cities where competition between separate ownerships still existed. These represented 3 percent of the 1500 cities with daily newspapers. In 1910 there had been 689 cities (57 percent of 1207) with two or more competing dailies. Before leaving the daily newspaper, however, we should note that the drop in numbers of daily newspapers from the 1910 peak has been only 20 percent and that the circulation of the survivors has increased from 22,000,000 to approximately 63,000,000.

Figure 2 shows a new concept: "media voices" replaces "daily newspapers" as the criterion for competition. By a "media voice" is meant any separate ownership in the field of local mass communication; "competi-

DAILIES

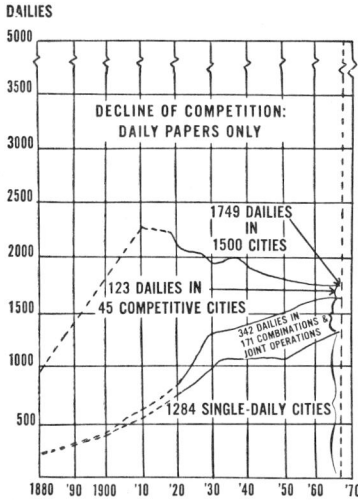

Figure 1

VOICES

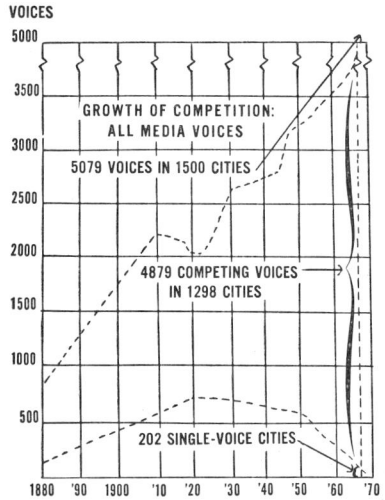

Figure 2

tion" means there are two or more separately owned newspapers, radio stations, or television stations in any combination. Thus the 1500 cities with daily newspapers had a total of 5079 media voices. Of these, 4879 were competing voices in 1298 cities. Only 202 were single-voice cities, and these were nearly all suburbs so close to central cities that outside voices are readily available, Professor Nixon reported. In addition, 1447 other cities had a local broadcast station. So the total of U.S. communities with daily mass communication was 2947.

The importance of having competition at the local level in mass communication revolves mainly around the problem of the citizen's access to news and opinion concerning local affairs: his schools, his urban renewal problems, his police force, his economic climate, his political choices. Here, as we have seen, Americans increasingly can turn to the competing voices of newspapers and broadcast stations to obtain checks and balances. Outside the local scene, diversity of news and viewpoints on state, national, and international issues comes readily from out-of-town newspapers and broadcast stations, magazines, books, film, and other cultural contacts. Here, too, the news and public affairs facilities of television and radio networks bring a diverse fare from that provided by the newspaper—and vice versa.

The expansion of group ownership of the mass media, including cross-media conglomerates, has been another much-debated subject. Such expansion in the mass communications industries, like others, has been encouraged by federal tax policies which make it advantageous for business concerns to invest their accumulated earnings in new enterprises, or for owners to sell their companies in a tax-free exchange of stock. As a result, a well-managed ownership like Time Inc. has branched out from its magazine base into book publishing, newspapers, radio, television, and film; the Hearst newspaper ownership also controls a major magazine group, radio and television stations, a news and photo service, a feature syndicate, and a paperback book publishing company; the Washington *Post* owns *Newsweek*; the Minneapolis *Star* and *Tribune* owns *Harper's*—and CBS owns the New York Yankees. In the 1960's the book publishing business became the favorite target of merger-minded enterprisers; in addition, such diverse competitors as Time Inc., the *Wall Street Journal,* the Los Angeles *Times,* the Associated Press, and the New York *Times* got into the book publishing act.

There is some merit to the criticism that the spread of group ownership and intermedia combinations places small groups of individuals in highly strategic positions. A Minneapolis citizen, for example, can find Cowles family members in ownership situations affecting both his morning and evening newspaper, his leading radio station, his CBS television network station, and his subscription to *Harper's* magazine. All these media outlets are operated independently of each other, it is true, but there is still an influence of ownership philosophy.

Newspaper ownership groups (two or more papers constitute a group) now control 63 percent of total daily circulation and 65 percent of Sunday's. But the largest—the Chicago *Tribune*-New York *Daily News* group—holds only 6 percent of daily circulation and only 16 of 159 groups control as much as 1 percent each of total daily circulation. Most of the groups permit local editorial autonomy on all issues as against the older policy of group unity on major national political issues characteristic of Hearst and Scripps-Howard papers. Other influential groups include those of Newhouse, Knight, Gannett, Ridder, and the British-owned Thomson organization.

Despite the large numbers of broadcast stations, the networks remain the most important forces within the industry. In entertainment, in public affairs, and in news, the viewer relies mainly on NBC, CBS, and ABC. Federal restrictions limit group ownership of stations to a handful. But cross-ownership has been constant, and newspapers and magazines are associated in common ownership with 25 percent of commercial television stations, 7 percent of commercial AM stations, and 9 percent of FM stations.

Regardless of intermedia ownership, control of the other mass media has always been limited. In magazine publishing, 10 large firms have dominated the field, and competition in subareas such as news magazines, women's magazines, picture magazines, and quality journals has severely declined. In book publishing, two dozen firms account for two thirds of the business each year. Eight large studios historically dominated the film industry, although their influence has been diminished by independent production by stars and the influence of television. The news media have their choice of two U.S. press associations, the Associated Press and United Press International. Certainly tendencies toward domination of the limited numbers of units within these fields, by common ownerships cutting across the media, constitute a challenge to society.

## AUDIENCE RESPONSES AND PREFERENCES

Newspapers, radio, and television come close to being universal media in the United States. Nine out of 10 American adults see a daily newspaper regularly; of those who do not, a majority read a weekly newspaper. Radios are found in 98.6 percent of homes, television sets in 96 percent. Again, the adult audiences come close to the total potential.

Magazines rank next in appeal; the best available survey figures show that 60 to 70 percent of adults read at least one magazine regularly. Approximately 50 percent of adults, when asked, say they have attended a movie during the previous month; 25 percent say they have read a book.

These figures constitute both a tribute and a challenge to the mass media. Public support, it might be said, becomes an embarrassment for those who must produce publications, programs, and films for such a diverse and overwhelming mass audience. One can hope to have 40,000,-000 readers of a magazine issue, like *Reader's Digest*; sell 10,000,000 copies of a paperback like *Valley of the Dolls*; produce a smash hit film like *The Godfather*; or have a TV audience like that for Bob Hope's annual Christmas show. But usually the problem is to satisfy mass audiences with a heterogeneous product: the newspaper, the daylong programing of television, the patter and music of radio, the general interest magazine. The object is to survive as a profit-making institution, holding enough audience to earn advertising and circulation revenues.

Readership studies, audience ratings, and other scientific methods determine audience preferences for mass media content. In the print media the final determination is how many copies of one's publication are bought; movies have their box office receipts for measurement; television and radio must rely upon audience ratings and critics' reactions, since programs are received free. But all these figures do not accurately reflect what people really feel about the media.

One study, repeated steadily since 1959, was made by Roper Research Associates and reported by them to the sponsors of the study, the television industry. In it, respondents were asked where they usually get most of their news of "what's going on in the world today" (a question minimizing the importance of local news, in which newspapers excel) and their 1971 reply was: from television, 60 percent; newspapers, 48 percent; radio, 23 percent; magazines, 5 percent; "other people," 5 percent (some listed more than one principal source). In another question involving which medium the respondent would keep if he could keep only one (a situation involving both news and entertainment ratings), the answer was: television, 58 percent; newspapers, 19 percent; radio, 17 percent; magazines, 5 percent.

Opposite results were found in a 1969 survey by the Louis Harris organization for *Time*, when it asked, "How upset would you be if your main news source were to become unavailable for a month?" The results: 44 percent said they would be "very upset" to lose their newspaper, and 33 percent would be "very upset" to lose their favorite television news broadcast.

Both studies disclosed that the public considers television "most believable" in a situation involving discrepancies between news media. The Roper study results were 49 percent for television, 20 percent for newspapers, 10 percent for radio, and 9 percent for magazines. The Harris study, while it shows a clear majority believing the newspaper is sometimes "unfair, partial and slanted," records only a third with a similar view toward television news.

There were other results in the Harris poll for media workers and scholars to reflect upon. Two out of three adults said they were better informed than they were five years earlier, a vote of confidence for the media. By a clear edge, respondents labeled television news "more full of violence" and "more full of sex" than newspapers. More than nine out of ten said they regularly watched television news: CBS, 35 percent; NBC, 35 percent; ABC, 13 percent. Asked to name favorite TV newsmen, 46 percent replied Walter Cronkite, 45 percent David Brinkley, 44 percent Chet Huntley, and 9 percent Eric Sevareid, with the rest trailing. By comparison, the late Drew Pearson led newspaper columnists in a similar question with a mere 7 percent. Among publications, Harris reported, *Time* and *Newsweek* were known by half the reading public, the New York *Times* by 30 percent, the *Wall Street Journal* by 28 percent, the *National Observer* by 14 percent, the Washington *Post* by 13 percent, and the Los Angeles *Times* by 12 percent.

## ECONOMIC PRESSURES ON THE MEDIA

Television's heavy impact on the time and attention of viewers is paralleled by the impact it has had on advertisers, the men whose dollars are essential in keeping all commercial media in operation.

Mass media must make a profit, like any business. Economic pressures dictate many of the decisions they make concerning program material and presentation. The degree to which advertisers apportion their budgets to the various media, and to the individual units within each medium, influences the attractiveness and effectiveness of the various outlets.

Before television, back in the mid-1930's, newspapers received 45 percent of all advertising expenditures in the United States, magazines 8.3 percent, and radio 6.5 percent. The remainder of the expenditures went to other advertising forms such as billboards and direct mail. By the end of the 1960's, television was getting 17.5 percent of the total advertising expenditures. This share had been drawn most heavily away from newspapers, which had fallen to 29 percent; magazines were down to 7.3 percent and radio to 6.4 percent.

Despite its decreased percentage of the total advertising expenditure, the newspaper industry experienced a large growth of dollar income because in the expanding economy and population the American business community put heavily increased expenditures into telling its story through the media. Although individual publications and stations had to fight aggressively through their sales staffs to obtain the revenue that would make their operations profitable, there were enough advertising dollars available for most of them to operate at comfortable and sometimes excellent profits.

## CRITICISMS OF ADVERTISING

The powerful consumer movement in the United States has drawn a sharp bead on advertising within the last several years, seeking federal sanctions against what it considers to be social ills encouraged by many industry practices.

Through advertising, it is maintained, companies enjoy almost a virtual monopoly on the kind of information available to consumers. Consumers are not exposed to contrasting viewpoints and are deprived of the diversity of opinion necessary for informed choices. This imbalance puts human and social interests second to private and political interests. Moreover, it is alleged, much advertising is deceptive and untruthful.

Under particular attack has been the advertising of cigarettes ("harmful to health"), over-the-counter drugs ("encouraging serious drug abuse"), gasoline, automobiles, soap, and detergents ("making misleading environmental claims"), and products used by children such as toys and breakfast cereals ("misleading and falsifying"). In addition, four major cereal manufacturers have been accused of having a joint market monopoly.

The Federal Trade Commission, in response to consumer complaints, has applied innovative sanctions and asked Congress for additional powers. These include the extension of FTC authority to cover intrastate, as well as interstate, commerce; to bring suits in district courts; and to issue trade regulations defining unfair or deceptive acts or practices, which would have the full force of law unless vetoed by Congress within 60 days.

In addition, the FTC has moved against what it terms "unfairness" in advertising, thus extending its powers to the more subjective area of the impression created by an advertisement rather than its literal truth. Its first citations were made against advertising in behalf of Wonder Bread, Lysol spray disinfectant, and Bayer, Anacin, and Excedrin analgesics.

Consent agreements that "corrective" notices would be incorporated in advertisements were obtained against Profile bread and Ocean Spray cranberry juice advertising. Under another consent agreement, six major cigarette manufacturers agreed to place conspicuous health warnings in their advertising. The FTC asked the Federal Communications Commission to require broadcast stations to run "counter-advertising" requested by public interest groups (see page 114). FTC orders requiring the public documentation of advertising claims included those directed against manufacturers of automobiles, air conditioners, electric shavers, toothpastes, and cough and cold remedies.

In addition to the measure which would extend the powers of the FTC, Congress also considered a truth-in-advertising bill as well as a measure establishing a Consumer Protection Agency. Also proposed was the establishment of a National Institute of Advertising, Marketing and Society.

The advertising industry supported some of the proposed federal strictures, but vigorously opposed the "counter-advertising" concept and granting the FTC authority to issue trade regulations with the full force of law. In addition, the American Advertising Federation undertook a study of advertising self-regulation resulting in the formation of the National Advertising Review Board, to deal with the truth and accuracy of national consumer advertising. Twenty percent of the board members represent the public. A system of local advertising review boards was contemplated.

In hearings before Congress, the FTC, and the FCC, industry leaders strongly defended the social and economic values of advertising. They warned that imposing broad restrictions on all advertising, because of the misleading or deceptive content of some, would destroy the integrity of the marketing process and the need to foster public confidence in the free enterprise system—which some saw as the real target of the most militant consumer advocates.

Other criticisms of advertising have been made. Some of the more common complaints and the replies that have been made to each in the literature of the field: (1) *Advertising persuades us to buy goods and services we cannot afford.* Persuasion is present, but never coercion; it is up to each of us to exercise self-control and sound judgment in our purchases. (2) *Advertising appeals primarily to our emotions rather than to our intellect.* Since all of us are motivated largely by emotional drives, it is only natural that advertisers should make such appeals. Again, a cautious buyer will avoid obvious "plays" to his emotions. (3) *Advertising is biased.* This, too, is natural; everyone puts his best foot forward in whatever he says or does. Being aware of this bias, we can discount some of the superlatives in advertising. (4) *Advertising involves conflicting competitive claims.* But advertising is "out in the open," never hidden as are some forms of propaganda, and we can decide for ourselves. (5) *Advertising is unduly repetitious.* That is because the public is essentially a passing parade, not a mass gathering; there are always new users whom the appeal has never reached. And slogans like "It Floats" have sold goods successfully for generations. (6) *Much advertising is vulgar, obtrusive, irritating.* Actually, only a handful of advertisers employ poor taste in their appeals; their excesses damage the higher standards of the many. And the very nature of radio and television, whose commercials cannot easily be turned off, accounts for much irritation; this complaint is seldom voiced in relation to printed advertising, which can be ignored.

There are other criticisms, relating primarily to the role of advertising itself rather than to its content. Certain economists, especially those who nourished the vision of a planned, controlled society, have charged that advertising is wasteful and unnecessary, adding to the cost of goods and services. This is true in some instances, when business uses the advertising tool foolishly or for the purpose of maintaining an inflexible high price on a product. But as a general criticism, it is answered with the

statement that advertising serves a socially desirable purpose: Our entire economy is geared to a fast turnover of merchandise; advertising provides selective buying information, assures us of uniform quality, saves us time in shopping, helps to lower prices through mass production and mass selling techniques, improves our standard of living by educating us concerning new products, serves cultural and intellectual ends as well as those of a purely material nature, and enables us to enjoy the mass media at small expense.

Other criticisms are directed at advertising by those who fear that their very lives are being manipulated by clever and unscrupulous Madison Avenue word-wizards whose only objective is to sell goods and ideas regardless of the social consequences. These critics are generally intellectual men and women who resist classification among the masses at whom the communications media are directed. Their intense desire to think and act of their own volition in an increasingly monolithic world leads them to attack advertising—"mass" by its very nature—at every turn, with little thought of the inevitable consequences of a society in which advertising became unduly shackled.

Many opinion leaders consider that advertising is almost wholly devoid of ethics. Frederic Wakeman's 1946 best seller, *The Hucksters,* spawned a series of anti-advertising novels. Advertisers and the broadcast industry shared blame for the rigged quiz shows and the disk jockey payola scandals of the late 1950's. The image of the earnest young man-about-Madison Avenue complete with gray-flannel suit, attache case, sincere smile, and lavish expense account is not one to inspire confidence. Set against the background of yesterday's patent medicine quackery, extravagant advertising, and the *laissez faire* doctrine of *caveat emptor,* and today's allegations of misleading drug and socially harmful cigarette advertising, the bill of indictments is devastating.

Add to that the questions of good taste in broadcasting—the jarring loudness of some commercials, the so-called insulting and obnoxious advertisements, the cramming of too many commercials into segments of broadcast time, and the clutter and length of some TV program credit crawls—and many persons have declared an anti-advertising Roman holiday. "TV is a series of tasteless and endless interruptions," cried one critic. "The people are tired of being screamed at, assaulted, and insulted by commercials," exclaimed another.

In addition to the Federal Trade Commission, more than 20 other federal agencies, including the Internal Revenue Service and the Securities & Exchange Commission, have taken some steps to regulate advertising. More than a dozen states have instituted taxes on advertising.

The federal government's interest in protecting consumers from business and advertising abuses has extended for some years. The Fair Packaging and Labeling Act of 1966 covered food, drug, and cosmetics packages, and the amount of label revision was enormous. A Commerce Department program to stem the proliferation of package sizes followed. In 1968 came the so-called "Truth in Lending" Act, requiring disclosure of the annual interest rate on revolving charge accounts. It was still all right to use the phrase, "Easy Credit," in an ad, but if specific language such as "$1.00 down and $1.00 a week" were introduced, the annual interest rate had to be stated. In 1971 Congress banned the broadcasting of cigarette commercials.

A National Consumer Foundation was proposed. One of its suggested functions would involve a national computerized vending machine system which, for a small fee, would disseminate product information compiled from government testing and from manufacturers. This proposal highlights a basic disagreement between government critics and marketing-advertising men. The former tend to emphasize the primary function of a product and the efficient matching of that product to customer needs, while the latter focus on product differentiation and the customer's own perceived best interest. For example, critics of product advertising generally would maintain that the consumer views soap as merely a cleansing agent. Marketers, on the other hand, would assert that the consumer considers scent, shape, color, and other characteristics, some ephemeral, equally as important as cleansing properties. In effect, declared two Harvard Business School professors, Raymond A. Bauer and Stephen A. Greyser, who have developed this thesis, businessmen and government leaders have two different models of the consumer world and hence "talk past instead of to one another."

Morton J. Simon, Philadelphia lawyer and author, has cited, in a *Printers' Ink* article, six principal reasons for the current unfavorable governmental climate toward advertising: (1) *Advertising is a horizontal industry*. It cuts across almost every business and service, so an attack on any industry almost always includes advertising. (2) *Advertising represents a lot of money*. It spends billions of dollars annually, and some persons view these funds as apparently untaxed and above the grip of the government. (3) *Advertising lives in a glass house*. By its nature it cannot hide its sins. (4) *The gray-flannel-suit image is pervasive*. Many consider that advertising men live lavishly and improperly on tax-deductible expense accounts. (5) *Advertising is not constitutionally protected*. Some in government believe that advertising is somehow tainted by its commercial purpose and therefore is not protected by the First Amendment; its legal status in this regard has not been made clear. (6) *Advertising has rarely lobbied*. Unlike most other major segments of the economy, advertising has maintained a Washington lobby only in recent years.

Before the consumer movement reached its full crescendo of complaints in the 1970's, most citizens were not very much concerned about advertising, a five-year study by the American Association of Advertising Agencies revealed. Bauer and Greyser, who helped direct the surveys involving 3382 interviews with men and women, discuss their findings in a book entitled, *Advertising in America: The Consumer View.* "Considering everything, we have no reason to believe that the public is substantially more or less critical of advertising and advertisements today than it has been at other times during the past two decades," the authors concluded. The study revealed that 78 percent of Americans considered that advertising is essential, 74 percent said that advertising results in better products, and 71 percent believed that advertising helps raise living standards. On the other hand, 65 percent agreed that advertising persuades people to buy things they shouldn't, and 43 percent felt that most advertising insults their intelligence. Critics then appeared to have little solid support from the public at large.

Although bowing to many of the demands of the present consumer movement, the industry insists that restrictive governmental actions will not insure the ultimate improvement of advertising practices. The answers, spokesmen contend, lie in advertising's own progress toward the achievement of high professional standards and in involving advertising fully, as partners with other segments of society, in the search for solutions to the vexing problems confronting the American people.

### EFFORTS TO IMPROVE

It is generally agreed that government can play only a minor role in efforts to improve the mass media, if they are to remain free. This means that efforts at improvement must come from within the media themselves or must be generated by groups outside the media that represent the general public. In each of the media there are groups and individuals who are contributing to the efforts to meet the challenges raised by society.

One group is composed of the various trade associations. For newspapers there are the American Newspaper Publishers Association, representing the dailies; the National Newspaper Association, for weeklies and small dailies; and two subsidiary national daily groups, the International Circulation Managers' Association and the International Newspaper Advertising Executives. There are also strong regional associations—Inland Daily Press Association, Southern Newspaper Publishers Association, New England Daily Newspaper Association, Northwest Daily Press Association—and state associations (usually emphasizing problems of weeklies).

The trade associations for other media include the National Association of Broadcasters, the Magazine Publishers Association, the American Book Publishers Council, the American Educational Publishers Institute, the Motion Picture Association of America, the American Business Press, Inc., the American Association of Advertising Agencies, and the Advertising Federation of America.

Each trade association speaks for its industry in affairs of general interest to the members. The staffs represent the industries when necessary at congressional hearings and before other government bodies. The associations develop promotional materials for their media and operate central offices which act as clearing-houses for information about the industries. The daily newspapers organized a Bureau of Advertising which promotes their media; the Magazine Advertising Bureau, the Radio Advertising Bureau, and the Television Information Bureau do the same in their fields. The National Association of Broadcasters, the Motion Picture Association of America, and the American Association of Advertising Agencies have developed codes of conduct. While they are primarily concerned with business matters, many of the associations sponsor discussions aimed at improvements of their media and encourage individual activities aimed at raising the standards of members.

There are also groups of editors and newsmen. Most prominent is the American Society of Newspaper Editors, limited primarily to editors, editorial page editors, and managing editors of dailies of 50,000 or more circulation. The ASNE formulated the "Canons of Journalism" in 1923 and attempted to regulate the professional conduct of its members but found it could not expel an accused editor. Its thoughtful discussions in annual meetings of news and editorial problems are reproduced in book form in the *Problems of Journalism* series. The monthly ASNE *Bulletin* analyzes problems confronting editors and the press.

Editorial page editors and writers also formed the National Conference of Editorial Writers, which meets annually in sessions featuring small-group critiques of the editorial pages of the members. It publishes a quarterly, the *Masthead,* and has a code of principles "to stimulate the conscience and the quality of the American editorial page." Managing editors of newspapers belonging to the Associated Press have organized the Associated Press Managing Editors Association, which has made a continuing study of the AP news report and has published the *APME Red Book* reporting on committee findings and convention sessions.

The Radio-Television News Directors Association is the equivalent organization for the electronic media. It has sought to elevate standards through adoption of a code of principles and has been instrumental in forwarding the position of news and public affairs broadcasting in the industry. Among magazine people, the International Association of Business Communicators has set standards of performance and has held annual sessions for men and women who edit company publications. The Public Relations Society of America requires practitioners to pass written examinations before they may be certified as accredited members of the organization. All three groups issue magazines for their members.

The American Newspaper Guild has done much to improve the standards of the newspaper business through the raising of salaries and has attempted to carry out programs of self-improvement. Its publication is the *Guild Reporter*. Membership is limited primarily to workers in larger daily newspapers and the press associations. Its role as a trade union will be discussed in greater detail in Chapter 9, which is devoted to the newspaper industry.

There are other groups: the professional journalistic societies, Sigma Delta Chi and Theta Sigma Phi (only for women), both more than 60 years old and both operating chapters for working journalists as well as on campuses; Pi Delta Epsilon, honorary collegiate journalism fraternity; Kappa Tau Alpha, journalism scholastic society; Alpha Delta Sigma, professional advertising fraternity; Gamma Alpha Chi, professional advertising sorority; Pi Alpha Mu, professional fraternity for men and women in the publishing, advertising, and journalistic management fields; Kappa Alpha Mu, professional photographic fraternity for men and women; Di Gamma Kappa and Alpha Epsilon Rho, professional broadcasting organizations; and the Public Relations Student Society of America. Most of them issue publications, the *Quill* of Sigma Delta Chi being the best known.

The Nieman Fellows, consisting of newsmen who have been given a year of study at Harvard University under the Nieman Foundation program, issue a quarterly, *Nieman Reports*. The *Columbia Journalism Review,* published by the Columbia University Graduate School of Journalism, offers a quarterly analysis and criticism of media performance. The monthly *Chicago Journalism Review* was started by a group of young Chicago newspaper reporters, disgruntled by press coverage during and after the street demonstrations connected with the 1968 Democratic national convention, mainly to criticize news media performance. Other such reviews followed. A few metropolitan radio and television stations have instituted programs designed to criticize press coverage, and some metropolitan underground newspapers do likewise. Publications of the Freedom of Information Center at the University of Missouri School of Journalism monitor developments in the mass media. A number of university journalism schools and departments publish periodicals containing media appraisal, among them being the *Montana Journalism Review,* of the University of Montana School of Journalism, and the *Iowa Journalist,* of the University of Iowa School of Journalism. Other roles of journalism educators and the cooperation extended to them by the mass communications industries are discussed in Chapter 19. The *Saturday Review* and other magazines frequently print articles dealing with the media. Copley Newspapers publishes *Seminar,* a quarterly review for newspapermen, and the Gannett Co., Inc., issues *Gannetteer,* a monthly magazine.

In a broad-based program designed to increase the number of highly competent journalists, the Ford Foundation since 1965 has granted millions of dollars for postgraduate journalism education. The projects include an urban journalism program through the Northwestern University Medill School of Journalism, expansion of the Nieman program bringing young newsmen to Harvard University for a year's study, further development of the Graduate School of Journalism at Columbia University, a public affairs reporting program in cooperation with the American Political Science Association, a variety of study and seminar programs for newsmen of the South in cooperation with the Southern Regional Education Board and the Southern Newspaper Publishers Association Foundation, and a Nieman-like program of study for experienced journalists at Stanford University.

The Newspaper Fund, supported by the *Wall Street Journal,* the *National Observer,* and *Barron's National Business and Financial Weekly* —all Dow Jones and Company publications—has spent more than $3,000,000 since 1958 in attracting talented young people into newsroom careers. For 13 years the fund's program revolved around six major programs: providing a clearing house of career information, summer study on college campuses for high school and junior college journalism teachers, summer intern programs with scholarships for college students, recognition to high school teachers for outstanding performances, urban journalism workshops for minority high school students, and an editor-in-residence program to bring working newsmen to college campuses in cooperation with the American Society of Newspaper Editors.

A concerted effort to attract black and other minority young people into careers in journalism was begun in the late 1960's by a number of media industries, professional groups, and communications educators.

In recent years increasing interest has developed toward the establishment of local press councils and a national public commission of the mass media in order to provide independent appraisal of the media and an opportunity for the public to air grievances against media treatment. The Commission on Freedom of the Press had recommended such an agency in 1947 after a three-year study financed by Henry Luce and headed by educator Robert M. Hutchins. The proposal was not accepted by the media. Journalism educators and a few media leaders revived the idea in 1967. Press councils on the West Coast and in southern Illinois were established by the Don R. Mellett Fund of the American Newspaper Guild. A group of journalism educators, foundation representatives, and others, with a $10,000 grant from the Rockefeller Fund, in 1972 studied the feasibility of establishing a National Media Center. The center, with working journalists fully involved, would coordinate research, award prizes, conduct study programs, critique performance, and act as people's ombudsman in dealings with the mass media. The National Advisory Commission on Civil Disorders proposed the establishment of an Institute of Urban Communications to monitor the media's handling of race relations. A study group of the National Commission on the Causes and Prevention of Violence in 1970 proposed the establishment of a National Center of Media Study. In all of these proposals, except the idea of a press council, which a few newspapers approved, the media held that it was their responsibility alone to assess their performance and that involvement of any "outside" group likely would infringe on the constitutional guarantee of freedom of the press.

In all the mass media there are conscientious and talented men and women who are as anxious as any of the philosophical critics of the press that a better job be done of informing the public and of giving it the basis for making proper decisions. They need the help of all readers, listeners, and viewers who make up the general public which the mass media serve.

PART IV

# THE
# MASS
# COMMUNICATIONS
# INDUSTRIES
# AND
# PROFESSIONS

# Chapter 9

# *Newspapers*

Newspapers are the written record of contemporary civilization. They report in detail events large and small, from President Nixon's trip to China down to the traffic accident in the next block. Increasingly, despite the handicap of short-range perspective, they seek to relate these events to the flow of history as evaluators of the daily grist, not merely reporters of it. To do so challenges the technical skill and intellectual capacity of editors and writers because they operate under severe time pressure in a society that is undergoing immense changes. Theirs is not the luxury of contemplation but the urgency of getting words on paper before the next deadline.

For the majority of the population newspapers still are the basic news medium. Lacking the speed and visual punch of television news, they nevertheless provide greater depth and variety of reporting. Without newspapers, the American public could not be well informed. Reading a newspaper takes more mental effort than watching a television news program, but the effort is worthwhile.

Changes of a profound nature have been occurring in American newspapers. The growth of television news reporting has forced new approaches to the newspaper's methods of covering news. The suburban spread of our giant cities has led to the creation of new daily newspapers catering to the altered patterns of American living. After years of scant progress, the physical methods of producing newspapers have undergone exciting advances in the past two decades. Approximately 63,000,000 copies of daily newspapers are sold each day, reflecting a growth more than keeping pace with the country's population increase.

In this chapter we shall look at newspapers in operation. We shall observe the roles individuals play in producing them and discuss the problems that must be solved before the vibrating rumble of the presses begins.

The term "newspaper" covers a surprisingly broad range of publications. It includes the small weekly in which every task from gathering news to running the press is done by two or three people and the huge metropolitan daily with a staff of more than a thousand and a daily circulation of a million copies. Between these extremes are hundreds of daily and weekly newspapers of many sizes and degrees of prosperity.

No matter what their circumstances, all of them are akin: they are made of type, ink, and newsprint. They exist to inform and influence the communities in which they are published, and the men who produce them share a common urge to get the news and advertising into print. Into the pages of every newspaper goes an essential but intangible extra ingredient, the minds and spirits of the men who make it.

Newspaper work is an adventure, so full of fresh experiences that men and women who have been in it for years still come to work with a subconscious wonder about what unexpected developments the day will bring. It is based upon a firmly disciplined routine, because "getting the paper out" on time is paramount, and this can be done only if a definite work pattern exists in all departments.

The exciting things that can happen within that framework are innumerable. For the newsman there is the stimulation of being on the inside of big developments, of watching history being made, and of meeting intriguing people. For those who work in advertising and circulation, there is satisfaction in conceiving and executing ideas that bring in money and influencing people through skill with words. Working on a newspaper is an open invitation to create ideas and put them to work. The newspaper people who succeed best are those who handle the necessary routine meticulously and bring to their jobs an extra spark of creative thinking. Those for whom the atmosphere and work lose their excitement frequently move on to other media or occupations.

As one of the mass communications media, the contemporary newspaper has three fundamental functions and some secondary ones. The basic ones are: (1) to inform its readers objectively about what is happening in their community, country, and world; (2) to comment editorially on the news in order to bring these developments into focus; (3)

to provide the means whereby persons with goods and services to sell can advertise their wares. The newspaper's less vital roles are: (1) to campaign for desirable civic projects and to help eliminate undesirable conditions; (2) to give the readers a portion of entertainment through such devices as comic strips, columnists, and special features; (3) to serve the reader as a friendly counselor, information bureau, and champion of his rights.

When a newspaper performs all or most of these tasks well, it becomes an integral part of community life. For many persons the newspaper has a more vivid "personality" than any of the other media. The temporary disappearance of newspapers from a city, because of labor trouble or a mechanical breakdown, creates confusion in business life and in the ordinary flow of social and civic affairs. The subscriber without his newspaper feels as lonesome as a person whose best friend has left town.

The printed word has a lasting power far beyond that of the spoken word or the visual image. Readers can refer to it again and again. Stories printed in today's columns may be clipped and saved by readers for many years and may be readily examined in the newspaper's files decades later. This fact increases the reporter's feeling that he is writing history and contributes to the newspaper's position as a stabilizing, continuing institution in the community.

### GENERAL ORGANIZATION OF NEWSPAPERS

The newspapers in the United States can be divided roughly into three categories: weeklies and semiweeklies, serving small areas with limited circulation; small and medium-sized dailies, which comprise the great bulk of our daily press; and metropolitan dailies whose circulation areas have populations of 1,000,000 or more.

Each of these newspaper groups has a definite purpose and is tailored to the needs of the communities served. The size and frequency of a newspaper's editions depend upon the amount of advertising and circulation revenue it commands. Trying to publish a newspaper on a grander scale than its community can support is a sure and swift path to bankruptcy.

Most American newspapers have a page that is eight columns wide and 20 or 21 inches deep; the normal column width is slightly less than two inches. This is the traditional standard size page. During recent years, to improve ease of reading, many newspapers have been printing six wider columns on the standard size page, instead of eight narrower ones. Some use this device only on the front page and in other "showcase" spaces. The result is a more spacious, open appearance. This trend probably will continue. A small minority of newspapers are tabloid in format, usually five columns wide and 15 inches deep, or approximately half the size of a standard page. Although the tabloid size newspaper is easy for the reader to handle, the problems of printing it and the limitations on its advertising potential have kept many publishers from adopting this format. In spite of these limitations the newspaper with the largest circulation in the United States, the New York *Daily News,* is a tabloid.

Unfortunately, because of the editorial approach used in the past by some tabloid metropolitan newspapers, the word "tabloid" has taken on a connotation of sensationalism. This is unfair to many tabloids whose contents are no more sensational than those of standard-size dailies, even less in some cases. Equating physical size and content is a false approach. Some newspapers call themselves "compact" rather than "tabloid" to avoid this stigma.

No matter what their size, all newspapers have a fundamental organization in common. Each has five major departments: *editorial,* which gathers and prepares the news, entertainment, and opinion materials, both written and illustrated; *advertising,* which solicits and prepares the commercial messages addressed to readers; *production,* which turns the editorial materials and advertisements into type and prints the newspapers; *circulation,* which has the task of selling and delivering the newspapers to the readers of the community; and *business,* which oversees the newspaper's entire operation.

Newspaper stories are written to include the "5 W's and H"—who, what, when, where, why, and how. Their goal is to present a report of an action in simple, easily understood language that can be comprehended by a mass audience of different educational levels. Simplicity of writing is emphasized. If newspapers are to fill their role of communicating to the mass of the population, they cannot indulge in writing styles and terminology so involved that many readers cannot comprehend them. The best newspaper reporters are those who can accurately present complex situations in terms that are easily understood by the majority of their readers. Increasingly, emphasis is being placed on the "why" of news situations. The surface facts of what happened are essential, and must be presented in a balanced, full, and objective manner. Often these facts in themselves do not tell the reader the full story of what has happened. The facts must be put into perspective. The extra element of interpretation—the "why" of the situation—also is needed.

Writing a news story that gives the facts and background without showing the writer's personal feelings or "slanting" the story to fit the publisher's editorial policy requires skill and judgment. The paper's opinions about the news it is reporting should be reserved for the editorial page and signed opinion columns. These principles should apply on newspapers of all sizes. As a whole, American journalism in the second half of the Twentieth Century adheres to them quite well, although there are glaring exceptions.

Television's ability to give the public "right now" visual reports of events in progress has led newspapers to de-emphasize their publication of brief, last-minute bulletins. The day when a newspaper published an "EXTRA" edition with a huge headline and 200 or 300 hastily written words about a major news development is gone forever. Yet only a few decades ago this was the principal method for spreading the news around a city. Newspapers today put more emphasis on depth, less on synthetic excitement. The crisp, terse bulletins are replaced by stories explaining the background of the news events, the personality sidelights surrounding them, their relationship to other news, and future developments the news might cause. This change in newswriting technique has opened new fields for the thoughtful, competent writer.

Newspaper advertising is divided into two types, *display* and *classified*. The former ranges from inconspicuous one-inch notices to multiple-page advertisements in which merchants and manufacturers proclaim their goods and services. Classified advertisements are the small-print, generally brief announcements packed closely together near the back of the paper; they deal with such diverse topics as help wanted, apartments for rent, used furniture and automobiles for sale, and personal notices. On almost all newspapers except the very smallest, display and classified advertising are handled by different staffs. Most newspapers receive about three-fourths of their income from advertising and one-fourth from circulation.

Display advertising in turn is broken into two categories, retail and national, sometimes called general. *Retail* advertising, often called local, comes from the sources its name implies, local merchants and service companies. *National* advertising comes primarily from manufacturers and other commercial organizations selling brand-name merchandise and services over wide regions or the entire country. Much of this advertising is placed through advertising agencies. Local advertising is usually discussed in terms of column inches whereas national advertising is measured by agate lines, 14 to the inch. A column inch is a space of one column wide and one inch deep.

The organizational setup of all newspapers is basically the same, although naturally the larger the newspaper, the more complex its staff alignments. The top man is the publisher, and, in many cases, he is also the principal owner of the newspaper. On some papers the publisher's decisions on all matters are absolute, whereas in other instances he must answer to a board of directors. The publisher's task is to set the newspaper's basic editorial and commercial policies and to see that they are carried out efficiently by the various department heads. On quite a few newspapers, especially smaller ones, the publisher is also the editor; he is then usually referred to as "editor and publisher," a nice tribute to the importance of editorial content in the newspaper.

Frequently there is a business manager or general manager under the publisher to administer the company's business operations, which range all the way from obtaining newsprint to the purchasing of tickets as the newspaper's contribution to a community concert series. The heads of the advertising, circulation, and production departments answer to the publisher through the business manager, if there is one. But the editorial department, jealous of its independence to print the news without being subject to commercial pressures (theoretically), demands and generally gets a line of command directly to the publisher. When editorial and business departments clash, as they sometimes do over ways to handle news situations and expenses, the ultimate decision is made by the publisher. The titles of executive editor and managing editor are most commonly used to designate heads of the news operation.

## THE CHANGING NEWSPAPER PATTERN

The American newspaper industry consists of approximately 1750 daily newspapers and 9400 weekly newspapers, a total that fluctuates slightly from year to year but appears to be relatively stable for the foreseeable future. Although the widely publicized death of long-famous metropolitan newspapers has given a misleading impression, the newspaper industry is in a healthy and expanding condition. Near the close of the 1960's the U.S. Department of Commerce listed it among the top 10 growth industries in the country. More daily newspapers, with greater circulation, are being published than at the end of World War II.

Sixty years ago the number of newspapers was larger: 2200 dailies and 11,800 weeklies. Many of these newspapers were economically weak, however, and had sprung into existence as new cities developed during the country's westward population expansion. In many cases, two or three newspapers were started in a newly developing area; almost inevitably the weaker ones failed to survive. The present total of daily and weekly publications has been fairly steady for quite a few years.

Nearly a thousand of the daily newspapers are published in cities with less than 25,000 population. Almost half of the American dailies have circulations of 10,000 or less. Few more than 125 of the 1750 have circulations above 100,000. Thus, while the greatest public attention is focused on huge metropolitan newspapers like the New York *Times* and the Chicago *Tribune,* their role in the total industry is relatively small physically. In the early 1970's, there were 1500 American cities with daily newspapers, an increase of more than 100 in 25 years. Since the total dailies published was about 1750, many of them by the same ownership within a city, this leaves few cities with competing daily newspapers.

If there is an average American daily (and the individualistic patterns of publishing make the description of an average or typical newspaper almost impossible), it has a circulation of not more than 10,000 copies and serves a city of about 20,000 and its surrounding trade area. A typical weekly has a circulation of about 1500 to 2000 copies in a small town and its surrounding countryside dotted with smaller villages. Neither has direct competition in its own community. Less than 5 percent of daily newspaper cities and weekly newspaper towns have competing newspaper ownerships.

These figures, often quoted by critics of the American press ownership pattern, are in one respect quite misleading. Far more competition for news and advertising exists in these "one-paper towns" than the statistics indicate. The small city dailies extend their coverage into the "weekly" towns with local news correspondents and advertising solicitors. In turn, the larger daily newspapers frequently make heavy inroads into the small daily cities with news bureaus and regional news pages designed for these cities. It is a matter of intense pride for a small city newspaper staff not to be beaten by the "intruder" on a story in its own backyard. The "intruder" in turn, being less deeply rooted in the small city, sometimes will break a story containing intricate local personal relationships that the small city daily has been hesitant to publish. Nothing upsets a local editor more than to hear a townsman say, "Why, there's more news about Jonesville in that out-of-town paper than you print in that sheet of yours."

Although many of the best-known American newspapers are morning publications, evening newspapers dominate the field, more than four to one. A tabulation early in the 1970's showed approximately 330 morning newspapers and 1440 evening papers. In some cases the morning and evening papers were under a single ownership. Morning papers are especially numerous in the metropolitan areas, and are gaining strength there at the expense of the evening papers. During the period 1950–1968, which saw the death of many metropolitan newspapers, the toll was much greater among the evening publications. In cities of more than 1,000,000 population, 16 evening papers ceased publication, as compared with only 6 morning papers.

The most spectacular manifestation of the changing American newspaper pattern in the last two decades has been in the great cities. One famous newspaper after another has been forced to quit publication, leading poorly informed observers to the false conclusion that the American newspaper industry was dwindling. What actually has happened is that newspapers have been heavily affected by the changing patterns of American life. Forty years ago the bulk of metropolitan populations lived within a few miles of the city's center. They did their business and shopping in the downtown district. The efforts of the newspaper in newsgathering, circulation, and advertising were concentrated close in. As the move to the suburbs accelerated, the metropolitan newspaper's problems increased, especially for the evening papers. Operating costs kept rising while the newspaper's audience kept moving farther from its production plant. Newspapers had to be hauled greater distances to readers, through heavy traffic. The downtown stores opened large branches in suburban shopping centers; new peripheral governmental agencies were created, which had to be covered for news. The new suburbanites developed loyalties to their outlying communities instead of the central cities. Because large companies moved their plants and offices to the metropolitan fringes, offering their employees better parking facilities and working atmosphere, many suburban residents no longer commuted to downtown. Higher purchasing power and income concentrated around the fringes, not in the core area. Through no particular fault of their own, afternoon newspapers in the largest cities found themselves being undercut by these changes.

Quickly, suburban community daily newspapers were created to serve this new audience. Some were long-time weeklies that went daily. Others were entirely new. Their growth has been one of the major publishing success stories of the last quarter-century.

This pattern has been especially pronounced in metropolitan areas with populations in excess of 5,000,000—New York in particular—and to lesser degree in the 2,000,000 to 5,000,000 population regions. It has been less noticeable in the 1,000,000 to 2,000,000 population areas, where massiveness has not yet robbed the regions of their personality. Between 1950 and 1968 the number of metropolitan newspapers in New York was reduced from eight to three; in Los Angeles, from five to two; and in Boston, from seven to four.

The metropolitan morning newspapers weathered the upheaval better than the evening papers, partly because they had less pressure during the night hours in distributing their papers to the outlying areas, and partly because they faced less competition from television as a purveyor of last-minute news and time-consuming entertainment. Most metropolitan newspapers that have survived, and adapted themselves to the changed conditions, have been showing circulation growth.

The 2 charts shown on page 181, based on research done by Professor Kenneth R. Byerly, show with specific figures the trends we have been discussing.

As the population grows, newspapers in general can look forward to continued circulation increases.

The chief immediate reason for the disappearance of many newspapers is the constantly rising cost of production. Had this not occurred, many of those that died could have overcome the other problems we have been discussing. The wages of the men who write and print the papers, the cost of newsprint, the metal for the typesetting machines, gasoline for the delivery trucks, taxes, the news and picture services—

## DECLINE OF METROPOLITAN DAILIES, 1950–68

|  | 1–2 Million Population | 2–5 Million | Over 5 Million |
|---|---|---|---|
| *Number* | | | |
| 1950 | 32 | 27 | 20 |
| 1960 | 28 | 23 | 18 |
| 1968 | 27 | 18 | 12 |
| *Circulation* | | | |
| 1950 | 5,509,172 | 6,422,174 | 11,512,992 |
| 1960 | 5,796,995 | 6,299,965 | 10,679,664 |
| 1968 | 6,039,144 | 6,036,830 | 8,868,577 |

## GROWTH OF COMMUNITY DAILIES, 1950–68
(within a 50-mile radius of metropolitan centers)

|  | 1–2 Million Population | 2–5 Million | Over 5 Million |
|---|---|---|---|
| *Number* | | | |
| 1950 | 73 | 124 | 108 |
| 1960 | 74 | 121 | 113 |
| 1968 | 77 | 117 | 116 |
| *Circulation* | | | |
| 1950 | 1,253,947 | 2,008,029 | 3,022,957 |
| 1960 | 1,513,535 | 2,449,283 | 4,049,556 |
| 1968 | 1,706,821 | 2,898,934 | 4,958,643 |

these and a hundred other expenses of a newspaper have become higher and higher. The price of newsprint has tripled in the past 30 years, for example, but the price at which most newspapers are sold to the public has not risen at the same pace. Nor has the cost of an inch of advertising. Thus to maintain the same profit margin as he had 30 years ago, the publisher must sell more newspapers and more advertising or find ways to cut his production costs. Competition by television and radio for the advertiser's dollar has given the publisher another thorny problem.

In many cities where two newspapers were competing for advertising and circulation, and both were struggling to stay solvent, the two owners have seen the financial advantage of combining forces into one publication. One sells out to the other, or they make a partnership arrangement of some sort. The city is left with only one newspaper. Critics of the American press look upon the rise in the number of one-newspaper cities as an unwholesome trend because it subjects the readers to the whims of a monopoly publisher if he chooses to twist or conceal news. There is reason for worry in this trend. Competition between two or more newspapers to cover the news usually gives the readers better assurance of being kept fully informed about what is happening in their community.

There is a substantial argument on the other side, however. One strong newspaper in a city, if the publisher and editor are conscientious men sensible of their responsibilities, can often provide better news coverage and community service than two weak ones. Also, a financially strong paper is sometimes more willing to attack entrenched and harmful interests in a city, because it is able to absorb the financial retaliation its foes aim at it by trying to undercut its advertising and circulation income. A paper that is weak financially is usually a timid paper editorially.

Concurrent with the reduction to one newspaper in many cities is the rise of local news coverage by television and radio stations. Thus in many cases the citizens do have an alternate source for local news. In the event that a newspaper attempts to ignore or twist a local news situation for a policy reason, an attitude much less frequent than the more vehement critics of the press claim, the news coverage by television and radio stations, plus that of "imported" newspapers mentioned previously, can expose this irresponsible action.

The local newspaper's greatest advantage is its more detailed presentation of hometown news, which many readers consider the most important ingredient. If a hometown paper is forced to quit business, its former readers still have access to a metropolitan paper that satisfies part of their needs but, despite special efforts it may make, cannot fill entirely the demand for hometown news. From a cold-blooded, dollars-and-cents standpoint, this sometimes means the elimination of marginal newspaper operations, just as marginal grocery stores are driven out of business by the supermarkets.

In examining the structure of the newspaper industry in the United States, two things should be remembered: (1) Newspapers do not necessarily increase in excellence as they grow larger. Some of the finest, best edited, and most influential papers in the country have relatively small circulations. (2) As a commercial venture a large newspaper is not necessarily more profitable than a small one. Many small-city dailies return a greater annual profit to their proprietors than certain metropolitan dailies with famous names, although the latter have vastly heavier investments in equipment and manpower. In relation to their investment some weekly newspapers are among the most profitable of all publishing operations. They are less glamorous places to work than the metropolitan papers, and usually their technical standards are lower; but as business ventures they may be superior. Often they are closer to the real needs and feelings of their communities than the huge dailies.

The majority of American newspapers are owned by people whose principal business is putting out the newspaper. Control is usually held tightly by an individual, a family, or a small group of investors whom the publisher has invited to share in the ownership. Ownership by publicly-held corporations grew substantially during the early 1970's, however. Recently, as the trend of American business has been toward development of huge conglomerate holding companies with investments in diverse fields, this influence has been felt in the newspaper business. Some of the largest newspaper owners, such as the Times-Mirror Co. of Los Angeles, have invested in many fields besides newspaper ownership and have offered their stock on the public exchanges. Conversely, a few widely diversified corporations have attempted to venture into newspaper ownership as part of their "package." Still other large fundamentally newspaper corporations, such as the Gannett, Newhouse, and Thomson enterprises, have made heavy investments in newspaper properties from coast to coast; usually, however, they emphasize that editorial and advertising control of their individual newspapers shall be kept in local hands. Most of today's newspaper group operations, unlike the William Randolph Hearst and Scripps-Howard chains of an earlier era, concentrate their efforts in smaller nonmetropolitan areas. Their political influence on national affairs thus is proportionately less.

An effective newspaper's editorial policy should not be subject to the whims of stockholder battles. Despite the recent trends, newspapers still are more the reflection of personal ownership than almost any other segment of American business, and owners as a whole are not anxious to share ownership unless financial necessity requires that they do so.

The market prices of successful newspapers have risen so sharply that it is difficult for an individual to purchase an important daily newspaper property today unless he is very wealthy or has substantial financial backing. A small daily with a circulation of 5000 will cost at least $150,000 if it is in a "live" business community. The sale price of a major metropolitan paper is at least $25,000,000. Weekly prices are lower because the papers usually have less mechanical equipment and are situated in towns where the advertising potential is limited. The selling price of an average moderately successful weekly is about $25,000 to $50,000; prices go to $100,000 or more in some cases. Although there still are occasional stories of men who start a small local newspaper on a shoestring and build it into a notable financial success, these have become rarities.

Starting a small daily newspaper from scratch today with a capital outlay of less than $200,000 is virtually impossible because of the high cost of mechanical equipment; most likely the figure would be higher. The publisher must also be prepared for operating losses until his advertising income is developed. Establishment of a completely new metropolitan newspaper would require an outlay of $10,000,000 or more before the publication could stand on its financial feet, which explains why no new papers are being born in our large cities.

Despite all the difficulties, newspaper publishing remains an attractive business. Few great fortunes are made in the field today, but well-managed publications in active communities yield their owners a substantial living with a strong measure of prestige attached. There are instances where a hard-working weekly publisher has improved his capital position by as much as $75,000 over a 15-year period of economic growth in his community.

### OPPORTUNITIES IN NEWSPAPER WORK

Breaking into newspaper work today is relatively easy. Publishers keep urging journalism schools to supply them with new talent, and there are numerous opportunities for college graduates who have majored in other fields. With 1750 daily newspapers and 9400 weeklies in operation, normal turnover creates hundreds of openings each year. The "help wanted" ads in the industry's trade journals are evidence of this. Weeklies and small dailies are the most frequent users of journalism school placement services, both for news and business department personnel. In addition, the prosperous era through which newspapers have been passing has brought sizable staff additions. Increasingly newspapers seek employees for all editorial and "front office" departments who have had at least some college education. Many editors make college training a requirement for all reporters they hire. This does not necessarily mean journalism school experience, however; an applicant who is well trained in liberal arts, with emphasis on English and political science, is welcomed in most newsrooms.

Employment opportunities became especially good for minority groups, blacks in particular, during the early 1970's as newspaper proprietors belatedly sought to achieve better balance of races and backgrounds on their staffs in keeping with national trends. Competent black reporters and editors were in great demand. Smaller newspapers had extreme difficulty in keeping the black reporters they trained because these men and women were lured away by the more glamorous metropolitan media at higher pay. An estimate accepted by the American Society of Newspaper Editors in 1972 put the number of persons in the national news force at 40,000, of whom fewer than one percent were black, Mexican-American, Indian, Cuban, or Oriental.

Ironically, with the market for minority editorial workers wide open, relatively few were available for hiring. The colleges were producing few qualified and interested minority candidates with journalism training; editors, insistent upon maintaining professional standards, hesitated to hire inadequately educated staff members just because they were from previously ignored minorities. The ASNE placed the recruitment of blacks and other minorities as one of its top priorities for the decade. On newspapers with a substantial percentage of black staff members, there was pressure to promote more of them into decision-making positions.

Broadly speaking, the specialized Negro press of the country has not reached the technical and professional levels of the general daily press, and has not been an especially fruitful recruiting source for the large daily newspapers. The development of such excellent Negro publications as *Ebony* has improved this situation.

The role of women in the newsrooms has grown dramatically. Long gone is the day when feminine staff members were relegated to the women's department, except for an occasional "sob sister" feature writer on the news staff. Competent women have approximately equal opportunities with men to be hired on most newspapers and to receive solid news staff assignments. Many cover regular beats with frequent bylines or write columns. Nudged by the women's liberation movement, city editors have found that they can send women satisfactorily on assignments they formerly thought suitable only for men and that the women are eager to go. Because of seniority systems and management habits, women are advancing slowly into decision-making positions, but the number who hold jobs that influence news policy is growing.

**News and editorial.**   There are two main divisions of newsroom work —*reporting,* which includes gathering and writing news and feature stories and the taking of news and feature photographs; and *desk work,* which is the selection and preparation for printing of the written material and photographs submitted by the reporters, photographers, and the wire and syndicate services. The men who do the desk work are called editors.

This distinction between the newsgatherers and the news processors is quite sharp on large daily newspaper staffs. Some editors will go a year or more without writing a single news story, and metropolitan reporters have nothing to do with the selection of a headline or page placement of the stories they write. On smaller papers the distinction is less pronounced, and in many cases an editorial man spends part of his day as a reporter, photographer, and writer and the other part in selecting and processing the news for publication. The smaller the paper, the greater the need to be the proverbial "jack of all trades."

Some men and women find their greatest satisfaction in being reporters all their lives—probing for information, being close to events as they happen, and mingling with the people who make news. Theirs is the most exciting part of newspaper work, when big stories are breaking, and they are the ones the public knows as newspapermen. Few laymen have any concept of the inside office workers who really put the paper together. Many of the finest reporters in the country abhor the idea of being bound to a desk all day, shuffling paper and fighting the mechanical demands of type and newsprint. In fact, some cynical metropolitan reporting veterans have a tendency to look upon desk men as slightly deficient in intelligence and very deficient in a zest for life.

The fact remains, however, that a reporter rarely is promoted directly to a high editorial place on a large or medium-sized daily. The top jobs go to the men who have had desk experience. They are the organizers, the planners, the men and women who think automatically of whether a headline will "count" and whether all the essential stories for an edition are moved out to the composing room before deadline so the papers will come off the press on time. By the same token, few desk men are truly successful unless they have had a thorough grounding in reporting, so they can know the problems a reporter faces on a story and can feed him useful suggestions.

A beginner can start as a city hall beat reporter for a small daily; he can also start as the telegraph editor, handling the news wire and writing headlines. If he chooses and sticks to reporting, he may graduate eventually to a metropolitan reporting staff; if he selects the editing path, he may advance to a large paper's copy desk. Or, in either capacity, he may remain with the small daily and soon rise to editorial management status.

On most daily newspapers there are specialized editing-reporting jobs, where the editorial worker gathers his own news and also helps in preparing it for print. The woman's page, the sports page, the business page, and the entertainment page fall into this category. Some men and women prefer to become specialists and do their reporting in one area. The woman's pages of a modern daily offer many opportunities for stimulating writing; sports always has been a magnet for prospective young men reporters. Business news has become a specialty on many papers, with staffs of as many as six or eight assigned to the area. Some metropolitan papers offer opportunities for critical reviewers of films, television, the drama, and books. There are also varied opportunities to specialize in one of the broader general news areas: politics, science, labor, religion, urban and racial problems, space and aviation, social work, and public health. Many a general assignment reporter has become a recognized expert in one of these fields and thereby has found a satisfying career.

A very important area of work is that on the editorial page. Editorial page staffs run to eight or ten men (and occasionally a woman) on metropolitan papers which pride themselves on the quality of their opinion offerings. Some specialize as writers of editorials on international affairs; others specialize in economics and business, or perhaps local subjects. The editorial page director coordinates their work and consults with the publisher on major policy decisions. Editorial page staffs of this size usually have a make-up editor who selects the column materials and "letters-to-the-editor" and produces the page. They also may have a staff cartoonist. Papers which place less emphasis upon the editorial page will have fewer editorial writers. And at the smaller daily level, there may be only one editorial writer, plus a managing editor who also attempts to comment on the day's news. Weekly newspaper editors sometimes write and publish regular editorial columns; others prefer to write what they call "personal columns" in a more informal style.

The opportunities to advance on an editorial staff come in many forms. A reporter may eventually earn a staff assignment in Washington, at the United Nations, or abroad; an increasing number of these jobs is becoming available. He may work his way up through the desk jobs to become city editor or even managing editor; he may become a top-flight political or science writer; or he may move into the editorial page staff or one of the specialized departments for a stay of many years. Much depends upon his temperament, and a bit of luck. As a rule the editorial management chooses for promotion, when an important vacancy occurs, a man or woman with all-around experience and a record of dependability and creative thinking.

**Photography.**   The newspaper photographer fills a large and growing role on the staff of every daily newspaper, large or small, as the field of photojournalism expands. On a newspaper, the photographer's primary task is to record in a single picture or a sequence, rapidly and factually, the news and feature developments of the day that lend themselves to pictorial treatment. He may take pictures for the news, sports, woman's page, and entertainment editors, as well as for the promotion and advertising departments. On large staffs, employing 20 or more photographers and technicians, individuals may develop specialties and be assigned primarily in these fields. One man demonstrates a knack for catching vivid sports action from unusual angles; another may be especially skillful at taking fashion and social pictures to avoid the "waxworks pose" that is so deadly in many prearranged feature photographs.

Planning of photographic coverage on good newspaper staffs is as meticulous as the arrangement of coverage by reporters. Memorable news photos usually are the result of having a photographer assigned to the right place at the proper time, plus the photographer's instinct for the climactic moment in the news situation and his technical ability to take an effective picture when that moment comes.

Newspaper photography has advanced far from the days when an aggressive copyboy of limited education could be taught the rudiments of a camera and turned loose as an ambulance-chasing photographer. Today many news photographers have college educations or have attended professional photography schools. They look upon photojournalism as a satisfying career and know that their income will increase with their skill. News photography is not a field for a shy person. The photographer must be ready to fight for his picture at times. However, the widely held concept of the photographer as a rough, brash fellow shoving heedlessly into the middle of things is inaccurate and misleading.

On the larger papers, the photographer's equipment ranges from the 5 × 7 Big Bertha camera with a 28-inch lens to the 35 mm or 2¼ × 2¼ camera. The trend is toward the use of small, inconspicuous equipment. His assignments range from aerial photos to close-ups of tiny objects such as rings. Two-way radio may keep him in constant touch with his office. Smaller dailies may have only one or two photographers, and on many weeklies the editor takes his own pictures. The reporter who can take photographs, and the photographer who can report, are in especial demand on small papers and are often paid more than those with a single ability.

Newspaper photographers receive the same salaries as reporters under Guild scales. They frequently supplement their salary checks with overtime assignments and with after-hours jobs such as photographing weddings. Free-lance photographers, not on the newspaper payroll, are paid for newsworthy pictures that they submit for publication. Large papers also employ picture editors, who give and coordinate assignments and supervise the publishing of all pictures, including photo pages.

The movement of experienced photographers between media compares to that of writers and editors. A photojournalist may remain on newspapers for his entire career. He may move to the photographic staff of a television station or a magazine. Perhaps he may choose to enter the commercial or industrial photographic field. Wherever he goes with his camera, his newspaper experience in judging situations and people quickly is invaluable. (See Chapter 12.)

**Advertising, circulation, management.** Although news reporting is the most glamorous and best publicized part of newspaper work, there are many other opportunities for young men and women in advertising sales and copywriting, circulation, promotion and public relations, personnel, research, production, and general business management.

The advertising department is one of the most attractive for sales-minded persons. A good newspaper space salesman must be much more than a glib talker. He must know as much as possible about the paper's policies and features. He must be able to supply the potential advertiser with abundant and accurate figures about the paper's circulation pattern and totals, the advertising rates, and the kind of merchandising support the advertiser will receive. He must know at least the rudiments of layout and art work. In addition, he should be an idea man, enthusiastic and able to give the merchant ideas about how best to use his advertising budget. Selling newspaper advertising requires the art of persuasion, a briefcase well loaded with facts and ideas, and a strong personal belief that the newspaper space he is selling will move goods off the merchant's shelves. The more he knows about his client merchant's business and problems, the more effectively he can serve him. In fact, it is not unusual for an advertising man to join one of the firms to which he has been selling advertising.

Advertising work for weeklies and small dailies is an excellent training ground for any kind of advertising man. Some young college graduates become advertising managers of weeklies, handling all types of business for their papers, from classified ads to the major local accounts. The same sort of opportunities for diversified experience come on small dailies, although as they increase in circulation the dailies tend to specialize in their advertising staff functions. On smaller papers, the advertising salesman is likely to be his own copywriter; on larger dailies there are positions for copywriters, both men and women, and artists.

Many advertising men get their start in the classified department of larger newspapers, where they deal with many small accounts in a wide variety of fields. A certain amount of classified advertising comes in voluntarily, but most of it must be solicited. Classified is sold on a day-to-day basis with deadlines only a few hours before publication. Salesmen have territories and detailed lists of accounts to cover, much like a reporter's beat.

Classified advertising is closer to the people than any other type of advertising. A three-line ad offering a desirable item for sale at a reduced price will cause the private advertiser's phone to ring dozens of times within a few hours after the paper appears. Conversely, the failure of an advertisement to get results may cause the advertiser to grumble, "That paper is no good!" A classified copywriter who learns the tricks of concise, alluring wording can help the advertiser, his newspaper, and his own career. Readership tests show that classified sections are among the best-read in a newspaper.

The young salesman is often promoted from classified into the local display department, and later perhaps into the smaller and more select national (or general) department. In the classified department he scrambles to meet his daily quota of lines for the next day's paper; in the national advertising department he works with manufacturers and distributors of brand-name products, often weeks in advance of publication. He is selling schedules of multiple insertions, sometimes in color. A newspaper's national sales staff works in conjunction with its national newspaper representatives, who solicit advertising for it in other major cities.

Promotions to the top ranks in the business department of a newspaper come for those who have demonstrated their ability in classified, local display, and national advertising. Heads of those departments report to the business manager, one of the key men in the organization.

The circulation department offers some opportunities for college-trained men with organizing ability, promotional ideas, and a liking for detail. Men who have a knack for working with carrier boys on a friendly basis, much like a coach with a high school football team, are in demand. While the top circulation jobs on large newspapers carry high salaries, the number of jobs available in this department for the college-trained man is somewhat less than in editorial and advertising. Few women work in circulation except in clerical capacities.

On larger dailies there are well-paying and interesting jobs in such supplementary departments as promotion and public relations, personnel, research, and administration. Some newspapers put out their own institutional publications for employees.

Roughly half the jobs on a metropolitan newspaper are in the production department, yet few men with college training in journalism find a place in this half of newspaper operation. The men who work in the composing room, the platemaking department, the engraving section, and the pressroom are drawn largely from the trade schools and apprenticeship programs. The work is mechanical in nature, demanding a high degree of technical skill. The men who hold top positions in the production departments usually come up through the ranks, although graduate engineers sometimes find their way into newspaper production offices.

Cost control is extremely important in newspaper production, just as in any manufacturing operation. Elaborate accounting sheets are kept, showing the costs of setting a column of type, making up a page, printing a thousand papers, increasing the size of an edition by two pages, working a press crew overtime because of a missed deadline, and a hundred other expense factors. All these costs are weighed carefully in setting the newspaper's advertising rates. If the publisher pegs his space rates very low he will attract extra advertising, but he may find that he is spending more to print each advertisement than he is being paid for it. If a loosely run production department has such large costs that the publisher must charge unusually high advertising rates to cover them, he forces the advertisers to use other media.

Most editorial people on large newspaper staffs, it might be added, know little and care less about such production and cost problems. They regard the business aspects of publishing as something remote and of scant concern to them. This is unfortunate, especially if they have thoughts of striking off on their own some day on that small country weekly of their dreams.

In a typical medium-size city newspaper with 50,000 circulation, figures reported to *Editor & Publisher* showed that, during the decade from the late 1950's to the late 1960's, overall operating costs rose 84 percent. Those in the editorial department increased 121.23 percent during the 10 years, from $285,000 to $630,500. This trend has continued. Editorial department operating costs are the highest figures on the newspaper's books. Reading space in the newspaper increased 30.6 percent, permitting publication of additional news each day. These statistics give some indication of the business pressures under which a publisher operates, and the large role the news department plays in them.

**Salaries.** Newspaper salaries, while not at the top of the list, compare favorably as a whole with those in other businesses and professions that require a good education and creative thinking. They have improved quite sharply during the past 25 years.

The activities of the American Newspaper Guild have been an important factor in this improvement. Organized in 1933, during the depression when editorial salaries in particular were low, the Guild has campaigned as an organized labor union for higher wages and more favorable working conditions. It has called strikes against newspapers to enforce its demands. A rise in newspaper salaries was inevitable, even without the existence of the Guild, or the industry could not have held its workers as economic conditions improved. But the activities of the Guild speeded the process.

Today the Guild has 30,000 members, mainly on larger papers. Its contracts with management cover salaries, vacations, severance pay, and working conditions. The salary levels are minimums, covering all men and women in the categories specified. Some Guild contracts cover just editorial departments; others, all nonprinting employees. The basic contract provides a graduated pay scale, with automatic annual steps from the starting minimum through five or seven years to a top minimum. Salary advancement faster than, and beyond the top of, Guild scales is by individual negotiation with management.

It is quite common for a good newspaperman with several years' experience to earn at least $10,000 a year. Salaries rise well above this figure as experience grows, especially on large newspapers, where top journeymen earn up to $20,000. Executive salaries exceed this figure considerably. A Newspaper Fund survey disclosed that in 1968 the annual starting salaries for college graduates on daily newspapers averaged $6000 for news personnel and $6300 for advertising employees. Weeklies offered 1968 news graduates an average of $5700 and advertising graduates $5800. Master's degree holders fared far better at a starting average of $8000. Early in the 1970's in some cities top Newspaper Guild minimum salaries for reporters with five years or more of experience exceeded $15,000, and weekly pay of $400 ($20,800 a year) was reached in a Guild contract for the first time. This was at the Washington *Post*. The average weekly salary for top level reporters under Guild contracts in 1972 was $220.96.

Salaries on newspapers without Guild contracts usually are in line with Guild papers of similar circulation. The size and location of the newspaper have heavy influence on the salary levels. Obviously a smaller city newspaper with limited resources cannot pay salaries like those in New York.

Newspaper salaries in general are comparable to those paid in broadcasting, but lower than on large magazines and in public relations. This fact often lures the young graduate directly into the public relations field, usually an unwise decision because a few years of the discipline and challenging experiences of news reporting will make him a more effective worker in whatever field he chooses later.

The Guild salaries are for 37-to-40-hour weeks, for average people. Superior people get above-minimum salaries. But as in all professions they must expect to work more than a mere 40-hour week to get extra pay. Any newspaperman can add to his income by becoming a specialist, doing outside writing and speaking. He thus enhances his value to the newspaper and likely becomes one of the above-minimum newsmen, who constitute a third to a half of many metropolitan staffs. Another route to the top pay levels is through skilled desk work, where a pronounced shortage of qualified personnel has existed in recent years.

Although many men and women spend their entire careers in the newspaper business, others move on from it into related fields. Newspapers are one training ground for workers in all mass communications media. In the newsroom they learn the art of reporting, the basic skill for all communication, and in the advertising department they develop their techniques of selling and presentation.

Why do men and women move from newspapers into related fields? Generally they are drawn by higher pay, the possibility of increased freedom as writers, or the opportunity to go into business for themselves. Public relations offices, magazine staffs, and radio and television news staffs are heavily loaded with former newspapermen and newspaperwomen. The press associations reach into the newspapers for their staffs; in turn, there is a steady movement of experienced press association men to the newspapers in the higher bracket editorial posts. Some faculty members in journalism schools are recruited from newspapermen who return to college for graduate work, then stay on to teach. Advertising agencies draw much of their manpower from the staffs of daily newspapers. Some newsmen enter politics, obtaining appointive jobs through friendships made as reporters and editors, and possibly later running for elective office. The newspaper has always been a fountainhead from which manpower flows into all areas of mass communications.

### HOW NEWSPAPERS ARE PRINTED

Johann Gutenberg's introduction of movable type in the 1440's and 1450's was the first, fundamental step toward the modern printing process. Before that, all books had been hand-lettered laboriously on sheets of vellum or parchment. By assembling pieces of movable type on the flatbed of a machine resembling a wine press, inking them, and pressing down a sheet of paper on them by a screw-and-lever arrangement, Gutenberg could print an entire page. The process was laborious; perhaps 600 impressions could be made in a day of hard work. His most renowned printed products were the cherished Gutenberg Bibles.

Slow as this process was, it caused a social revolution in Europe. For the first time, printed messages became widely distributed among a population that was predominantly illiterate. The ideas they contained stirred intellectual ferment.

Few important improvements in printing methods took place during the next 350 years. Printing as we know it began developing in the early 1800's, concurrent with the industrial revolution. An iron press was developed in 1798, permitting greater pressure and larger forms. The Washington Hand Press, which appeared in 1827, made possible as many as 250 impressions an hour. This was the press carried by itinerant printers on the great American trek to the West, and on which many pioneer newspapers were born.

Not until mechanical power was applied to running a press could sufficient speed be developed for daily newspaper production. In 1811 a German, Friedrich Koenig, produced a flatbed cylinder press that could be run by steam. Then in 1846 R. Hoe & Co. created a type-revolving press. The type was locked into forms placed on a slightly curved cylinder, against which revolved several impression cylinders. The weakness of this method was that no multiple-column headlines, illustrations, or advertisements could be used. All type still was being set by hand, letter by letter.

Two further inventions followed which made newspaper printing similar to today's traditional methods. First came stereotyping. Impressions were made from the flatbed of type on papier-maché matrices. Curved solid printing plates were made by pouring molten metal against the matrice, at great pressure. These plates were locked on a rotary cylinder on the press, inked, and pressed against the paper. Thus the actual printing was not done from the original flatbed of type. Soon the use of continuous rolls of newsprint was introduced, so the revolving plates printed one newspaper after another at high speed. By the 1870's a press could print 18,000 copies an hour, making possible the growth of mass circulations. Presses today run at more than twice that speed. Newsprint made from wood pulp was developed.

The next great revolution in newspaper printing took place when machines were invented to replace the slow process of setting type by hand. In the old days a printer meticulously picked one letter at a time from slots in a wooden case—capital letters in the upper portion, small letters in the lower part. This is the origin of the terms upper and lower case for capital and small letters. After use, the letters had to be redistributed in the case by hand. Then in 1886 Ottmar Mergenthaler's Linotype machine came into successful use by newspapers. Operated by a keyboard, it released a series of indented letter matrices. These were assembled in a row; hot metal was squirted against them; and a complete solid line of type emerged. The matrices were redistributed automatically by the machine for reuse. The speed of type production in a composing room was increased immensely. Soon the Intertype and other automatic typecasting machines followed. Color printing on rotary presses began in the 1890's, and use of photoengravings became feasible about the same time.

By 1900 most of the basic daily newspaper letterpress printing processes had been developed. For the next half-century few significant changes were made. While other manufacturing industries experimented and developed spectacular new techniques, newspapers stood almost still mechanically.

Fortunately there has been a resurgence of ingenuity and progress in the last 25 years.

First came typesetting by tape. Instead of fingering a Linotype keyboard and releasing one matrice at a time, an operator punches the words of a news story on a keyboard which perforates a continuous roll of tape. This is known as TTS, teletypesetting. Each letter is represented by a different combination of punch holes. These tapes are fed through the Linotype or Intertype machines, automatically releasing the matrices at high speed. One operator can monitor two or three linecasting machines at once. Recently computers have been harnessed to the typesetting task, making it even faster. A tape keyboard operator must make each line come out even, adjusting or "justifying" the spaces between words and inserting hyphens at the ends of the lines. This slows his work. With computer typesetting, the operator punches a continuous tape without worrying about justifying the lines and starting new lines. His and other tapes are fed through the computer, which justifies and hyphenates the tapes, putting them into high-speed linecasting machines ready to run. This type of printing is called the "hot type" method because it uses heated metal. New "cold type" techniques are eliminating the familiar hot metal type in many newspaper plants. Punched tape is run through high speed photo-electric typesetting machines that produce long strips of type on paper in column width, ready to be pasted onto makeup sheets. These paste-up pages then are photographed either onto printing plates for the offset printing method or onto the recently developed plastic printing plates that can be placed on traditional presses in lieu of the old heavy lead stereotype plates.

Offset printing is based on lithography, an older process in which printing was done from the smooth flat surface of stones. In surface printing, the image is placed on the stone by a greasy substance which has an affinity for ink. The nonprinting surface is covered with a thin film of water that repels the ink. Thus only the image is printed on paper when pressure is applied. The same principles are used on the offset printing press. The image is transferred from the printing plate cylinder to a rubber blanket attached to a second cylinder. It is then printed on the paper which is carried on a third impression cylinder. Development of offset presses capable of printing on a continuous web of paper was a major step in adapting this process to newspaper printing.

The advantages of offset printing in clarity and flexibility have caused a great upsurge in its use by newspapers, especially weeklies and smaller dailies. Some large circulation dailies adopted it after production problems were solved. By 1973, about one third of the American dailies and three fourths of the weekly newspapers were being printed by offset. Other papers adopted one of the plastic plate processes, of which the Grace Letterflex is best known. Use of these lightweight, photo-sensitive plates enabled them to avoid the heavy expense of replacing their presses with the offset variety.

Next, the electronic revolution reached the newsroom. Editing machines made it possible for copy to be processed from the reporter's typewriter, after correction by an editor, directly into the photo-electric typesetting machines, eliminating much of the tape punching. Optical character readers and video display terminals are two forms of the new equipment that appeared in newsrooms. Reporters and editors had to learn the tricks of producing copy on these ingenious machines.

Transmission of paste-up pages from one city to another by facsimile, to speed the printing of national publications in several plants simultaneously, is in use. Some metropolitan newspapers employ this process to move photographic copy of complete pages from their main offices to satellite printing plants in the suburbs.

## THE WEEKLY NEWSPAPER

In thousands of American towns the weekly newspaper is at the core of community life. It is the chief source of information about the activities of individuals and organizations, and the merchants look to its advertising columns as a major tool for selling goods. In the files of a small-town weekly are recorded the vital statistics of the town's life—the births and deaths, marriages, social events, tragedies, and the ludicrous moments that give life zest. The editor knows almost everyone and they all know him; the relationship between the small weekly newspaper and its audience is closer than in any other type of publishing. Even when it is overshadowed by a big city daily a few miles away, the weekly newspaper often has a secure place in the heart of its community and can continue to thrive. The chief stock in trade it has to offer is names: subscribers reading about their neighbors and about themselves. The larger the newspaper, the less impact the names in news stories have on the readers, because they do not know all the people mentioned. This personal link is an advantage the community weekly paper has over its larger, more sophisticated big city cousin.

The weekly newspaper is editing and publishing in its simplest form, although anyone who believes that putting out a weekly is easy has been badly misled. All the jobs involved in any newspaper must be done: getting news and editing it, selling advertising, handling circulation, and seeing to it that the paper is printed on time. On the large daily there are many people to handle each of these operations, but on the weekly everything is done by a handful of workers. The editor may also sell advertising, read proof, take pictures, haul the papers to the post office for mailing, and pitch in to help the printers put type into the forms on publication day. In some cases he also runs the press. The 40-hour week is only a dream to the men who edit and publish weekly newspapers. After the day's work at the office is finished, the weekly editor covers civic meetings, attends social functions in the hope of getting news, and listens to the complaints of fellow townsmen who consider him a referee of local disputes. The very fact that he is a newspaperman adds a certain aura to his name.

Many weekly newspapers are published by husband-and-wife teams. In some cases they share billing in the paper's masthead as joint editor and publisher; often the wife's aid is more informal, such as helping in the office with the advertising and circulation billing or gathering local news items by telephone. The work hours she contributes reduce the cost of hired help that much, and in an operation where the margin of profit is small that saving may have a significant influence on the year's earnings.

Another common arrangement is a partnership between a printer and a front-office man. One handles the mechanical operations while the other does the editorial and advertising work. In the past many weeklies were started by printers who set most of the type themselves and hired some relatively inexperienced person at a low salary to handle the front-office duties. A more common procedure now is for the publisher to be an advertising man who has decided to strike out on his own and who either handles the editorial work himself or hires someone to do it.

Most weekly publishers are also in the job printing business, and indeed they make a large percentage of their annual profit from this side of the operation. The same printing plant which publishes the paper once a week also prints programs and yearbooks for local clubs, wedding announcements, business cards, and other types of printing needed in every community. By doing job work the publisher keeps his machinery busy and has enough work to give his printers full-time jobs. The shop foreman, or the publisher himself if the paper is small enough, organizes the flow of printing work so the commercial jobs mesh with the weekly production of the paper. Relatively few daily newspapers do extensive job printing work unless they have a separate division especially set up for it with equipment of its own, because the task of producing a daily paper is too great a burden on the equipment.

Weekly newspaper publishing is a risky enterprise for a man who thinks only in editorial terms; he must learn the business tricks of obtaining revenue from advertising and circulation or his paper won't stay alive very long.

One of the clichés of newspaper work is the big city newsman who dreams of getting away from the hustle and bustle and settling down to an easy life in a small town with a weekly newspaper of his own. He envisions himself as a man of power in the community, leisurely writing editorials and going fishing for the weekend as soon as the week's edition is printed. Nothing could be further from the truth. The minute one week's edition is out he begins churning out copy for next week's paper so the machine operator can set it into type without drawing overtime pay on press day; talking to county political leaders about printing the delinquent tax list, a lucrative annual plum for newspapers in many communities; or soothing an angry mother whose daughter's name was misspelled in a wedding story. Instead of fishing he may spend his Saturday trying to collect a bill from a delinquent classified advertiser, repainting the office furniture, or attending a church picnic to prevent gossip that he was ignoring that particular denomination.

Good clues to the type of opportunities for ownership available in the weekly field are to be found in the columns of the *Publishers' Auxiliary,* a trade publication in the small newspaper field. The advertisements of newspapers for sale contain such phrases as these: "profitable if publisher can help some in back shop" . . . "golden opportunity for good man-and-wife team" . . . "present owner here 50 years will sell onefourth interest with option on balance to qualified printer-manager who can eventually take complete control. Will sell paper separate without plant to good newsman" . . . "lots of legal advertising, lots of printing, machinery in good condition. Present owner must slow down."

As an indication of the jack-of-all-trades ability required on small weeklies, here is an actual example of the setup of a weekly paper in a small southern town. The staff consisted of five persons:. three were apprentice printers who did job printing as well as making up the newspaper; the fourth was a part-time woman who wrote society news, which she brought to the office once a week. The remaining staff member was editor, columnist, advertising solicitor, proofreader, reporter, photographer, typesetter, pressman, and bill collector. This wasn't much of a newspaper by usual journalistic standards, but it did manage to come out every week and provide the community with information it could receive in no other way.

The weekly editor and publisher cannot easily escape his audience, as can the metropolitan newspaperman. His contacts with the community are too many and too deep. Even though these sometimes are a nuisance so far as demands upon his time are concerned, they are the very essence of his success.

Most weekly newspapers are published on Thursday, not merely from tradition but for a sound commercial reason. It is the day on which the local merchants want to reach readers with news of their weekend sales. The grocery stores in particular key their marketing pattern to their Thursday newspaper advertisements, offering special items on sale Thursday through Saturday. This pattern runs through newspapers of all sizes, in fact; Thursday is usually the biggest advertising day of the week, and as a result the papers issued on that day have more pages. Recently, however, food stores in some parts of the country have switched their advertising to Wednesday afternoons, some even to Tuesdays, in the struggle for competitive advantage.

**Basic printing methods.** The operating schedule of a weekly newspaper is determined largely by the capacity of its mechanical department. Many weeklies are published with an absolute minimum of equipment. Since printing equipment is so expensive that a struggling newspaper cannot afford the luxury of all it needs, the men who put it out must adjust their work schedules to fit the amount of type the machinery can produce.

Before offset printing became such a popular method, two kinds of newspaper presses were in general use in this country. One of these is the flatbed type, which is rapidly becoming a rarity except in remote areas. On this the pages of type are laid flat on a tray, side by side, and the web of newsprint from a large roll is pressed down on them by a roller moving back and forth. A simpler flatbed press, still used by small weekly newspapers, prints on single sheets of newsprint rather than on a roll. This is direct printing; the paper is in contact with the original type. The other, faster method is the rotary press, not commonly used by weekly newspapers. Flatbed presses are used on weekly newspapers because they cost less, and most weeklies have press runs too small to obtain the full advantage of rotary press operation.

With the rapid growth of offset printing, the appearance of American weeklies has improved. Because of a weekly's relatively small investment in printing equipment, the changeover is easier for it than for a daily. A common practice is for a number of weeklies to be printed in a common offset plant. Each paper maintains an office in its own community; there it carries on all the local business and editorial functions. Either by standard typesetting machines or the use of photo-typesetting machinery, it prepares camera-ready paste-up pages. These are transported to a central offset printing plant in a larger city, where they are run on the press overnight and brought back to the local community for distribution the next morning. Some central printing plants handle the entire job. Using copy submitted to them in typewritten and other rough form, they set type, paste up the pages, and print the finished newspapers. This enables the weekly newspaper to take advantage of offset printing without making a heavy plant investment.

**The weekly's editorial problems.** When we add up all the difficulties the weekly newspaper publisher has in keeping his small enterprise operating at a profit, it is not surprising that the editorial aspects of his newspaper sometimes suffer. The editorial department costs money but takes in nothing—nothing directly, that is, except for the fundamental fact that without it there would be no newspaper. The tendency of many weekly publishers, especially those whose experience runs largely to printing or advertising work, is to "get by" with the lowest editorial cost possible. They employ inexperienced help to write a few columns of front page news a week and fill the inside pages with "canned" material from commercial sources and articles contributed by local residents. The latter material is put into the paper with a minimum of editing. As a group, weekly newspapers are a dull looking lot.

Weekly newspapers do not have the news reports of the press associations to help fill their pages. Everything they print must be written locally or obtained from such sources as the editor can develop. Some small printing plants, operating with only a single typesetting machine, cannot produce enough type for the paper unless the printers work overtime at bonus wages, and so the editor must depend upon matted feature "boiler plate" material to fill the gap. Much free advertising disguised as news slips into print in this manner.

Because a portion of our weekly newspapers is forced to operate on such an extremely skimpy basis, it should not be assumed that all do so. The range in editorial excellence among weeklies is very wide. Notable examples of splendidly edited weeklies are to be found throughout the United States, as can be seen by an examination of the entries submitted in the annual contests conducted by the state press associations. The writing, editing, and makeup in these weeklies is the equal of that found in many large dailies.

Rarely are weekly newspapers of the crusading type. Most editors see their role as that of printing the constructive, orthodox news of the community without dealing in what often is called sensationalism. Their circulation is almost exclusively among families, and their personal contacts among the townspeople are so intimate that they sometimes omit stories which might be embarrassing. Also, in a tightly knit small community the commercial and social pressures on an editor to "stay in line" are exceptionally heavy. In some cases the newspaper's profit margin is so thin that the publisher cannot risk irritating an important advertiser by printing something he dislikes.

Often the editor-publisher is so busy with his business responsibilities that he neglects the editorial vigor his newspaper should have. This is understandable but nevertheless is a decided weakness in the functioning of our weekly press. Without resorting to big-city street sensationalism, many weekly editors could serve their communities better if they dealt more bluntly with local problems and tackled controversial issues head-on. The American weekly press as a whole is conformist and conservative.

**Circulation for weeklies.** The advertising rates a newspaper can charge depend upon the number of copies it sells, so it follows that the task of building the largest circulation possible is fundamental. This is a serious problem for most weeklies, because the sales potential in a small community is limited, and because circulation building is a specialized skill in which many weekly publishers are not well versed. For many years most weeklies followed the traditional policy of selling subscriptions to local residents and delivering the paper each Thursday in the regular mail. All too often the publisher let his circulation lists get out of date and failed to push his annual collections. Some progressive weeklies switched to delivery by carrier boy, a practice which has worked more successfully in some communities than in others.

More recently, especially in the suburban areas, some weeklies have changed to a free distribution basis, having a carrier boy deliver a newspaper automatically to every home in the community. Those who have adopted this practice prefer to call it "controlled circulation" while their opponents use the derogatory term "throwaway."

The publisher who distributes his newspaper free accepts three financial disadvantages to gain one important advantage. His newsprint bill rises and his income from circulation virtually disappears, and if he distributes copies by mail his postal costs rise, too. But by convincing advertisers that he has blanketed the town with copies of his newspaper he can obtain a higher advertising rate and more linage. If he can raise his advertising income sufficiently, his net profit rises.

A common practice of such free delivery weeklies is to have carrier boys call at each home every month to collect a small sum, frequently

25 cents, from those householders who volunteer to pay. Technically the money is for the delivery service, not for the newspaper itself. Those who do not pay continue to receive the paper anyway unless they specifically order it stopped. Usually the boy is paid a guaranteed sum for his work, and anything he collects above that amount is turned in to the paper. Such free distribution methods are impractical for daily newspapers because of the high newsprint costs and the lack of circulation revenue. They work well on weeklies only in those areas where there is a large concentration of homes.

Many of the most profitable weekly newspaper enterprises are combination operations in which one company prints weekly papers for several communities in a single plant. Each newspaper has a separate identity and is filled with news of its own community, gathered by an editorial staff on the spot. The typesetting and printing are done in a centralized plant, sometimes quite a few miles distant from the town of publication. Advertising in one paper of the group can be published in one or more of the others for a small additional fee or "pickup rate."

The advantages of such an operation are many. Because each piece of his equipment is used with greater frequency during the week, the publisher can afford better printing tools and so can put out a more attractive newspaper. By coordinating the editorial and advertising efforts of the various papers, and picking up some news from one edition to another, he can employ better qualified staff members. Some weekly group plants operate almost on a daily newspaper schedule with rotary presses and tightly planned deadlines. Suburban areas lend themselves especially well to group operation.

The next step above the weekly newspaper is the semiweekly, published twice a week rather than once, frequently on Monday and Thursday, or sometimes with a Sunday edition. There are relatively few semiweekly and triweekly publications in this country, because usually a weekly which seeks to expand into broader fields makes the jump directly to daily operation. Many semiweekly papers are the result of the combination of two competing weeklies in a town. Some come into being when a publisher learns to his sorrow that his city cannot sustain a daily and so cuts back to twice-a-week publication.

The semiweekly is related to the weekly in content, rather than to the daily. Usually it receives no wire service reports and is dependent upon local news to fill its columns, like the ordinary weekly. Because it has many of the advantages of group weekly publication, the semiweekly's standards of content and appearance are relatively high.

## THE SMALL DAILY NEWSPAPER

The differences in operation of the weekly newspaper and the small daily newspaper are great, because the fundamental element of timeliness has been added. The principle of "today's news today" dominates the minds of daily newspapermen, no matter how small their paper may be.

Because the process of assembling and printing the newspaper is done six or seven times a week, instead of once, the thinking of the men who do the job is accelerated. Working on a daily does not necessarily make a reporter or an advertising solicitor a better newspaperman than his colleagues on the weeklies, but it does tend to make him a faster one. Deadlines take on a fresh, compelling meaning. A weekly may define its news deadline as "Tuesday afternoon," and still be able to slip through a couple of late columns Wednesday morning without seriously disturbing the rather flexible press time. Not so on the daily; if the copy deadline is 12:40 p.m., any stories sent out to the composing room after that minute may make the press start late. That in turn can mean missed bus connections and lost street sales for the circulation department. However, in the 24 hours before publication a weekly newspaperman turns out a large amount of copy, probably more than he would on a daily.

A substantial overlapping exists between the weekly and small daily fields, in the sense that weekly cities sometimes are larger than small daily cities, and some weeklies have more circulation and advertising linage than small dailies. Yet, given a choice of jobs at identical pay, the majority of newspapermen would probably choose the daily. They find more stimulation in the faster pace, in seeing their stories in print shortly after they have written them, and in having a greater kinship with world affairs through the presence of wire service news teletypes in the office.

What, then, causes some towns to have daily papers and other larger towns to have only a weekly? Essentially it is a matter of geography, supplemented at times by the commercial audacity of the publisher. When a good-sized town is close to a large city, competition from the big neighboring paper may make successful operation of a small city daily financially impossible. Yet there is room for a weekly newspaper to present community news and the advertising of local merchants. A small daily in a relatively isolated region may operate at a profit, whereas the same paper would fail if it were published in the shadow of a large city daily.

Perhaps there would be more daily newspapers in operation if more weekly publishers were willing to gamble by "going daily." But they look at their present comfortable incomes, calculate the sharply increased costs of daily operation, and worry about whether they can obtain enough additional advertising and circulation revenue to cover this expense increase. Many of them decide to play it safe and remain weeklies, even when a daily operation might succeed. The economics of newspaper publishing is such, however, that elemental research shows that many towns which support a profitable weekly simply could not support a daily. Nevertheless, across the United States there are quite a few cities which have both a daily newspaper and a weekly. The latter is usually financially weak and manages to stay in business by picking up the "leavings" in advertising by local merchants and public utilities.

The primary problem a daily newspaper publisher faces is that the cost of producing his paper goes on every day, regardless of how much or how little advertising each issue carries. A "fat" paper one or two days a week cannot carry all his burden if the other issues have only a skimpy advertising content. Most newspapers try to average at least a 50-50 ratio between the amount of editorial and advertising content. This may rise as high as 65 percent advertising or a trifle more on some days.

A small daily newspaper in the proper geographical setting can be financially successful in a modest way with 5000 circulation if it is efficiently operated. Of course, it cannot give its readers as much news, background material, and advertising as they would receive from a metropolitan paper. It can give them the highlights of world and national news from a press association wire without the detailed background they find in a large city daily, plus thorough coverage of local news and the advertisements of local merchants. For most residents in the community that is sufficient. If they had to depend upon a large city newspaper hauled in from 50 or 100 miles away, they would get more news about the rest of the world but would be deprived of news about their neighbors and local school, church, and civic affairs.

To illustrate how a very small daily works, here is the actual staff line-up and working procedure of a successful newspaper with a daily circulation of less than 5000. Notice that the staff members, although relatively few in number, work in their own specialized fields without the "doubling in brass" so necessary and so commonplace on weekly newspapers; an editorial man rarely handles any advertising work, and an advertising salesman rarely concerns himself with circulation problems.

This paper has four editorial staff members: the managing editor, a general reporter who helps with the task of editing certain pages, a woman's section editor who also handles some spot assignments, and a beginning reporter who handles local sports and the police and fire beats as well. All three men take pictures; the number two man on the staff does most of the darkroom work.

The key man on the editorial staff is the managing editor. His tasks are varied and complex. On a large daily they would be handled by several different men, perhaps including the janitor, but he manages to get them all done and still get the paper to press on time. He makes assignments for the reporters, selects and edits stories from the press association wire, lays out the news pages, writes headlines on news stories, handles telephone calls, writes an occasional story, confers with the business staff on future projects, writes editorials, checks with the composing room foreman frequently during the day, and, at deadline time, supervises the makeup of the front page. Several nights a month he covers civic meetings.

Usually the managing editor of even such a small daily has at least some college education and five years or more of newspaper experience. He is managing editor, city editor, and copy desk all rolled into one, a combination of tasks impossible to maintain on papers much larger than this. The newspaper has at least six pages daily and on heavy Thursdays runs 14 to 16 pages; on a few special days each year it may publish as many as 20 pages.

The advertising staff of this very small daily consists of a business-advertising manager who handles most of the large accounts, another display advertising salesman, a clerk-secretary, and a classified advertising manager. Also in the front office there are a circulation manager, two women clerk-bookkeepers, and a proofreader. In the mechanical department there are four printers and one press operator. This force of

17 men and women brings out a daily newspaper six afternoons a week which, although modest in scope, is an essential part of the city's life. This is daily journalism at its lowest level.

Nowhere can a young man or woman interested in editorial or advertising work get finer, more rounded experience than on such a small daily. Since mechanical facilities are limited, the flow of copy must be closely scheduled and controlled, giving the beginner valuable experience in the extremely important matter of meeting deadlines. He learns to "make do" with the time and equipment at his disposal. In the editorial department he has an opportunity to cover local stories, observe the workings of a press association wire, and write headlines. His mistakes in news stories are brought to his attention very quickly, since in the small city he is in frequent business and social contact with the people about whom he writes. Also he has an excellent opportunity to practice photography. His ability to take pictures will help him throughout his career; the field of photojournalism, in which a man uses both reporting and camera skills, is growing more important. If a beginner has that extra spark of creative imagination so sought after by newspapers of all sizes, it will shine forth more quickly on a small daily than almost anywhere else in journalism that the young man or woman might work.

**Small-daily editorial problems.**   Perhaps you wonder how a four-man editorial staff can produce enough copy day after day to fill the newspaper. A six-page paper with 50 percent advertising content requires 24 columns of editorial matter. Where does this small staff in a little city find that much news or more day after day, and get it all written fast enough to make the daily deadline? The answer is that it doesn't need to do so. Part of this editorial hole is filled with feature material purchased from the newspaper syndicates and part is filled by wire service stories selected from the global news reports on the AP or UPI teleprinter which chatters away hour after hour in the newsroom.

Comic strips and syndicated feature columns, such as political commentary and personal advice, may take five to eight columns of that space. Pictures require the equivalent of three or four columns. Some are local photographs taken by staff members or are supplied to the newspaper by commercial photographers; others are feature mats or glossy prints purchased from the news picture services. A three-column picture 6 inches deep occupies 18 column inches, or almost the equivalent of a full column of type. (A column inch is the width of a single newspaper column, one inch deep.) Whereas the weekly editor must fill his entire paper with stories written or assembled by his staff, the daily editor has the resources of the press association teleprinter. It is quicker and easier to tear a 500-word story off the teleprinter and send it out to the composing room than to report and write a local story of the same length. A daily newspaper undertakes to give its readers a picture of the entire world, and to do so it must use much of the material supplied by the wire service, which has correspondents throughout the United States and around the world. But because wire service copy is easy to use, some small daily editors tend to fill their pages with second-rate telegraph stories when their readers would rather have well-developed local "enterprise" stories and interviews.

The staff which has been described is about the smallest possible one with which to publish a daily newspaper. As the circulation of a paper rises, so does the size of the staff. Any newspaper with less than 25,000 circulation falls within the general category of the small daily; a very large percentage of them are in the range from 7500 to 15,000. A recent survey of newspapers in this latter classification shows that about a third of them have either six or seven men in the newsroom and most of the others report that they have eight to twelve men.

In these somewhat larger staffs, the tasks performed by the managing editor of the very small daily are divided among several men, and the functional organization which reaches its peak in the staff of a huge metropolitan newspaper begins to emerge.

The managing editor's primary purpose is to oversee all the operations. Under him he has a city editor to direct the work of the local reporters and photographers and a telegraph editor who does the detailed job of selecting and editing stories from the press association wire. As the staff grows, a copy desk is set up to handle the task of editing copy and writing headlines, thus relieving the editors of this onerous but extremely important work. With specialists at work, the result is a better edited newspaper. But our six-page, 5000-circulation daily simply couldn't afford to operate with such a large news staff, and anyway there wouldn't be enough work to keep all these specialists busy. So the jack-of-all-trades managing editor does a little bit of everything.

**Advertising staff.** Advertising staffs grow, too, as a newspaper's circulation rises. The survey of dailies with circulations of 7500 to 15,000 showed an average of four retail display salesmen on each staff. The number of salesmen in the classified departments varied from two to five. Although most of the sales personnel in display advertising are men, women play a large role in classified work. Much classified selling is done by telephone. A pleasant feminine voice, projected over the telephone by a woman trained in the techniques of selling, can bring much additional linage into the paper. In many cases the manager of the classified department is a woman, the department of an American newspaper in which women are most likely to reach the top position.

On small dailies, the sale of local and national display advertising is handled by the same men, working in the latter case with the paper's national sales representatives. Because of the volume of the work involved, larger newspapers divide their display sales staffs into local and national sections.

**Mechanical production aids.**  Along with the tape typesetting method and other recent production aids already described, small and medium-sized daily newspapers using letterpress printing frequently use the Fairchild plastic engraving machine to give their readers better photographic coverage. This enables them to publish photographs taken by their own staff members at relatively small cost. Operation of a zinc engraving department is beyond the resources of many newspapers. Until the Fairchild machine was developed, they could give their readers far fewer pictures than they desired. Use of a commercial engraver's services usually was slow and costly.

The Fairchild machine reproduces a photograph on plastic rather than on zinc; these plastics can be placed directly into the newspaper form and on the press. The process is an electronic one in which a light beam scans a photograph fastened to a revolving cylinder. A cutting needle makes an exact reproduction of the photograph on a sheet of plastic wrapped around the other end of the cylinder. Although there are limitations on the jobs it can accomplish, and some printers contend that the quality of the plastic mats is not quite the equal of metal halftone cuts, the Fairchild machine enables many small dailies to give their readers much better picture coverage than ever before. The machines can be leased from the company which manufactures them, at a fairly high monthly fee, or can be purchased. Any staff member can operate a Fairchild machine after one instruction session, so no special labor cost is involved.

A European engraving machine rather similar to the Fairchild process has been placed on the American market, but it has made only relatively small inroads into the Fairchild market.

**Selling the papers.** Circulation procedures on daily newspapers are much better organized than on most weeklies, because the task of distributing and selling the paper must be done every day. There are several commonly used methods of selling a daily paper. Most of these are based upon the principle of having the publishing company sell copies of the paper to a distributor or delivery agent at a wholesale price several cents below the announced price per copy. The selling agent—home delivery carrier boy, street corner vendor, or store—sells papers to the public at the published price; the difference between wholesale and retail prices provides his profit. Most daily newspapers sell for 10 cents a copy but offer reduced prices for home delivery.

The backbone of a successful circulation system in most cities is the home delivery subscription list. Single-copy street sales are affected from day to day by the weather, traffic and shopping conditions, holidays, and the nature of the banner headline. Home delivery papers are sold to subscribers on a weekly, monthly, or even an annual basis; they give the newspaper an assured income and a firm circulation figure to quote to its advertisers, who want to know exactly how many newspaper purchasers will receive copies of their messages.

A few decades ago in the fight to win circulation and outdo their rivals, some newspapers resorted to making exaggerated claims about their sales. Since advertising rates are based upon circulation figures and upon the cost of reaching each thousand readers, this led to many discrepancies and a chaotic situation in which honest publishers were placed at an unfair disadvantage by the unscrupulous operators. To correct this problem the Audit Bureau of Circulations was formed in 1914.

Newspapers which belong to the ABC, as all larger dailies do, submit detailed reports of their circulation every six months and open their books to a detailed examination by ABC auditors every year. Rigid rules are enforced. The organization puts limits on methods of solicitation, the number of low-cost subscriptions, bulk sales, and other devices used by some publishers to inflate their circulation figures. Types of circulation which fail to meet these standards are disallowed, and others of a somewhat transitory nature are appropriately indicated on the statements published by the ABC about each paper.

In their constant battle to build circulation, some daily newspapers use many kinds of prize contests; others never use this kind of sales stimulant. A favorite device is the picture puzzle series or rebus type of puzzle; this starts simply to attract contestants and grows more difficult as later puzzles are published. Readers who participate must buy the newspaper daily during the contest or subscribe for a stated interval. The prizes are high, totaling more than $25,000 in some metropolitan promotions, but are paid out only after an elaborate series of "tie-breaker" supplementary puzzles.

The experience of many newspapers is that such contest-created circulation does not turn into permanent readers. Yet in the fight to keep their sales figures high, some big city publishers keep throwing in one contest after another at great expense. Others use trick weekly crossword puzzles, called by such names as Cashword or Baffler, or give cash to readers who find their Social Security numbers or automobile licenses in the daily printed lists.

Although some publishers and circulators consider such promotions an essential part of their newspaper-selling methods, others prefer to build readership more slowly but solidly through their carrier boy and street-outlet organizations. The decision is usually made on the basis of the local competitive situation and the state of the paper's circulation health. No newspaper can afford to have its advertisers see that its daily sales are slipping. If that happens, the advertiser demands lower rates and the financial woes multiply. In the recent history of American newspapers there are many proofs of the fact that once a newspaper goes into a prolonged circulation decline, its prospects for survival are slim.

One widely used method of handling home delivery is known as the little merchant system. A carrier boy or girl has a route of several city blocks and is responsible for delivery of the newspapers over that route, as well as making weekly or monthly collections of subscription fees from his customers. The publishing firm bills him at the wholesale rate each month for the number of copies he draws from it, and he collects the full subscription price from the readers. The difference is his monthly profit. The more new subscribers or "starts" he obtains, the more his monthly income will be. In effect he is an independent businessman in a small way. The newspaper circulation departments conduct prize contests to stimulate production of new orders, giving rewards such as sporting equipment, bicycles, and special trips to ball games or popular recreation areas to boys who reach specified quotas. Some papers give special awards to carriers who succeed in obtaining a subscription from every house along their routes.

The underlying premise in this circulation system is incentive: the paper tries to provide an incentive to make it worth the boy's while to give up part of his free hours, or to rise very early every morning, in order to deliver papers. Many boys have paid part of their way through college with earnings from their paper routes. Not only must they build their routes by obtaining additional starts, but they must keep their subscribers satisfied by giving them prompt and dependable delivery service.

In this respect newspaper publishing is unique; it hires expensive, highly experienced men to create its product and then depends upon young boys, many of them not yet in their teens, to sell it to the public. In other types of business such a practice would result in commercial failure. Given proper adult supervision, however, it works successfully for newspapers because the product is partially presold. There is an appetite for news, and in most communities the newspaper is a household word; the carrier boy's task is to turn this latent interest among potential readers into actual subscriptions. His own boyish appeal is often the decisive sales factor. Some critics, however, contend that overheavy reliance upon juvenile salesmen has held back newspapers from reaching their full sales potential.

The circulation department of a daily newspaper provides good opportunity for young men with sales and promotional instincts. A successful circulator must also have ability to handle detail, since the department's work involves accurate record keeping. Men who rise to the position of general manager in newspaper organizations frequently start in circulation or advertising work. Within the circulation departments of larger papers there are positions as district supervisors who oversee groups of carrier boys, and street sales supervisors whose responsibility it is to see that the paper is properly distributed on news racks and sold by vendors at places where foot and automobile traffic is heavy.

Few people will come to a newspaper office to buy a paper; the paper must be taken to them, and it must be put before them while it is fresh off the presses. To most circulation men the most sacred minute in the day is the moment the press is scheduled to start. Their entire distribution system is keyed to a prompt press start; if the papers begin rolling off a few minutes late, they may miss train or bus connections for out-of-town delivery, or fail to reach a busy sales spot in time to meet the outpouring of potential buyers from a factory or office building. That is why editorial deadlines must be met so diligently. Publication of a daily newspaper is a tightly scheduled operation in which every step is calculated and timed as closely as in an automobile factory assembly line. Failure or delay in any step of this flow disrupts the entire operation, sometimes with a direct loss of sales.

### THE MEDIUM-SIZED DAILY

Between the small daily, which we have described in detail, and the widely publicized huge metropolitan newspapers are hundreds of medium-sized dailies which are the bulwark of the American press. They range in size from 25,000 to 150,000 circulation. Their publication locales may be state capitals, the industrial second or third cities in large states, or, increasingly, the fringe areas around metropolitan centers. In many instances their influence reaches far beyond the city limits because they are distributed by mail, bus, truck, and even airplane to large surrounding rural areas. A motorist driving along a country road can often judge the impact of the newspaper published in a nearby city by the number of brightly painted tubes nailed on posts outside the farmhouses to receive delivery of the daily editions.

Papers of this size are financially strong enough to have editorial staffs of considerable scope, usually with several men of outstanding ability. Some may eventually move on to metropolitan papers. Others are content to spend their working lives in the congenial atmosphere of a middle-sized paper in a community sufficiently large to have some urban flavor, yet small enough for comfortable living.

At first glance, the medium-sized daily operating under the shadow of a metropolitan giant would appear at a severe disadvantage. Usually it cannot offer the bulk that American readers too often associate with a desirable product. Frequently the result is just the opposite. The medium-sized daily prospers because it provides the reader with as much, or nearly as much, press association and feature material as he desires, and in addition gives him detailed news of his local community. Density of population in these fringe areas is sufficient to provide a strong circulation potential. The presence of branch outlets of major downtown stores offers large advertising sources. In Los Angeles, for example, one leading department store has 20 branches in suburban areas. Most of these place advertising in the community dailies—advertising revenue that might previously have gone to the metropolitan papers. Metropolitan newspapers in some cities, notably Chicago, have sought to counteract this trend by starting community dailies of their own, concentrating on local news, as supplements to their downtown general publications.

The standards of medium-sized dailies in content, policies, and personnel frequently are high. Their salaries, while not equal to the metropolitan levels, are generally good and living costs frequently lower. For a young reporter whose ultimate goal is metropolitan journalism, a period of work on a well-regarded medium-sized daily is excellent training.

Editors of suburban community dailies keep a keen eye on the news "play" by their metropolitan rivals. They can give their readers later news than the afternoon big-city newspapers can, because the latter are handicapped in distributing their editions through heavy city traffic. By establishing a later deadline, the fringe daily can take advantage of the quick delivery within its own community and beat the downtown rival with the latest news.

TYPICAL ORGANIZATION OF A MEDIUM-SIZED DAILY NEWSPAPER

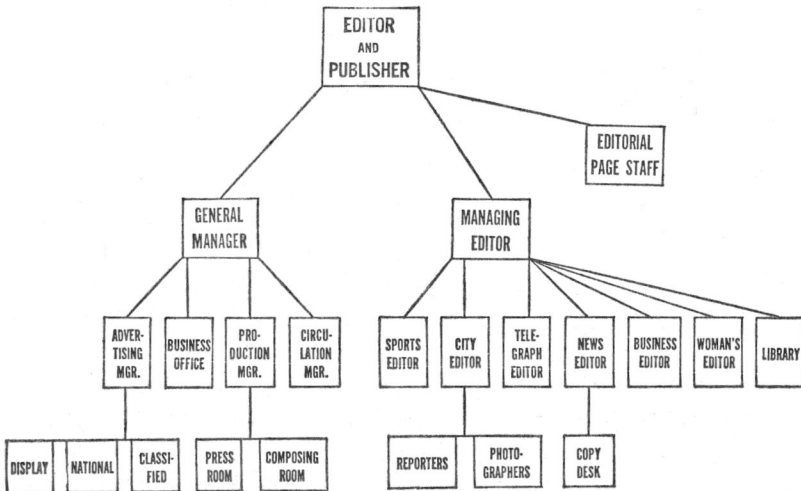

## THE METROPOLITAN PRESS

The newspaper as a mass communications medium reaches its highest development in our great metropolitan centers. Here the publishers and editors think of readers not in terms of thousands but of millions. Figuring three readers to each copy of the paper printed, which is a common rule of thumb in the profession, a big city newspaper with a Sunday circulation of a million copies is read by 3,000,000 people. The impact of a single news story flowing from the typewriter of one reporter, and published in such a huge edition, is easy to conceive.

Many newspapermen in editorial, advertising, and circulation departments look upon a metropolitan newspaper job as the goal of their careers, the ultimate whose achievement is the sign of professional success. Ironically, quite a few big-city newsmen in their quiet "bull" sessions between editions talk longingly of escaping the scramble of metropolitan journalism for what they envision as the calmer, more orderly and satisfying life on smaller papers. Given an opportunity to break away from metropolitan work, however, many of this wistful brigade either refuse to do so or drift back to the so-called "big time" within a few years. The tempo, adventure, and prestige of the metropolitan newspaper are alluring.

As stated earlier, metropolitan newspapers are the one group of the American press which has suffered severe attrition in the last quarter-century. Many of those bearing names which have been household words in journalism for decades have ceased publication, amid sentimental scenes of desolation and farewell in newsrooms that had seen the handling of so many dramatic stories in American history.

The underlying economic and social reasons for these newspaper consolidations and deaths already have been discussed; no matter how understandable, the passing of individual newspapers leaves a deep sense of loss among both readers and staff members. Even though it is a private business enterprise, a newspaper becomes such a deeply-ingrained part of public life that its sudden disappearance leaves a painful sense of loss.

Undoubtedly the best-known newspaper in the country is the morning and Sunday New York *Times*. The *Times* is edited as the country's newspaper of record, publishing lengthy texts of official documents and exhaustive reports on Washington and foreign developments. Its circulation

—approximately 1,000,000 daily and 1,500,000 Sunday—is nation-wide, appealing to readers who desire an abundance of governmental and cultural news. The *Times* is not written for a general mass audience, however, and many Americans find its stodgy makeup and bulky appearance less interesting than their own more personalized local newspapers. Like all newspapers, the *Times* commits its share of errors and shadings of news coverage. One embarrassing incident happened in the 1968 preconvention political maneuvering when it stated without qualification or quoting any source that Gov. Nelson Rockefeller would soon announce his candidacy for the Presidency. Two days later the governor did just the opposite, stating that he would not run. That year the *Times* also was accused of political sensationalism for its last-minute editorial attacks on Gov. Spiro Agnew of Maryland, the Republican candidate for Vice-President, using material that had previously been partially discounted. Perhaps such occasional missteps are not surprising in a publication of its immense size but they underline the point that no newspaper is totally accurate, no matter how great its reputation.

Few if any stories in a metropolitan paper are read by all who purchase the paper. Every reader is selective in the stories he chooses, picking a limited number of items from the huge tray of reading delicacies on the basis of his needs, interests, and even his whims. Even so, every story in a metropolitan paper, no matter how insignificantly it is displayed, is seen by thousands of readers.

Thus the reporter on a large newspaper assumes with good reason that his work is being absorbed by a very large number of persons. Yet the very size of the metropolitan region in which his paper circulates makes it impossible for him to have direct contact with his audience. Except for personal acquaintances and the handful of readers who are either irate or thoughtful enough to report their reactions to an individual story, the metropolitan reporter has little opportunity to determine how his stories are being received. This is one of the most striking differences between big-city and small-town newspaper work: the larger the city and the paper's circulation, the less personal contact there is between the newspaper's creators and its readers.

The young man or woman looking toward metropolitan newspapers as a place to work discovers two major differences from smaller dailies: greater speed and greater specialization.

Most small dailies have one basic edition a day, designed primarily for delivery to homes. Some may supplement this with a street sale edition in which the front page is remade with larger, flashier headlines and late sports results for sale to casual purchasers. Or they may have an early, skimpily organized edition for distribution to rural areas. In contrast, many metropolitan papers publish at least five editions within a period of eight hours. Afternoon papers are especially burdened with numerous editions because of the fast-changing nature of news during the daytime hours. This means high-speed work by the editorial staff, which must be constantly alert for last-minute news developments, and equally fast work by the circulation department in distributing papers to locations where crowds are gathered temporarily, such as homeward-bound commuter crowds. The edition schedule is an almost sacred document, whose stated deadlines govern the work of several hundred employees. If the press run of a big newspaper starts 15 minutes late, the recriminations can be heard all over the building and often precipitate a blunt-spoken post mortem in the publisher's office to determine the blame.

The final minutes before the deadline in each newspaper department are a-tingle with concentrated work. When the deadline has passed, and each department in the complicated process knows that it no longer can call back anything it has done or push something more into the paper, there comes a period of relaxation and waiting for the fresh edition copies to be brought up from the pressroom. Then the buildup process for the next edition begins.

A typical metropolitan deadline sheet has minute-by-minute rules telling when the final story must cross the city desk and move from the copy desk to the composing room; when the last photograph must leave the editorial art department for the engraving room; when the final page must move off the composing stone; when the last plate must be cast in the stereotype department; and finally what minute the press must start. For the system to work successfully the pages must flow smoothly through the complex assembly line at a designated pace. In a huge newspaper plant the production of a daily newspaper is a coordinated effort rarely exceeded in manufacturing, especially when we remember that the primary product fed into this conveyor belt system, news, is an intangible raw material difficult to find and hard to define. Few readers realize the immensity of effort and planning behind the daily newspaper tossed upon their doorsteps. Partly this is because newspapers have failed to tell their own exciting story well enough.

The young reporter who obtains a metropolitan job right out of school usually considers himself extremely lucky, believing that he is starting his career a big jump ahead of his classmates who go to work on weeklies or small dailies. Unfortunately for him, this is not necessarily the case.

He finds stimulation in associating with skilled veteran reporters and watching exciting stories move through the big paper's production line, on some of which he may do part of the work himself. But too often he finds himself shunted into a minor reporting job, like covering the overnight police beat, where he is unable to get the all-around experience his classmates are absorbing on smaller papers. Years may pass before he gets an opportunity to work on the copy desk, if, indeed, he ever does. Seniority plays an important part in assignments on metropolitan staffs, and unless he is fortunate or shows exceptional talent for writing, the young reporter on a large daily advances rather slowly.

Many editors and personnel managers of metropolitan papers advise beginners to work on small papers for from three to five years before trying the metropolitan field. Often a young man coming to a metropolitan staff with three or four years of smaller city work to his credit will advance faster than one of similar age who has spent those same years on the big-city paper. The all-around experience of a smaller paper prepares the young reporter to fill many different jobs as they become available.

**How a metropolitan news staff functions.** The key figure in the local newsgathering activities of a big-city paper is the city editor. He may have a staff of as many as 50 reporters, even more in a few cases, who are deployed at the most productive news sources or held in reserve as general assignment reporters to be dispatched as important stories break. The reporters who are placed on specific beats, such as the police department or city hall, are responsible for gathering all news that occurs in their territory and turning it in to the city desk. When time permits they write the stories themselves. But the urgency of deadlines often makes this impossible, so they telephone their facts to a rewrite man. These men are veterans, swift in their writing and quick at organizing a mass of facts into a story which reads smoothly and concisely.

When the story has been written, either by the reporter who covered it or by a rewrite man, it is turned in to the city desk. There the editor or an assistant reads it to catch errors, to be sure that it is easily understood and to look for "angles" which need further development. Writers and editors alike concentrate on finding a good "lead" for the story, an opening paragraph which summarizes the situation or entices the reader to continue further into the article.

Much reporting is done by telephone. The man assigned to a story calls as many sources as possible to cross-check his facts for accuracy and to make sure that he presents the best-rounded story he can. If he went in person to see each of these sources he would never get his job done in time for the next edition. Some metropolitan beat reporters, or "legmen," especially those on the police beats, may not write a story a week, even though they have worked on dozens of them by telephone.

While the city editor and his staff are gathering the local news, other groups are putting together the other parts of the paper. News from the rest of the country and the world clatters into the office over the wire service teleprinters and from special staff correspondents. This is edited and coordinated on the telegraph desk.

City news and telegraph stories pass across the news desk, where they are weighed for importance and general interest by the news editor. He assigns them appropriate size headlines and marks them into position on dummy sheets; it is these sheets that tell the printers how to assemble the mass of stories into the proper pages. The stories move along to the copy desk, usually semicircular with the supervisor or "slot man" in the middle. He is also known as the "dealer," because of the way he hands stories around to the "rim men" for editing. These language experts give the stories a final polishing and write the headlines. From the copy desk the stories are sent by pneumatic tubes to the composing room, where the process of turning them into type begins.

The sports department, woman's section, financial editors, and other specialist groups are also at work filling the pages allotted to them in a similar manner.

The man in charge of the entire news department is the managing editor, just as on the very small daily we discussed earlier. Only instead of doing the detailed work himself, he supervises the dozens of men and women who do it under his direction. The managing editor's post on a metropolitan newspaper is one of the most demanding and responsible jobs in all journalism.

## SUNDAY PAPERS—WORLD'S LARGEST

By far the bulkiest newspapers published anywhere are the Sunday editions of American metropolitan newspapers. These mammoth publications wrapped in sections of colored comics often contain more than 300 pages, nearly four pounds of reading matter covering everything from the current world crisis to interior decorating advice, theatrical notices, baseball scores, and weekly television logs.

There are about 20 such Sunday newspapers in the United States with 500,000 or more circulation, and several with more than a million. Even these mammoth figures, however, are greatly exceeded by the circulation of several English Sunday papers, printed in London and distributed throughout the British Isles.

The Sunday paper is designed for family reading and is distinguished from the daily editions by two elements: a high feature "package" and bulk retail advertising. As a medium for late spot news, the Sunday paper is less important than the daily editions because relatively less news occurs on Saturday (which it is covering) than on weekdays. Much of the material in the news sections is of a feature and background nature, stories for which there is no space in the smaller daily editions. Many newspapers print part of their Sunday editions well in advance because of the difficulties of printing such huge issues on the available press equipment on publication date. Stripped-down, predate versions of the New York *Daily News* Sunday tabloid, containing the colored comics and magazine features, are distributed to rural areas across the United States several days before publication day.

The Sunday editions of most newspapers have substantially larger circulation than the daily editions and sell for a higher price, sometimes more than double. Publishing a Sunday paper is a very expensive operation because of the heavy costs involved in buying the colored comics and nationally syndicated magazine inserts and in preparing the abundance of locally created feature material, such as the weekly television log and the staff-edited local magazine feature section. Newsprint costs on bulky papers are very high. Many smaller newspapers find such a publishing effort unprofitable, especially since they must compete against the metropolitan editions which are distributed over very wide circulation zones. As a result the Sunday field is dominated by the big-city newspapers which can afford to enter it; for most of them it is very lucrative, providing a substantial share of their annual profits.

Department stores have found Sunday editions to be one of their most effective selling tools. The paper is read at home in leisurely surroundings, and almost every member of the family peruses at least one part of the edition as it is scattered around the living room floor. So the stores put a heavy share of their advertising budget into the Sunday edition, often taking multiple pages or even entire eight-page sections to publicize their wares.

# Chapter 10

# *Television and Radio*

## BROADCASTING AND THE FUTURE

Television and radio are the electronic magic carpets that transport millions of persons each day to faraway places. They are the Twentieth-Century creations of the technological revolution that has transformed much of the world for the past two centuries, and their impact on our social, political, and cultural life has been profound.

It is estimated that almost 1,000,000,000 persons—the largest television audience in history—viewed the Summer Olympic games in Munich, Germany, in 1972. The electronic signals, mostly videotaped and timed to reach maximum audiences, were transmitted via satellite to approximately 100 countries. President Nixon's historic trip to China the same year drew huge audiences in many nations. In 1969 an estimated 500,000,000 persons watched and listened as earthmen first set foot on the moon.

The impending cultural, economic, and political impact of such a worldwide exchange of programs is certain to change the course of civilization. Future historians are likely to rank television as the most revolutionary and democratizing medium of our times. For example, in the United States alone, just as the press served as the democratizing agent in the early days of the Republic and as radio helped achieve a national consensus in the Franklin D. Roosevelt days of the depression and World War II, so television has brought to almost all Americans an awareness of their diversities and the common stakes they share. The worldwide impact of the medium is yet to come.

The spectacular growth of community antenna television systems (CATV) in the United States has in itself created a technological revolution that now challenges not only the established television industry, but all other forms of electronic communication as well. A nationwide system of subscription television (pay-TV) has been authorized by the Federal Communications Commission. And the steady increase in the number of Ultra High Frequency (UHF) stations, joining those transmitting the long-established Very High Frequency (VHF) signals, is providing a greater choice of programs for Americans.

Not to be outdone, radio has taken advantage of technological improvements in equipment, particularly miniature tape recorders, and the public's appetite for news, as evidenced by the proliferation of all-news and information stations, to provide virtually instantaneous coverage in the sound of news "as it is happening, from where it is happening." And "open mike" programs, described as the modern technological version of the town meeting and literally the voice of the people, have provided avenues for the expression of opinions in more than 2000 communities throughout the country.

**Video-cassette TV.** Marketing of the first cartridge television system for home use began in 1972. Video-cassette TV was heralded as making possible "a complete audio-visual experience center" serving as "a window to the world, a time machine recapturing events, a home monitor, and a family movie album."

By inserting a cartridge into a videotape player connected to his television set, a viewer may see and hear programs of his own selection, such as musicals, movies, educational materials, free commercial and government films, and TV programs recorded off the air. Videotaped "home movies," made with lightweight hand cameras equipped with microphones, also may be viewed.

Almost a dozen major companies battled for market supremacy. At the same time entertainment and information programs of all kinds were prepared on cartridges for sale and rent. Most of the programs were geared toward and priced for the business, educational, and government markets. In 1972 cassettes cost about $150 for a 30-minute program and $275 for a one-hour show. The industry was confident that prices would decrease and a consumer market would develop.

Quantum Science Corporation predicted that by 1980 approximately 3,400,000 video-players would be in use in 4 percent of U.S. homes and that the annual sales volume of video-cassettes would reach $1,800,-000,000. Marketing standardization, programing, and copyright questions were seen as the major problems to be overcome.

## THE SCOPE OF BROADCASTING

**In the United States.**    The stations' claim that "radio is your constant companion" is literally true. Every community in America is served by its own or a nearby station. Car radios, portable transistor radios, and multiple-set and intercommunication-wired homes provide constant contact with the unseen world of the wave lengths. Even television, despite its shorter range and fewer stations, is viewed in almost every part of the country, and community antenna systems soon will carry TV to virtually every hamlet.

Radio listening, after a temporary eclipse by television in the 1950's, came back strong with news, music, and programs designed for Americans' leisure habits. By 1972 approximately 62,600,000 homes, or 96.5 percent of all those in the United States, were equipped with one or more radio sets. The Radio Advertising Bureau estimated that more than 336,000,000 radio sets were in operation, a gain of about 68 percent in the last seven years. Of these, 240,600,000 were in homes and 95,400,000 in other places.

Frequency modulation (FM) broadcasting, whose development had been limited because of the national preoccupation with television, represented a major segment of the listening audience. Because of good music programing, stereophonic sound, virtually static-free reception, and the capability of attracting loyal specialized audiences, FM was growing rapidly.

More than 92,000,000 persons 18 years of age or older listened to radio every day, it was estimated. Radio listening in each home averaged about two and one-half hours a day, an increase of an hour in the last seven years, with morning and afternoon audiences exceeding those of television.

More than 62,000,000 U.S. homes, almost 96 percent of the total, had one or more of the nation's 88,000,000 television sets. For the first time, in 1971, color sets were estimated to be in more than half of U.S. television households. TV viewing per home totaled about six hours and twenty minutes each day.

By 1972 more than 6,000,000 homes in 49 states were wired to receive television on a paid subscription basis through 2750 community antenna television (CATV) systems. Community antenna homes were increasing at the rate of about 25 percent per year. Even in large cities, most conventional television sets can receive only three or four stations well, and the advent of color has made reception of a clear signal even more critical. On the other hand, CATV subscribers are able to receive all signals clearly, both VHF and UHF, picked from the air by a master antenna and sent by cable to their sets for a fee, usually about $5 per month. In addition, many CATV systems originate, on additional channels, neighborhood public service programs, educational programs, news, weather, stock market reports, and the like. CATV hookups for hospitals, police surveillance, direct-order marketing, and data transmission also were being developed.

Of the 699 commercial television stations on the air, 510 broadcast in the Very High Frequency (VHF) bands, using channels 2 through 13, and 189 broadcast on Ultra High Frequency (UHF) channels 14 through 83.

Of the 205 noncommercial television stations, 88 broadcast on VHF frequencies and 205 in the UHF band. The total number of TV stations was 904.

About 60 percent of the radio stations were AM stations—4354 in all. Of the 2777 FM stations, 2299 were commercial and 478 noncommercial. In only seven years FM broadcasting had grown from 25 percent to almost 40 percent of the total number of radio stations on the air.

Many independent television and radio stations were affiliated, by two-year contracts, with the National Broadcasting Company, Columbia Broadcasting System, and American Broadcasting Company. Others were served by the Mutual Broadcasting System and several smaller networks. The major networks themselves owned 20 AM, 20 FM, and 15 television stations. There were 113 regional radio networks and groups, and 12 regional television networks. Newspapers and magazines were associated in common ownership with about 7 percent of the AM stations, 9 percent of the commercial FM stations, and 25 percent of the commercial TV stations.

Television stations and networks grossed $2,808,200,000 and radio stations and networks $1,136,900,000 in 1970 time sales, *Broadcasting Yearbook* reported; and the industry as a whole was adjudged healthy indeed.

Broadcast stations and networks employed 115,000 persons. Although there were almost eight times as many radio as television stations, about 40 percent of the total broadcast personnel were employed at TV stations. The typical TV station employed about 50 full-time persons as compared with 10 at the typical radio station.

Although small in comparison with many other United States industries, television and radio were responsible for the livelihood of thousands of persons in related business. They included talent agents and managers, program producers and distributors, commercial and jingle producers, business and promotion film distributors, film processing laboratories, researchers, consulting engineers, management consultants, brokers, and station representatives, as well as employees of news services, associations and professional societies, unions, station finance companies, and public relations, publicity, and promotion firms.

Minorities played a larger role in almost all these businesses than in the past, and in the stations themselves. About 115 radio stations broadcast exclusively to blacks, and almost 300 more aired programs for blacks at some time during the day. Sixteen stations were owned by blacks, as compared with five in 1968. Black-oriented stations in 50 cities reached more than 80 percent of all blacks. Actualities of special interest were fed to the stations daily by the Black Audio Network.

**International broadcasting.**    The world is being wired for sight and sound. In the words of LeRoy Collins, former president of the National Association of Broadcasters: "Communications systems now circle the earth like the threads of a ball of yarn and bind this world together with invisible but nonetheless real threads. Events in the remotest part of the earth can be instantaneously and fully reported by the men who use them—broadcast men."

The growth in the number of television sets throughout the world has been phenomenal. From 65,000,000 sets worldwide in 1963, the total by 1970 approximated 175,000,000. Of these, the United States had about one-half, with Japan, the United Kingdom, Germany, France, Italy, and Canada following, in that order. Television was just gaining a foothold in the emerging nations, such as those in Africa.

Color television was spreading rapidly. Japan pioneered with color in 1960, followed by Canada in 1966. Then came Britain, West Germany, France, the Netherlands, Switzerland, Austria, Mexico, the Philippines, and Thailand. Converting to color recently were stations in Italy, Belgium, Sweden, Denmark, and Australia.

United States companies have been competing vigorously for several years in sales of filmed and videotaped programs to broadcasters abroad. By 1970 their sales in more than 100 countries approximated $100,000,-000, more than double that of 1962. Enhancing America's competitive position were the rapid growth of color TV abroad; the trend toward commercialization of TV channels in other countries, providing more money for buyers of American programs; the sales potential of satellite telecasts of special events, sports contests, and the like; and the growing availability of and need for educational films produced in the United States.

It was a two-way airlane, for by 1970 U.S. television was buying an estimated $30,000,000 in programs from distributors abroad. Of these, Britannia ruled the American airwaves with an estimated sales gross of $25,000,000, mostly in action-adventure and dramatic programs and series. Japan was exporting cartoons, and Australia and Canada were sending other types of specialized programs.

United States investors owned stock in stations throughout the world. Most were minority holdings, representing from 10 to 20 percent of total investment. The biggest investors were the three TV networks and Time Inc.'s Time-Life Broadcast International. The field also included such others as Screen Gems, Bartell Broadcasting, and Warner Brothers.

American advertisers were taking advantage of the world trend toward the commercialization of television. Permitting advertising only in recent years have been France, Holland, Hong Kong, Indonesia, West Germany, Italy, and Mexico. Sweden was the only leading nation still noncommercial.

Within less than a decade, color telecasts via satellite to and from most parts of the earth had become almost routine. It was only 1962 when Congress established the Communications Satellite Corporation as a private, profit-making corporation to own and operate the U.S. segment of this space communications system. An 80-member International Telecommunications Satellite Consortium coordinates the technology and the program exchanges. As a result, viewers virtually worldwide watched such events as the Vatican City conference, the funerals of President Kennedy and Winston Churchill, the Olympic games in Japan and Mexico, the investiture of the Prince of Wales, President Nixon's trips to China and Russia, and, most dramatically of all, the walk on the moon by the Apollo 11 astronauts.

## RISE OF THE BROADCAST MEDIA

Radio enjoyed only a quarter-century of commercial development in the United States before television emerged as still another of the major mass communications media. Various inventions during the nineteenth century paved the way for the perfecting of radio in the twentieth. Guglielmo Marconi's development of wireless telegraphy was followed by an improvement made by Dr. Lee De Forest in 1906 in the vacuum tube that made voice transmission possible. There was little interest in the possibility of mass radio listening, however, and Congress in 1912 empowered the Department of Commerce to issue licenses to private broadcasters and assign wave lengths for commercial operators primarily to prevent interference with government point-to-point message communication.

Many amateur enthusiasts built their own receivers and transmitters and finally Westinghouse, sensing a new sales market, applied for the first full commercial license for standard broadcasting. Its station, KDKA in Pittsburgh, began operating on November 2, 1920, by broadcasting returns from the Harding-Cox presidential election. An experimental station, 8MK, had begun daily operations from the Detroit *News* building on August 20, 1920, and in October, 1921, the *News* obtained its full commercial license for what became station WWJ.

The number of stations increased from 30 in January, 1922, to 556 in March, 1923. At the same time the number of receiving sets rose from about 50,000 in 1921 to more than 600,000 in 1922. National interest was heightened by the broadcasting of such events as the Dempsey-Carpentier fight in 1921 and the Army-Notre Dame football game and the World Series in 1923. Listeners delicately ran the "cat's whisker" across the crystals of their sets, trying to bring in a station on the earphones; many such sets were homemade. On certain nights local stations would remain silent so listeners could tune in out-of-town stations, and the excitement of picking up KDKA in Pittsburgh, or WBAP in Fort Worth, or WLS in Chicago, was a conversation piece the next day. The introduction of sets with loudspeakers increased the nation's pleasure.

At first, stations in scattered cities were hooked together to broadcast special shows with such stars as Paul Whiteman, Vincent Lopez, Ed Wynn, and Roxy and His Gang. Twenty-one stations from New York to California joined to broadcast Coolidge's second inauguration in

1925. The National Broadcasting Company, a subsidiary of the Radio Corporation of America, was formed late in 1926, and extended programing "coast to coast" in 1927. WEAF was the originating station for NBC's Red network and WJZ was the flagship for its Blue network. The Columbia Broadcasting System came into being in 1927. By 1934 CBS had 97 affiliated stations compared with 127 for the two NBC networks. The Mutual Broadcasting System was organized that year, primarily to provide network-caliber programs to smaller stations. Regional chains also developed. In 1943 an order by the Federal Communications Commission led to the sale of the Blue network and its renaming in 1945 as the American Broadcasting Company. The four networks continued to compete vigorously for outlets until by 1964 ABC-Radio had 424 affiliated stations; ABC-TV, 244; CBS-Radio, 225; CBS-TV, 200; NBC-Radio, 192; NBC-TV, 201; and MBS-Radio, 510.

Under the First Amendment to the Constitution, government is restrained from interfering with the freedom of the press or the freedom of speech. But while anyone with enough money is free to found a newspaper anywhere at any time, there are only a limited number of broadcast channels. The theory is that these channels belong to the people and since they are limited the people must allocate them through Congress. Thus, when stations jumped from one wave length to another to avoid interference, Congress in 1927 established a five-man Federal Radio Commission, empowered to regulate all forms of radio communication. The Communications Act of 1934 established a seven-member Federal Communication Commission to regulate the airwaves in the interest of the public. It has been in efforts by the FCC to define "public service" that controversy has arisen, such as Congress' requirement that equal time be provided for rival candidates for public office. The newspaper can publish what it desires in such matters, whether in the news, editorial, or advertising columns, subject only to public opinion and the laws of libel and obscenity. Broadcasting, however, because of its peculiar physical structure, must be regulated.

Many newspaper publishers began to view radio with some alarm as they noted the growing advertising revenue of the new medium since they were fearful that radio news might reduce the circulation of newspapers. A press-radio battle continued for nearly a decade, with the newspapers attempting to prevent the major press associations from selling their news reports to radio stations. It was a losing fight, however, and in

1933 a Press-Radio Bureau was established to provide the stations with two daily news reports and bulletins of "transcendent importance." The public demand for news by radio grew, and Trans-Radio Press, a unique newsgathering organization catering mainly to radio clients, came into being. In 1935 the United Press and International News Service began to service radio networks and stations with news that could be sponsored. The Associated Press soon followed suit, and the war was over.

By 1970 the Associated Press was sending its reports to 3100 stations and 1750 publications, whereas United Press International was serving 2300 stations and 1600 publications.

Radio developed its own stars, including such attractions of the 1920's as the A&P Gypsies, the Gold Dust Twins, Goodrich's Silver Masked Tenor, and Billy Jones & Ernie Haire ("We're the Interwoven pair"). The networks were on the air from 9 a.m. to 11 p.m., Eastern Standard Time, with a melange of humor, kiddie stories, soap operas, variety shows, interviews, poetry, dance bands, and symphony orchestras. The disk jockeys of affiliated stations were morning announcers, and local live talent generally was heard from 7 to 9 a.m. or so.

During the depression years of the 1930's radio provided inexpensive home entertainment. President Franklin D. Roosevelt's "fireside chats" helped allay fears that the nation's future was seriously threatened and, psychologically, bound the country together. In the field of entertainment, such personages as Will Rogers, the cowboy comedian-philosopher, with alarm clock at his elbow to clang when his time was up, and Eddie Cantor, banjo-eyed comedian singing "Potatoes are cheaper, tomatoes are cheaper, now's the time to fall in love," did their bit to bring their fellow countrymen out of the economic doldrums.

Radio was a part of almost everyone's life, and each program had its theme song. As one observer has written, "Five times a week, Kate Smith's moon came over the mountain—Bing Crosby's gold of the day met the blue of the night." Millions of listeners thrilled to "Gang Busters," "The Lone Ranger," and "Sherlock Holmes." They awaited the daily or weekly visits of Amos 'n Andy, Myrt and Marge, the Boswell Sisters, Boake Carter, Graham McNamee, Fibber McGee and Molly, Walter Winchell, Jack Benny, and Bob Hope.

In 1939 the almost hysterical tirades of Adolf Hitler formed an ominous backdrop to news of the march into the Low Countries and Poland, and the advent of World War II. Then, on an otherwise peaceful

Sunday, December 7, 1941, radio brought the catastrophic news of the Japanese attack on Pearl Harbor. Millions remained close to their radio sets during the eventful years of America's counterattack, invasions, A-bomb dropping, and eventual victory over both Nazis and Japanese in 1945. Commentators such as Elmer Davis, Eric Sevareid, Edward R. Murrow, and H. V. Kaltenborn gained immense followings with their daily quarter-hour interpretations of the news.

On June 8, 1948, comedian Milton Berle produced his first program for the young NBC-TV network. There were fewer than 1,000,000 sets in homes and bars, and the show was viewed in only 13 NBC-outlet cities. But almost the entire nation suddenly became aware of television and its potential, and the rush to build stations and buy sets was on. Radio was eclipsed. A year later TV was viewed in 2,500,000 or 6 per-cent of the nation's homes. The percentage rose to 19 in 1950, 70 in 1955, 87 in 1960, and 93 in 1965. Radio shifted patterns of operation and recovered to remain a prime U.S. necessity. Newspaper and magazine advertising and circulation also sagged, but recovered as a rapidly growing population continued its strong demand for all the media.

The story of television's development has largely been that of NBC, CBS, and ABC, which have spun electronic webs across the continent and dominated the stations because they provide most of the programing. It is also the story of the major advertisers and advertising agencies, which have influenced the nature of the programing so as to attract the most viewers. It is the story of the audience measurement agencies, such as the A. C. Nielsen Company, whose ratings have determined which programs shall continue to be broadcast.

The dominant figure in the industry was the late General David Sarnoff, former chairman of the board of RCA, which owns NBC. Sarnoff, sometimes termed Mr. Electronics, dominated much of the development of radio and as early as 1938 predicted the role that television would play. William S. Paley, chairman of the board, and Frank Stanton, vice chairman, have sparked the rise of CBS. A Harvard lawyer, Leonard Goldenson, and Robert Kintner, later president of NBC, rescued ABC from near-oblivion, largely because of a 1953 merger with Paramount Theatres, Inc., and heavy programing in Westerns.

Sylvester L. (Pat) Weaver, Jr., former NBC president, began the first nonexperimental pay TV venture in 1963. His West Coast company, Subscription Television, Inc., ceased operations in 1964.

## CABLE TELEVISION

An alternative communications medium with an exciting potential, cable television (CATV, from Community Antenna Television, the original use of cable in home television reception), began its long-awaited expansion in 1972. Prohibited since 1966 from importing distant signals into the top 100 television markets, CATV early in 1972 was given the go-ahead from the FCC to develop side by side with broadcasting.

The commission's authority to regulate cable television had been confirmed in 1968 by the Supreme Court, which at that time ruled that CATV broadcasts are not "performances" and thus not subjects for payment of copyright fees. Six main policy questions, however, had to be resolved, those relating to public impact, industry structure, access, copyright, and impact on existing media and regulatory framework.

For five years broadcasters, CATV operators, and copyright owners argued their respective causes. President Nixon in June 1971 created a committee to help iron out the problems. It was headed by Clay T. (Tom) Whitehead, director of the newly created Office of Telecommunications Policy. Working with FCC Chairman Dean Burch, the committee evolved a compromise agreement finally accepted by all groups.

The rules for the first time permitted CATV systems to operate with distant signals in the top-100 markets, thus providing a sound economic base for the industry. Provision was made to prevent cable TV from "jeopardizing the basic structure of over-the-air television," the most controversial aspect of the long dispute. The rules against CATV duplication of network programing were relaxed to allow same-day but not simultaneous showing of such programs. The use of non-network, syndicated programs was restricted to periods of one and two years or within the terms of existing contracts. Exclusivity restrictions did not apply to markets below the top 100.

Access at no cost was assured for the public, educators, and local governments. "The rules," said Chairman Burch, "will remove a bar to access for the public, so any member of the public can get on a television facility and communicate with other members of the public."

The cable industry, broadcasters, and copyright owners agreed to support separate CATV copyright legislation and work for its passage. Such legislation was regarded as imperative for CATV's growth.

The compromise was effected by the National Association of Broadcasters, the National Cable Television Association, the Association of Maximum Service Telecasters, and the copyright owners. Also approving the agreement were the eight major motion picture companies.

Left to a later decision were rules designed to afford radio stations some protection against the importation of distant radio signals and a sports-blackout rule for CATV along the lines of those in effect for professional sports.

The FCC already had adopted rules barring television stations from owning systems in their markets and networks from owning them anywhere. Under consideration was a rule to break up newspaper-cable cross-ownership in the same market.

All CATV systems having 3500 subscribers or more had been ordered by the FCC to begin local program origination on April 1, 1971. When a court order set aside that rule, the FCC appeared to take the posture that its then developing CATV proposals, coupled with local franchise requirements regarding program origination, negated the need to do more.

Although the cable systems had been designed and financed as passive delivery pipelines, many already were originating programs and gaining community support and participation in others. Some distributed popular programs, such as sports events, to other systems. All envisioned the leasing of closed channels to private users, such as banks and motion picture vendors, and to open-channel users such as supermarket chains and department stores. The door was definitely ajar for both *pay*-as-you-see and *order*-as-you-see television.

Declaring that "the television of abundance" was about to replace what it termed "the television of scarcity," a Sloan Commission report proposed a cable system for the nation that would include pay television as well as numerous other services. The system so envisioned would be capable, the report said, of bringing as many as 40 channels into 40 to 60 percent of U.S. television homes by the end of the decade.

Viewing cable television as a virgin field for the development of federal policy, a high-level administration committee appointed by the Office of Telecommunications Policy began in 1971 to prepare legislation that would provide a different kind of cable structure from the one which the FCC was building. Under this legislation CATV would be structured as a true common carrier, although not a public utility. The objective would be increased access to the medium and elimination of virtually all government control of content (except for the conventional sanctions against libel, obscenity, and incitement to riot). Since cable systems would be common carriers, there would be no need to bar networks, newspapers, and broadcast stations from owning CATV systems even in their own markets.

Such possible new national policy, however, was a matter for the future. CATV had gained the foothold it needed for development, and the possibilities for an increasingly wide diversity of programing and novel home communications services seemed almost endless. Whether the fledgling industry possessed the will and the imagination to fulfill the promise of its technology was a question yet to be answered.

## THE NEWS FUNCTION

The area of news and information is an important, aggressive, and prestige-building division of the television-radio programing structure. For the journalist, there are many types of programs suited to his talents. One type is the regular newscast, giving 5- to 60-minute summaries of happenings throughout the community, nation, and world. A second area is the background and interpretation program. It may be a newscaster's straight presentation of facts, a panel discussion, an interview, or a documentary. As an example, NBC's "First Tuesday" and CBS' "Sixty Minutes" gave a news magazine approach during prime evening time, providing information to groups with both general and special interests.

Another category for the journalist in broadcasting is the "instant" news event—man's first steps on the moon, the assassination of a President, a confrontation at a political convention. During these times, regular commercial programs are dispensed with to permit immediate news coverage to the American public. The pressure is strong on the newsman then; he must give facts and interpretation instantly, without a chance to edit his comments. Additionally, a type of program for the true reporter is the investigative area, uncovering new and often surprising facts about a public figure or issue. Many of these programs have their counterparts in the departments, columns, and features that appear in magazines and newspapers.

Television and radio alike spend a great deal of time and money **to** keep their audiences abreast of the news. Election-year coverage in 1968 cost the three major networks an estimated $30,000,000. The three television networks spend about $150,000,000 for news coverage annually, and the total news budgets of individual stations probably total an equal or greater sum. The technical items needed to cover a story for television—lights, cameramen, sound men, color film, processing and editing equipment—are costly. Network news operations show losses each year, in part because of another television requirement—mobility. "We spend more just getting the story from one place to another than other media spend covering it," said Richard Salant, CBS news president, in a *Fortune* interview. Miniaturization and lower costs in film and magnetic tape recording usage will ease some of the coverage costs.

To most broadcasters, the expense of covering news events is well justified. Stations and networks discovered quite early that news programs rank exceptionally high in public interest and render a public service while building a steady audience and steady revenues. A 1971 study by Roper Research Associates, the ninth in a series begun in 1959, found that television continued as the source of most news for the American people, a ranking it first achieved in 1963. The same study said that TV is considered the "most believable" news medium by 49 percent of the American people, as compared with 20 percent for newspapers, 10 percent for magazines, and 9 percent for radio. (See Chapter 8.)

"The TV news experience is the most real in comparison with any other medium, if it is presented properly," stated Dr. Phillip Eisenberg, president of Motivation Research, Inc. "It is the closest thing to the actual experience itself." Furthermore, Dr. Eisenberg noted, "one of the medium's great strengths is its ability to expose us directly to the personalities in the news. We see them and form opinions of them as people. The names in the news are no longer just names, they take on an immediate reality." Who can forget the jolting reality of Lee Harvey Oswald's murder on live television in Dallas in November, 1963, or the Apollo 11 astronauts' walk on the moon on live television July 11, 1969?

Television's excellence in covering live events today is unquestioned; it was not so in earlier days, however. During television's pioneer decade, many veteran journalists (including the much-revered interpreter of trends at home and overseas, Elmer Davis) concluded that the electronic infant would never amount to much as a conveyor of spot news. It was too slow, they said, compared to radio; it had too many limitations. By the time production techniques were completed for a TV news report, it would be entering the realm of history. Film coverage of necessity was restricted to planned events. Hence the medium threatened to give viewers a grossly distorted picture of the goings-on in the world. It would forever accent the trivial—bathing beauty contests, Paris fashions, new arrivals at the zoo. It would forever eliminate the significant—Communist witchcraft in the Middle East, recommendations of the Hoover commission on reorganization of the federal government, actions taken at last night's meeting of the local school board.

Happily, the early seers proved to be wrong. Television news was saved by technological improvements that have nearly solved the problems of slowness and mediocre coverage. The development of film of exceptionally high speed, eliminating the necessity for complicated lighting equipment in shooting a story, was a major breakthrough. The perfection of television tape was another. Refinements in both motion and still picture cameras contributed immensely to the common goal, as did the coming of age of TV mobile units. Faster transmission of films and pictures from the scene of an event to the network or station also played a part. Perhaps equally important was the improved training given newsmen and stringers in the use of camera equipment.

The clicking, rumbling teleprinters of the Associated Press or United Press International (and sometimes both) play a staccato rhythm night and day in the newsrooms of every television and radio station in the country. These newsgathering organizations provide the state, national, and foreign news reports that can be relayed almost instantaneously to the public. Regrettably, a considerable number of stations depend almost altogether upon giant press associations for their newscasts; in the lingo of the broadcast world their announcers simply "rip and read" these stories, frequently against a recorded background of wire machine cacophony and preceded by whistles, the ringing of bells, and other attention-compelling sounds. Many small stations also provide poor local news coverage, depending upon publicity handouts and upon rewriting the newspapers because they cannot or will not meet the cost of maintaining a news staff. By contrast, the quality stations rewrite wire dispatches, working in as much interpretative (not opinion) material as possible; their newscasts are presented in a more dignified manner; and they maintain staffs of varying talent and size in order to keep abreast of local news developments.

The most common types of radio newscasts are the 5-, 10-, and 15-minute sponsored programs. The networks use the hourly 5- and 10-minute newscast technique, a service that would have been impossible in the old days of the half-hour sponsored network music, comedy, or drama show, because of programing difficulties. The hourly 5-minute newscast is also a basic ingredient in what is known as "formula" radio. This is high-tension programing, with all announcements read at least 10 percent faster than ordinary, much playing of "survey" records—"the week's top 40 pop tunes"—and often double- or even triple-spotting of commercials between records.

Stations with larger staffs tend to produce 15-minute newscasts for airing early in the morning, at noon, in the late afternoon, and around 10:00 or 11:00 at night. The material for these newscasts is gathered in much the same manner as the newspaper employs. Reporters contact officials in such information-collecting centers as police departments; city, county, and federal offices; courts; chambers of commerce; industries and labor union headquarters. They either telephone accounts to a rewrite man or return to their newsrooms to write the stories themselves. Meanwhile, other developing stories are obtained by telephone from such sources as hospitals, funeral homes, weather bureaus, airports, and civic organizations. Many stations are staffed by men who have not only been trained to gather and write news but also to deliver it on the air. At other stations news scripts are prepared by trained journalists but the station's regular announcers broadcast the news. This system proves most effective when one writer, or set of writers, prepares copy regularly for the same announcer. Those writing the copy get to know the peculiar style, cadence, and microphone personality of the announcer, and they prepare their stories to fit the type of interpretation which they know will be given to the copy.

Reports direct from the scene of a news happening, radioed to the station from a mobile unit, frequently enliven newscasts. Often these reports are recorded earlier and interspersed into the regular newscasts. Reporters for stations which do not have a mobile unit frequently telephone their accounts; their narrations are recorded and may be placed on the air almost immediately.

Newspapers appeal to the sense of sight, and radio appeals to the sense of hearing; but television caters to both and offers the advantage of motion. The structure of television requires tight writing and editing. Many stories must be written to match the edited film or magnetic tape segment exactly. Television newscasts use short, conversational sentences and phrases; CBS' Walter Cronkite has pointed out that in an average half-hour television news broadcast, fewer words are spoken than are seen on two-thirds of a page of a regular-sized newspaper. Cronkite feels, however, that the half-hour is used well. In delivering the twentieth annual William Allen White Lecture at the University of Kansas in 1969, he declared:

> Look at what we do with that time. Twenty items in an average newscast— some but a paragraph long, true, but all with the essential information to provide at least a guide to our world that day. Film clips that, in a way available to no other daily medium, introduce our viewers to the people and the places that make the news. Investigative reports—pocket documentaries —that expose weakness in our democratic fabric. (Not enough of those, but we're coming along.) Feature film reports that explore the by-ways of America and assure us that the whole world hasn't turned topsy-turvy. Graphics that in a few seconds communicate a great deal of information. Clearly labeled analysis, or commentary, on the news.
>
> I think that is quite a package.

Whatever the technique, television news programs call for a maximum of cooperation among the director, camera crew, newscaster, and announcer (for the commercials). Each portion of the presentation must be carefully cued and timed for a smoothly produced show.

The production of television and radio newscasts for the networks requires the cooperation not only of large staffs, centered in New York City and Washington, D.C., but also of trained personnel scattered throughout the world. Events in other countries are filmed or taped and the footage dispatched by plane or satellite to the United States for immediate network use. Radio "pickups" can be made almost anywhere in the world and transmitted instantaneously to the American public, although these accounts often are recorded for rebroadcast at program time. Affiliated television stations throughout the United States provide man-on-camera narration and film clips which are interspersed into newscasts otherwise emanating from the principal network studios. Almost all of the highly skilled personnel required for network news programing consist of men who have obtained their basic training with local stations throughout the country or who have been engaged in competitive newspaper or press association reporting.

At one time there were great differences between the styles of radio-TV writing and newspaper writing, chiefly because broadcast copy was written for the ear and newspaper copy for the eye. Today, however, primarily as a result of the numerous readability studies of the 1940's and 1950's, much newspaper copy has been simplified to the point where it is just about as easy to comprehend as copy prepared for newscasts. With certain style exceptions, news that is easy to follow when it comes from the loudspeaker is also easily understood when read in a newspaper.

There are, of course, logical reasons for certain differences in the styles of writing news for the three media. Since many newspaper readers are inclined to be "skimmers" and to pay less than undivided attention to what they read as they ride on buses, planes, or commuter trains or while they sit at home absorbing the outpourings of television and radio sets and record players, newspaper stories must present their most important facts first—and fast. However, the newspaper reader has headlines and bold-faced paragraphs or subheads to help him grasp the significance of an array of facts. And if he doesn't get it the first time, he has a physical account to which he can refer again and again until it all becomes clear. So a newspaper account begins with the crux of a story and continues with facts ranked according to their importance; transitional phrases are dispensed with so that paragraphs may be rearranged or cut to fit allotted space.

The radio listener, on the other hand, must be prepared for the story with a clear and attention-arousing statement of what it concerns. He has some of the orientation aids the newspaper reader has—"headlines" at the beginning and end of the newscast, for example—but the brief stories with taped actualities require quick concentration if he is to get the message before they disappear—until the next newscast. Furthermore, key ideas (not words or phrases, but ideas) must be repeated in radio copy at times to put over a complex point. Such repetition would be both deadly and unnecessary in newspaper copy.

The television viewer ordinarily, though not always, gives his full attention to the televised news report. He doesn't have the newspaper's type guides to assist him in understanding the day's happenings; nor does he need them. Instead, he has a completely different set of tools—films, still pictures, symbolic art work, and background music—to help him follow what the newscaster is saying.

These different tools are also noted in the physical appearance of a television news script. News to be read fills no more than two-thirds of a regular sheet of paper; on the other one-third, usually the left side, instructions are written in concerning the use of film, tape, slides, special effects, and other television devices.

The newscaster has a rather strong contact with members of his audience at the time they expose themselves to the news, whereas the newspaper reporter does not have such a contact. To take advantage of this fact, broadcast news attempts to be conversational and highly informal. It is intended to sound like a story told by one good friend to another. It makes greater use of active voice and present tense than newspaper copy does; it rarely departs from simple, direct sentence structure; and it occasionally goes overboard in the use of colloquial and idiomatic expressions.

## THE EDITORIAL FUNCTION

Approximately one-half of the broadcast media in the 1970's were exercising their rights and privileges to present informed opinion. Individual news analysts such as H. V. Kaltenborn, Clifton Utley, Elmer Davis, John W. Vandercook, and Bill Henry had performed notable public service during the quarter-century when radio controlled the airwaves. Gradually, as television lured multitudes from their radio sets, these commentators lost their grip on the populace. TV, with its unique ability to bring the sights and sounds of live action into the home, soon found it had no place for the type of analyst who just sat and talked, except during events of transcendent news importance when, for example, the nation was nominating or electing its top executives and legislators.

In the field of the documentary, the versatility of films and remote pickups enabled television to score successes that its sightless partner could scarcely match, although radio continued to produce superb "actuality" shows—using the voices of participants instead of those of actors—and occasionally excelled in the presentation of public affairs programs.

From the long view, the only trouble with such outstanding TV originals as "See It Now" and "Wide, Wide World" was that they were expensive—and, hence, expendable. This resulted in their rather spasmodic appearance and disappearance. Sponsors felt a detectable reluctance to put on such programs for an appreciably smaller audience than that which could be attracted to low-budget westerns—despite the fact that one forum of enlightenment, CBS' "Twentieth Century," successfully bumped a horse opera competitor off home screens. A satisfactory solution to the problem has yet to be found.

The area of the opinion function in which the media are making continuous advances is presentation of owner viewpoints. Editorializing (the word most often used) consists of the advocacy of opinion that is clearly identified as the view of a broadcasting organization—as opposed to "commentating," in which the opinions expressed are those of an individual.

In 1941 the Federal Communications Commission decreed in its famed "Mayflower Decision" that licensees should not air their own editorial opinions. The decision concerned a Boston station held to be in violation of the Federal Communications Act because of its political broadcasting. In its opinion, the commission expressed concern that only one side of an issue might be placed before the public in one-station communities and in those in which the only newspaper and possibly the only station were owned by the same persons. In 1949, however, the FCC reversed itself, declaring that it would be in the public interest for stations to "editorialize with fairness." In other words, the FCC decided that if a broadcast licensee undertakes to present programing dealing with controversial issues of public importance, he must make reasonable efforts to present conflicting points of view on such issues.

For some years after the FCC reversed its decision, station managements made only limited attempts to offer their own "editorials of the air." There was no tradition to spur them on. Besides, effective editorials require careful research and expert writing. Since an editorial itself brings in no direct income, stations were reluctant to employ the extra manpower needed to do the job well. The first station to offer a daily editorial on television was WTVJ (Miami, Fla.) in September, 1957. Since then this station has achieved distinction in the field of the broadcast editorial, under the leadership of News Director Ralph Renick. WMCA, New York, became the first radio station to endorse a candidate for the Presidency with its editorial support of John F. Kennedy in 1960, and the station is a recognized leader in broadcast editorializing.

A strong movement toward the airing of editorials began in 1958. It subsided somewhat as 365 new stations went on the air in a four-year period, most of them lacking the maturity and staff necessary for effective editorializing. By 1967, however, a nationwide survey by the National Association of Broadcasters revealed that 57 percent of the nation's radio stations and 56 percent of its TV stations broadcast editorials either as regular program fare or on a sporadic basis.

The station owners viewed editorializing as part of their obligation to serve the interests of their local communities. They looked on editorials as making an important contribution to the public's understanding of issues and to provide an additional viewpoint for their audiences. Editorials also were regarded as enhancing a station's prestige and helping to build an audience. Stations that did not editorialize cited a lack of time or manpower for the extensive preparation to do an effective job. Some expressed the feeling that editorializing is not an appropriate activity for a broadcast station.

Most editorializing stations concentrated on issues of purely local interest, and the majority also preferred issues involving a wide difference of opinion. About half of the stations spoke out on statewide issues.

A followup NAB survey in 1968 found that about 70 percent of the public believes broadcasters should editorialize. About 80 percent of those aware of radio-TV editorializing said the editorials made them think more about the subject, 50 percent felt the editorials helped them make up their minds, and 25 percent said the editorials convinced' them to change their minds. Most felt that issues of any scope or subject, excluding those related to sex, were suitable for editorial treatment. Four out of five expressed the opinion that the stations themselves, rather than any agency of government, should regulate broadcast editorials.

Special editorial personnel or news staff members require more than five hours to prepare the average editorial for broadcast. In order to insure that the editorial is received as reflecting the viewpoint of management, and to maintain a desirable distinction between news and opinion, the editorial generally is delivered by the station manager himself, usually in two to three minutes of air time. Some stations present editorial cartoons and others read excerpts from letters from the public.

Many broadcasters who have failed to air editorials, or whose expressions have represented bland, "middle-of-the-road" points of view, have complained that the FCC's fairness doctrine is to blame. (See Chapter 6.) Why, they argue, should the station be forced to grant valuable air time for reply even if a reasonable determination can be made as to who should reply and on what specific issues? General Counsel Douglas Anello of the National Association of Broadcasters asked: "If a broadcaster can be forced to give time for the expression of a contrary point of view, isn't this comparable to the levy of damages for saying what you think?" Both actions, he declared, are equally inhibiting to free and open discussion. Fairness, he contended, should remain always a moral obligation, never a legal one. Furthermore, broadcasters are fearful that the FCC, which has power to revoke their licenses, may disagree with the stations' handling of certain controversial cases.

Former FCC Chairman E. William Henry has replied that it isn't the commission's fairness doctrine that is to blame for bland broadcast editorials and commentaries that lack a point of view—it's the broadcaster who is more concerned with his ratings than with winning a Peabody or Sigma Delta Chi Award. "The real difficulty," Henry said, "lies with broadcasters who aren't seriously committed to the journalistic function or to the exposure of controversy." Such broadcasters, he said, follow this rule: "Controversy may sell newspapers, but in this business it's the funny page that counts. Mr. Average Viewer will not consider buying your brand or Brand X when an editorial has just made him apoplectic."

Henry said the FCC has enunciated only the most general principles— "that the basic right to be protected is the public's right to hear both sides of a controversy, that a broadcaster has an obligation to respect that right, that he must make an affirmative effort to discharge this obligation over and above making his facilities available to contrasting points of view on demand. . . ." He added that the FCC has often upheld the broadcaster's judgment against the complaints of those whose ideas of fairness differed.

### ADVERTISING AND PROMOTION

Network advertising, national "spot" advertising, and local advertising provide the bulk of operating revenue for television and radio stations. Large stations may also receive income from such services as producing programs for clients, making transcriptions, and handling talent.

The advertising staffs of the national networks solicit advertising from companies whose products or services are marketed throughout the country. They provide a continuing flow of fresh, up-to-date information about the markets served by their affiliates, making contacts both directly with big companies and with the agencies that represent them.

National firms with large staffs of trained solicitors represent individual stations in calling on agencies and companies for business. They sell spot advertising, which may range from a series of brief announcements to full programs originating in the local studios and from filmed commercials to filmed 15- or 30-minute programs. These firms, located strategically in the major cities, make sales presentations for any or all the stations on their lists.

This leaves local advertising to be handled by the station itself. The commercial manager must build a staff of highly trained solicitors who often have a triple job to do: sell advertising in general, television and radio in particular, and their own station specifically. This is true because the local merchant may not be fully aware of the advantages of advertising and he may have practically no knowledge of what a carefully conceived television or radio advertising campaign may do for his business.

The salesman first learns all he can about his prospective client's business. In consultation with the local sales manager and station program director, he then prepares a suggested plan, involving possibly a regular program and a series of commercial announcements. If the plan is accepted, he oversees the necessary arrangements to ensure the effectiveness of the campaign. Skilled writers prepare the copy and continuity. After the advertiser is convinced that his campaign is selling his goods or services, the salesman seeks gradually to sell the sponsor additional broadcasting.

An important adjunct to sales is the promotion department. The promotion manager may be a staff member with no other responsibilities or he may be the general manager, the commercial manager, a copywriter, or a salesman. In order to attract both audiences and advertisers, the promotion manager prepares station advertisements and publicity stories for the local newspapers, for trade publications read by agency and company advertising men, and for use over the station's own facilities. In addition, he develops ideas for posters and other outdoor advertising; engages in such public relations activities as delivering speeches, answering station mail, and handling telephone inquiries; and attracts attention to the station and its individual programs through such devices as parades, stunts, and personal appearances by star performers. Journalistic training is almost imperative for successful performance in this capacity.

## PROGRAMING

Television and radio programs are planned, prepared, and produced by the programing department. On small stations, only a few persons may be employed to make commercial announcements, read news and sports summaries, select and play recordings, and introduce network programs. Large stations, however, may employ 75 or more persons to handle a variety of specialized jobs.

The programing policy and scheduling for a large station are handled by the program director. The traffic manager prepares daily schedules of programs and keeps a record of broadcast time available for advertising. The writing and editing of all scripts are the responsibility of the continuity director. Assisting him is the continuity writer, who prepares announcers' books containing the script and commercials for each program together with their sequence and length.

The director supervises individual programs. He may work under the supervision of a producer, who handles the selection of scripts, financial matters, and other production problems. At times these functions are combined in the job of producer-director. Program assistants obtain props, film slides, art work, and makeup service; assist in timing the program; and prepare cue cards. Some stations employ education and public affairs directors, who supervise most noncommercial programs such as those presented by churches, schools, and civic groups.

Television and radio staff announcers present news and live commercial messages, identify stations, conduct interviews, describe sports events, and act as masters of ceremonies. On the smaller stations they may also operate the control board, sell time, and write scripts and news copy. Announcers on small stations often obtain FCC licenses in order that they also may operate transmitters.

Large television and radio stations may employ a librarian to handle the music files, and also a musical director to supervise rehearsals and broadcasts. Television stations have film editors, who prepare films and video tape recordings for on-the-air presentation. The stations' files of films and tape are maintained by a film librarian.

Television performances which are aired either live or on tape require the services of a studio supervisor, who arranges scenery and other equipment; a floor or stage manager, who directs the movement of actors on the set and relays stage directions, station breaks, and cues; floormen, who set up props, hold cue cards, and perform other such chores; makeup artists, who prepare personnel for broadcasts; scenic designers, who plan and design settings and backgrounds; and sound effects technicians, who coordinate special sounds.

Working with all of these programing personnel are the engineers and broadcast technicians, who use their highly specialized knowledge to convert the sounds and pictures into electronic impulses that can be received by the public.

## OPPORTUNITIES AND SALARIES

There are hundreds of openings in television and radio news departments each year (and a few in the radio departments of press associations and in newsreel companies). To fill them, the news director or station manager usually turns to his file of job applicants, many of whom are seeking to advance from a smaller operation. Some small stations may employ a local high school graduate who has displayed an interest in "learning by doing." A number of quality stations, as well as others, recruit newsmen directly from departments and schools of journalism and communications. The most sought-after graduates are those trained at schools which have highly developed programs in television and radio news instruction. These graduates not only have learned to gather, write, and edit news but they have also been introduced to newsroom equipment and techniques and thus are enabled to perform specified chores almost immediately.

Because of the relative scarcity of instructional programs in television and radio news, however, many stations must seek out the graduates of print-oriented schools and departments of journalism and convert them into broadcast personnel.

If the recruit is employed by a radio station, he will be assigned to established news beats or given a rewrite job in the newsroom; if he doesn't already know how to operate a tape recorder, he will be taught how to do this and how to conduct a telephone interview to be placed on the air, or how to report from the scene of a news happening. If a television station employs him, he will be assigned to rewriting wire copy or will be handed a camera, either motion picture or still, and, if necessary, given minimum training in its operation. He then will be expected to report the news with both pencil and camera.

With the era of all-male news staffs at an end, many women gather and announce television news. Pauline Frederick, who has covered the United Nations for NBC for many years, has been joined by other women personalities such as Barbara Walters of the *Today* show. Countless women have become local celebrities on both radio and television.

Blacks and other minorities also are highly visible in television broadcasting. They are eagerly sought after by stations throughout the nation, who have "raided" newspaper staffs with substantial success.

According to their abilities, both men and women may advance from beginning jobs to become news directors, commentators, program directors, announcers, directors of public affairs and special events, and station managers. University speech and radio-TV departments provide training for most of the performing and production jobs in broadcasting.

Stations also are constantly in the market for competent advertising solicitors and continuity writers. Writing commercials requires a knowledge of selling, and more often than not such a job is filled by a woman. Salaries in these fields compare favorably with those requiring similar talents with the other media. Good promotion men and women with large stations commonly earn $9500 or more.

Beginning salaries for television and radio news personnel are comparable to, or slightly higher than, those paid newspaper reporters and editors. By 1973 these starting salaries were around $5500 to $6800, depending upon the size of the station, regional competitive factors, and the training of the applicant. After three to five years, salaries for radio news writers range from $7500 to $9000, while television news writers may exceed $10,000 on large stations. Talent fees for those with on-mike and on-camera assignments push their incomes even higher.

Wage scales in effect at NBC and ABC in 1972 ranged between $175 and $300 a week, compared with an average weekly salary of $220 paid top-level reporters under contracts won by the American Newspaper Guild. Additional fees of $9.60 per day were earned by so-called "desk men," who act as TV and radio assignment editors or "produce" TV network shows. Additional fees also were paid for network news "cut-ins." Newswriters at network originating points and at stations owned and operated by the two networks are represented by the National Association of Broadcast Employees and Technicians. The union's news jurisdiction includes all writing, editing, processing, collecting, and collating of news, including film. The bargaining agent for all the Columbia Broadcasting System writers, and for the NBC and ABC newsmen in New York City, is the Writers Guild of America.

Newsmen under individual contract to the networks to write and deliver their own news programs are members of the American Federation of Television and Radio Artists, the union that covers all on-the-air performers. AFTRA members may either prepare their own copy or read copy written by NABET members. AFTRA members are sometimes used as on-the-street reporters. They work under a fee system of talent payments for newscasts and air work toward a guaranteed wage. Individual contracts call for guarantees of $250 a week and higher. It is estimated that such veteran newsmen as Walter Cronkite and David Brinkley have reached total annual incomes in excess of $200,000 each.

As might be expected, personnel employed by large broadcast stations earn higher salaries than those paid by small stations. The range of television station salaries is roughly as follows: General manager, $17,000 to $45,000; station manager, $13,000 to $32,000; commercial manager, $10,000 to $23,000; program manager, $8500 to $15,000; promotion manager, $7000 to $13,000; chief engineer, $8500 to $17,000; news director, $8000 to $17,500.

Radio station salaries generally are lower. The range, roughly, is as follows: General manager, $8000 to $38,000; commercial manager, $8000 to $23,500; program manager, $6000 to $13,000; chief engineer, $6000 to $13,500; news director, $6000 to $12,000.

These salaries include fees and commissions, but not fringe benefits. Compensation varies widely according to geographic location, station and market size, program emphasis, and other factors.

Competent college graduates with bachelor's degrees should expect to receive beginning salaries ranging from $5000 to $7000 for most broadcast jobs, with annual raises of $10 to $15 per week the customary pattern. Master's degree graduates generally earn $1300 to $1800 more each year than those with bachelor's degrees.

The earnings of employees in television and radio broadcasting rank second highest in the entire industrial economy, Department of Commerce surveys reveal. Their average annual earnings are exceeded only by those of employees of security and commodity brokers, dealers, and exchanges.

## QUALIFICATIONS

Sound training in reporting and editing is essential for success in television and radio newsrooms. A knowledge of photography is desirable for those who aspire to positions in television. The successful newsman or newswoman must have curiosity, persistence, an interest in people, a good educational background and a knowledge of current events, an ability to write clearly and speedily, poise under pressure, and, if he is expected to read news copy, a voice of acceptable quality, inflection, and diction.

The newsman must be able to gather and write news quickly and under pressure. He must be able to edit the stories of others, including wire copy. He must have the ability to find local angles in national stories and to simplify complex matters and make them meaningful. He should quickly recognize feature angles in routine stories. If he reads his own copy on the air, he must do so with an acceptable voice.

Responsibility is a prime characteristic of the good newsman. He must be familiar with all laws applicable to broadcasting, including copyright, libel, and slander. In the handling of news, he must be well aware of broadcasting's responsibilities to the public and exercise judgment and good taste in selecting news items.

His must be a well-rounded knowledge that includes familiarity with general broadcast operations, including mechanical problems, and interest in current electronic developments and research methods. He must be familiar with the various techniques of newscasting, including first-person reporting, wire recordings, on-the-scene live broadcasts, and interviews. And he should know all about production matters such as the timing of a script, the placing of commercials, rehearsal, and coordination of the efforts of the newscaster, commercial announcer, and engineer.

An announcer must possess many of these same qualifications. In addition, he should have a pleasant and well-controlled voice, a good sense of timing, and excellent pronunciation. His English usage must be correct, and he should keep abreast of sports, music, current events, and the like. In television, high standards of personal appearance must be met.

An announcer should be a convincing salesman in presenting commercials and he should have a flair for showmanship. The ability to react quickly and imaginatively in unusual situations is important.

The television program director must have a comprehensive knowledge of all of the production techniques entailed in staging a performance before cameras and microphones, such as sets, graphics, script, makeup, lighting, music, and the like. He must be a master of detail and know how to work with all kinds of people.

The film director must have the same broad background as the director in TV, but he must also be acquainted with the special characteristics of film, including types of emulsions, camera limitations, special sound recording problems, and lab processing techniques. Often he must be both a writer and director.

The ideal advertising salesman is an enthusiastic, personable extrovert with a knack for making friends and a keen business mind that enables him to evaluate the needs of a particular firm and come up with a carefully planned program of television or radio advertising that will sell goods and services. He must be well trained in the basic functioning of advertising and must keep abreast of general business as well as media developments.

The copy and continuity writer, of course, must be a word craftsman, able to set a mood or epitomize a situation with a paucity of expression. He too must be well informed about the entire business of television or radio advertising.

The best promotion manager is an experienced journalist and an idea man. He can write news and advertising copy or dream up a publicity gimmick. He can design a highly complex campaign to project a favorable image for his station. He should know typography, layout, writing, editing, and public speaking and have a full awareness of public relations principles and practices.

# Chapter 11

# *Press Associations*

## THE ROLE OF PRESS ASSOCIATIONS

The clatter of press association teleprinters, delivering stories hour after hour with almost relentless precision, stirs a sense of subdued excitement in the newsrooms of the country. This is the world in action. Even veteran newsmen who work with the teleprinters at hand year after year always wonder subconsciously what dateline will emerge next on the continuous rolls of paper. The automatic keys spell out dispatches from Washington, London, Saigon, the state capitals, and a thousand other cities.

Supplying the news dispatches that come from the teleprinters in such abundance are the Associated Press and United Press International, the two largest, most intricate and fiercely competitive news-gathering agencies in the world. Without the service of a press association, a daily newspaper or broadcasting station would find distribution of a well-balanced news report to its audience virtually impossible.

The press associations take over where the local and area news coverage of the city desk ends. Even the largest dailies and the broadcasting networks with extensive staffs of their own correspondents in Washington and abroad are heavily dependent upon the press associations for domestic and foreign dispatches.

Intense hour-to-hour rivalry between AP and UPI exists in their effort to deliver dispatches that are comprehensive, accurate, objective, and perceptive—and to get them there first. Both services emphasize a writing style sufficiently simple and interesting to be understood by a mass audience.

This competitive urge is one of the attractions of press association work, especially for younger reporters and editors; it adds a zest to newsgathering which has disappeared to some degree from the local news staffs in many cities where only one newspaper now exists. Commercially, this competition to be faster and better than your rival has great importance, because the AP and UPI are in constant battle to take away customers from each other. (The AP calls them members; the UPI refers to them as clients.)

Although the services they deliver to newspapers, television, and radio stations here and abroad are similar, the two press associations are organized quite differently. The Associated Press, which is much older, is a cooperative newsgathering association. Each American newspaper which purchases its service becomes a member of the cooperative and has a voice in setting the association's newsgathering and financial policies; also, it is obligated to turn over its local news coverage to the cooperative. Television and radio stations taking AP service become associate members without voting rights; the total now exceeds that of newspaper members. The Associated Press was founded in 1848 by six New York publishers, primarily to cooperate in the gathering of news from ships arriving in eastern harbors from Europe. It has been in continuous existence ever since, having gone through several major reorganizations including one in 1900 which established it in its present form.

United Press International is a privately owned company, dealing on a contract basis with newspapers, television and radio stations, and other organizations which have need for a news report. Its individual clients influence the shape of the UPI news report only through their suggestions and criticisms, solicited by the UPI management, or through their ultimate power to cancel the service. An Associated Press member can withdraw on two years' notice; the usual United Press International contract with a client runs five years. The United Press was founded in 1907 by E. W. Scripps, the owner of a large group of newspapers, with the purpose of supplying news to papers which could not obtain Associated Press membership under the then-existing rules. In 1958 the United Press absorbed the International News Service, which had operated as a relatively weak third American competitor in the field since William Randolph Hearst founded it in 1909. The combined service became known as United Press International.

The Associated Press and United Press International are now comparable in strength, the UPI having improved its position by the merger with INS.

The Associated Press reported that during the early 1970's it was serving approximately 8500 newspapers and television and radio stations around the world; the United Press International reported it had approximately 6000 clients for its news and picture services. The UPI was operating in 114 countries and territories, the AP in 104. Both press associations leased more than 400,000 miles of telephone wires in the United States for transmission of news and pictures, and both used satellites, global radio teletype circuits, and underwater cables to send their news reports to and from Europe and Asia. For the United States alone, the two associations reported these figures: AP, service to 1750 publications and 3100 television and radio stations; UPI, 1600 publications and 2300 television and radio stations. Each had an annual budget above $50,000,000.

Regardless of whether it is called a member or a client, the net result for each daily newspaper is much the same. It receives the UPI or AP news report by teleprinter for a specified number of hours each day, for which it pays a fee based upon its circulation and the amount of news received. Prices range from roughly $100 to $400 a week for a paper of 25,000 circulation up to $6000 a week for the metropolitan dailies, depending on the special services purchased. Both news agencies offer supplemental sports and financial services.

Most small dailies, and even some very large ones, operate successfully with only one of the two major wire services. Of the 1750 American daily newspapers, approximately 45 percent subscribe only to AP, 30 percent only to UPI, and 25 percent to both services. More than 500 dailies purchase news from both to have a wider choice of news stories to publish. When both services provide stories on the same news events, as they do scores of times daily, the telegraph editor of the two-service newspaper selects the dispatch which arrives first, if an urgent news break is involved, or the one which seems to him more complete, concise, and interesting. Sometimes the two dispatches are combined to provide a more well-rounded and complete story.

The rival agencies keep close watch on selected lists of these two-service papers to determine the "play" their respective stories receive.

Bad "play" on a big story—or worse, being badly beaten by the rival agency on a news break—brings sharp backstage criticism from the New York home office down upon the head of the offending bureau involved.

## HOW PRESS ASSOCIATIONS FUNCTION

The news reports of each press association are carried to newspapers by leased telegraph circuits from offices scattered across the United States. The stories arrive in the newspaper office on a continuous roll of paper in a teleprinter, a machine resembling an automatic typewriter whose keys are activated by impulses transmitted over the telegraphic circuit from a press association office. This paper is cut into segments by the telegraph editor, who selects from it the stories he will publish in his newspaper that day. Originally transmission was on Morse dot-and-dash circuits, but these were replaced long ago by automatic teleprinters. When a major news break develops, the first portion of it is marked "urgent" or "bulletin" and transmitted along the circuit on a priority basis.

Each press association divides its flow of news into P.M. and A.M. reports, or cycles, the former for afternoon newspapers and the latter for morning papers. These reports always begin with a "budget," or checklist, of the most important stories that are to be transmitted. The budget represents a summary of the basic stories then available, or known to be forthcoming during the next few hours, plus sports and feature highlights. Usually it contains 10 or 12 items. The news editor is thus enabled to plan his makeup to ensure space for stories that he most likely will want to run. Since the large majority of American newspapers are published in the afternoon, and most news occurs during daytime hours, the P.M. reports are generally handled with a greater sense of urgency.

Basic stories on major news situations are transmitted early in each cycle. If later developments occur on a story, a new "lead" is moved on the wire. This reports the latest news on the situation and ends with a transitional paragraph which blends into the earlier dispatch at a specified place. On big, fast-breaking stories a press association may carry half a dozen leads in a cycle; these are edited so compactly that the dispatch which ultimately appears in a client newspaper reads with smooth continuity, even though it may contain segments of several leads.

Such methods are necessary because press association clients are constantly going to press and must print what is available on a given situation at press time. To use a phrase popular with United Press International, somewhere there is a deadline every minute. This is a major difference between press association and ordinary newspaper writing: the press association correspondent must keep feeding latest developments in a "spot" story onto the news wires immediately, even when their meaning and ramifications are not fully disclosed; the newspaper staff correspondent (called a "special" by wire service men) usually has more time before his deadline to digest and consolidate his information. Press association men always work under time pressure. When we consider this, the amount of background and interpretation an experienced press association man can weave into a fast-breaking story is remarkable.

The press associations have main trunk teletype circuits running across the country, serving the major metropolitan newspapers. From these main trunks, regional and state circuits strike off at relay bureaus to serve the smaller papers in different areas of the country. The editors who control the flow of news onto these secondary wires, known as "wire filers," must see that the newspapers on each receive a balanced menu of regional news along with the most important national and foreign dispatches. Thus an Associated Press member in Arizona will receive some stories of interest only to readers in the Southwest which will not be delivered to another member in Florida. These members will receive identical dispatches on the day's major news from Washington and London, however. Proper channeling of the daily news report, so that each newspaper gets the largest possible number of stories pertinent to its needs, is a basic problem for press association editors. Many stories are shortened when relayed on secondary circuits, because smaller newspapers do not have the space to publish them in full. Dispatches from the press association bureaus abroad are sent to the New York home offices for processing and filing on the domestic circuits.

As an example of the press association wire operation, a story originating in a small bureau may be distributed around the world, if various wire service editors along the way consider it sufficiently interesting; or it may never go farther than the circuit serving the newspapers in a nearby region. The bureau of origin transmits it on the state or regional wire. The editors at the control point for this circuit may consider the item to have national appeal and offer it to the editors in New York for nationwide transmission. When it reaches the New York general office, an editor may put it on circuits serving newspapers overseas. Every wire service story undergoes this selective screening process, by which the editors tailor the news report on each circuit to fit the needs and interests of its client newspapers.

Creation of teletypesetter circuits has been a major recent development in press association news transmission. On these circuits the news is delivered to client newspapers on a teleprinter roll, typed in capital and lower case letters with the lines justified to fit a newspaper column width for quick typesetting. Simultaneously, each newspaper receives the stories in perforated tape ready for use in automatic typesetting machines. Use of computers to justify the lines and insert hyphenation speeds up transmission. Under the original Morse code dot-and-dash system, about 35 words a minute could be transmitted. This was increased to 60 words on the all-capital letter teleprinters. Today computers and fast transmission circuits enable movement of special material such as stock market lists and baseball box scores at more than 1000 words a minute. The Associated Press and the Los Angeles *Times* in experiments have transmitted market reports at ultrahigh speeds of 50,000 words a minute, from one computer to another. After being stored in the receiving computer, the words come out on tape, to be run through ordinary typesetting machines. Further developments in uses of fast transmission are being explored.

## SPECIAL WRITING TECHNIQUES

It is evident that a news story which goes through all these vicissitudes of editing en route from reporter to client editor's desk requires special writing techniques. It may be published 500 words long in one newspaper and only 100 words in another. Thus the writer must keep his fundamental information near the top of the story so the dispatch can be trimmed easily without having any key facts omitted. A remarkable new computer system has been developed by the American Newspaper Publishers Association to do some of this story trimming automatically. If a wire service dispatch is 300 newspaper lines long, for example, the computer can shorten the story to almost any length the editor desires.

A press association reporter must write concisely, in simple sentences. Because his dispatches will be printed in newspapers of differing political persuasions and social viewpoints, he must be carefully objective in handling stories, even the complicated, controversial ones which require background and interpretation. The primary goal of press association writing is clear and swift communication of ideas and events, and the staff man's stock in trade is straight news, well written. More distinctive forms of self-expression find their way onto the wires, but those who wish to specialize in this type of writing usually choose other outlets.

Television and radio's instant news coverage of events in progress has had heavy impact on the press associations. Like newspapers, broadcast news staffs have changed their traditional operating methods, putting more stress on interpretative and analytical material.

Roger Tatarian, retired editor of United Press International, has described what took place in his organization during the 1960's. Much of what he states also applies to the Associated Press:

The UPI 10 or 15 years ago was basically happening-oriented. Its product was overwhelmingly based on action—action just over, action under way, or action imminent. This, in a word, is spot news. Spot news remains fundamental, of course, but the organization today is far more situation-oriented than it used to be. The restructuring of the report has been done in recognition that while newspapers can't usually be the first to disclose a major event to the public, it is in newspapers that these subjects can best be explored and reprised in a more meaningful way.

We are keenly aware that newspapers cannot compete with television or radio in giving readers an up-to-date account of a continuing thing like a space flight; or that a morning newspaper today can hardly report that Army beat Navy 20–7 yesterday when half the nation watched it on TV yesterday and the others who cared undoubtedly knew who won from radio. Our objective now is to write stories that are equally useful to those who know the central fact, and those who do not.

While the press associations permit their established writers more freedom in interpreting news situations now than in the past, they are on guard against political or social slanting of dispatches. The more complicated the world becomes, the more difficult it is for press associations to find a proper balance between quick-breaking facts and interpretation that gives them perspective without distortion. This calls for highly skilled reporting and editing.

## OTHER PRESS ASSOCIATION ACTIVITIES

Both the United Press International and Associated Press were founded to provide news for American newspapers. That remains their primary function, but they have branched out into several additional services. Each now delivers its news to newspapers and broadcasting stations in many foreign countries. A constant flow of overseas news comes to this country while news originating here is being dispatched throughout the world. Much of this global two-way news flow is accomplished by radio transmission, but because it is sometimes subject to interruption, both agencies also operate leased cable circuits under the Atlantic to London.

From New York radio teletype circuits operating around the clock transmit news both east and west for both the AP and UPI. In either operation, a transmitter on Long Island beams the signal by radio to Tangiers, where a relay station boosts the signal and beams it to Europe, the Middle East, South Asia, and South Africa. In London, the incoming beam is fed into teletype circuits covering more than 20,000 miles in Europe. In each country, the news is translated into that country's language and then put onto a separate national teletype network (translation into Spanish for Latin-American countries is largely done in the New York offices). The file to Asia is beamed by radio from San Francisco to booster relay stations at Manila and other points. Thus an important bulletin news story can flash by teletype within a minute or two on a Rome-London-New York-San Francisco-Tokyo transmission network. Pictures likewise are transmitted throughout the world by radio facilities.

The foreign bureaus of the American press associations usually are headed by an American, but they also employ local nationals in substantial numbers as reporters, editors, and translators. The number of foreign correspondent jobs available to Americans on the press associations is thus smaller than many people may believe. ·

In normal times approximately 500 U.S. citizens serve overseas as correspondents of U.S. media, the majority of them for the press associations. It is apparent that the commonly held desire of young newsmen to become foreign correspondents is not easily fulfilled. During the peak years of the Vietnam war the overseas contingent was much enlarged. Often sharp differences existed between the correspondents' reports from Saigon and the usually optimistic U.S. Army version of the conflict. As American troops were withdrawn, so were many reporters.

At many points around the world the American organizations are in sharp competition, in both newsgathering and sales, with such foreign news agencies as Reuters of Great Britain and Agence France-Presse. The impact of these foreign agencies upon the American press is negligible, however, since only a very few metropolitan papers purchase any of their material.

The American press associations have become important transmission belts for presenting a picture of life in America to foreigners. The hunger in many countries for news about the United States has been growing in proportion to this country's increasingly dominant role in world affairs. The Associated Press and United Press International carry a heavy responsibility in their selection and writing of news for the overseas audience, so that a well-balanced picture is presented. This does not imply censorship, the hiding of unpleasant news, or peddling of propaganda, but a judicious budget of stories to provide a multifaceted view of American life. For a great many citizens of foreign countries, press association dispatches provide the chief source of information about life, political policies, and attitudes in the United States.

The only foreign press association with important news outlets in the United States is Reuters, the British agency. The Reuters news report, which is edited principally in London, is purchased by some metropolitan American newspapers and TV-radio network news departments as a supplementary service.

Special news service for television and radio stations is a major part of the agencies' operations. This is transmitted on different teletype circuits from the newspaper service and is rewritten from the stories in the basic report to please the ear rather than the eye. The style is more conversational, with simpler sentence structure and less detail. Distribution of this specially processed radio report was inaugurated by the United Press in 1935. The Associated Press followed reluctantly five years later.

Another important service provided to newspapers by the press associations is news picture coverage. Both AP and UPI operate coast-to-coast circuits for transmission of news photographs, a growing number of them in color. The larger newspapers are connected with these circuits and receive photographs, about 80 or 90 a day, instantaneously as they are transmitted. Smaller newspapers receive selected airmailed packages of glossy prints or mats processed from the wire photo circuit by regional control points. The news agencies supply pictures to foreign clients by satellite, radio-photo, leased circuits, and mail.

Some newspapers purchasing the nationwide direct service receive the news photos in their offices over facsimile machines, which translate the electrical impulses of the transmission circuit into black-and-white photographs by means of a scanning device; these pictures are ready for immediate engraving and printing. Other newspapers obtain glossy black-and white photographs from negatives activated by the transmission circuit on equipment in their own plants. Both UPI and AP have staffs of photographers, who are assigned to stories much as are reporters. In addition, the Associated Press distributes many pictures taken by photographers on the staffs of member papers. UPI also supplements its staff picture coverage with photos from newspaper sources.

United Press International operates a daily motion picture newsfilm service for use on television news programs, an audio news service for radio station voice pickups on news events, and an Ocean Press radio news report to passenger liners at sea. Among its supplementary offerings the AP includes a color slide service for television stations, a mailed tape service, and a book division which produces a news annual and other special volumes.

On still another front, the Associated Press and United Press International, the latter through its subsidiary United Feature Syndicate, provide comic strips, women's features, political columns, and a host of other syndicated material for newspaper publication.

Thus the two organizations have journeyed far afield from their original purpose of providing dispatches for newspapers. However, the daily newspaper report continues to be the core of each agency's operations. The UPI and AP now serve not one but three of our mass communications media—newspapers, television, and radio, plus special services to magazines.

## CRITICAL VIEWS OF AGENCIES

Students of the American press sometimes are critical of the heavy dependence of newspapers and broadcasting stations upon the press associations; this criticism is aimed more at the role of the wire services than at their daily performance. There is an undercurrent of uneasiness among these critics because more than 1700 daily newspapers look to these two organizations for the great bulk of their nonlocal news. Anyone who listens to a succession of radio newscasts and hears the identical words from the radio news wires spoken to him repeatedly on different wave lengths realizes the dependence of radio stations in particular upon the press associations. In fact, an overwhelming percentage of the American people are largely dependent upon the two organizations, through their various newspaper and TV-radio ramifications, as well as their use by the weekly news magazines, for knowledge of what is happening in the world. In the eyes of the critics this constitutes a danger involving conformity of reporting and thought, and some question the qualifications of wire service newsmen to select the news which is transmitted.

The argument is more philosophic than practical. The economics of newspaper publishing makes it impossible for even the largest, richest newspapers to have staff reporters stationed around the world in sufficient numbers to give them exclusive reports, for the costs would be prohibitive. Therefore some form of cooperative newsgathering is necessary. And the men and women who select the news to be transmitted are as competent in performing this task as may be found; their judgment is constantly under question by veteran wire service officials and by the thousands of editors they are serving.

National concern about conduct of the Vietnam war and American policy caused close scrutiny of press association coverage from Saigon. Considering the difficulties involved, most informed critics gave the press associations good marks for their reporting from the war zone, particularly their efforts to reach beyond the official version of events.

So long as the United Press International and Associated Press remain free of governmental control or subsidy, operate in a highly competitive manner, and hold to their principles of objective news coverage, the perils of undue conformity are relatively small. The efficiency and far-reaching news lines of the press associations contribute greatly to the mammoth amount of information about the world available to readers and listeners throughout the United States.

The editors of client and member newspapers, and wire service executives themselves, subject the press association news report to a constant scrutiny for accuracy and completeness. When instances of insufficient or inaccurate coverage come to light, steps are taken quickly to remedy the weakness. The competitive factor is a very wholesome one. The Associated Press Managing Editors Association has committees of newsmen making year-around studies of AP operations.

The press associations are scolded at times by critics because they must depend upon the reporting services of part-time local "string" correspondents in some parts of the world. When a major story breaks in a normally quiet and remote area, they must use the sometimes inadequate services of these men until an American-trained correspondent can reach the scene. Press association executives answer by pointing out that it is economically impossible for them to keep highly qualified men in every country. Improved air service makes movement of expert reporters to distant scenes of action much faster now than in the past.

Another criticism of the press associations is shared by the newspapers themselves—an alleged preoccupation with "crisis" reporting. That means trying to find conflict and excitement in every situation, to the point of distorting the news. In particular this charge has been made concerning the handling of political and legislative news. It is stated that too much emphasis is placed upon the routine partisan postures of the two major parties. This allegation results from the striving of each association to find sharp "angles" that induce telegraph editors to print its stories instead of its competitor's. Recently, however, both wire services have been broadening their coverage by offering more thoughtful, interpretative articles in such fields as religion, race, education, labor, and social problems. They are much less open to charges of "crisis" overemphasis than they were a decade ago. The news services are also criticized for not carrying enough foreign news, to which criticism they reply that their newspapers will print only a limited amount of such news, and there is no use in taking wire transmission time to give them what they won't use.

Actually, the conformity in presentation of national and foreign news by newspapers is less than might be expected. Checks of representative groups of newspapers receiving the same wire service show a surprisingly wide variation in the stories chosen from the telegraphed news report by editors for publication in their newspapers. Stories selected for prominent front page play by some editors may be dismissed by others with brief mention on inside pages, or omitted entirely. This is not surprising when we realize that the press association wire delivers far more dispatches than most newspapers can use, and the pressures of local news vary from city to city. So do the news judgments of the individual editors.

Another way editors have found to broaden their national and foreign news coverage is purchase of a supplementary news service, such as those offered by the New York *Times* and the Los Angeles *Times*-Washington *Post* Service. These services supply to their clients by wire a daily news report that includes dispatches on major Washington and foreign events, plus background dispatches under many datelines. They leave the hourly spot coverage to the press associations, but seek to round out the picture with news material that is exclusive in each client's territory. Because of the cost, supplementary services are used primarily by the larger news-papers.

### JOB OPPORTUNITIES

The press associations are among the finest training grounds in the entire field of mass communications for young men and women interested in a career of working with news. The work is challenging. It puts a premium upon speed, conciseness, and judgment. Moreover, these organizations have a tradition of hiring young newsmen of limited professional experience and training them. Since the turnover in press association personnel is relatively high, there are quite a few job openings each year. Hiring of minority personnel, including women, is growing.

The beginner in press association work usually is given routine stories to rewrite from the local newspapers, items to check by telephone, and similar simple duties while he is getting the "feel." He must learn to look outward from his local community, to weigh each story for its interest to readers in other cities. He may have a period of wire filing, determining the order in which dispatches are to move on a state or regional wire, under the watchful supervision of his bureau chief. And at quite an early age, he may be named night manager of a small bureau, his first opportunity to exercise a limited amount of administrative responsibility. Because of the nature of press association work, wire service staff members do more editing and less original reporting than newspaper staffs do.

Those who stay with the press associations for a number of years, as many do, usually become managers of small or middle-sized bureaus or are transferred into such large offices as Chicago, Washington, or the New York general headquarters. After training in New York, a few are sent abroad to become foreign correspondents in the wire service offices overseas.

Salaries for press association work are approximately in line with those on large daily newspapers, with beginners starting at about $7000 a year. Under American Newspaper Guild contracts, salaries for key press association men and women in large cities reached the $300 a week ($15,600 a year) plateau during the early 1970's, plus pension benefits. Executive salaries ranged higher.

Although quite a few men and a few women spend virtually their entire careers in the press associations, there is a fairly heavy turnover in personnel. Some wire service men grow tired of the time pressures and the writing restrictions. They believe that while advancement is relatively fast when they are starting, it slows down as they mature.

They may find better salary opportunities in special reporting jobs and editorships on newspapers or in public relations, radio, television, and other related fields of mass communications. Many of the country's best-known reporters, writers, television commentators, and editors worked for the press associations in their younger years; almost unanimously they are grateful for the experience, especially for the writing discipline it taught them.

## NEWSPAPER FEATURE SYNDICATES

The other major source of editorial material used by daily newspapers from coast to coast, and tending to bring uniformity to the American press, is the feature syndicates. These sell to the newspapers a multitude of material for the entertainment and education of their readers, edited and ready for publication upon delivery. Comic strips and some other features are provided in mat and slick proof form; other text features are supplied in mimeographed form, in type and pictorial galley proofs, prepunched TTS tape, and "scanner ready" style for electronic editing.

An editor can load his paper as heavily with such syndicated material as his budget and his conscience will allow. The larger the feature "package" in a paper, the less space there is to be filled with locally created news and press association dispatches. A publication too full of such "canned" features gets a reputation of being more an entertainment medium than a newspaper and of being deficient in editorial enterprise. Readership polls show, however, that there is a very strong desire among readers for certain syndicated features, especially the better-known comic strips.

So the newspaper editor tries to strike a suitable balance. There is no firm rule of thumb about this; one good newspaper of substantial circulation and a reasonably large editorial "hole" (the space left in a newspaper after the advertisements have been inserted) will publish 16 comic strips daily while a comparable one runs only 10 or 12. The same is true of political columns and other material offered by the syndicates.

Examination of a typical well-edited newspaper with 50,000 daily circulation shows this material purchased ready-made from national feature syndicates: 12 comic strips, 12 cartoon panels, 5 political columns, medical column, personal advice column, crossword puzzle, astrological forecast, political cartoon, 2 entertainment columns, and juvenile information feature.

Some features, especially comic strips, have run in newspapers so many years that they have become household words, a commonplace in contemporary American life. Millions of readers every day look to see how Dick Tracy is getting along in his pursuit of a clever criminal, how the hillbilly Li'l Abner is faring in Dogpatch, and how Dagwood, the ordinary family man, is dealing with his domestic problems. The political opinions of columnists Jack Anderson and William Buckley, and the humorous satirical comment of Art Buchwald cause discussion among businessmen at lunch. Such free-swinging advice columns as "Dear Abby" are the pre-dinner fare of many housewives. An increase in subtlety and sophistication has been noted, with the rise of such strips as "Peanuts" and "The Wizard of Id," and the Jules Pfeiffer cartoons. Reflecting the changing social scene, comic strip artists have been using Negro characters in prominent roles since the late 1960's.

Approximately a dozen major syndicates provide the bulk of the features appearing in American newspapers, although there are more than a hundred smaller companies, some of which operate in specialized fields like boating and book serializations. The major syndicates have from 25 to more than 100 different features in the lists they offer for sale to editors. These include illustrated or text features on such diverse subjects as bridge, teen-age advice, beauty, Biblical tales, inspirational verse, automobile repairs, fashions, Hollywood gossip, Little League baseball, and handwriting analysis.

An editor who has trouble saying "no" to the sales talk of the syndicate salesmen soon finds himself overloaded with material for which the total weekly fee can run uncomfortably high. But an editor who can't say "no" is a contradiction in terms. On comics especially, many editors make a habit of dropping one feature whenever they buy a new one. Papers make occasional readership surveys to determine which comics and daily features are most popular. So attached do readers become to individual comic strips that the dropping of any single one almost always provokes a torrent of complaints; consequently, fewer changes are made than many editors desire.

Features are sold to newspapers for prices scaled to the paper's circulation. A famous comic strip that costs a metropolitan paper $50 or more a week may cost a paper with less than 10,000 circulation only $4. Although some features are sold for specific contract periods, many are on a "t.f." basis—the abbreviation for the phrase "till forbid"—meaning that the feature runs until the editor sends in a cancellation, usually on 30- to 90-day notice.

Competition among the syndicates to sell their features is intense. There are more than 250 daily comic strips on the market, many of which are also issued in color for Sunday comic sections; about 40 health columns, 75 religious features, and a dozen competing columns on stamp collecting. Although many well-established "name" features go on year after year, a new group of comic strips, panels, and text columns is brought onto the market annually. Features which lose popular appeal are dropped by the syndicates.

As a rule an editor organizing a comic page for his paper tries to offer readers a mixture of adventure continuity, serial stories similar to radio's soap opera drama with strong feminine appeal, children's interest, a strip slanted to teen-agers, and gag-a-day strips without continuity except in the characters themselves. Until a few years ago, most comic strips ran five columns wide; now almost all are in four columns. Closely connected with the comic strip is the cartoon panel, usually two columns wide, in which some familiar characters, such as Dennis the Menace, are involved in daily humorous misadventure; there is no continuity of action in these panels, which resemble those published in magazines. Several exceptionally popular comic strip and cartoon characters have been transformed into "live" versions on television, with uneven success.

The creators of popular strips like "Peanuts" earn large additional income through merchandising tie-ins featuring their cartoon characters.

The feature syndicates do not offer a very large potential for the young man or woman seeking a job. Their editorial and sales staffs are small and mostly drawn from professional journalists with several years of editorial or business-side experience. Most of the artists and writers whose material is distributed by these organizations do their work outside the syndicate offices and send or bring it in for editing and approval. Usually they work on a percentage arrangement with the syndicate, receiving a portion of the fees paid by the newspapers. Syndicate editing requires knowledge of the public taste, as well as the space problems, buying habits, and idiosyncracies of the various newspaper editors who are the customers for the syndicate products.

# Chapter 12

## Photographic Communication

### THE VISUAL DIMENSION

Photographic communication has emerged dramatically in recent decades as a key mode of mass communication—a visual dimension, capable of providing a wealth of description and detail not communicable through the written or spoken word.

The art of telling a story with photographs—both still and motion pictures—developed centuries later than the technique of telling it with words. Photographic equipment was relatively slow to become available, and the men who worked with pictures needed time to develop the editorial methods of photographic narration. The rapid development of equipment in recent years, and in man's comprehension of how to use his sophisticated new tools, however, made photojournalism a fundamental mode of mass communication.

Photojournalism for newspapers and magazines developed rapidly during the 1930's. Film, first used in the motion picture theater to provide entertainment, news, and documentaries for mass audiences, became in the 1950's and 1960's a dominant ingredient of televised news, public affairs, documentary, and advertising communication. *Photojournalism* thus has expanded in concept and function and today is part of the larger field known as *photographic communication.*

To have full knowledge of the communication process, the student needs to understand the functions performed by pictures, how photography developed, and the essentials of technique used by professional photographers and editors. This chapter discusses those topics, as well as the opportunities and working conditions for visual communicators.

Less than 150 years elapsed from the moment when a man first produced a photographic image until a fascinated world watched astronauts Neil Armstrong and Edwin Aldrin transmit a live television picture from the surface of the moon. In that century and a half the growth of photography as a medium of communication has been spectacular, especially when we realize that most of the progress has been made in the last 50 years.

## HOW PHOTOGRAPHY DEVELOPED

**Pioneering photography.**    Joseph Nicéphone Nièpce, a retired French lithographer, began searching for a method to capture the photographic image in 1813. Three years later he is believed to have succeeded in producing a negative image, but he could only partially fix the image after exposure—that is, desensitize it to light. In 1826 he made a photograph on a pewter plate showing a view from his workroom window. He called this process Heliographie (sun drawing).

Photography took a significant step forward with creation of the Daguerreotype by another Frenchman, Louis Jacques Mandé Daguerre, in 1839. In this process an invisible (latent) image was developed by using mercury vapor. The exposure time was reduced from eight hours to 30 minutes, giving photography a practical application. The Daguerreotype process had three great limitations: (1) the image could be only the size of the plate in the camera; (2) the image was unique in itself and could be duplicated only by reshooting; and (3) the image was a *negative*, coated on a mirrored metallic surface, so a viewer could see it as a *positive* only if the mirror reflected a dark background.

**Wet plates for the Civil War.**    The third important approach to photography was the collodion wet plate process, developed in 1851 by Frederick Scott Archer, an English sculptor. The collodion process required the coating of a glass plate with a light-sensitive solution which had to be kept wet until exposed in the camera and processed in a darkroom. Very sharp paper prints could be made from a collodion negative. A photographer could use this process outdoors to record exposures of only 10 seconds to a minute, a spectacular improvement in photographic speed. He was required, however, to work from a portable darkroom on location.

It was with this wet plate process, so clumsy by modern standards, that Mathew Brady produced his magnificent photographs of the Civil

War. A successful portrait photographer, Brady asked President Lincoln for permission to document the conflict. He sent out 20 teams of photographers, headed by Timothy O'Sullivan and Alexander Gardner, who followed the Union soldiers onto the battlefields and into their bivouacs. Brady's photographs have preserved for posterity a fascinating record of the war. For the first time, photography proved its value as a news medium.

**The flexible film.**    The next leap forward, opening the door for modern photography, came in 1889 when the Eastman Kodak Company, headed by George Eastman, introduced a transparent film on a flexible support. Creation of this film made the motion picture possible. It increased the picture-taking possibilities for still photographers, too; they could use smaller, less obtrusive cameras and no longer were burdened with heavy glass plates.

In 1912 the famous Speed Graphic press camera, which was to become the "workhorse" for news photographers for a half-century, was introduced. The small camera came into use in America in the 1920's. Ernst Leitz's Leica, a German camera using 35 mm film, was followed by another German make, the Rolleiflex, a larger 2¼ x 2¼ camera. Both remain popular in professional circles today.

The small camera freed the photographer from carrying bulky film or plate holders. It enabled him to operate less obtrusively, to take 36 pictures in rapid succession, and to use the fast lens to take pictures without flash in low-level lighting situations. The pictures thus were less formal, more candid, and honest. A German lawyer, Dr. Erich Salomon, who declared himself to be the first photojournalist, began using such a camera in 1928 as a photographer of European nobility. Two other Europeans who influenced the development of photojournalism were Stefan Lorant, who edited German and English illustrateds, and Alfred Eisenstaedt, a West Prussian, who moved from the Berlin office of the Associated Press to become one of *Life* magazine's first photographers.

Color photography became a commercial reality when the Eastman Kodak Company announced development of its Kodachrome color film in 1935. In the same year the first motion picture in Technicolor, a high fidelity color process, was presented on the American screen.

Two more fundamental breakthroughs in photographic equipment followed World War II. In 1947 Edwin H. Land introduced the Polaroid system for producing a positive black and white print 60 seconds after exposure. Soon this time was reduced to 10 seconds. Then in 1963 a 50-second Polaroid color print process opened new avenues for amateurs and professionals alike. The second of these breakthroughs came in the mid-1950's: the recording of moving pictures on magnetic video tape. This was an electronic approach; all the other advances in the photographic process had depended on chemistry.

**Photographs appear in newspapers.**   From a mass communication viewpoint, taking good photographs was not enough: a way had to be found to reproduce them in newspapers and magazines. Woodcuts had been used in the Civil War period, but they were slow to produce, expensive, and not exact. A direct photographic method was needed.

This was achieved by two men working separately, each of whom developed a halftone photoengraving technique. Frederic Eugene Ives published a halftone engraving in his laboratory at Cornell University in June, 1879, and Stephen Horgan published a photograph "direct from nature" in the New York *Daily Graphic* in March, 1880. Several years passed, however, before such photographs came into frequent use in newspapers; by the middle of the 1890's halftone engravings were appearing in supplemental inserts of the New York newspapers, and in 1897 the New York *Tribune* was the first to publish a halftone in the regular pages of a high-speed press run.

During the early years of the Twentieth Century, pictures in newspapers generally were used singly, to illustrate important stories. The newspaper picture page was developed during World War I, making use of special layouts and unusual picture shapes.

A major new force in American journalism, the picture tabloid, came into being shortly after World War I. In these newspapers with their small-page size and flashy makeup, designed to appeal to street sale readers, the photograph was given the dominant position, often overshadowing the text of the news stories. The tabloid front page usually consisted of a headline and a dramatically blown-up news photo.

The New York *Daily News* began publication in 1919, followed by Hearst's *Daily Mirror* and the *Evening Graphic*. Intense picture competition among these three New York tabloids led at times to the publication of photographs which violated the sense of good taste held by many people. The *Evening Graphic* illustrated major stories with faked composograph photos, and the *Daily News* shocked readers by printing a full-page photograph of the electrocution of Ruth Snyder, a murderess.

Of these three original New York tabloids, only the *Daily News* survives, still sharply edited but less flamboyant and less a "picture" paper than in its earlier days.

During the 1920's, when the picture newspapers were flourishing, experiments were carried out in transmission of a photographic image by wire and by radio. The first U.S. photos sent by wire were transmitted from Cleveland to New York in 1924. A decade of development passed before the Associated Press established its Wirephoto network on January 1, 1935. Distribution of news photos by wire enabled newspapers across the country to publish pictures from other cities only a few hours after they were taken.

**The picture magazines.** The expanded interest in all forms of photographic communication in the 1930's led Time Inc. to found the weekly picture magazine, *Life,* in November, 1936. *Life* was patterned after photographic publications developed in Germany and England. In 1937 the Cowles organization established *Look,* published every other week and more feature-oriented than *Life,* with less emphasis on news. *Look* ceased publication in 1971 and *Life* followed in 1972.

Both *Look* and *Life* emphasized editorial research and investigation preceding assignment of photographers to all but spot news stories. Photographers were well briefed as to the significance of a story before arriving on the scene to begin interpreting it with their cameras. In that sense photographers on the two magazines controlled a mind-guided camera. In its early years *Life* was even more stringent in controlling its photographers, suggesting to them before they left the office exactly how key pictures should be made. This practice diminished during World War II, which provided swiftly changing stories that did not fit an editor's preconceived plan.

From the mid-1930's into the 1950's a small group of well-known magazine photographers contributed to the development of the photographic essay and interpretative picture story. Dorothea Lange's sensitive images of America's depression conditions stand as examples of still photography at its finest. So also do photographs by Gordon Parks, whose creative abilities transcended the photographic medium to include writing, musical composition, and Hollywood film. Henri Cartier-Bresson, a French photojournalist, defined the "decisive moment" during this period, and Robert Capa showed how the still camera could record the reverberations of war. W. Eugene Smith and David Douglas Duncan were major contributors to *Life* during and after World War II. Smith's picture essays, including "Spanish Village," "Country Doctor," and "Nurse Midwife," stand as classics. David Duncan's word-and-picture reports of the Korean War have been matched only by his equally powerful Vietnam War magazine stories and picture books.

**Motion pictures emerge.**    Only two years after Eastman's development of flexible film, Thomas A. Edison developed the Kinetoscope in 1891, thereby laying the foundation for the motion picture. The Kinetoscope was a motion picture projector designed to show still pictures in rapid succession to produce the visual illusion of motion on a screen in a darkened room.

The Lumiere brothers presented the first public performance of a motion picture for pay in the Grand Cafe of Paris in 1895. Edison made jerky, primitive motion pictures of President William McKinley's inauguration in 1896, Admiral Dewey at Manila in 1898, and McKinley's speech in Buffalo, N.Y., shortly before his assassination in 1901. William Randolph Hearst personally took motion pictures of action in Cuba during the Spanish-American War. These early efforts showed the motion picture's potential as a recorder of history. Exhibition of commercial motion picture films began with regularity about 1900.

Edison's pioneer efforts at recording news events on film led within a few years to creation of the newsreel, a staple short item on virtually every motion picture theater program for half a century until the faster news coverage of television drove the last newsreel out of business during the 1960's. The first regular newsreel series is credited to the Pathé *Journal* of 1907. Among the familiar newsreel names in American theaters were Pathé, Fox Movietone News, Metrotone, and International Newsreel.

The documentary film, a more elaborate method of recording the lives and activities of real people, had its start in 1922. Hired by a New York fur company to film the life of an Eskimo family, Robert Flaherty overcame great technological difficulties in the Arctic climate to produce *Nanook of the North*. From this film developed the documentary tradition that has given film making some of its finest products.

During the depression years Pare Lorentz produced the film, *The Plow That Broke the Plains*, for the Farm Security Administration in the same spirit of the FSA team of photo documentarians who, under the guidance of Roy E. Stryker, made more than 272,000 negatives and 150,000 prints of the United States and its dustbowls and migratory workers. Lorentz's film, *The River*, in 1937 visualized the problems of erosion in the Mississippi River basin with more filmic power than his previous documentary.

A third form of factual storytelling on film, halfway between the newsreel and documentary, was the *March of Time*, a weekly news magazine of the screen. Started by Time Inc. in 1935, it played for 16 years. At its peak in the late 1930's and the early years of World War II it was seen by audiences of nearly 20,000,000 a week in more than 9000 American theaters. Louis de Rochemont, the producer, used real events and actors, skillfully blended, to present an interpretative account of an event in relation to its background.

When television became a commercial force in the late 1940's, the tools and techniques developed by the motion picture industry were adopted for presenting news on television. A motion picture camera was relatively small and portable, and film shot at news events could be shown on the television screen. Until remote telecasting became technically practical, visual presentation of on-the-spot news had to be done with motion picture film and, later, with magnetic tape.

The television documentary became an established part of the networks' programing. Some outstanding examples of the 1960's were CBS' "Hunger in America," done in the tradition of Edward R. Murrow's earlier documentary, "Harvest of Shame"; NBC's documentary on chemical and biological warfare, a part of its "First Tuesday" series, and "The Battle of Newburgh," shown on the NBC "White Paper" series; and a religious documentary, "A Time for Burning," aired over many educational stations.

## PRINCIPLES OF PHOTOGRAPHY

A photograph reproduced in a newspaper, magazine, or book is a two-dimensional representation of a subject that originally had four dimensions: length, width, depth, and existence and perhaps movement through time. Moreover, the printed image in almost every instance differs in size from its original model. Frequently it is a black-and-white representation of a subject with many colorful hues. The photographic communicator must master the technique of condensing these dimensions and conditions into a space having only length and width.

Photography is capable of high fidelity reproduction of very fine details and textures. A skillfully made photograph can communicate the essence of tactile experience. It can be controlled to represent a subject in various perspectives, determined by the photographer as he selects a particular lens and the camera-subject relationship for his picture. Black and white photographs provide the photographer almost unlimited control in representing the original subject in shades of gray and the extremes, black and white. Thus the photographer's technical skill and mental attitude influence the picture he takes. Two cameramen photographing the same subject may produce widely dissimilar pictures.

Since photography relies upon a lens to form a clear, sharp image and a shutter to control the length of time during which light strikes the sensitive film, two additional visual qualities are unique in photographic communciation. As the lens aperture is opened or closed to allow varying amounts of light to strike the film, a change occurs in the "depth-of-field," that is, the area in front of and behind the picture's subject that appears in sharp focus. The photographer may render only the subject sharp, with details in foreground and background blurred to reduce their importance. Or, by controlling the aperture size of the lens, he may render an entire scene in sharp focus, from the nearest to the farthest object shown.

By selecting a shutter speed for a picture, the photographer begins control over the fourth dimension, time. He may use a long exposure, in which case a moving subject might blur in the finished photograph, or a very short exposure time to freeze a moving subject at a precise instant. Having determined a shutter speed for the effect he desires, he must exercise an important selective act by deciding which moment to capture out of the millions available. The French photojournalist, Henri Cartier-Bresson, refers to this act as determining the *decisive moment.*

**Still pictures.**    Photographic communication for the printed page may be in the form of a single picture, a series, a sequence, or a picture story. The series of pictures can be distinguished from the sequence by noting that the series is generally photographed from more than one viewpoint and has been made over a relatively long period of time. The sequence is a group of pictures made from the same viewpoint and generally covering a very short period of time, such as a group of pictures on the sports page on a Sunday morning newspaper showing stages of a sensational touchdown run. Most picture magazines today present picture *series* rather than picture *stories;* the latter are the most complex form of photographic communication in the print media, requiring logical visual continuity built upon a well-researched idea. Excellent examples of the picture story include W. Eugene Smith's "Spanish Village" and David Duncan's "This Is War," both published in *Life* during the 1950's. In book form, Edward Steichen's *The Family of Man* has been widely acclaimed as a photo essay.

In attempting to recreate the essence of an event, the photographic communicator feels the need to couple his pictures with some sort of "sound track." He uses the written word in the form of captions, headlines, and overlines. When a viewer looks at a picture and reads its word accompaniment, his eye serves two sense functions. While he studies the image, it functions as a normal eye; when he begins reading words, his eye functions as an ear, picking up the sound track. This reading and seeing occur through time, thus further developing the fourth dimension in a two-dimensional photograph.

Wilson Hicks, for many years executive editor of *Life,* contributed in the introductory chapter of *Photographic Communication* a definition of the photojournalistic form. In its simplest unit it is a blend of words plus one picture. Words add information which the picture cannot give, and the picture contributes a dimension the words cannot. When the two have been blended, there emerges a greater meaning for the reader than he could receive from either words or picture separately. Hicks suggests that this blend develops a communicative overtone.

**Moving pictures.** While the characteristics of the still photograph apply to motion picture film and television magnetic tape, both of which are sequences of still pictures, there are important distinctions about the moving picture as a medium. Films and video tape reproduce natural movement and sound, two elements extremely difficult to communicate in still photography. The moving picture communicator in addition has as his most important tool his creative control over the fourth dimension, time.

An audience viewing a message on film or tape is captive to the communicator in terms of pace, emphasis, and rhythm. A reader can spend as much or as little time as he chooses in studying a picture, and he can do it whenever he desires, returning later for another look if he wishes. When he is a member of an audience in a motion picture theater or in front of a television screen, he does not have these options.

The producer of film and video tape is concerned with the continuity, the sequence of images. He knows how to use the "establishment" shot at the beginning of a particular scene and medium shots and closeups to continue the action, adding variety and emphasis. During the shooting and editing of film or tape, photographer and editor concern themselves with such visual techniques as screen direction, cutaways, cover material, reverse angles, and sound effectiveness. Film may be shot as silent footage, with a narrator adding description later in a studio, or it may be shot with natural lip-sync sound. Electronic video tape recording is used in place of film for some stories and advertisements on television. The first moon pictures sent back by Armstrong and Aldrin were an example of live presentation of moving pictures produced electronically without film or tape.

## FUNCTIONS OF PHOTOGRAPHERS AND EDITORS

Photographs are used just as are words, to inform, persuade, and entertain users of the mass media. Their effectiveness depends upon how well they are taken by the photographer and how well they are assembled for presentation to the audience by the editor. Each medium has its special problems of picture presentation that require special knowledge and experience in its field. Television is not radio with a picture of the announcer added; there is an important visual dimension. The still photograph is not "decoration," as it was in the newspaper and magazine early in this century. The development of candid photography with its quick, intimate glimpses of subjects off guard has given photojournalists exciting new possibilities by permitting them to avoid the stilted aspect so common in older pictures with slower cameras.

The daily newspaper photographer performs one of the fundamental tasks in photojournalism. On a typical day he receives three or four assignments, usually to happenings fairly close to his office. He likely will use a staff car, equipped with a two-way radio. His editor has given him a written assignment sheet describing the event and what he wants, and perhaps has discussed the job in detail. On many newspapers photographers use their own equipment, for which the publication pays a monthly depreciation allotment; on others, they use office-owned cameras.

Once at the scene, the photographer makes from 2 to 20 pictures, gathering names and important caption material. Upon his return to the office, the film will be processed, either by himself or by a laboratory man, and finished prints delivered to the editor. On most assignments, only one of the pictures he has taken will be published; in fact, frequently none of his pictures will be printed because of space limitations or the development of later, bigger news stories.

A photographer on a general magazine staff works on more elaborate projects than does the daily newspaper man, often requiring several weeks or even months to complete a single job. Assignments at times take him far from home. He is well briefed by researchers concerning the background of the story, and he receives large research folios for "homework." On a major assignment he will shoot from 1000 to 5000 images, sending them home to the editors in "takes"; they keep him posted on how his work has turned out. After all this effort, a dozen to a score of his pictures likely will appear in print.

*Life* had a staff of 15 photographers in the early 1970's, plus various contract and free-lance contributors. These men and women as a group were shooting nearly 1000 pictures a day—300,000 a year—for the magazine, which printed about 75 in each weekly issue. At *Look,* which had been published biweekly, about 150,000 photographs were shot each year by an eight-man staff.

The local television station news photographer works in a manner similar to that of his daily newspaper colleague. He has four to six assignments a day. He usually travels in a staff car, radio-equipped, and he carries both silent and sound 16 mm camera equipment. In addition, he may have an audio tape recorder to pick up background sound. As he works, he takes notes (spot sheets), including the names of those appearing in various scenes. The cameraman may work alone, with a reporter, or with a full crew to handle lighting and sound. After he returns to the station, his film is processed by a laboratory specialist while he may— or may not—write an accompanying script. Much depends upon the size of the station.

With so much more film being shot than can be used either in print or on the air, the role of the editor is essential. The editors of film and still pictures have three functions: to *procure* the pictures, by assigning staff photographers, buying material from free-lance men, and subscribing to syndicate services; to *select* the pictures to be used; and to *present* them in an effective manner.

Once the raw material has been obtained, the editor makes his selection from the entire "take" submitted. In the print media, he must crop and scale the pictures to emphasize their most interesting aspects and to work them into a layout. In television, the editor is concerned with juxtaposition effects from scene to scene and with time considerations. The presentation each editor puts together represents a blending of pictures and words, a designing of space and time.

## PHOTOJOURNALISM AS A CAREER

**Qualifications.** Stimulating opportunities await young men and women who decide to enter the photographic side of mass communications. The work at times is exciting, and always interesting; each day brings new assignments that give the photographer room for creative expression and the use of professional techniques.

Anyone contemplating such a career should be healthy and possessed of physical stamina, because the work can be dangerous on assignments such as fires and riots; and the hours frequently are irregular. The photographer must carry equipment that is cumbersome and, particularly in television news, often quite heavy. Both physical and emotional exhaustion can affect a photographer when he is involved in a long, difficult assignment.

The career photographic communicator also should have initiative, energy, and creative motivation. A degree of aggressiveness is necessary, but it should be tempered by thoughtfulness. Visual imagination is essential—the ability to see various interpretations of a subject in a given visual form. He should have an interest in design and the knack of examining pictures for their own special qualities. He must be curious about the world around him and have an ability to mix with people. Being able roughly to sketch scenes and individuals is an important asset, but by no means a requirement.

The photographic communicator should have a good general education. About one-fourth of his studies should be spent in learning how to relate his general knowledge to the discipline of photo communication. If he plans to work in the news and information function of the mass media, he should include courses in basic reporting, editing, law and history of the press, and graphic design and typography.

In his photography courses he must develop foundations in both the technical and visual dimensions of the medium. He should include courses in both still and motion photography, both black-and-white and color. Attention to the picture story, the documentary film, and advertising illustration is all-important. He should study the history of film and photography and also include courses in basic design.

Technical qualifications include an understanding of the photographic medium in terms of optics, lighting, color theory, and photographic processes, which include basic photo chemistry and physics. With the growing importance of electronics in nearly all areas of photographic communication, an understanding of electronic theory is desirable.

**Earnings.**   A college graduate with photographic skills will start on a daily newspaper at from $6000 to $8300 a year. An experienced newspaper photographer, with five years or more to his credit, may earn from $10,000 to $15,000 annually in large cities. The starting salary for a college graduate photographer on a local television station will vary from $5700 to $7800; after five years the range is $8000 to $12,000. A staff photographer for a general or specialized magazine can expect to earn $8000 to $15,000 in the early years of his career. His salary can rise rapidly, faster than in newspaper or television work. Top professionals on the *National Geographic* earn $15,000 to $50,000. Although his case is not typical, one talented B.A. degree holder in photojournalism earned more than $20,000 in his first year away from campus as a contract photographer for a national magazine.

Some photographers prefer to free-lance; that is, to work for themselves and sell their pictures to clients either directly or through picture agencies. The agencies take a commission of 25 to 35 percent of the selling price of the pictures. A free-lancer also may work on contract, under which a magazine guarantees him an agreed-upon earning in return for his guarantee to be available to it on call. A free-lancer usually begins as a staff photographer, then branches out on his own after he has established a reputation and a group of clients. Free-lance photographers can earn around $40,000 a year if very successful, although they start far lower in their early years. To be a successful free-lancer, a man must be a good businessman, knowing how to market pictures as well as take them. The American Society of Magazine Photographers sets minimum rates for its members. The rate in effect in the early 1970's was $150 per day plus expenses. Free-lancers charge $200 to

$250 a day in some cities, and occasionally up to $1000 to do a special one-day assignment.

Starting salaries for women in photographic communication are about the same as for men. However, feminine photographers find difficulty in becoming established professionally and need great perseverance. Among the renowned woman photographers who proved that it can be done are the late Margaret Bourke-White, one of *Life*'s first photographers in 1936; and the late Dickey Chapelle, who photographed the Vietnam conflict in its early stages.

Many women become successful free-lancers. In Miami a young woman accepts assignments from advertising agencies, public relations firms, regional publications, and, occasionally, a New York picture agency. Her travels take her across the Southeast and into Central and South America. While she is away, a telephone answering service accepts messages, relaying them to her daily. She stores her color film in a small ice box in her car and upon her return processes her film in a laboratory in her apartment.

**Case histories.**    Two additional examples will illustrate how the professional photographic structure functions, and how men may profit from skill and imagination. The first involves a free-lancer named Smitty, who lives in the West and is an enthusiastic amateur sailor. Through a contact established by a friend, Smitty was asked by a New York magazine editor to cover a sailing regatta in his area. The editor agreed to Smitty's charges of $150 a day plus expenses. This fee included delivery of contact proofs of his negatives. It was agreed that any enlargements and any color transparencies ordered by the magazine would be billed separately.

The magazine editor flew to the regatta and worked with Smitty for three days, indicating his needs but never interrupting the photographer while he was working. Eventually the story was published with a selection of Smitty's pictures and a cover color photograph.

He had sold the magazine only "first rights." This means that the magazine could be the first to use any pictures he shot on the assignment, but he retained the right to sell any of these pictures later to other publications.

Within a month after publication Smitty received requests from other publishers to use pictures from that story: from an American publisher regarding a book on sailing, from an English sailing magazine, and from a participant in the race who wanted to buy pictures of his boat. Six years after the regatta, Smitty still was selling pictures he had made on the occasion. The most recent sale was to another American sailing magazine, for use with a profile on the builder of boats which had raced there.

The second case concerns a staff photographer, named Stuart, with a Minneapolis television station. After routine outside assignments such as fires and accidents, he was given the opportunity to work inside, editing film for the evening news program on weekends. This work, however, did not satisfy Stuart's creative urge; he wanted to produce something more elaborate. He conceived the idea of producing a half-hour documentary film on the world of a four-year-old child. When approached on this idea, the news director said the station would provide film and processing, but would not give Stuart released time from his work or extra assistance to do the show.

For a year Stuart filmed his four-year-old son, including such events as the child's fourth birthday, bringing a baby brother home from the hospital, Christmas, visiting the zoo, entering preschool classes, and finally his fifth birthday. The photographer exposed nearly 10,000 feet of 16 mm color film, which was edited down to about 900 feet for a 30-minute show. This was a 10:1 ratio of film shot to film aired. While this might seem extravagant, a national network averages better than a 15:1 ratio. As a musical background, two friends played a specially composed theme for flute, helping to give the program continuity.

A local bank and a public utility company bought air time to televise Stuart's documentary during the Christmas season. The bank also purchased a copy of the film for promotion purposes. Later the film won a top national award for a locally produced documentary. The photographer's idea and diligence paid off splendidly in creative satisfaction, profit, and professional recognition.

These examples indicate the expanding need for versatile men and women with special training in photographic communication. Widening opportunities in the mass media and in related fields in government, business, and education make the future bright for those who know how to interpret life through the camera's lens.

# Chapter 13

# *The Film*

## THE ROLE OF MOTION PICTURES

"It is imperative that we invent a new world language . . . that we invent a nonverbal international picture-language. . . ." So writes Stan VanDerBeek, painter and experimental film maker. As corollary activities, VanDerBeek proposes using present audiovisual devices in the service of such a language, developing new image-making instruments to find the best combination of machines for nonverbal interchange, and establishing prototype theaters called Movie-Dromes to house these presentations—described as "Movie Murals," "Ethos-Cinema," "Newsreel of Dreams," and "Image Libraries."

While VanDerBeek's method is radical, the principle underlying his approach is as old as the motion picture itself. Early in the history of film, its practitioners and advocates recognized that the motion picture was truly an international language. And, while the "image-flow" described by VanDerBeek is as yet imperfectly realized, the desire for "peace and harmony . . . the interlocking of good wills on an international exchange basis . . . the interchange of images and ideas . . ." is as old as tribal man. Although, on the surface, VanDerBeek's "A Proposal and Manifesto" is naïve and idealistic, on a smaller, infinitely more conventional scale, the language of motion pictures *is* helping to bridge the gap among the people of different nations.

As motion picture critic Stanley Kauffmann observes, "Film is the only art besides music that is available to the whole world at once, exactly as it was first made." And film, like opera, can be enjoyed despite the viewer's ignorance of the language employed in the dialogue or narration. Kauffmann contends, "The point is not the spreading of information or amity, as in USIA or UNESCO films, useful though they may be. The point is emotional relationship and debt." To understand this observation, consider the Russian entertainment film *The Cranes are Flying* (1957), a romantic drama of life and death, of love and loss, set in the years 1941–1945 and played by Russian actors against a Russian background. If one empathizes with the young lovers, sharing their anguish at war and separation and their desire for peace and reunion, the viewer has been drawn into an emotional relationship with the characters that makes it impossible for him to view all Russians as unfeeling puppets solely committed in thought and deed to advancing the Communist state.

Although the advent of sound tended to nationalize film and reduce film's claim to being an international art as in the days of the silent movie, the current popularity of foreign films in America and the even more widespread distribution of American films in foreign markets demonstrate the primary role played by a film's visual elements, and the lesser importance of language as a communications device. In fact, when a motion picture is subtitled for distribution in a foreign market, the subtitles convey little more than one-third of the dialogue. Yet the meaning of the film is seldom, if ever, impaired, and its beauty is often enhanced.

The USIA film, *Years of Lightning, Day of Drums* (1964), illustrates the lesser role played by verbal language in motion pictures, even in a nontheatrical film. Approximately 40 percent of the film uses neither dialogue nor narration. Designed as a tribute to John F. Kennedy and as a vehicle to bolster confidence that the work Kennedy had begun would continue after his death, the film presents the six facets of the New Frontier, interlacing such programs as the Alliance for Progress, Civil Rights, and the Peace Corps, with sequences depicting the funeral. These funeral sequences are largely wordless, with the sound track carrying natural sound: the heavy footsteps of the marchers, the more staccato hoofbeats of the horses, and the steady, muffled drumbeat. Yet no words are necessary during these sequences. Death and bereavement are not uniquely American experiences. While the styles of burial and mourning may vary from country to country, the loss occasioned by death is a constant. Similarly, the scenes depicting the parades and enthusiastic crowds that greeted Kennedy on his international speaking tours need little narration—save the words spoken by Kennedy himself. The human face is the human face; close-ups of Kennedy's face, or of a nameless Filipino's or Costa Rican's, demand no verbal interpretation. Assembled from stock footage, *Years of Lightning, Day of Drums,* by sharing Kennedy's death with the foreign viewer, shares his political achievement and America's aspirations.

A note of warning: film is probably the most powerful propaganda medium man has yet devised. As a consequence, its potential for aiding or injuring civilization is enormous. In addition to supplying a verbal message through dialogue, narration, or subtitles, the film provides an instantaneous, accompanying visual message—supplying the viewer with a picture to bulwark what he has learned through language. Thus, his imagination need not conjure a mental image to accompany what words have told him; he leaves the theater complete with a concept and its substantiation. If a picture is worth 1000 words, a picture together with three or four carefully chosen words is worth 10,000 words. Makers of television commercials know this; so does anyone who has ever thought carefully about this compelling and utterly contemporary medium of communication.

In the past, American motion pictures have been associated with Hollywood. Persons desiring careers in the film industry saw and followed one road—and that road led to the golden West. But the situation has changed today. There are many roads leading to important and satisfying work in films–and not all end in Hollywood, as this chapter will reveal.

### THE ENTERTAINMENT FILM

**Hollywood: 1945–1965.** The late 1940's were boom years for Hollywood. At the close of 1946, box office revenues from United States movie theaters totaled a record $1,692,000,000—compared with $1,-187,000,000 in 1953, and $904,000,000 in 1963. During 1949, more than 90,000,000 tickets were sold weekly in American movie houses—as compared with 45,000,000 paid admissions each week in 1956, and 21,000,000 in 1968. Again during 1949, the major studios—among them Metro-Goldwyn-Mayer, Twentieth Century Fox, Columbia Pictures, RKO, and Warner Brothers—released 411 new motion pictures—as compared with 296 released in 1954, 235 in 1959, and 203 in 1963. Administered by the men who had established them, the major companies offered such escapist films as the horror-thriller *The Beast with Five Fingers* (1946) and the slick romantic comedy *June Bride* (1948) along with such provocative and candid films as *The Best Years of Our Lives* (1946) and *Crossfire* (1947) to a receptive and apparently uncritical American audience.

But then several events occurred which caused the near collapse of the Hollywood movie empire. First, television rocketed into prominence —quickly replacing the motion picture as a medium of mass entertainment. Successful prime-time network television series attract between 30,000,000 and 50,000,000 viewers—a number roughly double that of movie tickets sold weekly in 1968. And second, as a consequence of action taken by the federal government in the early 1950's, the major companies were forced to sell their chains of movie theaters—thus denying the studios an automatic outlet for their products regardless of intrinsic merit. In noisy desperation, Hollywood turned to the wide screen, undertook longer and more expensive film productions with star-studded casts, made use of more "adult" subject matter, advocated increases in ticket prices, started to produce 30- and 60-minute filmed series for television, and began selling already exhibited movies to the television industry. Between 1955 and 1958, Hollywood sold almost 9000 pre-1948 feature films to television, and by 1960 the major studios were vying with each other for sale of films produced since 1948.

The first of these retaliatory measures, the wide screen, has been called the most significant innovation in film technology since the advent of sound. Until the appearance of the first wide-screen motion picture, *The Robe* (a $5,000,000 Cinemascope film produced and distributed by Twentieth Century Fox in 1953), the standard screen shape had been a rectangle 20 feet wide and 15 feet high; this represents a ratio of 4 to 3, or 1.33:1—a proportion determined by the width of the film and going back to Thomas Edison and the Kinetoscope. The new wide screen changed the ratio to anything from 2.62:1 to 1.66:1, with Cinemascope settling at 2.55:1. Regardless of trade name and varying dimensions, however, most new screens are at least twice as wide as they are high.

Initial critical reactions to the wide screen were mixed, with some film makers insisting that the new screen size signaled the end of the close-up and rendered established directorial and cutting techniques ineffective. In time, however, the advantages and possibilities of the wide screen became apparent to film makers who have used its inclusiveness to achieve a naturalness and spontaneity, and its new dimensions to experiment with new kinds of visual compositions and new uses of the close-up.

In response to the wide screen and as a further effort to bring the American public back into the movie theaters, Hollywood began to produce longer and more expensive movies with casts of thousands and an abundance of well-known stars. Often, best-selling novels or successful dramas that called for copious action and spectacle provided the "story" for these productions—as in *The Ten Commandments* (1956), *Raintree County* (1957), *El Cid* (1961), and *Cleopatra* (1963).

During these years, the already complex machinery needed to produce a Hollywood picture was becoming even more complex, with producers, directors, writers, actors, cameramen, editors, stunt men, script consultants, script girls, costumers, set designers, wardrobe assistants, prop men, lighting technicians, makeup artists, carpenters, actors' agents, painters, publicists, and gossip columnists composing the Hollywood scene. Overseeing the vast collective enterprise that movie making had become were the studio presidents and executive producers—men like Jesse L. Lasky, David O. Selznick, Samuel Goldwyn, and Darryl Zanuck, who exercised ultimate authority over script, stars, and budget.

The collaboration and expense involved in a typical Hollywood film are revealed in the following example. A major Hollywood studio made a film which included a scene in a newspaper office. This consisted merely of an office boy tearing a bulletin off a press association teleprinter and rushing across the city room to hand it to the managing editor. The action required less than a minute on the screen and filled barely a page in the shooting script.

For authenticity, the film producers arranged to shoot this brief scene in the city room of a Los Angeles metropolitan newspaper, after the last afternoon edition. Technicians and stage hands brought in lights, sound equipment, and cameras. Lighting experts put masking tape over all shiny articles in the city room to reduce the glare. Desks were moved to make an easier path for the actor playing the office boy role. Clerical assistants, supervisors, and actors arrived. By the time the little episode had been shot, nearly 100 persons had been involved and several hours consumed.

This kind of procedure has made Hollywood films expensive to produce but technically expert. One reason for the huge overhead is the high degree of unionization among motion picture personnel. Few industries are so intensively organized; rigid limitations are enforced upon the duties each worker can perform and the kinds of physical properties he may touch.

A recent breakdown of the average production budget for a Hollywood movie indicates the large percentage consumed by sets and other physical properties, as well as studio overhead:

| | |
|---|---|
| Story costs | 5% |
| Production and direction costs | 5% |
| Sets and other physical properties | 35% |
| Stars and cast | 20% |
| Studio overhead | 20% |
| Income taxes | 5% |
| Net profit after taxes | 10% |

As a final measure, Hollywood sought to dramatize subject matter once denied film treatment as a result of the Production Code. In 1956, revisions in the code permitted depiction of drug addiction, kidnapping, prostitution, and abortion. Soon, movies treating narcotics addiction, like *Monkey on My Back* (1957) and *The Pusher* (1959), and films involving prostitution, like *Butterfield 8* (1960) and *Girl of the Night* (1960), were released bearing the Motion Picture Seal of Approval. Although the new freedom of subject matter resulted in the creation of a few artistic successes, Hollywood quickly managed to create new clichés from the once-forbidden subject matter at its disposal—proving once again that mere sensationalism is as empty as the most bland "family-type" situation comedy.

Not even the inclusion of such stars as Elizabeth Taylor, Doris Day, Cary Grant, Rock Hudson, Burt Lancaster, and Marlon Brando could remedy the decline in movie attendance. And gradually, Hollywood became aware that the casting of a star meant little in terms of the commercial success of its movies. Further, although selling old movies to television and producing filmed television series were profitable and aided Hollywood's faltering economy, such measures did not strike at the core of what was plaguing Hollywood.

Something was happening to the American movie-going public. It was changing, and although Hollywood was changing too, the movies and their audiences were moving in unrelated directions. What were these changes? It is true that the movie-going public was watching 15 or more hours of television a week. But what other reasons account for the decline of Hollywood in the mid-1950's and early 1960's? The increased popularity of foreign films, the rise of the American experimental film maker, different methods of distribution, and the growth of a visually more sophisticated audience—all these are partial reasons. In its own way, each has contributed to the decline of Hollywood and, paradoxically, to its reemergence in the mid-1960's as a vital force in film production.

## THE FOREIGN FILM

**Italy.** If Hollywood chose to ignore, by and large, the realities of the post-World-War-II world, that was not true of Italian film makers. Responding to the grim reality of a war-torn, impoverished Italy, Roberto Rossellini directed *Open City* (1945)—the first important film shot in a style quickly dubbed by the critics as neorealism. Combining stock newsreel footage with his own film (shot chiefly on the streets of Rome and scratched to resemble newsreels), Rossellini depicted the hardships endured by Italians during the Nazi occupation and their courageous resistance. To heighten the authenticity gained by actual locations and natural lighting, he used only a handful of professional actors whom he encouraged to ad lib, and chose ordinary Roman citizens as supporting players. While none of these techniques in isolation was new, none had been used so successfully together before; and *Open City* became, as the film historian Arthur Knight has said, "the key film in the entire neorealist Italian revival."

Equally as personal and visually intense, and equally as concerned with social realism, are two early films by Vittorio De Sica. In *Shoeshine* (1946), De Sica portrays the lives of a group of homeless Roman boys involved in the corrupt underworld of the Italian black market. *Bicycle Thief* (1947) treats the relationship between a father (played by a factory mechanic) and his son (played by a Roman newsboy) who together try to beat the apparently insurmountable odds occasioned by unemployment, poverty, and corruption.

Other directors central to this movement are Luigi Zampa (*To Live in Peace,* 1946; *Angelina,* 1947), Giuseppe De Santis (*The Tragic Hunt,* 1947), and Alberto Lattuada (*Without Pity,* 1947). Within a five year span, neorealism began to die out, its force vitiated by postwar recovery and renewed prosperity.

In recent years, amid a rash of conventional and often sensational films, the work of two masterful directors has emerged. Described as "second generation realists," Federico Fellini (*La Dolce Vita,* 1960; *8½,* 1962; *Juliet of the Spirits,* 1965) and Michelangelo Antonioni (*L'Avventura,* 1959; *La Notte,* 1960; *The Red Desert,* 1964; *Blow-Up,* 1966) have little in common except a compulsion to use the surfaces, rituals, and hidden recesses of contemporary existence as theme and subject matter, and a proven ability to use improvisation as an effective cinematic technique.

**France.**   Suffering from lack of funds and the shifting patronage of the French government, French film makers in the late 1940's and early 1950's were engaged in the production of drab imitation of American gangster films; sensational melodramas; *film noir* (the film of despair, represented by such works as Clouzot's *Manon,* 1949; Clement's *Les Jeux Interdits,* 1952); films based on successful or distinguished fiction (*Symphonie Pastorale,* 1946; *Devil in the Flesh,* 1947; *L'Idiot,* 1947); films embodying existential doctrine (*Les Jeux Sont Faits,* 1947; Cocteau's *Orphée,* 1950); films exploiting sex (initiated by Roger Vadim's *And God Created Women,* 1956); and a few individualistic works, such as the comedies of Jacques Tati (*M. Hulot's Holiday,* 1953; and *Mon Oncle,* 1958) and Robert Bresson's *Les Dames du Bois de Boulogne* (1944), and *Journal d'un Curé de Campagne* (1951).

But then, in 1958–59, the "Nouvelle Vague" erupted on the French film scene, with Francois Truffaut's *Les Quatre Cents Coups* and Alain Resnais' *Hiroshima Mon Amour* winning awards at the 1959 Cannes Film Festival. Other films which heralded the New Wave are Claude Chabrol's *Le Beau Serge* (1958), Louis Malle's *Les Amants* (1958), and Jean-Luc Godard's *Breathless* (1959). Although heterogeneous and resistant of labels in the manner of all creative artists, these New Wave directors do share many cinematic ideals as well as an outlet for these ideals in the influential film journal *Cahiers du Cinema.* Truffaut, Godard, and Chabrol had been film critics in the early 1950's, and they continued to write interestingly of the cinema. Describing his own procedures, Truffaut has said,

> I start with a very imperfect script, in which there are certain elements that please and stimulate me. Characters that strike some chord of response in me. A theme that lets me "talk about" something I want to film. As I work I find I am eliminating all the scenes of story transition and explanation. So it can happen that when the film is done, it is completely different from what it was proposed to say in the first place. The shooting of the film is that sort of adventure.

In *Breathless,* Godard took his camera onto the Paris streets. Using a hand-held Arriflex and a three-page script outline by Truffaut, Godard allowed the camera to follow the actions and reactions of Michel (a small-time gangster, played by Jean-Paul Belmondo) and his American girl friend (played by Jean Seberg), depicting a life devoid of logic or purpose.

Although the New Wave has dissipated itself (by 1964, Cannes was denigrating the very movement it had applauded five years earlier), these films and their directors have made great and irrevocable contributions to cinema art—in particular, in the imaginative and "free" camera work that characterizes New Wave films, in the encouragement of a liberated acting style dependent on improvisation and self-portraiture rather than on self-conscious or stagey performance, on the fanciful use of silent film techniques, on the absence of conventional plotting and continuity, and on a moving away from a cinema grounded in literature and drama to one that uses the strengths of the film medium to make its own powerful, highly cinematic statements.

**England.**    Films like *Blue Scar* (1948) and *The Brave Don't Cry* (1952), both depicting the life of coal miners; *Chance of a Lifetime* (1950), set in a small Gloucestershire factory; and such short films as Lindsay Anderson's *Every Day Except Christmas* (1957), concerning workers at Covent Garden, and Karel Reisz's *We Are the Lambeth Boys* (1958), in which a boys' club in London furnishes the principal locale, prefigure the realism of British theatrical films in the late 1950's.

*Room at the Top* (1958) was the first in a remarkable series of outspoken realistic films to gain widespread critical attention. Soon, motion pictures like *Saturday Night and Sunday Morning* (1960), *A Taste of Honey* (1961), *The Loneliness of the Long-Distance Runner* (1962),

*A Kind of Loving* (1962), *Billy Liar* (1963), *Morgan* (1966), *The Leather Boys* (1963), and *This Sporting Life* (1962) had established the reputation of their directors—Karel Reisz, Tony Richardson, John Schlesinger, Sidney Furie, Lindsay Anderson—and the significance of the British feature film. Describing their work as "free cinema," these directors brought to the screen a penetrating social realism focused on the English working class, preparing the way for the Beatles (who, themselves, are featured in Richard Lester's *A Hard Day's Night,* 1964; and *Help!,* 1965) and the ascendancy of Liverpool over Pall Mall.

**Other Countries.**   In Soviet Russia, film production is not only nationalized but the work of individual studios like Lenfilm, in Leningrad, and Mosfilm, in Moscow, is closely supervised by a specially designated state committee. Not unexpectedly, therefore, many Soviet feature films have either implicit or explicit social messages, like the strongly chauvinistic *The Turbulent Years* (1960). But there are also those films which focus on personal crises and solutions rather than on social problems. Among such are the previously mentioned *The Cranes are Flying* (1957), *Clear Sky,* (1961), *I'm Twenty* (1965), and such adaptations of literary classics as Sergei Youtkevich's *Othello* (1955) and Grigori Kozintsev's *Don Quixote* (1957) and *Hamlet* (1963).

Although the Polish film industry is also nationalized, Polish film makers have produced a sizable body of sensitive and cinematically expert films. Many, like *The Last Stage* (1948) and *Five Boys of Barska Street* (1954), depict Poland's immediate past (World War II, the Nazi occupation, concentration camps, and the politically troubled postwar years) with a frank and searching realism. Andrzej Wajda's *Ashes and Diamonds* (1958) provides a good example. Set in the late 1940's, the film depicts as its hero a basically apolitical young man who, acting upon orders from a right-wing political group, kills a Communist leader and is killed, in turn, by agents of the state.

A later film by Wajda, *Innocent Sorcerers* (1960), eschews any overt political concern, depicting the aimless, amoral, unsentimental existence of worldly and bored Warsaw young people, and shows the influence of the "New Wave" in both subject matter and treatment. Other important Polish directors are Roman Polanski (*Knife in the Water,* 1962), Andrzej Munk (*Eroica,* 1957), Jerzy Kawalerowicz (*Mother Joan of the Angels,* 1961), and Kazimierz Kutz (*A Pearl in the Crown,* 1972).

Although, as in Poland, the Czechoslovakian film industry is nationalized, a young group of Czech film makers has been producing some significant movies since the early 1960's—like Jan Nemac's *Diamonds of the Night* (1964) and Milos Forman's *Peter and Pavla* (1964) and *The Loves of a Blonde* (1965). But when Soviet intervention put an end to the increasing liberalization of the Czech government in 1968, the much-heralded "new Czechoslovak film" also died. Directors like Forman, Kadar, Barabas, and Taborsky no longer work in Czechoslovakia.

In Sweden, recent film making has been dominated by Ingmar Bergman, who uses film to explore such abstract and eternal problems as the meaning of life and death (*The Seventh Seal,* 1956), the nature of truth (*The Magician,* 1958), and man's tragic inability to communicate (*The Silence,* 1963).

The Japanese film has become best known to American audiences through the work of Akira Kurasawa. Like Bergman, Kurasawa depicts elemental problems and passions—using highly stylized, historical settings to underscore the timelessness of his themes. *Rashomon* (which won the Grand Prize at the Venice Film Festival in 1951) concerns the nature of truth, while *Throne of Blood* (1957), like *Macbeth* after which it is patterned, depicts the breaking down of morality through greed. But Japan has not neglected contemporary settings and subjects, as Kurasawa's *Drunken Angel* (1948), Imai's *Stained Image* (1953), and Toyoda's *Wheat Whistle* (1955) attest.

**American Experimental Film Makers.** While Hollywood in the 1940's and 1950's persevered in its chosen course, determinedly oblivious to innovations in European film making, a segment of the American movie-going public was well aware of their importance. Excited by the new techniques and possibilities for film, dismayed at the impersonality and inanity of most Hollywood movies, and aware that film is as much an art form as the novel, dance, or painting, numerous young Americans turned to film to give shape to their feelings and ideas, as their predecessors (and many of their contemporaries) had chosen the more conventional vehicles of drama, fiction, poetry, painting, or sculpture.

Much of the credit for publicizing and organizing the work and esthetic doctrines of America's experimental film makers goes to Jonas Mekas, himself a film maker, in addition to being publisher and editor of *Film Culture,* film critic for the *Village Voice,* and organizer of the

Film Makers' Cooperative and Distribution Center. In describing his own work and that of other independent film makers, Mekas has said:

Our movies come from our hearts—our little movies, not the Hollywood movies. Our movies are like extensions of our own pulse, of our heartbeat, of our eyes, our fingertips; they are so personal, so unambitious in their movement, in their use of light, their imagery. We want to surround this earth with our film frames and warm it up—until it begins to move.

Of extreme importance to the experimental film makers is the unambitiousness and intensely personal nature of their films, as described by Mekas. In many instances, desire and budget dictate that the film be the result of one person who functions as producer, director, cameraman, editor, and often distributor. The actors are often friends, and usually nonprofessionals. Most films are done on 16 mm. And, as in the "New Wave" films, there is an absence of chronological continuity and carefully plotted story lines, along with considerable use of improvisation and emphasis on spontaneous action and reaction rather than upon stagey performance.

As the "New Wave" is a convenient rubric that lumps together highly individualistic directors, so the New American Cinema Group—"a free organization of independent film makers dedicated to the support of the men and women giving their vision to the filmic art"—is a convenient label, embracing film makers with divergent purposes, talents, and methods. But, like the "New Wave" directors, the New American Cinema Group shares an outlet for its views, the magazine *Film Culture,* and evinces a common hatred and a common enthusiasm. As the French directors rebelled against film's prior dependency on literature and rejoiced in the cinema as an art form with its own esthetic, so the New American Cinema rebels against all that is unimaginative, standardized, and hopelessly phony about Hollywood and celebrates, too, the film as an art form.

Among the more notable experimental film makers are Jonas Mekas (*Guns of the Trees, The Brig*), Stan VanDerBeek (*Mankinda, Skullduggery, Summit, Breathdeath*), Stan Brakage (*Dog Star Man, Window Water Baby Moving, Scenes from Under Childhood*), Bruce Conner (*A Movie, Cosmic Ray, Liberty Crown*), Kenneth Anger (*Scorpio Rising, Inauguration of the Pleasure Dome*), Gregory Markopoulos (*Twice a Man, Serenity, Ming Green*), Charles Boultenhouse (*Handwritten,*

*Dionysius*), Shirley Clarke (*The Connection, Skyscraper, The Cool World*), and, of course, Andy Warhol and Paul Morrissey.

Parodying Hollywood's film factories with his own Factory, Hollywood's star system with his own superstars, Hollywood's trumped-up and ultimately phony retailing of sex and sex goddesses in *Screen Test,* and Hollywood's bad guys, good guys and Westerns in *Horse,* Warhol has been enormously and unabashedly prolific and successful. In all his films, whether in the early "documentaries" like *Empire, Sleep,* and *Eat,* or in the later "feature" films, *Kitchen, The Chelsea Girls, My Hustler, Bike Boy,* and *Lonesome Cowboys,* Warhol's constant subject has been the film itself. Using a variety of techniques, from a static camera focused on one object for more than eight hours, to cinéma vérité pushed to an extreme, to employing two screens and running two films simultaneously, Warhol has drawn attention through technique and subject matter to the films as product and substance, reveling in and revealing its particular properties as a physical entity.

The many purposes and styles of American experimental films range from social criticism using documentary techniques to embodiments of the subconscious through surrealism and myth to psychedelic experiments with light and color. At their best, the films of the avant-garde are exciting, fresh, sensitive, and fully able to transmit their maker's vision. At their worst, they are very bad indeed—as bad as the worst products of any art form—as trivial and boring, for example, as the worst Hollywood movie.

**Hollywood: 1965–1972.** In 1950, when a consent decree put teeth into a court decision calling for the major motion picture studios to sell their theater chains, a monopoly was broken up that had linked production with distribution and had fostered the exhibition of American motion pictures regardless of quality. And when this blow to Hollywood was followed by the ascendancy of television in the American economy and the American home, Hollywood began to retrench. In addition to cutting back on production, the major studios dropped contract actors, directors, and writers at option time. In 1950, there were 474 actors, 147 writers, and 99 directors under contract to the major studios; in 1955, there were 209 actors, 67 writers, and 79 directors; in 1960, there were 139 actors, 48 writers, and 24 directors. Three studios—RKO, Republic, and Monogram—stopped production entirely. And approximately 6000 movie houses closed their doors.

Into these troubled waters stepped the independent producers. Some of the independent production companies were formed by the stars themselves—among them Burt Lancaster, Frank Sinatra, Kirk Douglas, and Bob Hope. Other independent companies were started by directors —William Wyler, Alfred Hitchcock, Elia Kazan, and Otto Preminger. Some had been producers, like Sam Spiegel and Arthur Hornblow. Still others had been writers, like Richard Brooks, Joseph Mankiewicz, and Robert Rossen. In itself, the independent production company was not a new commodity in Hollywood. But the independent producer had never made any significant inroads in the Hollywood system until the 1950's. At that time, the major studios, having involved themselves in fewer productions, began increasingly to finance and then distribute films made by the independent production company. Gradually, therefore, the studios began to function like United Artists, which had been started in 1919 as a releasing company without studio facilities.

By accepting the lesser role of financier, promoter, and distributor, even at times leasing its own facilities to the independent production company, the major studios relinquished artistic control over the films they were underwriting. Control passed to the independent producer, creating a situation that allowed a film to have a style impressed on it by the men who made it rather than by a studio boss overseeing a dozen or more films simultaneously.

Although not all the motion pictures produced by the independent companies have been artistic or commercial successes, a good many independent productions are of outstanding quality and have increased the prestige of the Hollywood movie both here and abroad. Seven of the nine films winning Oscars as Best Motion Picture of the Year between 1954 and 1962 were produced by independents: *On the Waterfront* (1954), *Marty* (1955), *Around the World in Eighty Days* (1956), *The Bridge on the River Kwai* (1957), *The Apartment* (1960), *West Side Story* (1961), and *Lawrence of Arabia* (1962). Other successful independents have been *The Diary of Anne Frank* (1959), *The Hustler* (1961), *Advise and Consent* (1962), *Guess Who's Coming to Dinner* (1967), *In the Heat of the Night* (1967), *The Graduate* (1967), *Bonnie and Clyde* (1967), *Faces* (1968), and *Easy Rider* (1969).

And, in turn, the more interesting and stimulating movies have been bringing American audiences back into the movie houses. Only with

**a** difference. A recent survey disclosed that persons under 24 compose approximately 50 percent of the movie audience, and that 75 percent of that audience is under 40 years of age. Further, the people who go to movies at least once a month tend to be college students and college graduates. This means that movies are less a mass medium than an elitist medium—that is, less a form of mass art than of high art. In the inevitable rearrangement caused by displacement, television has become the mass medium. All this extends to the entertainment film great and as yet only partially fulfilled possibilities in educating its already educated audience to want movies that are even more truthful, inventive, technically expert, and intellectually arresting than those that have been produced so far. In part, the movie industry can thank television for its new, visually sophisticated audiences. It's in the cards that a generation weaned on television wants, as adolescents and adults, stronger stuff.

To accommodate the new audiences and the new movies, there were 14,300 movie theaters in operation in the United States as of June, 1970. Of this total, 9700 were indoor or "hardtop" theaters, and 4600 were drive-ins. From 1963–1969, roof-top theaters increased by an average of 4½ percent and drive-in theaters by an average of 21 percent. In all there were approximately 700 circuits, each with four or more theaters, operating about 53 percent of all movie houses. The remaining movie theaters were owned and operated by 6800 individuals or companies.

Within the past few years, elaborate movie palaces of the 1920's and 1930's, such as Time Square's Paramount, Roxy, Capitol, and State, have been torn down. Approximately 400 new theaters, both indoor and outdoor, were either opened, announced, or placed under construction in 1970. The day of the multi-auditorium theater was at hand. Most were twin-auditorium theaters, but some had three, four, and even six auditoriums. Along with these more ambitious projects were an ever-increasing number of mini-theaters, deluxe houses with audience capacities of 150 to 400 persons and relatively inexpensive to construct and operate. Of these 400 new projects, approximately 70 percent were in shopping centers, continuing a trend that had begun in 1962.

At present, American motion pictures continue to dominate the world market, being preferred in most countries to the indigenous product. It is estimated that U.S. films take up 60 percent of the world motion picture playing time, occupying 67 percent of motion picture screen time in England, 55 percent in Italy, 33 percent in France, and as high as 90 percent in other countries with less developed film industries.

All this should make clear that Hollywood did not die; the film capital only faded for a few years, and has come back reorganized, reoriented, and recharged—with a new face, a new outlook, and a new openness. And, while a way of life may have disappeared in the process, another life style, more suited to a world grown smaller through new communications technology and to a world with its eyes on the galactic stars and not on Hollywood's, has appeared to take its place.

**The International Movie.**   Part of the life style that characterizes the new Hollywood concerns the international movie. A step toward internationalization occurred in the 1950's. The independent producers, being unshackled to particular film studios, made movies in Europe and other foreign locations in order to profit from cheaper labor costs and national subsidies, to use actual locales, and to please the movie stars themselves who, by establishing residence in a foreign country, could avoid paying U. S. income tax on money earned while working abroad.

At present, changed tax laws and increased foreign labor costs have reduced the advantages of filming in foreign locations. But the transporting of Hollywood actors, directors, cameramen, and all the assorted personnel connected with movie production continues, and this trans-Atlantic and trans-Pacific traffic has helped to return movie making to its international beginnings.

The new mobility of contemporary movie makers has been aided tremendously by certain technological developments. Lightweight cameras and sound recording equipment, as well as "mini-studios" capable of being airlifted, are allowing movie producers to set up shooting where whim and geography dictate—which is often *not* in the Hollywood studio.

Further, such elements as the directors and writers, as well as the financial backing and distribution arrangements, have done their share to internationalize the industry. For example, *Blow-Up*, which won the 1967 Cannes Film Festival Golden Palm Award, was an English entry, with an Italian director (Antonioni), produced for MGM. *Taking Off*, which won the 1971 Cannes Jury Special Prize, was a United States entry directed by the Czech director Milos Forman. The 1966 Berlin Festival winner was a British entry *Cul-de-Sac,* made by the

Polish director Roman Polanski, who also directed *Rosemary's Baby*. The list could go on and on. Even such an American movie as *Bonnie and Clyde* was almost a French product. Its American writers, Robert Benton and David Newman, wrote the screenplay first for Francois Truffaut. When Truffaut rejected the script (he was then filming *Farenheit 451*), Benton and Newman approached Jean-Luc Godard, who was interested but ultimately decided against undertaking the project. And it was only at this time that Warren Beatty began negotiations, finally buying the script for $75,000.

The many film festivals prevalent today are additional evidence of the internationalism of the film industry. Festivals in Cannes, Berlin, Venice, San Sebastian, New York, Moscow, Montreal, Cork, Chicago, and Mexico have provided showcases for films from every nation and a meeting and market place for actors, directors, writers, and producers. "More and more," as Edward Lipton, news editor of *The Film Daily* points out, " 'country-of-origin' of a film seems to be becoming not so much cloudy as meaningless."

**Film Criticism.**   As film's potential for personal and artistic expression was realized, and as its capability for being more than a cheap entertainment medium for the illiterate was understood, an accompanying esthetic developed to explain and analyze the form and content of motion pictures. Vachel Lindsay's *The Art of the Moving Picture* (1915) and Rudolf Arnheim's *Film* (1933) are early examples of enlightened film criticism.

Good film criticism, like good literary criticism, serves two functions: (1) it explicates the work at hand, and (2) it elevates the public taste. The first function is the more obvious. As film techniques have become more complex, as film has probed deeper into human sensibility and experience, and as films have become identifiable as the work of a particular director who uses personal symbols in the manner of contemporary poets and novelists, effective film criticism seeks to explain this heightened complexity by clarifying techniques, images, and relationships of time, place, and character.

The second purpose is perhaps best explained by Walt Whitman's oft-quoted remark that great audiences make great poets. An audience knowledgeable about film history and techniques is in a position to recognize the second-rate, the false, the vacuous, the film that appears to be saying something but in reality says nothing, and the slick directorial tricks that attempt to hide the untrue. Great audiences make great poets (film makers) because they provide a need and a receiving ground for great poetry (films); they inspire the poet (film maker) to do his best by giving him a reason for being that transcends his physical identity. Advances in film technology and subject matter have occurred and will continue to occur because film artist and film audience have become knowledgeable together.

At its best, good film criticism is informative, expanding the reader's knowledge by relating the film at hand to other works of a particular film maker, or to other films of similar or dissimilar genre; it respects the film and glories in its potential realized; it bears the stamp of its creator's mind by possessing a distinctive style; it bridges epochs and nations by linking past with present achievement regardless of "country-of-origin."

In all this, the film critic must be distinguished from the film reviewer, who serves a reportorial function. Whereas the film critic seeks to analyze and explain, the film reviewer seeks to ascertain the merits of a particular film with the intention of warning his audience against an inferior, boring, or morally degrading film, or touting those films with a high entertainment value. Judith Crist has served this function in her weekly column in *TV Guide* and in her appearances on NBC's *Today* show. For the most part, movie reviewers write for the daily papers, previewing and describing films for their readers; they seldom go beyond the value of amusement as a criterion.

In contrast, film critics generally write for the magazines: *Film Quarterly, Cahiers Du Cinema* (available in an English edition), *Film Culture, Sight and Sound, New Yorker,* and *Esquire.* Richard Schnickel in *Life* and Arthur Knight and Hollis Alpert in *Saturday Review* have written weekly pieces that combine previewing a film with deeper, more thoughtful, analysis. Recent well-known American film critics have been Andrew Sarris, Stanley Kauffmann, Pauline Kael, Wilfrid Sheed, Jonas Mekas, and John Simon.

## THE DOCUMENTARY FILM

In both England and America, the documentary film came of age in the 1930's through direct patronage by the national governments, and matured, still under governmental auspices, during the troubled years of

World War II. Perhaps this is not surprising, as a documentary's purpose is always partially social—setting forth public and private crises and victories, showing us where man has been and what, inevitably, man will become unless proper action is taken.

In England, the earliest documentaries are associated with the Empire Market Board Film Unit, headed by John Grierson. Grierson's first film, *Drifters* (1929), shot on location on the North Sea, portrays the daily existence of the herring fishermen. When the E.M.B. Film Unit was shifted to the General Post Office in 1933, Grierson and the film unit continued the production of quality documentaries, including *Weather Forecast* (1934), *Song of Ceylon* (1934), *Coal Face* (1935), *Night Mail* (1936), and *North Sea* (1938). "By the time the war broke out," Arthur Knight writes, "the British documentary movement—headed by men like Paul Rotha, Stuart Legg, Basil Wright, Harry Watt, Alberto Cavalcanti, Arthur Elton and Edgar Anstey—had achieved a worldwide reputation and inspired scores of directors outside England to attempt documentary movements in their own countries."

In America, the depression and the New Deal gave rise to a remarkable series of documentaries. (See Chapter 12.)

World War II gave impetus to increased documentary film production—ranging from training films for United States servicemen to informative films for a civilian population needing instruction in wartime procedures. As well, Hollywood directors like John Huston, William Wyler, and John Ford began making films for the military. *San Pietro* (1944), *Memphis Belle* (1944), and *Battle of Midway* (1944) are memorable documentaries filmed on and around World War II's battlegrounds.

In England, the documentary film makers, now working under the aegis of the Ministry of Information, also turned their attention to wartime subjects, producing such films as *London Can Take It* (1940), depicting London during a Nazi air raid; *Target for Tonight* (1941), documenting an air force bombing mission; and *Desert Victory* (1942), an account of the North African campaign. Early in the war, the English independent film studios were mobilized to produce training films as well as to continue in the production of feature films. As Arthur Knight has observed, "for the first time, the documentary and fiction film makers of Britain joined forces. Some, like Alberto Cavalcanti and Harry Watt, moved from documentary to fiction; while fiction directors like John Boulting, Thorold Dickinson and Carol Reed became, at least for the time, documentalists."

Basic to many recent documentaries is a problematic cinema technique known as cinéma vérité, spontaneous cinema, or direct cinema. The term, cinéma vérité, applies to film which uses the camera to record reality in an unbiased and unmanipulated way. In presenting the essence of a situation, the director does not work from a preconceived shooting script, and, to all intents and purposes, he does not direct—if by directing one means organizing and controlling what happens before the camera. By making use of the new lightweight cameras and recording equipment, the film maker goes into the field where he and his camera act as witnesses and scribes. His intent is to provide either minimal or no interpretation and to retain the spontaneity and natural characteristics of the actual event.

In practice, documentary films exhibiting pure cinéma vérité are hard to find. Either consciously or unconsciously, most film makers impose an interpretation on their subject matter through in-camera editing, or editing after the film has been shot. Others "edit" reality before any filming occurs by carefully selecting the persons and objects to be photographed and only then applying cinéma-vérité filming techniques. For example, *Chronique d'un Eté*, by Jean Rouch and Edgar Morin, shows evidence of rather stringent preshooting "editing," although the most effective parts of the film result from the characters behaving in ways that could not have been predicted beforehand.

In contrast, *Showman* and *The Beatles* provide good examples of pure cinéma vérité. Directed and produced by Albert and David Maysles, these films have been criticized for their superficiality. But, the Maysles contend, their vow has been only to avoid interfering with the subject during filming; any superficiality, therefore, is inherent in the subject and is inevitably part of the truth that the film depicts.

Robert Drew, Richard Leacock, Donald Pennebaker, and Gregory Shuker have produced many outstanding documentary films under the label The Drew Associates. *On the Pole* depicts the ambitions, anguish, and ultimate failure of an Indianapolis race car driver named Eddie Sachs. *Primary* concerns the Hubert Humphrey–John F. Kennedy primary contest in Wisconsin. *Crisis* depicts the Robert Kennedy–Governor Wallace fight over the token integration of the Alabama schools. *The Chair* is about an effort to prevent a young Negro from going to the electric chair. *Jane* is a film portrait of Jane Fonda on the opening night of an unsuccessful play.

Other notable documentaries include Lionel Rogosin's *On the Bowery*, filmed on location in New York City. Still others are Allan King's *Warrendale*, which concerns the treatment of emotionally disturbed children, and Frank Simon's *The Queen*, on a "Miss America" contest for transvestites.

In recent years, television has provided a ready market for documentaries. A fine example of a television documentary, and one which also makes use of cinéma-vérité techniques, is "Royal Family," produced by a consortium of BBC and England's independent television companies and shown on American television September, 1969. Richard Cawston served as producer-director, working with an eight-man crew throughout an almost full year of shooting 43 hours of film. Cawston has attributed the success of this film to the royal family's freedom to talk without restraint, ad-libbing in front of the cameras, in the knowledge that Queen Elizabeth and Prince Philip had the right to veto any sections they found unacceptable in retrospect. "I decided it could be done only with some sense of humor and with a sort of cinéma-vérité technique," Cawston has said. "Therefore, nothing was really rehearsed. We would discuss beforehand what would happen, and then simply shoot it. It worked out very well."

Other television documentaries are considerably shorter and understandably more humble in subject matter and technique, ranging from film accounts of war maneuvers in Vietnam to Charles Kuralt's "On the Road" segments for the "Walter Cronkite Evening News." The television news magazines, like "Chronolog," and timely news specials provide excellent documentaries on such subjects as a U.S. Olympic skydiving team and a "Stone Age" New Guinea tribe, photographed with precision and sensitivity by a team of Japanese cinematographers. Other outstanding documentaries have been ABC's Cousteau and *National Geographic* series, Public Broadcasting Laboratory's "Birth and Death," and CBS's "Hunger in America" and "The Selling of the Pentagon."

Arthur Knight has conjectured that in the near future regional film makers may be celebrating their region through film as, traditionally, novelists, poets, and musicians have done. Certainly, the field for documentary production is wide open. Invariably, it seems, truth is stranger and more interesting than fiction. As a purveyor of facts and feelings, as a conveyor of an increasingly important photographic reality, and as a molder of public opinion, the documentary film is a powerful force in modern communications.

## FILMS FOR INDUSTRY, GOVERNMENT, AND EDUCATION

This is a mushrooming industry in which an estimated 1200 firms are at work in the United States, producing pictures on a multiplicity of topics for showing to industrial and sales groups, schools and universities, government and community organizations, the armed forces, and professional and religious bodies. These firms might be compared to the hundreds of small trade journals in the magazine field. Few of them are major organizations, but in the mass they form an influential channel for communicating information and ideas.

Nontheatrical film making is heavily financed by American industry, which has found in this type of motion picture a highly effective means for presenting its purposes, methods, and achievements. By 1969, nontheatrical film production had reached 13,700 a year. Most were produced on 16 mm film, the standard size for projection by small and portable machines. A few of the more elaborate were made on 35 mm, some even for wide-screen projection. This total includes some 9400 business and industrial pictures, 1900 government films, 1700 educational films, 250 for medical and health use, 300 for community organizations, and 150 religious films. More than $1,436,500,000 was being spent annually to produce these films and for other audio-visual aids, such as filmstrips, slides, and equipment.

The price of making and distributing a good company film averages nearly $100,000 with some major productions running close to $500,000. As many as 200 prints are made for some films to satisfy the demand. The average total audience for such a film is estimated to be 1,500,000. Many educational and instructional films are produced on far smaller budgets, some of them only a few thousand dollars, and are shown to more limited audiences.

Production of educational and informational films began with the development of the 16 mm portable projector in 1923. At present more than 750,000 projectors are in use in the United States, mostly in schools and businesses, but also in clubs, libraries, homes, and churches.

A large proportion of these nontheatrical films are available for use by organizations and private citizens free of charge. The cost is underwritten by business organizations as part of their institutional public relations budget; by federal, state, and local governments; by social or economic organizations which seek to present educational material in their particular fields; or by tax-supported institutions such as public libraries or adult education schools. There are 2600 film libraries in the United States distributing 16 mm films. *The H. W. Wilson Educational Film Guide* lists more than 20,000 films which can be borrowed. Some of the diversity and purposes of nontheatrical films sponsored by American industry is apparent from the following titles and descriptions:

*One Hoe for Kalaboe,* a 27-minute production in color telling the story of modern tool building and its effects on economies and civilizations. The film is produced by the National Machine Tool Builders Association.

*Adventures in Dairyland,* a Technicolor picture prepared by the American Dairy Association in which two city youngsters visit a Wisconsin farm and learn the methods of modern dairy farming.

*Working Dollars,* a 15-minute color cartoon story explaining how the stock market works and the advantages of the monthly investment plan. The film is financed by members of the New York Stock Exchange.

*The Gamblers,* a 19-minute film produced for the Caterpillar Tractor Company, stressing the importance of safety rules when operating landmoving machinery, and intended for construction workers or anyone who might find himself using, or around, heavy equipment.

All levels of government make some use of film in describing their function, in initiating the public to new programs and procedures, in influencing public opinion in order to shape voter attitudes, in training their employees, and in exercising an important public relations function. Typical of recent United States government films is *Janet and Genie,* a 28-minute color film sponsored by the U.S. Department of Agriculture, using animation as well as live actors to explain USDA's labels and grades. Representative of an informative film on the local government level is *The Cry for Help,* a 33-minute film sponsored by the Chicago Police Department and designed to help police officers develop a feeling of concern and understanding in dealing with the suicidal person. Except for the previously mentioned *Years of Lightning, Day of Drums,* however, the many U.S. Information Agency films released yearly are produced only for exhibition in foreign countries.

Representative of government-sponsored films on the state level are these produced by the Florida Development Commission:

*Emerald Isle,* depicting Marco Island, at the outer edge of the Ten Thousand Islands on Florida's lower Gulf coast.

*Changing Face of Florida,* portraying the Sunshine State's taking on a new look as industry discovers its advantages.

*Florida's Modern Forests,* showing the scope of forestry and its by-products. The film examines modern methods and techniques used in producing wood in Florida's forests.

*The Season People,* documenting the plight of Florida's migrant workers (produced for the State Board of Health).

In education, the film has many important advantages and functions. Well suited to depicting the passage of time and therefore to showing process and development, the film has the added advantage of being able to bring the outside world into the classroom. Of special interest are two new developments in educational films—full course films and single-concept films.

In many subject areas, entire courses have been put on film with the intention not to replace the classroom teacher but to allow him to function more efficiently. A recent series is the CHEM Study Films—26 films designed for a high school chemistry class and made under the auspices of the American Chemical Society. These films show advanced experimental techniques and the use of uncommon, costly equipment—photographing such relatively inaccessible subjects as giant cyclotrons, radiation laboratories, and industrial laboratories.

The single-concept film runs from 30 seconds to five minutes, and presents a single idea, problem, or skill. The single-concept film is the direct result of improved technology—(1) the relative ease with which sound can be attached to 8 mm magnetic-striped film, thus enabling the classroom teacher to make his own 8 mm sound films; and (2) the 8 mm instantaneous film projector which, by using cartridges, provides a "continuous loop" for repeated viewing and eliminates, therefore, cumbersome and time-consuming threading and rewinding of reels. According to the Educational Facilities Laboratories, the future use of cartridge projectors for 16 mm sound film "could do for individual movies (motion pictures) what paperbacks did for publishing."

Medical films are used to demonstrate operations, to show to those within the medical profession, and to inform general audiences about diseases and public health problems. Church organizations present religious films to dramatize the teachings of the Bible and to generate support for their missionary and welfare activities.

From this brief survey, the diversity and potential of the nontheatrical film is apparent. It is a growing field, well-financed in many instances, in which there is need for creative thinking. There are jobs available in it in many cities for young men and women who have the ability to tell a story in visual form and to convey facts and ideas in pictures. The creative person in nontheatrical work must be able to plan films (a journalistic job of determining what the story is and what can be filmed), conduct all necessary research, knit the facts together into a narrative or commentary script, plan production so that the story can be filmed economically and effectively, and communicate intelligently with the film's producer or director.

One obvious opportunity is to work on film production for a large company. Many corporations have staffs in their public relations departments in charge of audiovisual materials and film work; however, most assign the actual shooting of the picture to film production companies, which work with materials provided by the corporation public relations department. In some companies geared to Twentieth-Century communication methods, the film is being used to supplement the company newsletter or magazine.

## THE AMERICAN FILM INSTITUTE

The John F. Kennedy Center for the Performing Arts in Washington, D.C., is the headquarters for the American Film Institute, a private organization established in 1967 "to bring cinema to its fullest stature in the country of its birth; to preserve, stimulate, enrich, and nurture the art of film in America." The institute is supported by the federal government through the National Endowment for the Arts, by the Ford Foundation, by the Motion Picture Association of America, by corporate and individual donations, and by institute programs.

During its first four years the AFI helped preserve more than 8000 films, many thought to be lost forever; they have been placed in the Library of Congress. The 1653-page first volume of a comprehensive catalog of historical data on every film produced in the U.S. was published. An innovative conservatory for filmmakers was opened as a bridge between the film and television professions and the more than 400 colleges and universities offering courses in cinema and television. Training programs for teachers were started, grants were made to independent filmmakers, an internship program with leading professionals was inaugurated, historical research was supported, a Community Film Workshop Council was formed to provide training and jobs for new filmmakers from minority groups, and a repertory theater exhibiting outstanding film works was opened.

By 1970 the AFI was spending almost $3,000,000 a year and employed more than 80 persons in Washington, California, and New York City. More than 4000 persons became members when given the opportunity in 1971. George Stevens, Jr., AFI director, predicted that the institute increasingly would provide "an enhanced appreciation of film as an art form and a source of enjoyment and enlightenment" for millions of persons.

## OPPORTUNITIES

There are abundant opportunities for young men and women in both theatrical and nontheatrical film areas today. Many of those entering the field begin their studies at the more than 400 colleges and universities which offer work in film (see Chapter 19). Beginning salaries compare favorably with those of other mass communications industries and professions, and almost limitless financial returns may be achieved by highly creative and productive individuals.

A recent *Saturday Review* article affirms that "the opportunities for young film makers have never been greater, not just in theatrical motion pictures, but also in the burgeoning industrial, educational, and commercial film fields." The article continues, "Writers with an ear for the dialogue of the contemporary life problem and an eye for the contemporary setting are in demand." Even the "much maligned producer function" is being reappraised and its important role reaffirmed. Undeniably, while at one time getting into film work was a hit or miss affair, the college student today can find a well-paved academic route into one of the many careers available in the thriving and many-faceted film industry.

# Chapter 14

# *Magazines*

## THE ROLE OF MAGAZINES

Much communication of ideas, information, and attitudes among the American people is carried on through magazines. Hundreds of periodicals fall within this category, ranging from the slick paper picture weekly with circulation in the millions down to the small special interest quarterly which, though virtually unknown to the general public, may have very strong influence within its field.

The magazine exists to inform, entertain, and influence its readers editorially and to put before them advertising messages of national or regional scope. With a few exceptions, its outlook is national rather than local. Magazines never appear more frequently than once a week; thus they have more time to dig into issues and situations than the daily newspaper, and consequently they have a better opportunity to bring events into focus and interpret their meaning.

So many different types of magazines exist that making broad statements about their functions and goals may lead to inconsistencies. Some are published solely for their entertainment value and are loaded with material of little consequence. Others deal entirely with a serious investigation of contemporary problems, and many combine entertainment and service material with reporting and interpretation. It is valid to state that magazines have a much better opportunity than newspapers to serve as thoughtful interpreters and analysts of events and trends.

The men who create and write for magazines stand back a little further from the tumbling immediacy of events than do newspaper reporters and editors. Often the magazine writer moves into a situation as the spot news reporter hastens on to something new.

In the case of a mine disaster, for example, the newspaper stories tell of men trapped, the rescue efforts, and the emotional scenes above ground as the families await word of survivors. If at some later date there is an official investigation of the causes of the disaster, the newspaper will cover that, too, but by this time the urgency of the story has dimmed, and the headlines go to some new event. The magazine writer, with more time at his disposal and more space in which to develop background information, may spend weeks investigating all aspects of the disaster and gathering much information the newspaper reporter had no time to search out. The result may be a magazine article that brings the entire mine situation into focus and perhaps leads to reforms in mine safety procedures.

Each man has done his job equally well, but they are different jobs. The magazine writer probes the "why" of a situation and is an interpreter of events far more than a newspaperman can be. Occasionally, of course, a newspaper reporter is given the same amount of time to do his research.

The magazine with its more durable cover and bound pages has a semipermanence which the newspaper lacks. Magazines such as the *National Geographic* often are kept around a home for years, or passed from hand to hand. They are halfway between newspapers and books in this regard and also in content. Broadly speaking, the magazine examines a situation from the middle distance, and the book examines it from the higher ground of historical perspective.

There is another basic difference between newspapers and magazines. A newspaper must appeal to an entire community and have a little of everything for almost everybody. With a few exceptions, like the *Wall Street Journal,* a newspaper cannot be aimed at a single special interest group and survive. Yet hundreds of successful magazines are designed for reading by such limited-interest groups as gasoline station operators, dentists, poultry farmers, and model railroad fans. Therein lies the richness of diversity that makes the magazine field so attractive to many editorial workers. The possibilities for the specialist editor and writer are greater than on newspapers, although the total number of editorial jobs on magazines is less.

## TYPES OF MAGAZINES

Generalizations about content, style, and appearance of American magazines are dangerous because so many variations exist among the approximately 8400 periodicals now being published. That is the number given in Ayer's *Directory,* as distinguished from listings of newspapers with general circulations. Not all of the 8400 appear in magazine format, however; quite a few are tabloid or regular newspaper size. No more than 600 can be classified as general interest magazines. In contrast, there are 2500 specialized business and trade publications, 1300 in the field of religion, and about 800 agricultural periodicals, to list three·major subfields. Not included in these figures are some 9000 industrial, or company, publications designed for employees, customers, stockholders, dealers, and others. Many of these are issued in magazine format. Although all magazines share certain basic problems of production and distribution, their editorial content and advertising are of a hundred hues. Even trying to group them into categories becomes difficult because inevitably there is overlapping, and a few magazines almost defy classification.

A glance at the magazine rack in the corner drugstore shows what a kaleidoscopic outpouring of periodicals is being offered to the public. These are only a fraction of the magazines being published today. In fact, judging the magazine field by the publications available on general newsstands would be a grave error. The preponderance on the rack of so-called men's, fan, and "girlie" magazines, which survive only by sex-ridden headlines and other sensational newsstand-sale techniques, gives the casual observer the impression that magazines are a shoddy lot of trivia. This is untrue. Fortunately what appears on the stands is only a small segment of American magazine publishing. Many of the best and most significant ones are difficult to find on public racks because they are sold primarily by subscription or are distributed to special audiences.

Most magazines fall into these general categories:

**General interest.**    Two mass circulation magazines which sell 6,000,-000 or more copies per issue lead this group. They are aimed at the entire population and are edited to appeal to the interests of everyone, man and woman alike. One, the *TV Guide,* has a specialized function. The larger in circulation, the *Reader's Digest,* concentrates on informative and entertaining nonfiction. Two other general interest magazines, *Look* and *Life,* which blended textual material and elaborate photographic layouts, ceased publication in 1971 and 1972, respectively. When someone mentioned the word magazines, these mass circulation mixtures of information and entertainment with their sizable volume of colorful advertising usually were the first to come to mind.

**News magazines.** These weekly publications are designed to summarize the news and provide background, adding depth and interpretation that most newspapers cannot give. They publish articles on news situations, examine headline personalities, and discuss trends in such diverse fields as religion, labor, sports, and art. Atop this potpourri they sprinkle a spice of predictions about things to come and give "inside" tips.

The present group of news magazines got its start with the appearance of *Time* under the direction of Henry Luce and Briton Hadden in 1923. *Time* introduced a bright, flippant narrative style of news reporting, which includes a strong editorial viewpoint in its coverage. A more staid and conservative predecessor, the *Literary Digest,* was once an American household word. It ceased publication after a long slump that was climaxed by the monumental mishap of publishing a supposedly accurate national straw poll on the 1936 presidential campaign, predicting the election of Alfred Landon to the White House. Landon was overwhelmingly defeated by Franklin D. Roosevelt, winning only 2 of 48 states, and the magazine never recovered from this blow to its accuracy.

Leaders in the news magazine field are *Time,* with a circulation above 4,000,000, *Newsweek* at 2,600,000, and *U.S. News & World Report* at 1,875,000.

**Quality or class magazines.** These periodicals differ from the mass appeal high-circulation leaders in that they are oriented toward class or select audiences. One, *National Geographic,* doubled its circulation in the 1960's and at 6,000,000 copies stood in the top ten. Another, the literate *New York,* set a fast pace for city magazines. Most influential are the *Saturday Review,* the *New Yorker, Harper's,* and *Atlantic.* These serious-minded publications offer high-level reporting, opinion, or fiction to the general public, with emphasis upon literary, ethical, social, and political problems. Their circulations are substantial, ranging from *Saturday Review*'s 625,000 to *Atlantic*'s 325,000.

There also are smaller, more combative magazines of opinion, like the *National Review* and *Ramparts* and the older *Nation* and *New Republic,* which were once more famous than they are now. Periodicals of this type, important in the United States at the turn of the century, have not maintained the influence they have in Great Britain and the European countries.

**Women's interest.** Many of the largest, most successful magazines are aimed straight at the woman reader. Men who happen to pick up the

*Ladies' Home Journal, McCall's,* or *Good Housekeeping,* to mention the long-time leaders in the feminine field, feel as though they have accidentally opened the wrong door. The inside of a woman's magazine is a world of fashions, food, beauty hints, homemaking advice, inspiration, frank talks about personal problems, and emotional fiction. During the 1960's *McCall's* passed the 8,000,000 circulation point and *Ladies' Home Journal* exceeded 7,000,000.

At a time when most women's pages of newspapers were filled with stereotyped "society" news, the editors of women's magazines began to experiment. They quit publishing stilted love stories and flattering articles about the activities of social queens and used their space to serve the personal interests of women as a whole. They found that women in every category of life were interested in much the same things—how to improve themselves physically and emotionally and how to be better homemakers and career women. On this formula some of the country's greatest magazine successes have been built.

Another group of women's magazines, edited on a lower level, is aimed at the feminine desire to escape the humdrum of everyday life. These are the publications of romantic fiction, some of them published under the guise of "real life" stories. The movie and TV fan magazines, with their purported "inside" stories about the lives and loves of popular entertainment figures, are designed for the same market. Although these publications draw sneers from the critics and many better-educated readers, some of them have big circulations. Their brand of glamorized escapism fills a need in the lives of many women.

Still a third group of women's magazines concentrates on special categories of feminine interest and age groups, such as *Vogue* and *Harper's Bazaar* in fashions and *Seventeen.*

**Men's interest.**    Some magazines are aimed just as firmly at masculine readership. None of them reaches the circulation level of the most popular women's magazines. Men's magazines fall into two major categories: those concerned primarily with sports and he-man adventure and those which emphasize urbane sophistication, liberally illustrated with pictures of girls wearing as little as postal regulations permit. Among the leaders in sports are *Sports Illustrated, Sports Afield,* and *Field and Stream;* in the rugged masculine category, the leading magazines are *True* and *Argosy.* For many years *Esquire* set the pace in the sophisticated field, offering a mixture of high-quality articles and fiction, men's fashions and sexy drawings. More recently it has become more conservative—the metamorphosis that frequently follows success in the mass media field—and has come closer to the quality group in editorial tone. Its place in the barber shop magazine rack has been taken by the more uninhibited *Playboy* and its rash of imitators. *Playboy* was a 5,000,000 circulation phenomenon of the 1960's, a mixture of nude photographs, articles and stories, and rather pompous editorials based on a hedonistic philosophy. Even on newsstands which carry no other "girlie" magazines, *Playboy* always seems to have a prominent place.

Also important in the men's field are the mechanical and how-to-do-it magazines such as the perennial favorites *Popular Mechanics* and *Popular Science*, each with a circulation well above 1,000,000. Science fiction magazines also had a vogue for some years.

**Special interest magazines.** The hundreds of periodicals aimed at special audiences form a very large segment of the magazine industry. Some are little known to the general public because they are infrequently displayed on the newsstands; others fall in major circulation categories.

The latter type includes the "shelter" magazines about family living, headed by *Better Homes and Gardens* and *American Home;* farm magazines like *Farm Journal* and *Successful Farming;* such science-interest publications as *Scientific American* and *Science Digest,* and the Negro magazines, *Ebony, Jet,* and *Essence.* Others include trade and technical journals, professional and scientific publications, and publications aimed at readers with hobbies such as model railroading or stamp collecting. Religious magazine publishing is an influential and important field. There are both denominational and nondenominational publications, the largest of which—*Presbyterian Life, Catholic Digest,* and the *Christian Herald* —circulate to hundreds of thousands of readers. The rise of the supermarket as a magazine sales outlet led to development of such periodicals as *Everywoman's Family Circle Magazine,* and *Woman's Day* with more than 7,000,000 copies. *Boy's Life,* sponsored by the Boy Scouts of America, has a circulation of 2,500,000 to lead the youth group.

**Sunday supplement magazines.** Distributed as part of the Sunday newspapers in many large American cities are some large-circulation magazines. Faring badly in the competition for advertising revenues with television, the nationally-edited group lost the *American Weekly* and *This Week,* but retained *Parade* with 17,000,000 copies and *Family Weekly* at 8,000,000 at the start of the 1970's. A Negro-oriented supplement named *Tuesday* had 2,400,000 circulation. Gaining favor were the individual Sunday magazines of leading papers, such as the New York *Times,* Los Angeles *Times,* and Chicago *Tribune.*

**The business press.**   The fastest growing area in magazine publishing in the 1960's was that occupied by the nearly 2500 periodicals known as the business press. One small segment includes the general business or business news magazines, headed by *Nation's Business, Business Week, Forbes,* and *Fortune,* all above 500,000 in circulation. The rest are identified by the American Business Press, the industry trade association to which most of the larger business publishing houses belong, as "specialized business publications serving specific industrial, business, service, or professional business audiences." Nearly half of these business magazines are industrial, followed, in order, by merchandising, medical, export and import and international, financial, educational, and government.

Largest of the U.S. publishing houses in the business field is McGraw-Hill, with 38 publications, 800 full-time editors and reporters, a worldwide business news service, and such well-known magazines as *Business Week* and *Electrical World.* The next largest group publishers are Cahners Publishing, Chilton, and Miller Publishing. Some well-known titles are Chilton's *Iron Age,* Fairchild's *Women's Wear Daily,* and *Modern Medicine.* All told, the business press has a circulation of more than 60,000,000 and puts out more than 800,000 editorial pages per year, the work of 14,000 editors.

**Company publications.**   These are magazines published by corporations for distribution to their employees and customers, usually without charge. Their purpose is to present the company's policy and products in a favorable light and to promote a better sense of teamwork and "belonging" among the employees. They are known also as individual magazines; the term "house organ" which once was widely used for them has fallen into disfavor.

This field of industrial publishing has made large advances as corporations have become more conscious of their public relations. Many of these company publications are edited by men widely experienced in general magazine work, who have been given ample funds to produce magazines of sophisticated appearance and high-grade editorial content. More and more companies are coming to the realization that they must hire professional people and set their standards to compare with general magazines on a broad basis. As one leading industrial editor, himself a veteran of general magazine staffs, expressed it, "No longer can the mail clerk or the personnel manager be regarded as an authority in the field of industrial editing. The emphasis definitely is on editing—and on journalism." When hiring staff members, the editors of the better industrial magazines give particular attention to men and women who have strong newspaper writing and editing backgrounds. As the field of industrial editing grows, it can be expected to draw with increasing frequency upon well-trained newspaper people who wish to move on into another related field. Some journalism graduates, particularly women, move directly into industrial editing. In many such publications articles of general interest, unrelated to the company's products, are included, and company "propaganda" is kept at a very subdued level. Some large corporations, in fact, publish a number of magazines aimed variously at customers, stockholders, and employees. For example, the International Harvester Company and the Ford Motor Company publish some two dozen employee magazines each at different plants. Some of the more elaborate company publications, intended to reach the public as well as employees, have circulations above a million.

Company publications are of many sizes and shapes, and it is difficult to say at any given time how many of them qualify as magazines. Many appear in newspaper format. One recent estimate put the combined circulation of major company periodicals above 100,000,000. American business and industry invests more than $500,000,000 a year in these 9000 publications with some 15,000 editors and staff members.

## HOW MAGAZINES ARE MARKETED

The magazine industry rests upon twin foundations, circulation and advertising. General practice is for the publisher to sell each copy to the reader for less money than it costs to produce it. He closes this gap and makes his profit through the sale of national advertising. Failure of the magazine to attract and hold advertising is fatal and accounts for the disappearance of several well-known magazines during the past quarter-century.

Since hundreds of magazines, plus other media, are competing for the advertiser's dollars, the successful publisher must convince the advertiser that purchase of space in his pages is a good investment. This proof is based largely upon his circulation figures. Either he must show very large mass distribution figures among a general readership or a firmly established circulation among the special interest group to which his publication appeals editorially.

These economic principles have a powerful influence on the entire shape of the magazine industry. A magazine either must be designed for appeal to a well-defined segment of the population, such as outboard boating enthusiasts or members of a fraternal order, or it must be of such broad interest that it will attract huge numbers of general readers. In the latter category, the circulation figures of the leading magazines run high into the millions.

*Reader's Digest,* founded and long directed by DeWitt Wallace, is among the most fabulously successful magazine ventures of the twentieth century with a circulation of 18,000,000 copies for its basic domestic monthly edition plus another 11,000,000 for its overseas editions. *Reader's Digest* started the trend toward pocket-size magazines. For many years it was published without advertising, almost alone in this respect among consumer magazines. But the rising costs of production that have plagued all publishers eventually caught up even with this giant, and it now sells advertising space. Many lesser magazines are created in just the opposite way: the publisher sees a field of special interest in which he judges that sufficient advertising support can be developed and so brings out a magazine aimed at that audience.

Recent studies show about 50 other magazines with circulations of more than a million. *TV Guide*'s many editions total nearly 15,000,000. *McCall's* is in the 8–9,000,000 bracket; *Better Homes and Gardens* and *Ladies' Home Journal* are in the 7–8,000,000 class, and *Life, National Geographic, Good Housekeeping,* and *Playboy* are at the 5–6,000,000 level. *Redbook* and *Time* top 4,000,000. Rising population in the United States makes the big publishers hopeful of even greater circulation figures in the next decade. They constantly seek to increase their circulation by costly sales promotion devices. In *Life's* case, however, the publisher decided to cut back circulation 2,500,000 to make advertising rates more attractive.

The death of a half dozen mass circulation magazines such as *Saturday Evening Post, Collier's, Coronet, American, Look,* and *Life* in recent years has created the false impression that hard times have hit the big magazine field. The figures just quoted and other evidence, such as all-time record revenues, show that this is not the case. Individual magazines have suffered because of changing public tastes and marketing conditions, including increased postal rates and the loss of much advertising to television, but the general interest magazine field as a whole is healthy. Editors have had to make major changes in content to counteract the element of fictional entertainment brought into their readers' lives by the television screen. Extremely heavy production and distribution costs means that when a major magazine gets out of step with the reading public's tastes, it either dies, like the *Saturday Evening Post,* or it goes through many vicissitudes in trying to solidify its audience.

Hundreds of smaller magazines operate profitably year after year by concentrating in their special fields. Since advertising rates are based largely upon circulation, many advertisers cannot afford to buy space in magazines with circulations in the millions, where the rate for a single black-and-white advertising page ranges from $20,000 to $45,000 and for color from $30,000 to $65,000. Instead they spend their money in publications they can afford and which offer them an audience especially adapted to their products. To counteract this, some of the mass circulation giants are offering advertising space on regional or fractional split-run bases. More than 250 magazines offer such special rates, accounting for some 20 percent of total magazine advertising revenues by 1970. *Look* had 75 regional editions, *Life* had 26 marketing areas, and *Time* offered seven regional areas and 11 metropolitan zones. *Life,* for example, had the highest page rate for a four-color advertisement, of $64,200 for its total circulation; but a Minnesota company could place a four-color ad in that state's 150,000 copies for some $2500.

One of the largest magazine publishers today, in terms of total income, is Time Inc. Started in the early 1920's, when *Time* made its shaky appearance with a new style of news magazine, this corporation grew spectacularly. Its picture weekly, *Life,* held top place among all magazines in gross advertising revenue from the 1950's to its demise in 1972. *Time* now holds that position. The firm also publishes *Fortune,* devoted to the business world; *Sports Illustrated;* and a new venture, *Money.*

The Hearst magazine group is affiliated with that newspaper publishing family's empire. The chain includes such large and profitable properties as *Good Housekeeping, Cosmopolitan, Harper's Bazaar, Popular Mechanics, Sports Afield,* and *House Beautiful.* Its group of more than a dozen publications also lists magazines in the motoring, medical, and leisure fields.

Other major groups include the McGraw-Hill trade publications, headed by *Business Week;* the McCall Corporation, with *McCall's* and *Redbook;* Meredith Publishing Company, with *Better Homes and Gardens* and *Successful Farming;* the Johnson Publishing Company, with *Ebony, Jet,* and *Tan;* and the Condé Nast publications, *Glamour, Vogue, Mademoiselle,* and *House and Garden.*

In some of the smaller group publishing operations, the same man will edit two or more magazines. Sometimes a company will publish three or four periodicals in the same field, such as crime or confessions, diverting manuscripts from one to another to fill its formula requirements.

Magazines are sold by two principal methods, single copy sales on newsstands and mail delivery of copies to subscribers. Mass circulation magazines consider newsstand sales more important than subscriptions. Some trade publications are distributed free of charge to controlled lists in order to give the advertiser a large audience for his product. Circulation is one of the most costly and complex problems a magazine publisher faces. Copies of each issue must be distributed nationwide and must be on sale by fixed dates each week or month. Copies unsold when the publication date for the next issue comes around must be discarded at heavy loss.

Newsstand sales of magazines are handled through news wholesalers. Intricate arrangements and "deals" are made to assure good display at outlets, since many sales are made on the buyer's impulse as he walks past the colorful array on the racks. This makes attractive cover design and provocative, attention-getting titles and sales catchlines on the covers extremely important. Even the conservative quality magazines have entered the battle for newsstand sales with brighter colors and more compelling headlines. Out of this scramble for attention came that American phenomenon, the cover girl, whose voluptuous charms are credited with selling millions of magazines. Some periodicals operate entirely on street sales whereas others, especially among the trade and professional fields, are sold predominantly by subscription. Consumer magazines as a whole probably get slightly more than half their sales from subscriptions. Across the United States there are more than 110,000 retail magazine sales outlets, many of them in supermarkets.

Unlike newspapers, a large majority of magazines do not own their own printing facilities. The editors and advertising staffs prepare each issue in their office and then send the material to a commercial printer who holds a contract to produce the magazine. In fact, a few large printing houses with high-speed color presses do the printing for most of the major national magazines. This freedom from the heavy initial investment in printing equipment enables new publishers to start magazines with limited capital; however, unless the new venture embodies an attractive basic idea or "angle," and is well edited, the printing and circulation bills can soon eat up the adventurous newcomer's capital. Although there are notable examples of successful magazines starting on small sums, even in these days of high costs, the odds against success with a national magazine by a new publisher are great. New publications created by established publishers are always preceded by detailed research of the market possibilities and extensive promotion.

Because of the necessity for quick nationwide delivery, some magazines are printed and distributed regionally. The plates are prepared at a central plant and then flown to presses in several parts of the country for simultaneous printing. Thus identical copies can be delivered to subscribers in New York and Los Angeles on Tuesday morning, although they came off presses situated 3000 miles apart. Some magazines handle overseas editions similarly.

## ADVERTISING AND PROMOTION

Magazine advertising has played a significant role in the growth of the American economy and the distribution of consumer goods. Many manufacturers have concentrated their advertising budgets in the magazines for two reasons: the periodicals have nationwide distribution, thus carrying the story of an advertiser's product from coast to coast, and by use of color printing processes on smooth paper stock magazines are able to present more alluring advertisements than newspapers can on their coarser, uncoated paper.

Use of selected newspapers enables an advertiser to pinpoint his market areas across the country, whereas magazine advertising gives him a general nationwide audience. A major corporation introducing a new product frequently uses both media, providing different copy and layouts to fit each; television programs and radio spot announcements are used simultaneously with the printed advertisements if the company can afford such a mammoth expenditure. This technique is used by automobile manufacturers to introduce their new models.

The other important advantage of magazines as advertising outlets is their ability to provide the advertiser with special interest audiences. The other media cannot do this, except in a very limited way.

For those who desire to build a career on the business side of publishing, magazines provide job opportunities in advertising selling and circulation, as well as in sales promotion. The promotion department utilizes the findings of the commercial research department to exploit the magazine as an advertising medium and handles major promotion and publicity campaigns. Salaries for jobs in these business departments are very attractive.

### EDITORIAL CONTENT AND OPERATION

The editorial content of American magazines is predominantly nonfiction. About three-fourths of the material printed in consumer periodicals is factual, and the percentage is even higher in the trade and professional journals. Many magazines carry no fiction at all.

Editorial operation of magazines varies greatly, depending upon the size, type, and frequency of the publication. Generally, editorial staffs are relatively small. A magazine selling 4,000,000 copies can be prepared editorially by a smaller staff than the one needed to put out a newspaper which sells a half-million copies. This is possible because much of the material published in many magazines is written by free-lance writers, either on speculation or on order from the editors. These writers are paid fees for their work and do not function as members of the staff.

The magazine editor's job is to decide what kind of material he wants to publish, arrange to obtain it, and then present it in his "book" in a manner pleasing to the reader's eye. Most editors work from a formula; that is, each issue contains specified types of material in predetermined amounts, arranged to give a desired effect. Articles and stories are selected for publication not only on their merit but for the way they fit the formula.

The editor has a staff of assistants to screen free-lance material, work with writers, think up ideas, and edit the material chosen for publication.

An art director arranges attractive layouts and chooses the covers. A cartoon editor selects such drawings if the periodical carries them. On many magazines a substantial portion of each issue is written by staff members.

The skillful, imaginative use of photojournalism has contributed heavily to the acceptance gained by many magazines in recent years. Combining technical efficiency with an appreciation of the aesthetic and the dramatic, the photojournalist is an able communicator with a camera. He performs his art as powerfully for the advertiser as for the editor. His work is best exemplified by the sequence of well-planned pictures that, combined with the correct proportion of textual material, tells a story with unified effectiveness. Most magazines have their own staffs of professional photojournalists, but free-lance photographers, often working through agents, provide many striking pictures. Rates range in excess of $300 per page for black-and-white pictures, $400 for color pages, and $500 for cover shots. Charges may be assessed for time taken in shooting the pictures at rates in excess of $150 per day. Picture editors make assignments and select the photos wanted for publication.

A key part of most magazine operations is the editorial conference, a session in which the editors discuss the forthcoming issue, make decisions on the material to be used, examine proposed layouts, and agree upon projects for future issues. Magazine projects frequently are planned months in advance of publication. On some staffs one editor makes the decisions on nonfiction ideas and articles and another is responsible for the selection of fiction. Details of editorial procedure vary from one magazine to another, depending upon the type of contents, size of the staff, and personality of the chief editor.

The news magazines operate somewhat differently. All their content is written by staff members, who are responsible for designated categories of material and for specific assignments, somewhat like a newspaper. Bureaus around the country submit material as ordered from the home office, which then is rewritten and condensed to fit the available space. The magazines also lean heavily upon press association material. News magazines operate on a rigid schedule in order to put the latest information on the newsstands throughout the United States.

A problem that news magazine editors and writers face is "writing around" the time lag between the closing of the editorial forms and actual distribution of the magazines to the public. There is constant danger that a late development on a major story will make part of the magazine's contents look outdated, even ridiculous. Regional printing has reduced this time lag considerably.

Most magazines have at their command large amounts of free-lance material submitted by writers who hope to "strike it lucky" and sell their work for a substantial sum. As most editors will testify, a relatively small amount of the unsolicited material unloaded on their desks by the mailman each day ever reaches print. Not that most of it necessarily is badly written or devoid of fresh ideas, but much of it does not fit the magazine's formula. Either it covers a subject the editor does not regard as suitable for his audience, is not written in the style he seeks in order to give his publication "character," or is about a subject similar to something the magazine has run recently. An article rejected for publication in one magazine may be purchased immediately by another. The problem for the free-lance writer is to have the right manuscript in the right editorial office at the right moment—not an easy task. Professional writers usually submit their articles in outline form or just a brief writeup of the idea.

Since editors have found that they cannot depend upon unsolicited free-lance material to fit their individual needs, they go in search of what they want. They assign article ideas to writers they know, and then work with them until the manuscripts have the desired flavor and approach. Or the idea might be assigned to a member of the staff and developed in the same manner.

Very few men and women in the United States, perhaps only 250 or 300, make a living as full-time, free-lance magazine writers. Probably fewer than a hundred of them earn $10,000 a year. Although an established writer may be paid from $1000 upward per article, the uncertainties of the craft are many and the number of big money markets is relatively few. Most of these full-time magazine writers work largely on assignment, being commissioned by editors who know and like their work to prepare articles on ideas proposed by the editors or ideas approved by them. In many cases the free-lance writers use agents to sell their output to editors on a commission basis. Almost all fiction in big magazines is sold by agents, and many professional article writers use their services. The agent functions to a degree as an adjunct of the editorial staff; he screens the output of his clients, channeling the worthwhile stories to appropriate magazines. The better-known agents are quite selective in the authors they will handle, and having a well-known agent is a helpful endorsement for a writer.

Even an assignment from an editor, faithfully carried out, does not assure that the article will be printed. It may be rejected at the last moment as "not quite what we had in mind," or the editor who ordered it may be replaced by someone who doesn't care for the idea. The vicissitudes are many in the life of a free-lance writer. It is normal practice for the magazine to pay for an article or a piece of fiction upon acceptance of the final draft.

Much of the contributed material published in magazines is written by men and women who do free-lance work on a part-time basis as a sideline to their regular occupation. Newspapermen, members of other mass media, teachers, attorneys and other professional men, even housewives with a flair for writing try their hands at free-lancing with varying degrees of success.

There are hundreds of places where magazine material can be sold. Competition to place articles and fiction in the mass circulation magazines is intense, and the material purchased must be excellently written and extensively researched. Preparation of a major magazine article requires so much skill and time that the work for the top dozen magazines is done largely by the small group of full-time professionals and staff members. However, the part-time free lancer can hit even the biggest magazines with short material, such as anecdotes, personal experiences, and humor. With a little luck and a large amount of perseverance, a writer can sell numerous articles to smaller magazines and specialized periodicals. However, the pay in these smaller markets is not large, ranging from $50 for a 2500-word article or short story up to about $500. Rates of payment for the confession-type magazines are three to five cents a word. At the upper end of the scale, where the competition is intense, the mass circulation magazines pay from $1000 to $3000 or higher for an article. The rates are flexible because the editors will pay extra if they consider that the material is exactly right for them or if the writer has a well-known name worth publicizing on the cover. One of the best ways for the newcomer to break into the market is to submit short-item filler material for which many magazines pay $10 or more.

A successful magazine writer must do more than conceive fresh ideas and write good articles based on them; he also must be a close student of his market. "Study the magazine; see what type of material we use and how we present it," is the advice of editors to those who would write for them. It would be a waste of time and postage to send an article on fishing to a women's magazine, unless perhaps the writer could think up a feminine angle such as how a woman should behave if her husband invites her along on a fishing trip. The usual procedure on major articles is for the writer to query a magazine with his idea; then if the editor indicates interest, the author either submits a detailed outline or the complete article.

There also is a market for the sale of pictures by free-lance photographers to company and trade magazines.

## JOB OPPORTUNITIES

The magazine industry provides interesting, stimulating, and generally well-paid jobs for thousands of men and women. On some periodicals the editorial staff members do extensive writing, handling special departments and articles, whereas on others the editors are engaged largely in selection and editing of submitted material.

Magazines offer larger opportunities for the woman editorial worker than newspapers do. The percentage of staff positions held by women is greater and the opportunity for advancement to high editorial positions is much brighter. Feminine associate editors, managing editors, and even editors-in-chief are not uncommon.

Although there is no certain formula for the man or woman college graduate to use in seeking a magazine job, the surest way to draw attention to yourself is to sell the magazine some articles or stories. The very fact that the editor buys the material shows that he approves of the writer's work. Personal contacts developed in this editor-writer relationship sometimes lead to staff positions. In some of the large magazines young men and women get their start in the research department and other jobs around the fringe of the editorial staff.

Large magazines draw many of their staff members from the trade magazines and company publications, much as metropolitan newspapers hire reporters who have had training on smaller dailies. The mechanical techniques of magazine editing and design are complex and can best be learned by experience on smaller publications.

Industrial magazines are among the finest training grounds for magazine workers. This is a rapidly expanding field, as more and more corporations realize the value of issuing a periodical for customers, employees, salesmen, stockholders, and other groups the management wishes to impress. These are divided into internal publications, for distribution within a company, and external ones, which go to nonemployee readers. Many are combinations of these approaches. The type of distribution influences the kind of editorial matter used and to some extent the size of the staff. The best available estimate puts the number of editorial employees on company publications around 15,000. Although many of these publications are prepared by a single editor, with clerical help, the more elaborate ones have a staff of six or eight editors. They use the same technique of design, multicolored art work, and editorial presentation as those employed by the better-known consumer magazines.

External publications usually are published by manufacturers who hope for repeat sales of their products of relatively high price. The automobile manufacturers are among the most lavish publishers in this field; magazines like the *Ford Times* and *Dodge News* are widely circulated to maintain contact with users and to promote sales and service.

Many fraternal and nonprofit organizations publish magazines, too, in order to maintain the bond with their members or supporters. Such periodicals as *American Legion* and the *Rotarian* publish a rather broad range of general articles which their editors consider of interest to their readers and interweave promotional and fraternal material about the sponsoring organization.

A college degree, or at least a partial college education, is almost essential for the editorial job applicant in the magazine field. Although quite a few industrial editors have moved into that work from other corporation departments, a recent survey shows that three out of four editors of these industrial magazines are college graduates. The percentage in consumer magazines is probably even higher.

Work on specialized magazines, both of the industrial magazine and trade varieties, sometimes requires technical knowledge in such fields as engineering, electronics, and chemistry. It is natural for a young man or woman seeking a job to enter whatever trade field holds particular interest for him or her. No matter what technical knowledge may be necessary, however, the fundamental requirement in all magazine work is a sound training in English. With this foundation and a willingness to work hard at learning the rudiments of a specialized field, the aspiring trade journal or industrial editor can progress steadily. A knack for simplifying technical material for the layman reader is a desirable asset. College courses in economics are valuable in almost any kind of magazine work because so much of the material printed in magazines deals in some way with the operations of American business. Many schools offer industrial and technical curricula to help their students prepare for industrial journalism.

Pay scales on magazines are generally attractive and rise to high figures for a small number of men and women in the top editorial positions of the mass circulation magazines. The chief editor of a major consumer magazine may receive a salary of at least $25,000 a year, going to more than $100,000, if he is a veteran with a proven "touch" or if he directs the work of a magazine group.

These high salaries carry with them a substantial amount of job uncertainty. If a magazine begins to lose circulation or advertising, frequently one of the first corrective moves is to change editors, even though the fault may not lie in the editorial department at all. When a magazine is struggling to work out a new formula to regain readership, it may try several editors before finding one who can do the job. The pay offered to college graduates as beginners is in line with that offered by other media.

Salaries in the trade and industrial magazine fields are somewhat lower but still good, and the job security is better. A recent survey by the International Association of Business Communicators shows that salaries for industrial editors range to $15,000 a year or somewhat higher. The salaries received by editors of large farm publications range from $15,000 to $25,000.

Editorial and business offices of most large national magazines are in New York and other eastern cities. Trade publication headquarters are situated throughout the United States, depending in part upon the market being served. There are numerous editorial links between magazine and book publishing, since much magazine material eventually finds its way into book form. This leads to some movement of editorial workers from magazines to book publishing firms and occasionally back in the other direction. Many writers and editors move into magazine work from positions on newspapers; in fact, most magazine staff writers and editors have a background of newspaper work.

# Chapter 15

# *Book Publishing*

## THE ROLE OF BOOKS

Books are a medium of mass communication that deeply affect the lives of all of us. They convey much of the heritage of the past, help us understand ourselves and the world we live in, and enable us to plan better for the future. Books are a significant tool of our educational process. And they provide entertainment for people of every age.

The nation's educational, business, professional, and social life could not survive long without books. Judges and attorneys must examine law tomes continually; doctors constantly refer to the repositories of medical wisdom and experience; governmental officials must remain aware of all the ramifications of legislative fiat. Teachers and pupils alike find in textbooks the vast knowledge of history, philosophy, the sciences, literature, and the social sciences accumulated throughout the ages. Men and women in every walk of life read to keep abreast of a fast-changing world; to find inspiration, relaxation, and pleasure; and to gain knowledge. Books, without doubt, explain and interpret virtually every activity.

Creative writing has been one of the principal hallmarks by which each succeeding world civilization has been measured; the works of Plato and Aristotle, for example, both reflected and refined the quality of early Greek life. Social historians long have examined the creative literature as well as the factual records of a civilization in their efforts to reconstruct the life of the people of a particular time and place. In the United States today the finest published fiction has a reverberating impact upon our society; the ideas and the techniques employed have an enormous effect on the theater, movies, television scripts, and magazine pieces. Many outstanding productions result from the book publisher's enterprise in encouraging and promoting new as well as established authors. Creative writing enhances most of the art forms by which our civilization will one day be judged.

Whether they are paperbacks or hard-cover volumes printed on quality paper, books provide a permanence characteristic of no other communications medium. The newspaperman and the radio-television commentator write and speak in the main to an ephemeral audience. Those who write for magazines may anticipate longer life for their messages. Books, however, such as the superb copies of the Bible produced by Gutenberg in the fifteenth century, have an almost endless existence.

Clarence Day put it so aptly: "The world of books is the most remarkable creation of man. Nothing else that he builds ever lasts. Monuments fall, nations perish, civilizations grow old and die out and, after an era of darkness, new races build others. But in the world of books are volumes that have seen this happen again and again and yet live on, still young, still as fresh as the day they were written, still telling men's hearts of the hearts of men centuries dead."

For the mass communicator, books and book publishing provide several important functions. They not only serve as well-springs of knowledge for him as for all men, but through translation and reprinting book publishing may convey his own ideas to billions of people throughout the world. And in the publishing trade itself the journalist may find a rewarding outlet for his skills in editing and promoting the distribution of books.

In the writing of books, journalists such as Harrison Salisbury, David Halberstam, Tom Wolfe, Walter Lippmann, John Gunther, John Hersey, and William Allen White, to name only a few, have vastly increased the size of the audience for their reporting efforts and each has produced an impact in the world of ideas that almost invariably accompanies the creation of a widely read book.

Because of the relative slowness of writing, editing, and publishing a manuscript, books lack the characteristic of immediacy possessed by other media in conveying messages to the public. What may be lost in timeliness, however, is often more than compensated for by the extreme care possible in checking facts, attaining perspective, and rewriting copy for maximum effectiveness. This sustained, systematic exposition of a story or of an idea (with the reader's concomitant opportunity to reread, underscore, and study at leisure) is afforded only by books among all the media of communication.

Unlike most newspapers, but like many magazines, books may have a highly selective audience that makes it not only unnecessary but also undesirable to aim the communication at a fairly low common denominator of reading or listening ability. Nevertheless, authors and publishers definitely are engaged in mass communication, even though their efforts at times may be, directed toward only a very small segment of the public.

## A COMMON HERITAGE

Newspapers, magazines, and books had a common beginning, and the paths to the attainment of their present central roles in civilization were beset by mutual problems pertaining to printing and distribution. The art of writing itself has been traced well beyond 4500 B.C. when the ancient Egyptians carved hieroglyphic, or pictograph, messages in stone and the Babylonians formed their wedge-shaped, or cuneiform, letters in clay tablets. In China scholars used ink made from tree sap to write on slips of bamboo or wood. The first books may possibly have consisted of a number of these bamboo slips, each about 9 inches long, tied together by a thong. When learned men such as the philosopher Me T had to load their bamboo books into several carts to transport them from place to place, it was apparent that a new writing material was needed. The Chinese are credited with the invention of paper, and Egypt later developed the first cheap writing material, made from papyrus plants growing along the Nile.

Europeans, however, did not begin making paper until the fourteenth century. Their books had been hand-written and illustrated on vellum or parchment, usually by the monks. Gutenberg's invention of movable type opened the door to the printing of books on paper, of which his famous Bible of 1456 is an example. Several million volumes came off European presses by 1500; this printing of books in large quantities paved the way for the religious reformation and made possible popular education.

Both books and newspapers, which developed as news books and broadsides, were considered threats to the authority of church and state. In England Henry VIII started the control of the press with a list of prohibited books in 1529. The censorship restrictions which continued until 1694 were aimed as much at books and pamphlets as at newspapers.

The human target often was the same, for the occupations of bookselling and journalism were closely allied throughout the early period. The book-shop was the center of literary culture; the printer was often also the bookseller; it was he who got out the news broadsides and news books. The heavy emphasis upon book advertising in early newspapers also testifies to the link.

Book and newspaper publishing were also closely identified in early United States history. The first book published in the American colonies came off the Puritans' Cambridge printing press in 1640. Early book publishing in each colony often was of a religious tone, but local histories were also produced. Then, as the journalists took over, the horizons widened. Benjamin Harris, who got out one issue of his *Publick Occurrences* in Boston in 1690, was a bookseller importing from London. Editors such as James and Benjamin Franklin had sizable libraries and reprinted literary material in their papers—including Daniel Defoe's *Robinson Crusoe*. The patriot journalist Isaiah Thomas was also an important book publisher; his shop at Worcester produced the first American novel, the first American dictionary, more than 400 technical books, and 100 children's books. Thomas was the first American to publish Blackstone's *Commentaries,* Bunyan's *Pilgrim's Progress,* and Defoe's *Robinson Crusoe* in book form. He himself wrote a two-volume history of American printing.

By 1820 more than 50,000 titles, including books, magazines, and newspapers, were listed as American. Readers were still buying 70 percent of their books from European publishers even though American book publishing was increasing 10 percent in a decade. Names such as Emerson, Thoreau, Poe, Cooper, and Whitman emerged in the realm of American literature, giving both books and magazines a great lift, even though English writers such as Dickens remained favorites. By 1850 and later some publishing houses, including Harper's and Scribner's, were active in both the book and magazine fields. Book publishing, however, came to require distinctively specialized equipment and editing knowl-edge, and the two areas of book publishing and journalism gradually became separate.

The great cultural stirring following the Civil War brought a sharp expansion of both scholarly book publishing and publication of literary and popular books. Works in science, history, and philosophy came from the presses along with millions of encyclopedias and even more dime novels. Free public libraries, spreading across the country after 1880, played an important part in stimulating book publishing and reading. Henry James, Mark Twain, and William Dean Howells became leading names in American literature. At the turn of the century the "muck-rakers" produced books as well as countless newspaper and magazine articles to expose instances of corruption and greed in American life— among them were Lincoln Steffens, Jack London, Frank Norris, and Upton Sinclair. Thus the print media continued to share a common background in their use by American writers to discuss the social, political, and economic problems of each generation. Social historians must examine all the print media to gain a full understanding of the development of our civilization.

### THE SCOPE OF BOOK PUBLISHING

Today, book publishing is a pygmy among American industrial giants; it represents only a tiny fraction of the country's more than $800 billion economy. Yet some 2,500,000,000 books and approximately 38,000 new titles (including 26,000 brand new ones) are issued annually by more than 1500 firms. Actually, some 900 publishers bring out nearly all of these titles, and the top 100 publishers issue about 60 percent of them. In general (trade) publishing, fewer than 5 percent of hardbound books sell more than 5000 copies in the life of the particular title.

Because of the availability of all types of specialized services, most publishing companies are concentrated in New York, Boston, Chicago, and Philadelphia.

Textbook publishing produces over one-third of the industry's annual gross income of almost $3,200,000,000. It is estimated that 700,000,000 new textbooks are sold each year. About 290,000,000 copies of hardcover adult general trade books are sold annually through bookstores and book clubs, and by direct mail. Children's books sell close to 170,000,000 copies.

Book publishing offers a number of intriguing specialties. Many publishers concentrate successfully in special areas. Medical, religious, garden, law, music, and art books, suspense stories, westerns—all may constitute special departments of publishing firms. University press publishing, concerned mainly with materials by and for the use of scholars, attracts many interested in embarking on a publishing career. Subscription-reference book publishing is one of the largest and most remunerative special areas with sales exceeding $600,000,000.

Approximately 7 percent of the total volume of books, largely texts, scholarly works, and paper-bound reprints, are exported to overseas markets for a revenue in excess of $200,000,000 a year.

There are more than 9000 outlets for hard-cover books in the United States, including more than 2300 general bookstores, about 200 college stores, and about 900 book divisions of department stores. Around 200 book clubs receive nearly $300,000,000 a year from readers. More than 70,000 libraries acquire books. Among them are about 5800 public library systems and more than 4000 branches; 2200 university, college, and junior college libraries; 4000 "special" libraries such as law and medical collections; and around 55,000 libraries in elementary and secondary schools.

The inexpensive paperbound book today is a vital part of every branch of book publishing. In fact, paperbacks have been with us both here and in Europe since the early 1800's, with a major splurge here taking place in the 1870's and 1880's. In 1885 about one-third of all titles published were bound in paper; the same is true again today.

Since World War II the sale of paperbacks, in drug stores, news stands, supermarkets, airports, regular bookstores, and elsewhere has cut deeply into the sale of magazines and second-hand books but is often deliberately coordinated with the sale of hard-cover books. In 1971 paperback sales by publishers were in excess of $257,000,000. The sale of paperbacks to libraries, to elementary and secondary schools, and to colleges and universities has increased dramatically. Printed from rubber plates on high-speed rotary presses, these volumes are to a large extent books that have previously succeeded in the conventional format, but many are brand new titles, some for popular entertainment, some for use in schools and colleges, some for home guidance and instruction. The prices of all paperbacks have risen markedly, but there is still a meaningful price gap between them and the cloth-bound books. Publishers generally are pleased that the huge sales of paperbacks have increased reading, proliferated the use of books, and, as a result, made all forms of publishing more profitable.

Most leading book publishing firms that started 100 or more years ago began as either printers or booksellers. Today, with the exception mainly of Doubleday and some university presses, book publishers have removed themselves from the printing field. The temptation to feed the hungry presses and pressroom gangs by taking on inferior and unsalable manuscripts was one of the principal contributing reasons. And only Scribner's, Harcourt Brace Jovanovich, Doubleday, and McGraw-Hill operate bookstores of their own. A merger trend during the 1960's caused the submergence of such separate entities as Macmillan, Appleton-Century-Crofts, Row, Rinehart, World Book, D.C. Heath, Ginn, and D. Van Nostrand. These consolidations mainly occurred after Wall Street "discovered" the publishing field despite its relatively small size. Beginning in 1959, publishers were offered the chance to "go public," that is, to convert their proprietorship into shares that would be traded and priced on the stock market. More than 20 firms responded. Not only did publishers themselves diversify their product offerings by buying companies that produced materials in other media, but conglomerates and communications firms acquired publishing companies. Many integrated firms, however, ran into trouble, and by 1973 the merger trend virtually had ended. Corporate management often was unable to cope with the variety of diversified business and was troubled by something as highly specialized and individualistic as book publishing. It was frequently found better to run an acquired company as a subsidiary, and many acquisitions were spun off as not satisfying growth requirements.

Only about 3000 booksellers are deemed worth calling on by the regular salesmen from general trade publishing firms. As George Gallup has pointed out, Denmark, a nation with a population smaller than the state of New Jersey, has 650 bookstores. If the United States had the same number in proportion to population, we would have in the neighborhood of 23,000 bookstores. This same Gallup survey showed, too, that fewer books are read in America than in any other major English-speaking country. In England, for example, where the typical citizen has far less schooling than has the typical citizen here, about three times as many people were found to be reading books at any given time, and in Canada almost twice as many people read books as in this country. The statement is sometimes made, in defense of American readers, that both fiction and non-fiction, later to appear in book form, are first read in the popular magazines and that Americans do as much *reading* as other nations when newspapers and periodicals are also taken into account. But we are concerned here more with a qualitative than a quantitative judgment. Relatively little first-class fiction or nonfiction, other than material written primarily to entertain, is issued and read except in book form—hard-bound or paperback.

## THE CHALLENGE OF PUBLISHING

Is book publishing a business or a profession? What strong attraction does it hold for the thousands who have made it their life's work? Chandler B. Grannis, in his Columbia University Press book entitled, *What Happens in Book Publishing,* has the following to say about the basic nature of publishing:

> Book publishers may be overheard referring to their work, loftily, as a profession; realistically, as a business; ruefully, as a gamble. It is essentially a business, of course. It is something of a gamble, too, in that it involves considerable risks, even when its effort is directed towards educational or specialized audiences that can pretty well be estimated in advance. But it is a business that has strong professional overtones; it serves all the professions and it has room for a remarkable number of professional skills and nonpublishing professional backgrounds. Moreover, it faces a responsibility to society akin to the responsibility faced by educators.

The fascination of book publishing may lie in the undercurrent of excitement that accompanies the discovery of new authors and the sparking of ideas in them. Or perhaps the fascination stems from the very diversity of the industry, for a wholly different batch of new products must be promoted and sold each season. (What other manufacturer of physical entities can make such a claim?) The gambling aspect to which Grannis refers may account for part of the interest: who knows whether a book will flop financially or will sell a half-million copies? A strong appeal also undoubtedly lies in the highly individualistic, nonscientific nature of book publishing, with important decisions often based on intuition as well as an analysis.

Vice Admiral H. G. Rickover, U.S. Navy, emphasized the professional nature of book publishing in an address before the Publishers' Lunch Club in New York City. He complimented the publishers for printing books "on any subject under the sun" and for publishing controversial books and books that appeal to limited audiences, "though you know full well they may bring you no profit." He likened this concept of professional service to that of "good physicians whose practice habitually includes patients too poor to pay their medical bills."

Warning that technology is undermining human liberty by creating giant, bureaucratic organizations that often are oblivious to human needs, Admiral Rickover said that book publishing, because of its professional, individualistic spirit, is one of the few remaining strongholds of free men against huge enterprises that tend to consider only economic rights. Said Rickover:

> Your business is conducted more nearly as a profession than any other business I know. I assume this is due, in part, to the kind of work you do; in part, to the human scale of your enterprises. So far, you have avoided the organizational giantism that is so prominent a feature of American life.
>
> Huge organizations have difficulty maintaining a professional viewpoint; chiefly because, in our country at least, such organizations are customarily run not by the people who do the productive work but by a special category of career men whose particular *metier* is to rule large-scale enterprises—the "pure" administrators. To them, the decisive consideration is the good of the organization, by which they nearly always mean whatever enhances its power and profit. Administrators are rarely receptive to the professional viewpoint which has an ethic of its own; an ethic that, to professional people, supersedes material considerations.
>
> It is then perhaps not surprising that when communications enterprises grow overlarge, and therefore succumb to the rule of "pure" administrators, they tend to interpret freedom of speech and the press as an *economic* right, the right of communications media to decide what to say or print and, conversely, what to play down or omit entirely. All too often, the determining factor will be profit, not principle. In contrast, *you* see more clearly that freedom of speech and of the press is a great constitutional right and has as its correlative the obligation to give the public the truth in all matters—all of the truth, no matter how controversial, how distasteful to powerful pressure groups. Book publishing is today the main bulwark of freedom of speech and the press, in the original sense of the expression which meant not an *economic* but a *human* right—the right to be informed and the right to be heard. I hope you will never grow so large that you lose your basic professionalism.

William Jovanovich, president of Harcourt Brace Jovanovich, has called attention to the creative craftsmanship that must be displayed by all persons engaged in the production of books. Addressing a conference of editors, designers, and production men, he declared:

> The essence of our work is that the skill and imagination of writers and artists and publishing people are eventually transpired into learning and insight by readers of books. As an end in itself, you and I would wish to seek new forms of communication and to fashion words and lines into aesthetic and

meaningful patterns. We are compelled to this, beyond the goads of the market place, because we are dealing with a noble thing: the book.

Is it not a wonder to watch an idea nurtured, made viable? Is it not a sustenance to be so engaged that an idea is made whole and visible by words and lines and is given permanence by ink and paper and cloth so that at last there is a book that will stand in welcome readiness on a shelf, will be carried to and from in a hurried young hand, and will perhaps bring to old eyes of an afternoon the picture of bright mornings in the beginning?

### STEPS IN PUBLISHING

All books begin with an idea, germinated usually by the author or by an editor employed by a publishing concern. If the author has the idea, he generally prepares a précis and perhaps several sample chapters and submits them to a literary agent or publisher. If it is the editor's idea, he seeks out the writer who he believes can best develop the book he has in mind. Publishing firms vary in the number of editors employed and the duties with which they are charged. In general, however, the editor works closely with an author in the preparation of a manuscript, and he also may shepherd the work through various business and production stages. The editor must keep abreast of matters of public taste and interest and be able to anticipate insofar as possible the types of books that will find markets in the months ahead. Reference, technical, and textbook editors, having specialized subject matter, often employ professional readers, but trade editors, especially in fiction, are less likely to employ outside advice.

A common fallacy held by each summer's crop of job applicants in book publishing is that a publisher, or an editor, is simply a person of taste who sits with his feet on his desk waiting for hungry authors to seek him out with best-selling manuscripts. Book publishing, however, is like an iceberg. The part that shows, namely books that are reviewed in mass media journals and magazines and that are sold in the general bookstores, constitutes only about 8 percent of the over-all dollar volume in books. For every editor who breaks bread with a Philip Roth or a Norman Mailer, there are hundreds who are editing reference works or working with college and school textbook authors. For most publishing houses, the over-the-transom manuscript is almost never publishable. The beginning reader of these voluntary contributions soon becomes appalled with his screening operation.

Accepted manuscripts are turned over to copy editors, who search for grammatical, spelling, and punctuation errors; corroborate facts; correct discrepancies in style (such as writing 20th Century in one chapter and twentieth century in another); perhaps cut the copy to a predetermined length (despite the author's probable scream of anguish: "Sir, would you cut the Bible?!"). The copy editor must also coordinate entries in the bibliography with the citations in footnotes (if the book has them); insure that chapter headings correspond with tables of contents; relate pictures, tables, charts, and the like with the text; query the author if necessary; read the galley proofs including indexes; check corrections made by the author in the proofs; and in general satisfy himself that the text is as accurate as possible.

The production department, which may consist of from three or four to two dozen or more persons, normally serves as the book publisher's liaison with the printer. Highly specialized employees oversee the designing of the book, obtain art work if necessary, estimate length, select the type and paper, and order the typesetting, printing, binding, and preparation of the cover and the jacket. Every book presents an individual problem and every stage of production must be worked out carefully in advance.

Long before the book has been produced, plans are under way for its distribution. The sales department studies possible markets and lays its campaign plans in cooperation with advertising, promotion, and publicity personnel. The "travelers" who visit bookstore buyers throughout the country are called in for conferences concerning the entire list of books being prepared for sale. In accordance with the advertising budget established for the book, based on anticipated sales, media are selected and dealer aids such as posters, circulars, or mail enclosures are prepared.

The publicity department writes and mails news releases, arranges author interviews and other appearances, sends copies to reviewers, announces the book in trade magazines, arranges for exhibits at conventions attended by book sellers, and works on other "angles" to promote the sale of the book. The primary responsibility of the promotion department is to establish a climate of acceptance for the new title, employing every possible means at hand.

The larger accounts may be called on by the publisher's salesmen 15 or

20 times per year. The men work normally on salary or commission or a combination of the two, and frequently carry the lines of two or more houses. There are more than 700 men currently so employed. In addition, of course, some salesmen call on book sellers in behalf of jobbers and other outlet accounts.

There are today more than 1000 college travelers and these men perform a distinctly different function. Calling on the nation's college professors, they make certain that their clients are acquainted with or have complimentary copies of textbooks appropriate to the courses they teach. Travelers seldom if ever write up bookstore orders themselves. They must hope that the professors they visit, who usually have freedom of textbook selection, will give them their share of business via the local college bookstore. The college traveler also acts as a manuscript scout for his firm since all of its college textbooks are, of course, written by college professors.

The more than 2000 school book agents work through state, county, and city adoption systems in selling their wares except where local boards of education, teachers, or superintendents are involved. School textbooks are largely written by staff members of a publishing house working in active collaboration with professional teachers.

Many other ramifications involved in producing and selling books are not covered in this sketch of the principal steps in publishing. It is an intricate business, and many years are required to learn the ground rules.

### HOW THE MASS COMMUNICATOR FITS IN

The kinship of book publishing to other mass media activities should be apparent. There are writing and editing to be done; copy editing and proofreading; illustrating and designing; and advertising, publicity and other forms of promotion, printing, and distribution. There must be shrewd insight into what the public is interested in, and why; the newspaper city editor's sense of rapport with his readers finds its counterpart in the identification of the book editor with the tastes of various segments of the book-buying population.

It is true, as pointed out earlier in this chapter, that book publishing is a step removed from the operations of the other media that have a genuinely mass audience to deal with continually; books often are read by highly selective groups. Yet, reporting and editing and preparing advertisements for any of the other media can provide an ideal background for the performance of those duties in the book publishing field. The writer for newspapers, magazines, and radio-television, for example, inevitably gains insights into human life that can be drawn upon to advantage at the book editor's desk. As a student as well as a practitioner of effective writing, he can recognize craftsmanship in others and can quickly spot good or poor writing in the manuscript he is reading. The editor's experience in rewriting the work of others can enable him to shore up the weak spots he finds. As a journalist, he has learned to respect facts and documentation and will insist upon high standards in the materials that cross his desk in the book publishing offices. He knows the principles of style and grammar; he can supervise the work of copy editors, as well as proofreaders. His experience in having worked with printers and with other high-priced craftsmen, including photographers, artists, engravers, and pressmen, will assist him well in the all-important area of reducing job costs. As a reporter or editor for a newspaper, magazine, or radio or television station, he has drawn paychecks from a profit-making organization and has gained an appreciation of sound business methods that serves him well in dealing with authors who may never have earned bread and butter in the ordinary business world.

The knowledge of typography that the mass communicator learns in journalism school or on the job will be of use to him in the ordering of printing for a book and the production of its cover and jacket. The advertising staff man or woman can draw upon this same knowledge of typography, as well as other journalistic techniques, in the preparation of direct mail folders, posters, and advertisements for newspapers and magazines. He will find that the same principles of copy, layout, illustration, color, and selection of paper and ink apply in the preparation of advertisements for new books.

The man or woman writing news releases and other publicity materials, and contacting the various media, will likely be a former newspaper editorial employee. There is no substitute for such experience in fitting a person for effective promotion, publicity, and general public relations duties. The cliché, "I was a newspaperman once myself," can truthfully be voiced by most employees in these departments.

## RUNGS ON THE JOB LADDER

Horace Greeley's celebrated admonition, "Go west, young man!," still applies to beginners in the book publishing trade. Even the publisher's son "hits the road" west—or north or south, as the case may be—to learn the business from bottom up. Traveling to the cultural oases of the nation—wherever books are bought, sold, and read—is the normal beginning pursuit for men who seek careers in book publishing. The theory (and it has been proved a thousand times) is: You can't become a good editor sitting in a New York or Boston office; you can learn the facts of bookselling life only by prolonged and intimate acquaintance with a constantly changing market, finding out what will sell, and what won't, and getting a pretty good idea of "why" in both cases.

It's a rigorous, timetabled sort of life, but after three or four years the traveler, now well seasoned, may wish to swap his suitcase for a swivel chair in the home office, qualified to serve as an editor or in some other specialized capacity.

Scores of men, however, make lifelong careers as travelers. They enjoy being their own bosses and being free from office routine. Although traveling is the best way to enter publishing, it also may serve as an end in itself.

Most travelers are personable, college-trained lovers of books whose starting salaries generally range upwards from $6000, depending on their age, experience, and potential. All their expenses while on the road are paid, of course. An experienced traveler may net between $10,000 and $25,000 or even more annually.

Moving in to the main publishing offices, he most likely will put his road experience to work in textbook, general trade, or the editorial, sales, or advertising department. Or he may elect to enter the production department. Eventually, he may become a department head, later perhaps an officer and director of the company. The creativity and business knowledge that could propel him to such heights merit accompanying income boosts to the $25,000, $35,000, or maybe even the $50,000 range.

That is the male route to the top. The women skip the road work, but frequently have an equally humble beginning as typists who earn $5500 a year. With a toehold thus established, they become secretaries earning $7000 to $8000 per year. Indirectly and gradually, they display an interest in subject matter, tackling the pile of unsolicited manuscripts that almost every mail delivery augments. They make brief reports of the value of these manuscripts; as their judgment is corroborated by an editor, they are given more creative tasks. Some demonstrate an admirable ability at correcting grammatical errors and punctuation faults and become copy and proof editors. Others prove they can rewrite portions of manuscripts with distinction. Those with an even more scholarly bent may exhibit proficiency in researching facts in encyclopedias and other reference works.

There is a fairly definite ceiling for opportunity at this point in their development, but some ascend the publishing ladder as editors. More women find success in editing or producing children's books than in any other field of book publishing. Countless others, however, move into well-paying advertising and publicity jobs. They write news and feature copy, prepare advertising materials, compose jacket blurbs, engineer radio and television personal appearances and lecture tours, and otherwise exhibit ingenuity in promoting the sale of books. For these services they may be paid from $7000 to as high as $25,000 annually.

Hundreds of persons free-lance as copy editors, taking manuscripts home with them to earn $3.50 to $8.00 per hour. Those who read galley proofs often work at the printer's plant.

The type composition, printing, and binding of books is done largely by a few hundred manufacturers, mostly in the East and Midwest. These firms require, in addition to their mechanical workers and craftsmen, people who can work with a publisher client: they include estimators, design and layout consultants, proofreaders, schedulers, and warehouse and delivery planners and supervisors. Some men and women who enter the graphic trades provide invaluable liaison with the publishing world. In addition to the book manufacturing specialist firms, there are thousands of typographic, printing, and binding plants, large and small, of which many do at least some book work. Persons who demonstrate a real ability in the graphic arts area are well rewarded financially in such commercial enterprises.

#### QUALIFICATIONS

A good education, high intelligence, a love of books, and an ability to keep abreast of the latest trends and developments in all phases of human life but particularly in the area of one's specialization are prime characteristics of a good editor. He need not be a creative writer; in fact, there is little place in book publishing for the varying temperament that frequently afflicts (or aids) authorship. Persons with highly individual ideas and taste are sometimes less willing to remain anonymous and to play second fiddle to authors with quixotic personalities. The good editor has the capacity to deal in calm, unruffled fashion with the prima donnas whose genius or near-genius often spells the difference between profit and loss in a publishing year. ("Sir, don't you dare change a word of this manuscript!" "I insist on an advertisement on every book review page in the country!")

The ideal copy editor is a perfectionist who can detect the slightest deviations in style and form. He has the forbearance to leave original writing alone; yet his necessary alterations are so skillfully done that no author objects. He has a mania for the exact word and can verify a fact with expedition.

Whether he wishes to become a general editor, a copy or proof editor, an advertising specialist, or a publicity or promotion man, the college graduate who aspires to a career in book publishing will profit by an education, as well as experience, in mass communications. He will seek to acquire a sound background in literature, history, languages, the natural and social sciences, philosophy—in fact, in all areas of knowledge that comprise a liberal education. He will not overlook his professional education, for the insights, skills, and fundamental knowledge gained in the classrooms and laboratories of a school of communications should prove of inestimable value throughout his career.

# Chapter 16

# *Advertising*

## ADVERTISING AND THE FUTURE

Advertising has come to play a unique and central role in the functioning of the American economic system. Our skills in producing goods and services have grown so great that *production* no longer is our primary concern, as is still the case in most countries. Instead, *distribution* has the principal task of maintaining a high level of employment and general prosperity. And the distribution of goods and services depends largely upon the effective use of advertising in the media.

As Frederick R. Gamble, former president of the American Association of Advertising Agencies, has pointed out:

Advertising is the counterpart in distribution of the machine in production. By the use of machines, our production of goods and services has been multiplied. By the use of mass media, advertising multiplies the selling effort. Advertising is the great accelerating force in distribution. Reaching many people rapidly at low cost, advertising speeds up sales, turns prospects into customers in large numbers and at high speed. Hence, in a mass-production and high-consumption economy, advertising has the greatest opportunity and the greatest responsibility for finding customers.

Advertising men are a creative and resourceful lot, but even they have not been able to find the proper words to describe adequately the tremendous rise of advertising since World War II. In 1947 American business spent slightly over $4,000,000,000 to cry its wares. By 1971 advertising exceeded $22,520,000,000 a year, a figure expected to rise to $25,000,000,000 or more in 1973. An advertising environment, like it or not, was a way of life in America. A Harvard study, for example, indicated that the average adult was exposed potentially to 500 ads daily in television, radio, newspapers, and magazines. Throw in billboards, direct mail, and such specialty items as book matches and ballpoint pens, and you have perhaps 1500 ad exposures each day.

The packages in which most products are displayed so attractively in these days of self-service constitute another form of advertising. The more than $14,000,000,000 spent annually in the packaging of products is certain to increase substantially.

In the United States advertising is serving a population now exceeding 200,000,000 and expected to reach 240,000,000 within 20 years. The child and youth market has swelled immeasurably, and medical science is helping to increase the ranks of the middle-aged and the elderly. The production of goods and services inevitably must expand tremendously, and advertising will expand right along with them.

An historic surge of research and development by American industry, education, and government has produced more efficient manufacturing as well as countless new products. Research expenditures now exceeding $15,000,000,000 each year have revolutionized much of American business. For example, in only a decade we increased the production of plastics by 300 percent, electronics 240 percent, and aluminum products 200 percent. The manufacturing and marketing of semiconductors alone is a half-billion-dollar per year business. Approximately 10,000 new products account for 10 percent of all sales each year, and the volume of new products is increasing rapidly. Advertising, along with its marketing aids of sales promotion, product design, packaging, point-of-purchase displays, product publicity, and public relations, has its work cut out for it.

J. Davis Danforth, formerly executive vice president of one of the largest advertising agencies, Batten, Barton, Durstine & Osborn, Inc., took a look at the future in a speech before an advertising group, and declared:

If our national productivity increases, as most economists predict, advertising will have to grow to move the mountain of goods which will be produced. New color television sets, fuel injection automobiles, hundreds of new appliances that are in laboratory stages now, millions of new homes with advanced radiant heating and cooling equipment, and the astonishing new furnishings that will go into them . . . and we'll have to help sell them all!

We will be selling windows that close themselves when it rains, and food that will be practically nonperishable, irradiated by electronic rays to keep it fresh almost indefinitely. Perhaps you will shop by TV by just sitting at home and dialing a number, color TV will hang in a picture frame on your wall, phones will come equipped with viewing screens so you will be able to see as well as hear (is that good?). Already we can dial long distance almost anywhere in the country without ever contacting an operator. We will have doubledeck streets in the high traffic centers, daily newspapers may be printed in color, and perhaps you will have a unit in your house so that your morning newspaper will be printed right in your own home while you are sleeping. With the new science of geriatrics, everybody is going to live longer—maybe even advertising men! . . .

Advertising men almost certainly will want to live longer, for they will be caught up in the key roles of helping to bring about the dazzling pattern of living for the future. Hundreds will find their opportunities overseas, for American business has truly gone international. Every one of the 100 leading corporations in the United States is involved with international trade, and most of them have their own manufacturing facilities overseas. Well over 100 American advertising agencies are represented abroad, and the top 10 agencies alone place more than $1,950,000,000 in international advertising each year. As more and more countries become industrialized and personal incomes increase, American business and American advertising men will explore new frontiers of worldwide expansion and opportunity. These pioneers of the future will be paid well, in both money and satisfaction, for their abilities to help move the products of a new age into the hands of people everywhere. Small wonder that advertising as a career is appealing to an increasing number of the most mentally alert and imaginative of today's youth.

## THE LURE OF ADVERTISING

Few careers provide the day-by-day job satisfactions inherent in advertising. Each sales problem that must be solved and each advertisement that must be conceived, produced, and presented to the public challenge the creativity and the skill of the men and women so engaged. The industry richly rewards those people with imagination, those with the ability to think for themselves. It brings a sense of fulfillment to those who have cultivated the "whole man"—who have achieved a liberal education through delving into philosophy, foreign languages, literature, art, music, astronomy, and other such fields. It enables them to call upon their own inner resources, to test new ideas and new approaches, and to seek results through subtle means as well as directly. Like fiction writers, they have the opportunity to *create* the mental images they want to evoke in the minds of the public.

There's an intensely satisfying thrill in seeing one's ideas assume form and substance in an advertisement or an advertising campaign that actually produces the intended response. There's an accompanying thrill in viewing the creativity of others. "It's probably terrible to say this, but I buy the *New Yorker* to read the ads," exclaimed a young advertising career woman. The advertisements, she explained, excited her aesthetic sense and produced the same stimulation that a young voice student must experience upon hearing a famous operatic singer. The most creative television and radio commercials elicit a similar response.

Since most advertising has a positive social value in bringing a higher standard of living to America and in helping to satisfy people's desires and needs, many engaged in the industry tend to identify their own efforts with these larger objectives and thus find increased satisfaction in what they are doing. Bruce Barton, who with two partners in 1919 formed an advertising agency which has since become one of the largest in the world, recalled an incident that illustrates this point. He wrote an advertisement for a life insurance company, addressing it to young husbands and fathers. From Rio de Janeiro came a reply from a 38-year-old New Jersey man, married, and the father of three children. He wanted, and obtained, a policy that would guarantee his family an income of $3000 a year in the event of his death. A few days after the policy was written, the man had a wisdom tooth extracted; the cavity became infected and he died. "That incident made a deep impression on me," Barton later wrote. "Many times in the intervening years I have been reminded that somewhere in New Jersey there are a mother and three children, now grown up, who, without the slightest suspicion of my existence, have had their whole lives changed by the fact that one day I put together some words that were printed in a magazine, and read in a faraway country by their husband and father, who was influenced to do what I suggested."

## HOW ADVERTISING DEVELOPED

Until the advent of mass selling in the nineteenth century, advertising played only a minor role in the conduct of business. In early Greek and Roman days signboards were placed above the doors of business establishments, and town criers proclaimed that merchants had certain wares for sale. These were merely means to attract customers to a shop, however; in contrast with modern advertising and sales techniques, the display of merchandise and personal selling were depended upon to make the sale.

After the invention of movable type, accelerated printing in the mid-fifteenth century, handbills, posters, and then newspapers were used in increasing quantities to advertise products. Advertisements appeared in early American newspapers, but the volume did not grow to sizable proportions until trade began to flourish in the metropolitan centers in the early days of the republic. Almost all selling was local until about 1840, when the development of railroad transportation enabled industry to send its products to consumers far from the manufacturing plants. National advertising resulted as businessmen used both magazines and newspapers to broaden their markets. The first advertising agency in the United States was organized by Volney B. Palmer in 1840 or 1841. His agency, and those which followed his, did not prepare copy but served primarily as publisher's representatives. Some 30 agencies were selling space for more than 4000 American publications by 1860. Since there were no public lists of these publications and no way of substantiating circulation claims, the agents could manipulate their buying and selling of space to substantial personal advantage.

In 1869, however, George P. Rowell began publishing *Rowell's American Newspaper Directory,* a rather complete list of newspapers together with careful estimates of circulation. The same year F. Wayland Ayer founded N. W. Ayer & Son, Inc. (with his father) to buy space in the interest of his clients rather than to sell it for newspapers, and his agency began its continuing directory of all periodicals in 1880. Soon other agencies were started along professional lines of providing planning and space-buying services for their clients. There was an upsurge in the use of pictorial art in advertisements, and the nation began to be conscious of the first widely quoted slogans such as Ivory Soap's "99 $^{44}/_{100}$ Per Cent Pure" and "It Floats," Eastman Kodak's "You Press the Button— We Do the Rest," and "Good Morning, Have You Used Pears' Soap?"

As newspaper and magazine circulations increased and new technological advances were made, advertising at the turn of the century developed new slogans, better copywriters and artists, and a greater analysis of products, media, and markets. A crusade was begun in 1911 against the gross exaggerations and misleading claims of some advertisers, notably those selling patent medicines. Various advertising organizations were formed which helped elevate the ethics of the business. To promote truth in advertising many states adopted a model statute proposed by *Printers' Ink* (a magazine for advertising people later entitled, *Marketing/Communications*, but no longer published), at the behest of the Association of Advertising Clubs. The first Better Business Bureau was formed in 1913, and the next year saw the establishment of the Audit Bureau of Circulations, a nonprofit organization making unbiased periodical audits and statements concerning a publication's circulation.

The advent of radio and a steady improvement in the techniques of advertising, such as copy-testing, the study of psychological appeals, and plans for integrated campaigns, characterized the 1920's. Advertising fought to hold its own during the depression years of the 1930's against both the near-paralysis of business and the organized objections of consumers to what they considered to be improper practices in advertising. In 1938 the Wheeler-Lea Act was passed to protect the consumer against false advertising by business firms, mainly in selling foods, drugs, and cosmetics. During this decade, however, advertisers increasingly used research methods, such as readership studies and audience measurement.

During World War II the War Advertising Council was established by advertising agencies, media, and advertisers as a voluntary contribution to the total war effort. So successful was the council in promoting the sale of war bonds, donation of blood, rationing, and the like, that it has been continued in peacetime as the Advertising Council to promote America's welfare. During the council's lifetime the advertising-communications industry has contributed more than $4,000,000,000 worth of service and facilities to one overall effort: to persuade Americans, through advertising, to take those actions which would improve the lot of their fellow citizens, the nation, and themselves.

Our booming economy after World War II produced rapid growth in all areas of advertising. Staffs were enlarged, branch offices of advertising agencies proliferated, and small agencies formed networks to provide reciprocal services for their clients in cities across the country. The development of television as an advertising medium accelerated the trend to larger agencies, however, because it increased the complexities of advertising. Television arrived at a most opportune time, for advertisers were introducing hundreds of new products and consumers were eager to learn their merits. The older media, also growing, soon adjusted to television, although radio and the national magazines felt the new competition most keenly. Advertisers turned increasingly to research to provide facts about their products and to discover the motivations of consumer markets.

Advertising in the 1970's was confronted with the staggering task of helping to move into the hands of consumers an unprecedented volume of manufactured goods. More money was entrusted to advertising personnel, and their responsibilities mounted. Management demanded more efficient methods of measuring the effectiveness of advertising as distinguished from other marketing functions. Many large agencies "went public," that is, converted their proprietorship into shares that would be traded, and priced, on the stock market. In order to generate greater profits for principals and stockholders, some agencies began diversifying into side businesses, such as retail stores and product manufacturing.

The computer, long used for such housekeeping chores as accounting, billing, and reports, came into more sophisticated use to provide breakouts and analyses necessary for sound manufacturing and advertising decisions. As information multiplied, the computer helped management, advertising, and marketing men understand the new world of product proliferation, market segmentation, automated distribution, population shifts, and the profit squeeze. A national computer network was established, using high-speed data transmission telephone lines and other communications facilities. The computer was used to analyze consumer surveys, to assist in media buying, to calculate television program cost efficiencies in relation to client objectives, and in numerous other ways.

At the same time, the attention paid to creativity, cleverness, and wit in the preparation of print and broadcast messages and campaigns led to a widely discussed "cult of creativity" in the industry. Television commercials in particular were often so full of wit and humor that many viewers considered them more entertaining than the programs. Prime examples were the creations of satirist Stan Freberg for Jeno's Pizza and Chun King products, the far-out ad campaign and marketing overhaul for Braniff Airways, and the advertising prepared for such companies as Avis, Volkswagen, and Benson & Hedges. Many new agencies were established as the most creative advertising personnel went into business for themselves. On the other hand, some advertising men decried the extensive use of wit and humor, contending that it might be entertaining but that it doesn't always sell goods and services.

As American business rapidly increased its operations overseas, new patterns of diversification were introduced into agencies. An example is Interpublic, Inc., comprising a group of components active in producing various marketing-communications services on a farflung scale. The new technology, coupled with a dynamic, fluctuating world economy, was rapidly sweeping advertising into uncharted, troubled, but rewarding waters.

Some of the criticisms leveled at the advertising industry, and the chief problems confronting it, are discussed in Chapter 8. The threat of government regulation loomed as the largest of these problems as the powerful consumer movement with its multiple pressures on industry spread rapidly. How to recruit, and hold, able young men and women so as to refresh and replenish the industry's $15,000,000,000 pool of advertising talent was another major problem. "Talent napping" was a continuing practice, and the agencies' annual turnover rate stood at 35 percent. Mounting areas of friction between clients and agencies, caused by poor communications, account conflicts, the feeling by some clients that agencies overcharge or are overpaid, failure to agree on how to measure the effectiveness of ads, and other reasons, contributed to the annual shifting of about 20 percent of all advertising accounts in the nation from one agency to another. The problems in this mercurial, exciting business were many; but few deserted it, and the level of earnings continued to rise.

## THE SIZE OF THE ADVERTISING FIELD

**In the United States.**  More than 400,000 persons are employed in all phases of advertising in this country. This estimate includes those who create or sell advertising for an advertiser, medium, or service, but not the thousands behind the scenes such as printers, sign painters, and clerical help.

Manufacturing and service concerns employ the largest number of advertising workers. Next, in order, are the mass media, including radio, television, magazines, outdoor, direct mail, and transportation advertising departments. Following them are retail establishments, advertising agencies, wholesalers, and miscellaneous specialty companies.

Almost 75,000 men and women are employed in the 4800 advertising agencies in the United States. Of the approximately 20,000 newcomers attracted into the advertising business each year, about 1500 are hired by the advertising agencies directly from college.

**International advertising.** United States advertisers, agencies, and advertising personnel have been engaged in international advertising for nearly two-thirds of a century. Today our participation is steadily and dramatically increasing. Standards of living in Europe, the Far East, Latin America, and other heretofore untapped marketing areas are constantly improving. The literacy rates have been rising, and the growth of both print and broadcast media in many countries has provided a larger audience for advertising. American wares are in great demand. We are exporting billions of dollars worth of products each year. These join the flow of goods produced by overseas plants in which Americans have invested more than $50,000,000,000.

As a consequence, giant corporations such as IBM World Trade, Standard Oil (New Jersey), Coca-Cola Export, General Motors, and Monsanto, long in the international field, are being joined by countless other companies seeking their share of the world market. IBM World Trade alone has more than 330 sales locations in 106 countries, 238 data-processing centers, and approximately 87,000 employees, almost all of whom are nationals of the countries in which they work. In 1968 its gross earnings abroad were $2,040,000,000.

The J. Walter Thompson Company and McCann-Erickson (International) in 1971 had about a third of all the advertising business of the ten largest "international agencies." The clients of these two agencies exceed 1000. Since its first foreign office was opened in London in 1889, the J. Walter Thompson Company has sent hundreds of its American employees abroad to staff them. Today more than 4500 employees work in 38 offices in 22 countries. McCann-Erickson (International) staffs its more than 50 foreign offices largely with nationals of the 22 countries in which they are located. The firm is a part of Interpublic, Inc., the parent company of 10 such corporations and divisions. Together, the J. Walter Thompson Company and McCann-Erickson (International) handle well over $650,000,000 a year in billings outside the United States, an increase of almost $450,000,000 in a three-year period. Ted Bates & Company and Young & Rubicam have overseas billings in excess of $360,000,000 annually.

The smaller domestic agencies operate overseas in four ways: through subsidiaries, of which they own part or all of the stock; through "exclusive" affiliations; through "account" affiliations with overseas agencies which may also work with other U.S. agencies; and through "export" media, such as *Life International, Reader's Digest International,* and *Vision.* The fourth method often is used along with any of the other three.

The total number of advertising employees serving overseas with U.S. companies and agencies has never been estimated. Despite automation, or partly perhaps because of it, the number is certain to increase. L. T. Steele, executive vice president of Benton & Bowles, Inc., has summed up the opportunities in this fashion:

> Young people coming into advertising . . . will discover, in the international scope of the business, a whole world of opportunities. Advertising men and women of our generation are rightfully proud of their contributions to the American economy. The new, young breed will extend these contributions to many other economies in other countries. If we, in our time, have found excitement, stimulation, and rich rewards in our careers in advertising, think how much greater their achievements can be!

It is they who will truly be co-architects of the world of tomorrow.

## WHAT ADVERTISING PEOPLE DO

Advertising may be defined as the dissemination of sales messages through purchased space, time, or other media to identify, inform, or persuade. What people do to accomplish this objective can be described by examining briefly the roles they play in advertising agencies, in advertising departments of the mass media, in retail store and company advertising departments, and, finally, in the planning of a national advertising campaign.

**Advertising agencies.** An agency first studies its client's product or service to learn the advantages and disadvantages of the product itself in relation to its competition. It then analyzes the present and potential market for which the product or service is intended. Taken into consideration next are the distribution and sales plans of the client, which are studied with a view to determining the best selection of media. A definite plan is then formulated and presented to the client.

Once the plan is approved the agency staff writes, designs, and illustrates the proposed advertisements or prepares the broadcast commercials; contracts for space or time with the media; produces the advertisements and sends them to the media with instructions; checks and verifies the use of the ads; pays for the services rendered and bills the client; and cooperates in such merchandising efforts as point-of-purchase displays.

Who are the persons who perform these services? The answer varies, since advertising agencies range in size from the so-called "one-man" agency with an owner and one or two assistants to organizations employing a thousand persons or more. The executive heads of an agency are usually people who have proved they can produce sales for their clients through print and broadcasting and who are capable of procuring new business for the agency. They may be organized as a plans board, giving general direction to such departments as research, planning, media, copy, art and layout, television production, print production, traffic, merchandising, checking, and accounting.

The key man in "servicing an account," that is, in providing liaison between the agency and the client, is the account executive. He must have a general knowledge of all phases of advertising, merchandising, and general business practices, as well as an ability to aid creatively in solving a client's special advertising problems and in planning campaigns. The account executive calls upon the agency's various departments for assistance and correlates their efforts in behalf of his particular client.

Copy and art chiefs are responsible for the actual creation of advertisements. The copywriter is a salesman, inventor, interpreter, perhaps an artist, but in particular a gifted writer. The art director is a salesman, inventor, interpreter, perhaps a writer and sometimes a producer, but always one who is visually sensitive, and he can usually draw. He sees to it that all the visual elements come together at every phase of the work, from rough layouts to finished ads. He supervises every aspect from the graphic approach to selection of type. For television, he begins by making a storyboard, the series of pictures representing the video portion of the commercial. Often, too, he helps choose the film techniques, the type of music, and the models.

The broadcasting department selects, recommends, and contracts for the programs best suited to the product to be advertised. The agency also creates the television and radio commercials and supervises their actual production.

From the moment an ad is designed and written to the time it actually appears, in magazines and newspapers, or on billboards, it is in the hands of the print production people. They are up to date on typography, printing, photoengraving, electrotyping, and allied crafts and processes. They know what is practical for reproduction and help to guide the creative departments in planning their work. They buy graphic arts services and materials and see assignments through to completion.

Because so many agency functions, including copy, art, production, and media, are involved in the same assignment—that of producing a single ad or commercial or an entire campaign—it is vital to keep everyone working smoothly and on schedule. Planning the flow and timing of all the work is the function of traffic or traffic control. Whether it is a one-man operation or a sizable staff, traffic sees that everyone does his part on time in order to meet deadlines and publishers' closing dates.

The marketing research department gathers the facts that make it possible to solve sales problems. Research findings provide vital intelligence for the agency. Facts—for instance, about what type of people use a product and why—may help provide creative people with the central idea for an advertising approach. Or media people may plan an entire advertising campaign, based on research about the way people read certain magazines or which television stations they watch.

Media people select and buy print space for ads and air time for commercials. They get the facts and figures from the research department. They must be able to sense the moods of magazines, the psychological environments of TV shows, the editorial authority of any given newspaper. They choose from daily and weekly newspapers, national magazines, business magazines, radio stations, television stations, outdoor posters, and direct mail lists, picking the most effective ones, or combinations, for each advertisement and product. And they must be able to stay within a budget.

Agencies also have people who handle sales promotion, merchandising, public relations, fashion, home economics, and personnel. And with the growth of international marketing, most major agencies have established offices or affiliates abroad that offer short- or long-term opportunities to live and work overseas. Then too, like other firms, agencies need comptrollers, secretaries, general office workers, bookkeepers, and billing clerks.

The Advertising Checking Bureau determines if the advertisements have been used by the media as planned. The agency's commission then is computed. This is generally 15 percent of the medium's published

ADVERTISING AGENCY ORGANIZATION CHART

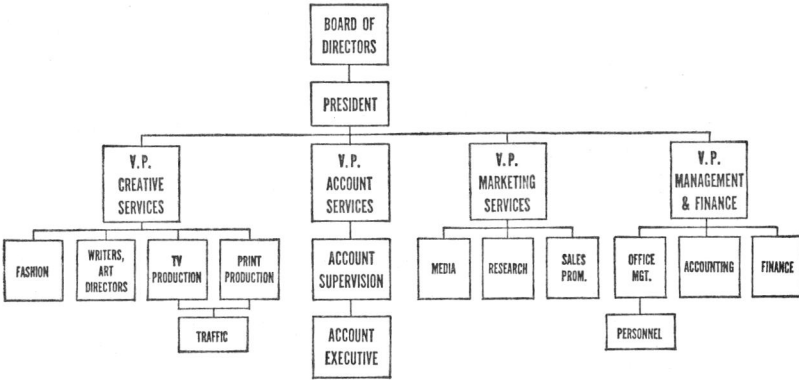

rate; if the advertising space or time cost $100, the agency collects that amount from the client and pays the medium $85. Most agencies today operate under the commission system because the bulk of their compensation comes from commissions allowed by media. This averages about 75 percent of income. The remaining 25 percent compensation to these agencies is from clients. It consists of fees, plus out-of-pocket expenditures, for special services and collateral work performed at the client's request, and service charges, or commissions as they are more commonly called, added to the cost of materials and services purchased in the preparation of advertising. The suppliers of materials and services used in preparing advertising, typography, plates, filmed commercials, artwork, printing, etc., do not allow a commission to the agencies as do the media. When these charges are billed to the advertiser, commission generally is added. Until recent years commission was usually 15 percent on the net bill, but it is becoming more standard to make the commission 17.65 percent in order to receive 15 percent on the gross bill.

After all expenses have been met, the agencies generally wind up with 2 to 3 percent net profit on their gross income each year.

**Advertising departments of mass media.** All the media employ space or time salesmen, and almost all engage national sales representatives to obtain advertising for them. The principal function of the time or space salesman is to show how the medium can assist in the sale and marketing of the product or service to be advertised. He provides fresh, up-to-date information about the markets that his newspaper, magazine, or station covers and about the medium itself. This information comes from the research men in his advertising department. His calls are not limited to the advertising agencies that generally represent the largest accounts; he also makes certain that the advertiser himself is aware of the particular advantages of his medium in selling his product or service.

Each salesman can provide general information about newspaper and magazine readership and the ratings accorded radio and television programs. These facts are coordinated by his own research and promotion departments and by national trade associations or bureaus representing each medium. Formerly, the salesman worked on a commission basis; the trend today, however, is to place him on a salary, with perhaps a bonus arrangement as well. He thus is less apt to "oversell" an account and drive away future business.

Informing and persuading generally are his chief functions in the offices of advertising agencies and in the advertising departments of large companies, since trained personnel there usually plan campaigns and prepare copy. Managers of smaller firms, however, may ask him and other media staff members, such as artists and copywriters, to carry out these latter functions. In addition, the medium provides promotion, market research, and merchandising services.

The newspaper advertising salesman often works first in the classified department, where he solicits and writes copy for the large variety of advertisements that are "classified" according to category (for rent, for sale, jobs wanted, etc.) He may move to the local retail display department, handling larger accounts, or to the general advertising staff, which cooperates with national advertising representatives in servicing nationwide accounts. Or he may be hired by an agency that wants an advanced-level staff man who has worked with the media.

Television obtains roughly 80 percent of its income from network and national spot advertising; the rest comes from local advertising. Radio, on the other hand, gets approximately 60 percent of its income from local advertising. Major advertising agencies contract for the network time, dealing directly with the networks themselves, which pay the individual stations at a specified rate for the time used. National sales representatives solicit agencies to obtain nonnetwork, or spot, advertising, which may range from a brief announcement to an entire program originating in the studios of the station. Local advertising is sold by time solicitors and prepared usually by copywriters employed by the station. Many advance to the position of commercial manager and eventually to that of general manager of the station.

Most magazines deal directly with national advertisers or indirectly through national representatives. As is true with the other media, copywriters, artists, and production, promotion, and merchandising personnel supplement the sales force. And there is a similar ladder of promotion to executive positions.

**Retail store advertising.** Retail firms employ more than 80,000 persons in their advertising departments. These range from one-man staffs to those employing dozens of persons. In a large store the advertising manager works closely with sales promotion and marketing specialists. In one large Chicago department store, the staff consists of a copy chief, production manager, and proofreader; an art director and assistant art director, together with six layout artists, five "finish" artists, and two apprentices; and five copywriters, mostly women with a high degree of creativeness who specialize in women's and children's apparel, men's apparel and accessories, and home furnishings. In addition, two copywriters are assigned to the basement store and the suburban store. Other journalistic personnel may be found in the public relations and publicity office and in the radio-television division preparing special product demonstrations.

**Industrial and trade advertising.** The public is well aware of consumer goods advertising: we see and hear advertisements almost every moment of the waking day, and often advertising jingles course through our brains even as we sleep. Not so with industrial and trade advertisements, for they are not addressed to the general public. *Industrial advertising* is employed by producers of industrial goods, such as steel, machinery, lubricants, packaging, and office equipment, in order to sell these products to other industries. *Trade advertising* is employed by the producers and distributors of branded and nonbranded consumer goods in order to reach the retailers and wholesalers of consumer goods. They, in turn, sell these goods to their own customers.

The industrial or trade advertising department may employ only one man, the advertising manager, or as many as 400 or more persons. The typical department, however, employs about seven persons. These are likely to include the advertising manager, secretarial help, a writer, perhaps an artist, and one or two persons engaged in marketing research, media evaluation, or production work.

The department handles inquiries and prepares catalogs and technical data sheets, direct mail, exhibits, and sales promotion materials such as slide films, movies, and props for sales meeting. It likely will engage in market research, but most departments obtain market data through business paper research services, without charge.

Almost all industrial and trade advertising departments employ outside agencies to handle trade advertisements. More than half the advertising placed in business publications comes from general agencies. Others identify themselves as industrial advertising agencies, although most of them also handle consumer goods advertising. They specialize in industrial, technical, scientific, commercial, and merchandising products and services. A few agencies confine themselves to such fields as financial or pharmaceutical advertising.

The industrial agency is most likely to emphasize the services of account executives who work directly with the client, write copy, and make media-buying analyses and decisions largely on their own. There is a minimum of creative direction by an overall planning board. Between 20 and 50 percent, or more, of industrial agency income is derived from fees rather than media commissions. This is caused by the fact that commissions are limited, generally amounting to only $150, often even $25 or $50, per insertion. And an agency may be called upon to prepare between 50 and 100 different advertisements each year per $100,000 in annual space expenditures. With costs for research, layout, merchandising, and public relations running high and commissions low, the charging of supplemental fees for these services is a necessity.

**Planning a national campaign.** Selecting appropriate media for a particular advertising campaign demands great business acumen and reliance on research studies. If an advertiser decides to use magazines as his vehicle, for example, he must next decide which class or group, such as women's magazines, to choose, and then must select the specific publication, such as *McCall's*. The size of the advertisement and the frequency of publication also must be determined. Similar choices must be made for all the media to be employed.

In introducing its 1970 Maverick automobile, the Ford Motor Company combined thorough market research with an advertising, sales promotion, and public relations campaign that achieved outstanding results. In so doing it followed a course of action that only five years before carried its Mustang automobile to third place in the industry in its first year on the market. Once again, the company aimed for the youth market, but this time created an automobile designed to cut deeply into the sales of such small foreign-made cars as the Volkswagen.

Ford bought simultaneous prime time on all three major television networks and figured it would reach 84 percent of all television homes an average of six times each with Maverick commercials during its follow-up TV campaign. On the announcement weekend alone the company bought more than 100 commercial minutes on the NBC "Monitor" radio program, as well as spot radio announcements on CBS and on the news and sports shows carried by more than 500 Mutual network stations.

Advertisements were placed in 2575 newspapers reaching three-fourths of the nation's households. Three-page cover spreads were purchased in major magazines as part of a magazine schedule designed to be read by 162,000,000 persons. More than 22,775 "paper Mavericks" appeared on billboard posters expected to be seen by 92 percent of the nation's population 13 times each month. Dealers displayed posters entitled, "It's a Little Gas" and "Ford's Answer to the Gold Drain."

An estimated 100,000 college students on spring vacation viewed the Maverick at announcement day showings, complete with novelty giveaways, on Florida, Texas, and California beaches. More than 500,000 posters featuring "the world's great mavericks," such as W. C. Fields, Will Rogers, Jean Harlow, and Sigmund Freud, were distributed on 350 college campuses.

An early news conference for magazine writers and photographers was followed two months later by a barbecue announcement party on a western town movie set at Carefree, Arizona, attended by more than 100 newsmen from all the media. A 60-second television newsfilm of the Maverick in action was serviced to 143 major television stations and to the networks, which distributed the clip to their 401 member stations. Network news divisions sent film to 70 foreign countries. Radio and television interviews with Ford officials were tailored especially for major stations. Maverick news and feature stories and pictures appeared in newspapers and magazines with combined circulation of more than 200,-000,000.

The results? Ford dealers sold Mavericks faster than they could be produced, more than 115,000 in the first four months. Similar campaigns were waged by other American car manufacturers in combatting the foreign car market.

Few advertising and promotional budgets can be this extensive. The procedure, however, is the same in each: The judicious expenditure of an allotted sum in a carefully coordinated campaign, involving research, marketing, advertising, and public relations personnel, and using every medium necessary to accomplish the specified sales objective.

### QUALIFICATIONS

Men and women with a wide variety of interests and talents qualify for careers in advertising. As the American Association of Advertising Agencies puts it:

Whether your career interests lie in marketing or management, design or decimals, psychology or public service, fashion or finance, computers or copywriting, people or products, ideas or imagery, the medium or the message, personnel or photography, communications or commerce, sales or show business, math or music, graphics or global markets, packaging or printing, research or retail promotion, television . . . or you name it . . . the multifaceted world of advertising offers opportunities to get involved in all these areas—and more.

The advertising world is made up of people who have creative, analytical, selling, or management abilities. Successful advertising people are said to be constructive, adaptable, and eternally curious. They must be constructively optimistic because they are called on to originate ideas and to initiate action—to visualize in full operation something that has not yet been started. They must be adaptable because of the infinitely varied problems and the different types of persons that they meet almost daily. And they must have an unceasing interest in people and things and the operation of business in general and the industry in particular. They must keep abreast of developments in advertising and remain keen and interested students in many fields throughout their careers.

Imagination, foresight in sensing trends, the ability to reason analytically, and a sense of form are characteristics of advertising men and women which are frequently cited. Also emphasized is a broad general education in the liberal arts, obtained either in conjunction with the offerings of schools of communication or commerce or entirely in the

humanities, social sciences, or sciences. Generally, professional preparation in advertising opens doors most quickly.

Young men and women with talent and ability rise rapidly in advertising, particularly in the agency field. More than one-fifth of the
agencies which belong to the American Association of Advertising
Agencies are run by executives who were under 40 when they stepped
up to the chief executive's chair.

Women play important roles in practically every phase of advertising.
Many women graduates go to work immediately as copywriters for
department stores and other companies and for the agencies. A few sell
space and time for the media or enter the classified advertising departments of newspapers. A number of national advertising campaigns have
been masterminded by women, functioning as account executives. The
advertising directors of some of the largest department stores are women,
and women also have achieved success as media buyers for agencies.
More and more women are being made vice presidents of agencies and
several very successful women now head firms of their own.

Rewards, both financial and psychological, come quickly for those
persons who are imaginative and quick-thinking, can work under pressure, and have a bent for solving problems. About half the people in a
typical agency, for example, are professionals or executives. The sharing
of ownership and profits with such key employees is practiced more
often in agencies than in most businesses.

## SALARIES

The overall trend in advertising agency salaries is up, surveys have
disclosed. These advances include across-the-board increases, partly to
take care of cost-of-living hikes. The main reason for the raises, however, lies in the fact that most agencies today are handling far more
business than they did before and immediately after World War II.

Agencies in metropolitan areas (New York, Chicago, Los Angeles,
Detroit, and Boston were those surveyed) pay from 10 to 15 percent
higher salaries than those in smaller cities. In both metropolitan and
nonmetropolitan areas, respectively, salaries now vary little from one
section of the country to the other. In both large and small cities, however, one fact stands out: the heavier the gross billings by an agency,
the greater the salary scale. There are agencies that gross less than

$250,000 a year, whereas those in the giant category take in $10,000,000 and more with the largest going above $250,000,000.

Suppose the young advertising graduate goes to work for an agency grossing between $1,000,000 and $2,000,000 in a *nonmetropolitan* area; what may he expect in pay? If he avoids, as he should, an apprenticeship at a discouragingly low wage, he may be made a junior copywriter at $5000 or $6000. Junior copywriters for agencies this size average $7000, and earn up to $11,500. When he advances to senior copywriter, he will find a minimum of $7000, an average salary of $11,000, and a top of $15,000. As an account executive in an agency this size, he may expect an annual salary varying from the $12,500 average to as much as $21,000. If he becomes a part- or full-time owner, he will be in the $25,000 to $60,000 bracket.

At the level of the agency grossing $10,000,000 or more a year, our advertising graduate will find higher pay scales. Here the minimum for junior copywriters is likely to be $7000 a year, with an average of $9000 and a top of $15,000. For senior copywriters, the minimum figure is $11,000, the average $17,000, and the top $23,200. Account executives average $19,900. Copy chiefs earn $19,500 to $35,000. Creative group heads average $26,300, with a high of $32,800. Account group heads earn $21,000 to $43,000, with an average of $32,300. The research analyst range is $8800 to $11,000. Top executives and senior partners take home pay checks ranging up to $100,000 or more a year.

As his skills and experience increase, the advertising specialist will find that he possesses knowledge for which there is a great demand. In moving from one agency to another, often taking accounts with him, he will naturally move into higher pay brackets.

A somewhat similar promotion situation is true in media and company advertising departments. The top advertising executives in the offices of newspapers, magazines, and other media, and in client companies, likely will earn only about two-thirds of what their counterparts with the agencies receive. Other factors, however, such as security and fringe benefits, often more than make up for the lower salaries.

In the general magazine field, advertising directors earn from $9000 to $45,000, depending largely upon circulation. Business paper advertising managers may earn from $8000 to $32,000. Advertising managers for newspapers will be paid about the same. And commercial managers for radio and television stations may be paid from $6500 to $25,000.

Salaries paid beginners in advertising departments of both print and broadcast media generally exceed those for beginning news personnel, whose starting salaries by 1971 were varying widely from $6000 to $7400 a year. Starting salaries for trained advertising personnel in 1971 averaged $6718 for dailies and $6882 for weeklies. Manufacturing companies were making similar offers to advertising graduates in many cases; retail store salaries for copywriters ranged lower, however, with women receiving perhaps $4800 and men $5300 to start.

Those who rise to the position of advertising manager of an individual company may expect salaries ranging from $7000 to $75,000 a year, depending on the size of the business and the responsibilities involved. By contrast, 15 years ago the advertising director of even the largest company received only about $30,000 a year.

Men and women who join the advertising staffs of these companies have excellent opportunities to advance to high positions regardless of the types of power echelon jobs they fill. Jumps directly to the position of advertising manager have been made by copywriters, account executives, salesmen, sales promotion people, merchandising managers, and advertising production managers.

## Chapter 17

# *Public Relations*

# *and Information Writing*

### WHAT IS PUBLIC RELATIONS?

One of the most rapidly growing and attention-exciting fields in mass communications is that loosely identified by the term "public relations." Some 100,000 men and women are engaged in some form of public relations work for thousands of institutions of every conceivable type—business firms, trade associations, civic organizations, colleges, social work groups, churches, trade unions, government bureaus, and schools. The best organized area is that of corporate public relations.

Probably no term which became so commonly used in the past few decades has been more misunderstood than "public relations." Many a businessman assumed that a skillful publicity writer who could concoct interesting stories for the papers was a public relations man, not realizing that publicity writing needs to be done with purposeful planning as a "tool" operation in an overall public relations program. Groups ranging from church congregations to tavern owners' associations decided that they had better do something about their "public relations," and they debated exactly what they meant. Few understood the social science theory, stemming from a study of public opinion processes, which should guide a proper and beneficial public relations program.

The public relations function is defined as the planned effort to influence and maintain favorable opinion through acceptable performance, honestly presented, and with reliance on two-way communication. It necessarily must be a "management" function; that is, the planned effort must be based on established and agreed-upon policy statements which reflect the operating principles and the working practices of the company, organization, or group. In this aspect, public relations is one of the operating concepts, or business philosophies, of management.

Corporate public relations is also a specialized staff function in management, drawing heavily on journalistic and social science techniques. The professional practitioner must ascertain and evaluate the opinions of various "publics" or groups (e.g., employees, stockholders, dealers, customers, residents of a given community) which collectively make up an institution's total public if communication is really going to be "two-way." He must counsel management on ways of dealing with public opinion as it exists at a particular time and suggest points at which the policies and procedures of the company should be revised if the management wants to earn an "acceptable performance" rating from groups it seeks to influence. Finally, he plans and executes a program of action to develop effective two-way communication which will result in mutual responsiveness, understanding, and acceptance. The staff function is to represent the public to the management and the management to the public so that there will be a two-way flow of both information and attitudes.

At this highest level of corporate public relations, a public relations executive is a top-level management man. He deals directly with the president, board of directors, and chief operating officers of a company. Basic principles of operation are fashioned which will guide everyday working practices, and no major decision is made without considering its public relations effects. The public relations staff acts as a balance wheel to protect, insofar as possible, the conflicting interests of the company's various publics: the shareholders who want the best possible return on their investment, the employees who want the best possible wages, the customers who want good service or products at the lowest possible cost. The public relations staff must act, too, as a constant guardian of the program's integrity, since other people do the actual "acceptable performing" in direct communicative contact with employees, customers, and others with whom the company deals. It is the public relations staff, of course, which maps out the ways of reaching the company's various publics through formal communications—printed materials, films, meetings and talks, and through use of the mass media: newspapers, radio, television, magazines.

Historically, this concept of public relations developed only recently. The term "public relations counsel" was first used by Edward L. Bernays, one of the pioneers in the field, in 1923. At the same moment an influential literature of public opinion theory was appearing in response to a growing realization of the important role of public opinion in modern society. The experiences of Bernays, Ivy Lee, T. J. Ross, and other pioneers had taught them that publicity in itself was not enough; there needed to be a consulting operation. The need for a company or institution to have such counseling, and to make a planned effort to influence and maintain favorable opinion, was slowly accepted as the professional public relations practitioners translated the theories of public opinion scholars into practical arguments and corporate programs.

Long before the term "public relations" was invented men had performed the communicating functions, because they had a general understanding of the importance of public opinion. Much of the communicating, however, was what is called *casual publicity;* age-old, this is publicity without any planned objective or social purpose. *Informational publicity,* through which an organization tells its story to the public, is a second or midway level of activity. Bernays, Lee, Carl Byoir, and other early public relations counselors had been educated to the importance of basing an opinion-forming campaign upon full dissemination of information during World War I, when George Creel developed an admirable informational program for the government (the work of the Committee on Public Information). It was only one more step to the two-way aspect and the corporate policy-level planning of *public relations counseling.* Development of market research and of customer opinion surveys came during the 1920's, followed by the working out of sound opinion measurement methods in the 1930's and 1940's—the now-familiar Gallup and Roper polls. The use of scientifically determined samples of a total population or public has enabled researchers to find out what the general public thinks about a given issue or what it knows about a given subject. Such a study of an employee group, for example, can be followed by depth interviews with individuals which probe to find out why attitudes are held or how facts have been learned.

Political and social pressures arising out of the modern environment accounted for this growth of public relations activity. The country had become industrialized, and society was more and more complex and interdependent. The public interest and the private interest had to be more nearly reconciled; individuals and institutions found the amount of their activity which could be termed strictly private in its effects was steadily declining. Government was called upon to intervene in economic and social affairs—social security, labor relations, and other areas. In the corporate realm, the idea that the public had a stake in how owners and managers conducted their affairs came to be accepted, if only because pressures of public opinion threatened to bring (or brought) governmental regulation of business activity in increasing volume. Gradually some businesses and other organized groups—educators, doctors, banks, stockbrokers—came to see the values of two-way responsiveness, of seeking to reconcile private and public interests in behalf of the general welfare.

But such transitions occur slowly, and only a portion of the converts to public relations planning have known how to fashion proper programs. Today all the historical levels of publicity and public relations activity are still represented. There are thousands of casual or opportunistic publicists who were once called press agents but who now prefer the more elegant "public relations" label. There are thousands more who are information writers who do creditable enough jobs but who have no share in policymaking and so likewise should not assume the full "public relations" label. There are thousands of men and women who operate behind a façade of a public relations program—complete with everything except the integrity of the operating concept of the management. Finally, there are effective public relations directors and staffs operating to the best of their abilities under the basic concept as described and public relations counselors who offer sound advice and programs of benefit both to the client and to society, not merely publicity gimmicks.

It is important that persons interested in service to society, as journalists are, see and understand these various levels of what is loosely called "public relations" work. As either news media people or potential public relations people, they should understand the theoretical bases of a proper public relations philosophy and be able to differentiate between the useful and the useless and even dangerous activities.

A man who undertakes community relations work in behalf of an industrial firm or public utility that is anxious to contribute to the welfare of the city in which it is located, as a "corporate citizen," can make effective contributions to civic progress. A woman who develops a working statement of the objectives of a social work organization, such as Family Service, and who interprets the work of that group to the community with two-way communication as a goal, likewise has a satisfying job. A public relations counsel who persuades a company to undertake a comprehensive scientific sample of employee attitudes, as a basis for developing better programs of work supervision and promotion standards, has contributed to cooperative good will within that company.

On the other hand, the seven press agents who each received $50 a week to get the name of one New York restaurant mentioned in the gossip columns scarcely are doing work of benefit to society. Nor are the hundreds of publicity bureaus which flood the mails with press releases of the horn-blowing or inconsequential type prized by some clients. It should be perfectly obvious that the so-called public relations staffs employed by some companies and organizations to manipulate public opinion, or to apologize as best they can for the group's antisocial activities, are detrimental to society. The activities of the press agents are less obviously detrimental, but they can be so if they clog the avenues of mass communication. Information writers should strive to give newspapers and other media material of interest and value to readers; they should not, as one California publicity firm did, brag publicly how it obtained 650 inches of space in Los Angeles papers which would have cost $8775 in advertising money in behalf of a client's real estate promotional activity. Such stupidity on the part of men who call themselves public relations experts merely infuriates conscientious newspaper editors who hate being made to look like suckers.

An important step in professionalization was the 1968 decision of the 6000-member Public Relations Society of America to begin an accreditation program requiring the passing of an examination, written and oral, to obtain active status in the society. By this means leaders in public relations hoped to raise professional standards and identify trained men and women. The program gained strong acceptance among PRSA members.

## TYPES OF PUBLIC RELATIONS WORK

The largest single area of public relations work is in corporate public relations. Thousands of United States industrial firms, banks, trade associations, cooperatives, stores, and other businesses have organized their own public relations departments. The public relations director and his staff work as employees of the organization. About 85 percent of the companies which have public relations programs have company public relations departments. These often may be combined in the organizational structure with advertising, or with personnel.

Similarly, staff positions within the organization are maintained by chambers of commerce, federal government bureaus, state government offices, universities and colleges, community chests and social work organizations, labor unions, farm organizations, medical associations, bar associations, and countless other groups. These may be fully planned public relations efforts or middle-level information-writing assignments.

Smaller numbers of public relations men and women work as independent counselors, or members of an advertising agency staff with public relations specialization. The public relations counsel, studying the client firm from an independent outside role, offers program planning and management-policy advice to the firm's executives. He is paid on a fee basis, as a consultant. About 30 percent of United States companies having public relations programs utilize the services of a public relations counseling firm; about 40 percent use the services of public relations workers in advertising agencies. But only 15 percent rely exclusively on these types of public relations direction. Some 40 percent of company public relations departments buy the services of a counselor or an advertising agency in addition to their own activities. There is an increasing relationship between the marketing, advertising, and public relations fields.

There are large public relations firms, such as Carl Byoir & Associates, Ruder & Finn, or Hill & Knowlton, in which staff members do specialized assignments (information writing, radio and television contacts, magazine article preparation) as well as client counseling. There are individual public relations counselors, with only a one-secretary staff, who handle all aspects of a client's needs. Public relations specialists working within an advertising agency may give advice at a policymaking level, may help prepare a publicity campaign, or may handle the stories about company products for trade journals. But whether they are doing counseling work or tool-type operations, they likely will be described as "public relations men." Here lies the difficulty of nomenclature which confuses the picture of what public relations work is.

## VARIOUS PUBLIC RELATIONS ASSIGNMENTS

Let us consider, for example, a university journalism graduate who goes to work for a public utility, such as the telephone company, after preparing himself for publishing, broadcast, or advertising work. He joins the staff of one of the Bell operating companies, perhaps as a member of the three-man employee magazine staff. His next assignment is in the company news bureau, preparing news stories for the home-town newspapers in cities where the company operates—stories about personnel changes and promotions in the local telephone office, about retirements of old-time employees, about additional services or improvements in long-distance dialing, and so on. He is working at the "tool" level, using his journalistic skills. He is not immediately making policy, although he attends staff meetings in the public relations department at which policy is argued. He is being indoctrinated in company policy and procedures, and he is beginning to understand the total nature of the company operation.

Next he may be sent to the community relations section, where he is more of an "idea" man. He consults with the local office manager in a town where customer attitude survey studies have shown dissatisfaction with service or misunderstanding of billing procedures and rates. They decide they need better employee communication and arrange for foremen to hold group meetings; they check to see if the local managers are making effective use of the company's films which can be shown to civic groups; they plan an institutional advertising series in the local newspaper which will explain the company's costs and the needs for revenue if. the town is to have the best possible telephone service; they check through various ways in which the company can show responsiveness to the community.

Now he returns to employee relations work, perhaps as editor of the magazine, or as an information specialist who develops manuals and programs for the use of supervisory management. He attends employee meetings as a consultant to the operating programs. He suggests ways in which employees can be made more interested in the company's financial problems. He may help run "indoctrination sessions" for higher supervisory personnel in which the public relations objectives of the company are explained. Why should a local manager spend time working with the local newspaper editor? How should he go about it to be welcome as a news source? Why should the manager belong to the Lions or Kiwanis Club and spend time "doing good"? The employee relations specialist tries to relate the facets of the total public relations program to the personal interests of employees.

There are other assignments—if he has had advertising experience, our public relations man may be placed in charge of institutional advertising or of the product news bureau in a manufacturing firm. If he has training in sampling procedures and statistical method, he may take charge of the customer attitude survey and its interpretation. He may become director of the company's radio and television programs. He may head the audio-visual section, handling films, slides, and pictures. He may return to the news bureau as director in charge of the major company stories. He may edit the company's annual report for a time and do shareholder-relations work. He may become a "policy thinker"—preparing speeches for the company president, writing a manual explaining the public relations policies of the company, working with various executives on long-range planning. He might in time become assistant director of the department. And he might finally become vice-president in charge of public relations, and a member of the key company management group. Or, he might move on to the central public relations staff of the parent company, American Telephone & Telegraph. More likely he will remain in a median-level assignment, rounding out a comfortable and satisfying career as a telephone company employee who serves the community and other employees in a specialized staff role demanding technical journalistic skills and policymaking ability.

Another example might be of a young woman journalism graduate who is not convinced she wishes to do newspaper work, but who has acquired some understanding of newspaper routines through her classes and a vacation stint on a small paper. She is more interested in magazine writing and layout and begins as assistant editor of a company employee magazine. A year later she becomes editor. After she has married, she has time to do some work at home, on a part-time basis, and finds a local hospital needs a woman to edit its informal staff bulletin, handle the printing of occasional brochures and reports, and represent the hospital with the local newspaper when newsworthy events take place. She is able to advise the hospital administrator on both printing matters and news policy and develops some interesting stories of value both to him and to readers.

A third example might be a five-year veteran of metropolitan newspaper work who is offered a position with a major automotive company. He starts in information work, quickly moves into employee relations, and becomes assistant director for a major branch plant. Three years later he is shifted to Detroit, where he becomes assistant manager of the company's public relations department. He decides he would prefer to enter a counseling firm and becomes an account executive for one specializing in automotive clients. At 35 he is a vice-president of the firm and receives as much pay as a major executive of the largest metropolitan dailies. When he visits his old newspaper shop, he feels a little "tug" for having left the mainstream of news work, but his work and pay satisfactions are far more than enough to keep him satisfied with his career choice. In a counseling firm he is freer to carry out his own plans and ideas than in a company staff role. But he also needs to be more daring, for he has less personal security.

Technical writing for agricultural organizations, aviation firms, manufacturing companies serving scientific audiences, and other groups proves interesting to some journalists. The United States Information Service overseas, other federal government agencies, state tourist bureaus and industrial development departments, and some city school systems employ information writers. Colleges and universities, state health departments, the Red Cross, and many other service organizations do likewise. These usually are writing and editing assignments, but sometimes there is opportunity for making policy suggestions, and always there is a chance to do an effective job of working with the news media.

There are those who like to handle what might be called "promotional publicity"—building a story in behalf of a client, creating frothy feature stories, publicizing a queen contest, and otherwise earning a fee without too much effort or any serious thinking. This can be a pleasant enough career if the press agent—for that is what he is—stays in the good graces of the newsmen upon whom he depends and does not drop into the habit of handling dubious stories. But in middle age, the press agent might find himself outwritten by younger and fresher competitors and earning less money than his college classmates who chose more productive and serious roles in public relations.

## OPPORTUNITIES AND SALARIES

Several thousand United States companies and firms maintain fairly well-developed public relations departments—the number employing at least some public relations personnel has never been accurately determined. Firms which in 1945 had but a single public relations man by 1970 had full-blown departments ranging from 25 to 100 employees. Companies which did not organize their departments until the late 1950's —and there were many of them—still were in this growing stage. Men hired as information writers by smaller organizations, and who advanced to policy levels, were able to employ younger men and women to do writing and editing work, employee communication assignments, and similar jobs. The best estimate for public relations counseling firms is some 2000, and several hundred advertising agencies offer public relations services.

A survey of 166 manufacturing corporations made by the Public Relations Society of America showed that companies with more than a billion dollars of annual sales had public relations staffs averaging 65 in number. Those at the hundred million to half-billion sales level had a dozen or so staff members. Smaller companies averaged four public relations workers. Such large counseling firms as Carl Byoir and Hill & Knowlton employ more than 300 persons; but many independent firms are essentially one- or two-man operations. A survey of advertising agencies showed those which had public relations sections employed from 3 to 10 persons, although the Young & Rubicam agency had more than 100 in its public relations department.

Salary levels of corporate public relations men and women tend to be equated more with general levels of business salaries than with those in the news media. As a result, the average veteran public relations man in a major company probably earns half again as much as an average newspaperman, at the time each has reached his peaked and has leveled off. A salary of $15,000 to $20,000 might be expected by a moderately successful public relations man in a large company after perhaps 15 years of service; a moderately successful newsman who stayed close to the established minimum salary for large metropolitan newspapers might range from $10,000 to $13,500 in peak pay. His superior colleague on the newspaper staff probably would receive above $15,000 and might be happier doing his chosen work than shifting to public relations. So might a moderately successful newsman, despite the pay differential for, despite the many common basic qualifications, public relations work requires personal outlooks and abilities differing from those of newsmen.

Should the corporate public relations man advance to executive levels he will earn a salary ranging from $20,000 to $40,000 a year. Independent counselors report incomes of from $7500 a year to $35,000, depending upon their success in attracting clients and their firm's size. Those who remain at the employee magazine, information writing, and technical writing level earn from $8000 to $15,000 a year, with a few rising to $20,000. Those who stay in public relations work for smaller companies and noncorporate organizations also tend to remain in this more average salary bracket. Many a young newsman who was attracted to public relations work by a $10,000 salary offered by a smaller organization has found that it was a top salary as well as a beginning salary. He then has found it difficult either to return to newspaper work or to join a larger company's public relations staff. For although the larger companies have openings at advanced levels, they prefer to fill them with persons with media training—newspapers, radio and television, magazines, advertising—or with persons specially trained in such areas as speech, film, and communication research. Public relations does not have the turnover and exchange of personnel prevalent in the advertising agency field.

Beginning salaries in public relations departments tend to equal or exceed those in the mass media. Journalism graduates are offered starting salaries by such large employers as General Electric Company well in excess of starting newspaper pay. For those who are convinced their futures lie in corporate firms this is a tempting offer, particularly if they feel they lack the zeal for news work. But 15 or so years later the company may give a prized promotion of executive level to a staff member who was well seasoned in the mass media and pass by the man who came to it directly, on the theory that the ex-newsman had plus values and more rounded abilities to direct all phases of the public relations program. A news, advertising, or broadcast student who has had only introductory courses in public relations likely should avoid immediate entry into the field, particularly in "go-nowhere" jobs with smaller organizations, and instead should gain apprentice experience in the mass media. Those graduates of highly developed public relations educational programs, however, often find considerable success in moving directly into the public relations field.

## TALENTS AND EDUCATIONAL PREPARATION

Anyone who aspires to the corporate level of public relations work, involving policymaking for management, obviously must have excellent preparation. He should have a good grasp of the communications skills and an understanding of the mass media. He should be well grounded in the social sciences: economics, psychology, political science, sociology, history. He will have to know how to deal with people, as well as with facts.

Writing ability is mentioned more often than any other by public relations men asked by the Public Relations Society of America in a representative sample survey to rank skills needed in their work. Seven out of ten listed writing ability as one of four or five most important skills. Tact in dealing with people and creative ability ranked next. Speaking ability also was ranked high. General intelligence and good general background came next.

More than 90 percent of this sample of public relations men had attended college, and 29 percent had taken graduate work. The three leading major subjects in college were journalism, 32 percent; English, 28 percent; business administration, 24 percent. Slightly more than half, 53 percent, had been in newspaper work; 43 percent had been in advertising or merchandising; 10 percent had been in magazine work; 6 percent had been in radio, television, or movies. Only 43 percent had been in full-time public relations work prior to the job they then held.

Some basic courses a future public relations worker should include in a college program would be newspaper reporting and editing, broadcasting, principles of advertising, marketing, public opinion, public speaking, principles of economics, American government and history, general psychology. By the very nature of his chosen field, the public relations prospect cannot overspecialize in his educational training. He must be careful to select a broad band of social science courses, in addition to his communications concentration. If he is in the news-editorial or advertising area, he will include basic courses in the other area. If he is in business administration, he will want to include several basic journalism courses, and vice versa. If courses in public relations theory and methods are offered (and they are more commonly offered by journalism schools than by business schools), he will, of course, take them. In a few instances, he will find a major offered in his field.

College graduates who prepare themselves both in communications skills and in general background knowledge are in demand even though they may be inexperienced. A survey of public relations departments and firms by the Public Relations Society of America showed that one out of every three persons hired is a college graduate without experience. Entry is easiest in advertising agencies, industries, and institutions; it is less easy in public relations firms, welfare organizations, and governmental units. These employers, having typically smaller staffs, are more likely to demand previous media experience.

Although writing skill ranks highest in the minds of public relations men, there are openings on large company staffs for those who write adequately but who prefer other types of work. Specialists in survey and statistical work, good speakers who have organizational ability and training in group discussion, radio-television and film specialists, persons who have specialized in corporate organization or labor relations—these are some who can find a place in the public relations field and advance to high levels.

# Chapter 18

# *Mass Communications Research*

## THE NEED FOR RESEARCH

The rocket-like growth of the various forms of mass communications in the mid-twentieth century has resulted in an increasing need for better knowledge of the processes and effects of mass communications. A core of specially trained research men and women has arisen to search for and supply this knowledge to working communicators.

Take the magazine or newspaper editor, for example. He needs to know such things as these:

How many persons read my publication? (Typically, each copy has several readers so the total audience may be something quite different from the total circulation.)

What kinds of persons read my publication? (The New York *Times,* for example, is aimed at a different audience than is the *Daily News;* the audience of *Holiday* is almost completely different from that of *Jack and Jill.*)

How am I doing as an editor? Am I printing the kinds of things my audience wants to read about? Are my stories easy to read or hard to read?

How can I improve the content of my publication? How can I improve the presentation of this content in terms of layout and typography?

The broadcaster, the advertising man, and other communicators have similar questions to ask.

Time was when an editor could know many of these things pretty well by personal contact with the people of his community or area. By informal means, through his experience, he developed a rough idea of the composition of his audience and how they liked his publication. This unsystematic, informal "intuitive" method is no longer adequate for the modern communicator for several reasons:

1. *The increasing number of communications media.* In the present-day community, the average person has access to many media—local and out-of-town newspapers, several television and radio stations, and hundreds of magazines, books, and films.

2. *Increasing competition among the media for the attention of the public.* Since no individual has enough time to read or listen to all the media, or even to pay attention to all the output of just one medium, this means he must select a small fraction of the available output and ignore the rest. This leads to intense competition among the different media to capture as much of the public's time and attention as possible—obviously, the newspaper or magazine or station which succeeds in satisfying the needs of the public, whose messages are interesting and easy to absorb, will get a good share of public attention. Those which do not succeed in doing this will eventually fall by the wayside.

3. *The increasing number of people in the audience.* An editor or broadcaster has from several thousand to several million people in his audience, and the tendency is constantly toward larger audiences. No communicator can possibly have personal contact with everyone in his audience and knowledge of all their varying needs, likes, dislikes, and opinions.

4. *The changing tastes of the public.* People are becoming better educated and more sophisticated; they travel more, know more about the rest of the world, and are constantly developing broader interests through exposure to more communications from outside their immediate environment. Any communicator's audience is in a constant state of turnover and interest change. He cannot base his decisions on what he knew to be true ten years of five years or even one year ago. It is a "fickle public" in the sense that it is constantly changing in taste and mood.

These are all good reasons why the effective communicator—whether he be advertising copywriter, editor, or broadcaster—can no longer rely on "hunch" and "intuition" alone to capture and hold the attention of the public. As Harry Henry says in *Motivation Research:* "There are examples, of course, of 'hunch-merchants' who hit on successful ideas with enormous success, and finish up as classic case histories. But no case histories are written up of the 99 equally self-confident but not so lucky venturers whose only spell of glory is in a brief trip to the bankruptcy courts."

In the face of all these changing requirements, then, just how does the modern mass communicator get the precise information he needs to make his medium a successful one? He turns to communications research, a specialty which has grown up in the past two decades, to help answer some of the questions which he doesn't have the time or training to answer for himself. The communications researcher is just one member of the team of writers, editors, artists, advertising men, and others working together to help a medium do its job, which is to transmit information, opinion, and entertainment to a mass public. Or again, he may be a scholar in a university setting whose main objective is that of adding to our general knowledge of the communication process.

## WHAT IS COMMUNICATIONS RESEARCH?

A broad definition of research is simply "careful investigation" or a diligent inquiry into any subject. This broad term would include almost any kind of study—the literary scholar who reads through all of Shakespeare's works, the biographer who finds out all he can about a famous man, or the historian who compiles a history of American newspapers.

Mass communications research has taken on a somewhat more specialized meaning, however. First of all, it is usually (though not always) considered as *behavioral* research—the study of human beings (rather than inanimate or nonhuman objects). It is a branch of the behavioral sciences such as psychology, sociology, and anthropology.

Thus we see it is also *interdisciplinary* research. That is, it borrows the tools and knowledge of various other fields of study which will help in the understanding of mass communications problems. It does not confine itself to any particular point of view or theory or subject matter. It may borrow from linguistics, general semantics, philosophy, economics, or any other discipline which might help communications effectiveness.

It is *scientific research,* since it uses scientific methodology in solving communications problems. As in any science, its aim is to explain, predict, and control. In achieving this end, its methods must be objective (as opposed to subjective) and systematic (as opposed to unsystematic). Although most mass communications research is done on specific problems, the goal—as in any scientific field—is to formulate general principles and theories which can bring about more effective communication.

Being scientific, it is, of course, *quantitative research*. Random sampling methods, the laws of probability, and mathematical statistical techniques all help to make more precise and meaningful the findings from any particular investigation.

It is generally *primary* research rather than secondary. That is, the mass communications researcher customarily gathers new and original information rather than relying on printed source material. This is not always the case, however, since one may, for example, have to consult year-by-year statistical figures gathered in the past by other researchers in order to spot a trend over a period of time.

And, of course, the subject matter of communications research is *communication*. More specifically, it is concerned with *mass* communications, the communications behavior of large numbers of people, particularly those who make up the *audiences* for the different media. But other groups can be studied, too, of course—newspaper reporters, news sources, magazine editors, or public relations men, for example. In order to understand the behavior of groups, however, it is usually necessary first to understand individual behavior.

To summarize the definition of mass communications research: It is generally the scientific study of the mass communications behavior of human beings, usually in current situations requiring the gathering of primary quantitative information. It also includes the study of the communicators, their media, and the content of their messages.

This is not the only definition that might be legitimately applied. It leaves out other kinds of research done in the field of journalism and mass communications (e.g., historical, literary, biographical, legal, economic, international aspects), which are discussed in Chapter 19 on journalism teaching, and editorial research of the "fact-checking" variety. It also includes some topics which might be claimed by other disciplines. It is, however, a reasonably comprehensive definition of the specialized type of mass communications research which has grown up recently.

## AREAS OF COMMUNICATIONS RESEARCH

Communications research may be categorized generally within the four aspects of the communications process described in Chapter 1: the *com-*

*municator,* the *message,* the *channel,* and the *audience.* Extensive research has been done in each area, with the ultimate goal being the explanation or determination of *communications effects.*

**Communicator research.** C. I. Hovland's studies on the effects of the prestige of the source and the order of presentation of persuasive arguments are classic examples of communicator research. The question is, simply, what can the source do to make his communication more effective? In our everyday conversation and attempts at persuasion, we apply the "prestige principle" and attempt to lend credence to our arguments by citing expert or prestigious sources such as television, a newspaper, or a U.S. senator, in support of our information and points of view. Communicator research may compare different methods of a single communicator, one individual with another, or one institutional source, such as a magazine, with another source. It is logical that one way to improve communications is to find out what kinds of people are best suited for the job. What are the essential characteristics of good reporters or editors or advertising men? What "blocks" to effective communications exist in the ranks of existing job holders, as the result of lack of capacity or training, and what training can best be offered to future professionals? By finding out these essentials, better selection and training of communications personnel can take place.

**Message research.** The effects of different forms of the same message may be compared through variations in style, length, degree of difficulty, and the like, with attention paid to comprehensibility, interest, and attention value. We often vary our personal conversations as to complexity and word usage in terms of some determination of the sophistication of the intended receiver. With scientific content analysis we can easily determine the relative degree of difficulty of any message, and we can make inferences about the intent of the communicator as well.

**Channel research.** The channel through which a message is transmitted is highly related to the effectiveness of the message. This is due in part to the differing characteristics of the various media, which perform somewhat differently the functions of informing, interpreting, entertaining, and selling. By their character, content, style, and geographic coverage, media, to a great extent, are able to select their desired audiences. Advertisers are especially interested in determining which media can best deliver their messages and in knowing something about the people who comprise the potential audience of a medium. And in face-to-face communication, we often use facial expressions—a smile, for example—to much greater advantage than a flow of pleasant words.

**Audience research.** All communications research, in the end, attempts to determine something about audiences. Communicators need to know the behavior, interests, habits, potential, wishes, tastes, attitudes, and opinions of the people whom they seek to reach. Of great interest is the extent to which messages about products or ideas change the opinions of people. Knowing the number and description of people in a medium's audience is especially useful to advertisers to help them reach the right kind of person for their products. A baby-food manufacturer, for example, may want to know which of two magazines of equal circulations is better for him to advertise in; if magazine A has primarily an elderly audience and B has primarily young married women, he can easily decide which is better for his purpose. Such studies are also useful to editors in the selection of editorial content; a farm journal audience may change in reading interests due to shifts in composition and in living standards, for example. In another area, the reading likes of young newspaper readers are quite different from those of older folk, and some editors have recognized this by including specially edited "teen-age" pages.

The overall goal is to find out how mass communications affects audiences, just as we individuals need to know how our words affect other individuals with whom we communicate. The object of mass communications is to affect human behavior and attitudes. The object of communications research is to find out how and to what degree human behavior and attitudes are affected by mass communications.

## COMMUNICATIONS RESEARCH METHODS

Communications research, with its subject being human communications behavior, uses the same basic research methods as other branches of the behavioral sciences. And, depending on the needs of the researcher, any of the following methods may be applied to practically any problem.

In *survey research* the scientific sample is studied to gather demographic information or sociological facts as well as psychological information—opinions and attitudes. As opposed to the status survey, which produces an inventory of facts, survey research gathers both factual information and the opinions of subjects. Thus the researcher is able to talk about the relationships among variables, for example, the relationship between educational level and media usage, or between sex and opinion concerning a particular political candidate.

A similar method, but one in which independent and dependent variables are related and hypotheses tested, is the *field study.* Whereas in a third method, the *field experiment,* the independent variable is introduced by the researcher in an environment in which considerable control of extraneous variables is possible, the field study is ex post facto. In both the field study and field experiment an attempt is made to establish causal relationships between independent and dependent variables. The most closely controlled method of study of causal relationships is the *laboratory experiment,* in which all except the independent variable to be studied are eliminated.

The survey is frequently used to determine relationships between demographics and mass communications behavior, as in determining the relationships of sex and age to television program viewing. An example of a field study is a case in which it is hypothesized that the grade performance of school children has a stronger and more consistent relationship to the extent of usage and comprehension of mass communications than do other variables in the school and home environment. In a field experiment, one might designate two groups or communities which are highly similar in relevant characteristics and introduce variables, such as two forms of advertising of the same new product, to determine which form of advertising is more conducive to the purchase of the new product. Both the field study and the field experiment are difficult to control because variables other than those studied may affect the measured or dependent variable without the researcher's being able to know what really happened.

The *laboratory experiment* provides the best opportunity for control of variables since the researcher can be practically certain that the causal variable he introduces actually brings about the measured effect. For example, using two equivalent or matched groups, one might present a message in oral form to one group and in written form to the other. If a standard test then demonstrates that comprehension was consistently higher for the oral message group than for the written message group, one could be reasonably certain that the oral message was more easily understood by people like those in the two groups.

## EXAMPLES OF COMMUNICATIONS RESEARCH

Research can be, and has been, used by every kind of communicator—newspaper and magazine editors and writers, television and radio broadcasters, advertising men, public relations men, government information specialists, book publishers, and film producers. Some examples will show the usefulness of this kind of research in practical situations. With the exception of content analysis, almost any of these examples of kinds of research could be performed by using any of the previously described methods of communications research.

**Readership studies.**    Sometimes called "reader traffic" studies, these tell the editor how many and what kinds of people have read *each item* in his publication. For example, story A had 40 percent readership whereas story B had 10 percent, picture A had 37 percent readership whereas picture B had 12 percent. Such information, gathered by trained personnel in personal interviews with representative samples of readers, provides a check on editorial judgment. It is useful to the editor in following trends of audience interest, in evaluating effects of typographical makeup and display of stories on readership, in deciding which of several syndicated features he wants to retain or drop, and so on. Effectiveness of various types of advertising also can be studied.

Similar research is conducted on television and radio programs. The various "rating" services can determine how many sets were tuned in to each of a number of programs, how many people were listening to each set, and what kinds of people they were. One TV-radio research service gets its information from an electronic device permanently attached to the television or radio sets of a sample of households. Another "rating" service makes personal telephone calls to homes while programs are on the air. Another method is to have listeners keep diaries.

**Graphics research.**    Typography, layout, and makeup fall within the area generally called "graphics" by the print media. By experimentation with different methods of presentation, the researcher can tell the editor the most effective means of presentation of a given item. A book publisher or magazine or newspaper editor may choose to test, say, audience preference for one kind of typeface as compared with another; the use of one large illustration instead of several smaller pictures; or the effectiveness of a news item published in an area two columns wide and

5 inches deep, as contrasted with the same item set in one column 10 inches deep. Much research has been done on the legibility of type-faces and aesthetic preferences for them.

Advertising men, too, are strongly interested in graphics research. Which ad gets across the most information—an ad with a big picture and a little text, or a little picture and a lot of text? Such research may be done by "split-runs" in the publication, so that the alternatives are presented to two different samples of readers whose reactions then can be compared after a readership survey, or by experimentation with a relatively small group of persons before publication.

Graphics research has its parallel in the broadcasting media. Research can tell whether three minutes of commercial time are most effective at the beginning of a program, at the end, or spread through it. Or it can tell whether, on a radio newscast, a summary of "headlines" at the start of the program will increase interest in the news items which follow.

**Advertising research.** The various media and almost all advertising agencies conduct advertising research to help them in their job of persuading people to buy. *Market research* has been carried on since the start of the century and was the forerunner of other public opinion research. It includes consumer surveys on potential markets for new products, dealer studies, customer attitude surveys, and studies of effectiveness of brand names and package designs. Media use by advertisers is determined in part by market research results, and various media seek to point out their usefulness by undertaking market research studies for particular advertisers' products. *Copy research* includes analysis of advertisement readership studies, pretesting of advertisements, evaluation of printed advertisement campaign effectiveness, and graphics. In broadcasting, commercials and programs may be tried out on small samples of listeners by use of response recording devices. The same is true of films.

**Public opinion research.** Every communicator is interested in knowing the state of public opinion about himself or his medium. The publisher wants to know how the public "feels" about his newspaper, magazine, or books. The broadcaster and film producer are equally sensitive to public approval. Public relations and advertising men want to know if they have succeeded in creating a favorable "image" for their companies or products in the public mind. Surveys of attitudes held by specific customer groups, and by the public generally, give them some answers.

Communicators are interested in public opinion from an additional viewpoint—that is, public attitudes toward social and economic issues, government officials and their policies, and important events. The familiar national polls conducted by George Gallup, Elmo Roper, and others offer a check on prevailing opinion. And since public opinion is news in itself, the polls are sold to many newspapers; in addition, some newspapers conduct their own polls and report the outcomes as news stories. Large companies subscribe to opinion-survey services as a part of their public relations programs. Government also uses public opinion research —the United States Information Agency has a survey research division whose sole function is to measure public opinion toward the United States in other countries, and the effects of our various foreign information programs including the Voice of America. Politicians are increasingly using public opinion surveys to gauge campaign progress and important issues.

**Content analysis.**   Much can be learned about a publication merely by studying its contents. (This falls somewhat outside the definition of "behavioral" research.) Content analysis provides a clue to an editor's or writer's intentions and to the kind of audience which a publication or broadcast attracts. Combined with readership studies, it gives clues to what people want to read about. This form of research can be especially valuable when more precise kinds of research are inappropriate or unavailable. For example, a content analysis of German wartime broadcasts gave the Allies useful clues as to the enemy's war strategy. An analysis of Soviet "cold war" propaganda helps the U.S. Information Agency in the formulation of its own propaganda, since it reveals the themes which are currently being stressed and enables us to combat them.

**Communications "effects" research.**   As mentioned before, every communicator is interested in the effect he achieves on an audience with his message. Did people pay attention to the message? Did they understand it? Did it change their opinions or add to their store of useful information? Did they take any action as a result? Various research tools are used in answering these questions in a more precise way than any communicator can do intuitively, no matter how astute he is. This is the most rapidly growing area of the communications research field.

**Creative research.**   Most of the research enumerated thus far deals with familiar and continuing problems, using fairly standardized research techniques from job to job. However, one of the most satisfying aspects of communications research is in doing original, imaginative thinking and investigation. The creative researcher tries to think of different ways to do a particular communications job and then tests the alternatives to see which is the most effective. He critically analyzes the long-standing traditions and accepted practices of the media and then tests these "tricks of the trade" to see if they are really the most effective ways to communicate. He devises new and original research techniques and methods to solve particular problems. He keeps abreast of developments in related disciplines such as psychology and sociology, applying the findings and theories from those fields to communications problems. Creative communications researchers also make valuable contributions to theory and practice in those related disciplines. They both borrow from and contribute to other areas of knowledge.

These are just a few general classifications of the wide variety of activity that goes on under the name of mass communications research. They are not mutually exclusive—a readership study, for example, is just one form of audience research. All of these mentioned are concerned, directly or indirectly, with "effects" research. Most of them could be classed under public opinion research. They all overlap and interact.

A glance through a few issues of the *Journalism Quarterly* and *Public Opinion Quarterly* will reveal in more detail some of the directions that mass communications research now takes. Although the questions or problems explored do not differ greatly from those explored 20 years ago, the emphasis now is on the use of more scientific methods of studying those questions. Earlier expressions of subjective opinion by communications experts are being subjected to scientific scrutiny and the "folklore" of the media are being validated or disproved.

### OPPORTUNITIES IN RESEARCH

Research is being conducted in every kind of communications and business enterprise today. All of the media are engaged in research to some degree: newspapers, magazines, radio, television, publishing houses, film producers. So are the supporting agencies: press associations, advertising agencies, public relations firms, specialized commercial research firms. So are manufacturers of consumer and industrial products, retail and wholesale business firms, the federal government, and colleges and universities.

Surveys have shown that four out of every five United States companies have a department (one man or more) engaged in market research, which almost always includes some form of communications or opinion research in its activities. Even among the smaller firms—those with sales under $5,000,000 annually—three out of every five have a research department.

Advertising agencies are the most avid users of research; more than 90 percent of all United States agencies have a research department. And almost as many publishing and broadcasting organizations employ researchers.

Naturally, the larger the firm, the more likely it is to have a research department. However, both it and the smaller firm frequently turn to commercial research firms, whose sole business it is to conduct research for outside business clients. Most medium and large cities in the country today have at least one commercial research firm, and the number of such firms is increasing yearly. Many of these firms serve clients on a national basis, and a few conduct research in foreign countries. Some of the largest are the Opinion Research Corporation of Princeton, New Jersey; International Research Associates and Alfred Politz Research of New York City; A. C. Nielsen Company in Chicago; and Field Research on the west coast.

Advertising agencies tend to have larger research staffs than other kinds of businesses; the largest agencies employ an average of 50 persons in their research departments. Large publishing and broadcasting firms average four research employees, but a few have departments more the size of those in the agencies.

How is the pay for the worker in communications research? Because of the extensive amount of advanced training and specialized knowledge required, researchers are well paid compared with other mass communications personnel. The holder of a master's degree who has specialized in research may expect a starting salary of $8000 to $10,000 a year. The more advanced student in communications research—who has completed most or all of his doctoral training—can initially command $10,000 to $12,000 a year. These figures vary, of course, with location and size of firm. With the gaining of experience, communications research specialists rise in salary to $25,000 or higher. Research analysts exceed the $10,000 level. Women are frequently employed in analyst positions, less often in the top research posts. They formerly were paid about 10 to 15 percent less than men; the difference has narrowed considerably in recent years.

Opportunities for advancement in mass communications research are good, because of the expansion taking place in the field. Not only can research be a rewarding and satisfying vocation in itself, but it also serves as a stepping stone to other kinds of work, both in the creative and business aspects of communications. One example is Dr. Frank Stanton, who started in research and became head of the Columbia Broadcasting System. Two others are A. Edward Miller, who became publisher of *McCall's,* and Marion Harper, Jr., who became head of McCann-Erickson advertising agency.

Another excellent opportunity for researchers exists in schools of journalism and mass communications. More and more universities are adding communications researchers to their staffs, both to do research and to teach and train students in the skills involved. In addition, such schools often contract to do research for the media or for civic and governmental agencies. A doctoral degree is generally considered a requirement for such a faculty position.

## TRAINING FOR RESEARCH POSITIONS

Until just after World War II, most scientifically trained researchers on mass communications problems came from psychology and sociology. The importance of research as a specialty has since led some of the nation's leading schools of journalism and mass communications to set up graduate programs in quantitative scientific research methods.

In some of these schools, mass communications research is offered as just one of several communications fields which a graduate student may elect in his course of study; in others, the entire graduate program is devoted to courses in behavioral research theory and methodology with a minimum of emphasis on the "communications" aspect. In almost all of them, however, the research specialization requires a sampling of appropriate courses drawn from several different disciplines and a heavy emphasis on statistics and scientific method courses.

A typical graduate program calls for a major in mass communications or journalism with a minor in psychology, sociology, or statistics. Various other departments—anthropology, philosophy, economics, political science, marketing, to name a few—may also figure in the program to a lesser extent, depending on the individual interests of the student. Some individuals prefer to major in social psychology or sociology, and minor in communications or journalism.

It is generally considered desirable—though not necessary—for graduate students in communications research to have professional experience in one or more of the mass media. The first wave of communications research Ph.D.'s—those receiving degrees in the 1950's—almost without exception had practical journalism experience, as newspaper reporters and editors, radio newsmen, and so on. The value of a practical journalism background lies in the greater awareness of crucial communications problems, a better knowledge of the questionable assumptions of the trade, and a generally better critical perspective based on an understanding of journalistic processes and folkways.

However, it should be emphasized that prior journalistic experience is not a requirement, but merely helpful, for the person interested in mass communications research. He or she can acquire knowledge of the media and of journalistic techniques in journalism courses and in post-degree professional work. It should be noted, too, that the only distinction between the graduate program of a mass communications researcher and that of the less-specialized behavioral scientist is the former's preoccupation with mass communications as the subject matter of his research; in practice, he is qualified to do almost any kind of social research he wishes.

# Chapter 19

# *Mass Communications Education*

## THE ROLE OF EDUCATION

Informing and enlightening the public is a difficult task. Few can succeed as practitioners in mass communications without mastering the principles and practices of broad areas of knowledge that comprise the basic ingredients of a college education. Society has become so complex, its specialties so numerous, and its varying relationships so involved that only a person with a sure intelligence and a comprehension of many facets of human activity can understand the meaning of events. And without understanding, any attempt at reporting or interpreting is not only superficial but actually dangerous to the security of a democratic nation.

It is true that the exceptional individual can acquire a broad education without entering the portals of an institution of higher learning. A number of men and women with limited academic backgrounds are exerting genuine leadership in the editorial offices of the country today. But for most of us the only certain path to the acquiring of knowledge about our world lies in formal courses of instruction in the social sciences, the natural sciences, and the humanities. Here we discover the precise methodology of the researcher and the scientist and the skills of the writer or artist; we have guided access to the accumulated wisdom of the ages; we learn what men have considered to be the good, the true, and the beautiful; and we study the behavior of man, both as an individual and in his relationships with others.

Acquiring such a basic education has special importance to the future journalist. For one thing he is exposed to areas of thought and criticism that give him the opportunity to become a cultured person of discrimination and taste in his own right. From these experiences he should be able to acquire a sound working knowledge of society and a sensitivity to its many problems that will enable him to exercise the type of forthright citizenship so essential in our democracy. If his exposure to the processes of education has been productive, he will be enabled, in the words of Newman, "to see things as they are, to go right to the point, to disentangle a skein of thought, to detect what is sophistical, and to discard what is irrelevant."

Education, however, assumes an even greater importance to the future newsman or newswoman: almost every bit of knowledge and every insight that he acquires in college, from a study of the love life of the oyster to Thorstein Veblen's views on "conspicuous consumption," eventually seem to become grist for the mill as he reports and interprets the kaleidoscopic nature of life in the most practical of working assignments.

For example, in covering a state legislative hearing concerning a new sales tax proposal, the reporter should be aware of the various types of taxation and how they operate; assigned to interview an Oak Ridge physicist, he should know something about atomic power and its uses; reporting a discovery in the field of medicine, he may put his knowledge of biology or chemistry to work; an interview with a famous author may call forth his familiarity with the methods of literary criticism or a knowledge of current trends in writing; in handling a story about Saudi Arabian oil operation he must recall his studies in history, geography, and possibly geology; interpreting the new city budget will demand a knowledge of economics and accounting; covering a musical concert, a dramatic production, or the opening of an art exhibition, he will be grateful for any background which he may have acquired in those fields; and on and on. The journalist eventually puts all his education to use, and fervently wishes he knew more.

## CHANNELS OF EDUCATION FOR MASS COMMUNICATIONS

Men and women desiring to equip themselves for journalistic careers in mass communications may follow several avenues in reaching their goal. The most common method is to enroll in a school or department of journalism or communications offering a four-year program leading to a degree in journalism. Approximately 300 colleges and universities in the United States provide such courses of study. Some of these institutions have provided separate administrative units (colleges, schools, divisions) for their journalism or communications instruction. The majority have located the school or department of journalism or communications within the liberal arts college. In either case, a student typically takes no more than 25 to 30 percent of his course work in journalism or communications; the remainder is spread through the social sciences, humanities, and natural sciences, as well as physical education or military fields, in accordance with the university's requirements for both breadth and depth of study in the various areas of learning. In effect, the student elects a major specialization in professional studies which give him instruction in basic communication skills and in social science-oriented courses which relate journalism and communications to society. He does this just as other students elect a major concentration in geology, physics, political science, or English—and he is no more "specialized" in one subject than are they.

Many practitioners in mass communications are college graduates who have pursued noncommunications majors in liberal arts colleges. Seldom, however, does such a student consciously plan a mass communications career when he embarks on his college studies; almost always he acquires this goal late in his college career, or he turns to a communications career after his graduation. Some employers among the mass media seek out such students, in the belief that their background in a general liberal arts study best equips them for full development within their organizations. It seems more reasonable, however, that the men and women who acquired both professional and general liberal arts education while enrolled in schools and departments of journalism, television-radio, speech, or communications would be better prepared for professional work and would be employed more readily. This fact has been corroborated by numerous surveys.

Journalism educators know about this increasing reliance by newspapers upon their graduates through the operations of their placement offices. The placement service is one of the most important functions of a journalism school as far as the prospective graduate is concerned. Employers rely upon the schools to recommend applicants for both beginning and advanced positions and make calls directly to the journalism offices rather than to the college's general placement service. Surveys taken each year by *Journalism Quarterly* show that the schools receive far more requests than they can fill, particularly for beginning men and women workers. A large journalism or communications school will handle several hundred requests each year, the majority coming from newspapers. During the 1960's no journalism graduate went without a starting job if he or she really wished to apply for work, and most had choices of alternative offers. There has been steadily increasing use of the journalism school placement services by press associations, television and radio stations, magazines, advertising agencies, major industrial companies seeking advertising and public relations personnel, and others wishing to employ graduates with communications skills.

Many students are introduced to the mass communications field through study at the more than 500 four-year institutions in the United States that offer some journalism courses but not a full major. High schools and junior colleges provide the beginning courses for thousands of other students. Some work on campus newspaper, yearbook, and television or radio staffs, or find part-time employment with local newspapers and broadcast stations while still in school. Since the nation's journalism schools graduate only about 8000 students each year, far fewer than the number required by the media and related fields, many students from these nonjournalism-major institutions and from the junior colleges and even high schools find jobs in communications.

Students desiring careers in advertising and communications management frequently find the courses of study they want under the professional and liberal arts listings of schools and department of journalism, speech, radio-television, and communications. Much of this training for jobs in the nonmechanical and noneditorial aspects of the media, however, also is offered through schools of business. In many universities a cooperative arrangement exists so that, regardless of the type of degree sought, such students obtain their specialized courses in both business and communications areas. The business major must become familiar with the peculiar problems and structure of the branch of the communications industry he proposes to enter; the communications major must learn principles of sound business practice. Along this same line, the future advertising man, whether enrolled in business or communications, must learn writing and editing while at the same time mastering the principles of marketing and retailing, and such business "core" subjects as accounting, business law, finance, management principles, and statistics.

With the tremendous expansion of industry since World War II, public relations has risen to prominence as a career sought by thousands. Most schools and departments of journalism offer one or two orientation courses in combination with preparation in basic journalistic training; they and those schools with more fully developed curricula suggest programs emphasizing electives in economics, psychology, sociology, and other social sciences. Few schools of business offer separate courses in public relations although they incorporate course units emphasizing the theory and over-all knowledge of public relations essential to successful management. Journalism school courses seek to offer the student both this background and the instruction necessary for becoming an actual practitioner in public relations.

In the broadcast area, students desiring careers in performance and production generally concentrate on courses in speech and radio-television. Those desiring to become radio and television newscasters and writers combine journalism, speech, and radio-television courses. Those headed for sales, promotion, public relations, and management positions may choose to major in business with allied instruction in journalism and radio-television. Those entering educational broadcasting frequently obtain teaching certificates while also acquiring a background in radio-television and speech. Television production students likely will take as much work in theater and dramatic literature as possible. The possible variations in these emphases are almost endless, depending upon the students' objectives. Common to all of these career paths, however, is a strong background in the liberal arts. The interlocking nature of broadcast instruction is a factor in the recent development of schools or colleges of communications, linking speech, radio-television, film, advertising, public relations, and journalism.

Courses in the film are offered by radio and television, communications, journalism, theater arts, and education schools and departments. They range from a single film appreciation course in some institutions to multiple courses in production, history, and aesthetics leading to a film major in others. Among institutions emphasizing study in the film are Southern California, University of California at Berkeley, Boston, Indiana, Columbia, New York, Northwestern, Michigan State, Kansas, Georgia, and San Francisco State College.

Combination programs have been developed at many universities to enable the student interested in a career as a communications specialist in such areas as agriculture, home economics, medicine, or science to obtain basic proficiency through courses made available in two or more departments, schools, or colleges.

In-service training programs by newspapers have expanded rapidly in recent years. One of the most elaborate of these programs, which primarily involved indoctrination into actual working conditions, was a 21-week, on-the-job study course provided by the Gannett Company, Inc. The Copley Newspapers had a similar, extensive training program for new employees.

Summer internship programs with dailies and weeklies supplement classroom and laboratory instruction in many states. Juniors, who already have received basic instruction in news writing and editing, accept jobs at salaries averaging $90 per week; in some instances, when close supervision can be provided and study reports written, academic credit also is awarded. Faced with a shortage of qualified applicants for news jobs, many newspapers accept interns with the hope of inducing them to return after graduation for full-time employment.

In an effort to identify talent at institutions with no journalism programs, the Newspaper Fund, Inc., of Dow Jones and Company, publisher of the *Wall Street Journal,* has awarded $465,000 in intern scholarships to more than 900 students in such colleges and universities since 1960. Outstanding interns won $38,500 additional. An editing program, begun in 1968, has resulted in awards of $140,000 to 241 students, mostly from journalism schools and departments.

Some magazines, broadcast stations, and advertising agencies also offer summer training for college students, as well as "refresher" experiences for instructors. Many students work part-time at journalistic tasks throughout the year, some even accepting jobs with their home-town newspapers while in high school. Working on a high-quality college newspaper is also an internship, with the added value of being tied closely to a parallel course work program.

## HOW COMMUNICATIONS EDUCATION DEVELOPED

Journalism, a comparative fledgling among university disciplines, gained its foothold on college campuses about a half-century ago. Formal education for journalism was inevitable in the face of the steadily increasing complexities of the twentieth century which demanded better-trained personnel on American newspaper staffs. None other than General Robert E. Lee first proposed a special college education for printer-editors. That was in 1869 when the general was president of Washington

College, now Washington and Lee University, in Virginia. Little came of his proposal. Other early attention was given to printing instruction, such as that beginning at Kansas State College in 1873. It was 1893 before the first definitely organized curriculum in journalism was established in the Wharton School of Business at the University of Pennsylvania, an effort which languished in 1901.

In 1904 the first four-year curriculum for journalism students was organized at the University of Illinois, and journalism instruction began the same year at the University of Wisconsin. Four years later the first separate school of journalism was founded at the University of Missouri by an experienced journalist, Dean Walter Williams. In 1912 the Columbia University School of Journalism, endowed with $2,000,000 from Joseph Pulitzer, opened its doors. A survey disclosed that more than 30 colleges and universities were then offering courses in journalism.

The first courses were largely vocational in nature as pioneer teachers in the field endeavored to prepare college students for careers on newspapers, then the unrivalled medium of mass communication. During the 1920's, however, emphasis on technique lessened and curricula began to reflect an increasing interest in the social, ethical, and cultural aspects of journalism. Dr. Willard G. Bleyer, director of the University of Wisconsin School of Journalism until his death in 1935, is credited with leading the movement away from a preoccupation with techniques. Also influential was the exposure to methods of teaching the social sciences that journalism insructors were receiving in graduate programs. Courses in the history and the ethics of journalism became popular, and they were followed by studies of the newspaper as a social institution, of the interpretation of current affairs, and of public opinion.

These courses, together with those dealing with foreign news channels and legal aspects of the press, heightened respect for journalism as a discipline among other college teachers. At the same time products of journalism departments were earning a grudging acceptance from curmudgeons of the editorial offices who, as Horace Greeley put it, learned their journalism through eating ink and sleeping on the exchanges. Teachers began to offer courses to prepare students for careers in newspaper management, advertising, photography, and other such specialized fields. And while recognizing the importance of the humanities and the natural sciences in the total educational program of their students, teachers came to achieve the closest working relationships with the social sciences.

As both the breadth and depth of subject matter in journalism increased, master's degrees were offered. In 1935 the Pulitzer School at Columbia restricted its year's course to holders of a bachelor's degree, and the Medill School of Northwestern University established a five-year plan for professional training in 1938. Graduate study for journalism majors developed at a rapid pace after World War II, as the schools themselves and some of the media units began to urge advanced study in both journalism and the social sciences. Many of those who obtained master's degrees entered journalism teaching, but increasing numbers spent five years of study in preparation for professional journalism careers.

At the doctoral level, most graduate schools which recognized journalism instruction followed the lead of the University of Wisconsin in providing a minor or a double minor in journalism for candidates who generally majored in such fields as history or political science. The University of Missouri, however, awarded the first degree of Doctor of Philosophy in journalism in 1934, and by the 1940's other programs were under way. Some were based on strong supporting emphasis in the social sciences; others related the study of mass communications to psychology and sociology as a behavioral science. By 1970 the Ph.D. degree in mass communications or journalism was offered at 17 universities: Illinois, Indiana, Iowa, Michigan State, Minnesota, Missouri, North Carolina, Northwestern, Pennsylvania, Ohio, Southern Illinois, Stanford, Syracuse, Temple, Texas, Washington, and Wisconsin.

Some Ph.D. degree holders entered the communications industry, but most joined journalism faculties of colleges and universities. The number of journalism professors holding doctorates rose from 25 in 1945 to 117 in 1954 and 302 in 1969. The great majority of other journalism teachers in colleges held master's degrees, in addition to several years of professional experience in the media generally required by the schools.

It has been pointed out that early journalism instructors concerned themselves almost entirely with effective teaching and curricula development. Soon, however, the service obligations of journalism training units became apparent. As a result, there developed seminars and workshops for all branches of mass communications personnel, conferences for high school teachers and pupils, and other assorted projects.

Research, the third obligation of the university, developed somewhat slowly. For many years journalism scholars applied themselves largely to a study of the history of mass communications media. A development of the last two decades has led to the amassing of a substantial body of literature in communications research. Journalism scholars adapted the techniques of the behavioral sciences and joined sociologists, psychologists, statisticians, and other such investigators in unearthing a wealth of insights into the problems that face the communicator and his audiences and the effects of the communicated symbols on attitude and behavior. To many, the world of the statistician's chi square and variance and multiple regression seemed far-removed from the usual paths of journalism instruction, but research scholars are slowly penetrating hitherto unknown areas of communications and achieving a new respect for journalism as a scholarly discipline that can be a science as well as an art.

Important communications findings are also being developed by research personnel who are not required to use precise quantitative measurement tools; examples are studies in the broad realm of American civilization and in such areas as economic and political history and cultural anthropology.

Research personnel are sought after by both industry and the teaching profession, and salaries for men and women who have mastered the techniques required frequently range in the $15,000 to $25,000 realm.

The growth of the philosophy that journalism schools should develop research scholars capable of critical analysis of the media and their social environment coincided with television's rise and the increased importance of departments of speech and radio-television in providing study for broadcast careers. New, integrated instructional units in communications emerged, a few merely for administrative convenience, but most of them prepared for serious study of communication as the common denominator linking several academic departments.

Michigan State University brought its speech, journalism, advertising, and TV-radio instruction together into a College of Communication Arts, with a research unit at its center. The University of Texas similarly combined its speech, radio-television-film, and journalism programs into a School of Communication. Other universities at which "Communications" or "Communication" first became the identifying part of the title of a unit concerned with journalism and broadcasting included Illinois, Stanford, Washington, Florida, Arizona State, Brigham Young, Iowa

State, Kentucky, Minnesota, Washington State, Houston, and Boston. Almost 50 others have done the same since 1969. Educators with a background in speech, as well as in journalism, assumed leadership of other units, including those at Colorado State University and University of Houston. Other journalism schools with a longtime interest in broadcasting instruction have included Georgia, Indiana, Iowa, Kansas, Minnesota, Missouri, Montana State, Northwestern, Ohio, and Pennsylvania State.

## ORGANIZING FOR HIGHER STANDARDS

The beginning student in mass communications soon may find himself as confused about the organizational structure of journalism education as were newspaper readers during the 1930's. Then a plethora of New Deal agencies known principally by their initials—NRA, HOLC, FERA, WPA, CCC—sprang into being. When the student hears reference to AEJ, ACEJ, AASDJ, or ASJSA, he should know that these are the alphabetized symbols for the four leading organizations in journalism education today.

A desire to exchange information and raise teaching standards prompted the organization in 1912 of the American Association of Teachers of Journalism. Five years later the American Association of Schools and Departments of Journalism was created. By establishing certain standards for institutional membership, the AASDJ acted as a recognizing agency in the field. Eight schools and departments were approved by AASDJ at the time of its organization; by 1970 membership numbered 57. In 1924 the two associations jointly established the *Journalism Bulletin,* devoted to investigative studies in journalism; in 1928 the name was changed to *Journalism Quarterly.*

Efforts by AASDJ to work more closely with the press and to improve teaching standards culminated in January, 1939, with the organization of what is now known as the American Council on Education for Journalism. Present at the historic Chicago meeting were five journalism educators and representatives of five associations: the American Society of Newspaper Editors, American Newspaper Publishers Association, Southern Newspaper Publishers Association, National Newspaper Association, and Inland Daily Press Association. Subsequently, the National Association of Broadcasters, Magazine Publishers Association, and Public Relations Society of America became full members. As industry support broadened, six other organizations were admitted: the International Newspaper Advertising Executives, International Association of Business Communicators, National Conference of Editorial Writers, National Press Photographers Association, Radio-Television News Directors Association, Associated Press Managing Editors Association, and the California Newspaper Publishers Association.

ACEJ works for the improvement of education for journalism and conducts a program of evaluation in accredited universities and colleges throughout the United States. In this program, ACEJ cooperates with the National Commission on Accrediting and other national and regional accrediting organizations and collects and makes available information about journalism education programs that are of value to schools and departments of journalism. Other activities include the distribution of career booklets for high school students throughout the United States. In 1970 the council consisted of nine educator and nine industry representatives.

A second administrators' organization, the American Society of Journalism School Administrators, was established in 1944, partly in protest to what its members considered a trend toward monopoly of journalism education among the schools that comprised AASDJ. The expressed purpose of ASJSA was to encourage the exchange of ideas and information about journalism administrative and teaching problems. Its primary interest lay in undergraduate teaching, its secondary concern in research and advanced-degree guidance. Members represented schools or departments in accredited colleges and universities that offered four-year programs leading to a degree in journalism.

Emphasizing service to all its members, ASJSA established a mimeographed publication, the *Roundtable,* to exchange "how we do it" ideas. The chief publication was the *Bulletin,* a semiannual printed publication which became a quarterly when its name was changed in 1958 to the *Journalism Educator.* The organization also sponsored a summer intern program for journalism teachers in cooperation with industry. ASJSA membership had reached 82 by 1972 and included two Canadian administrators.

Major structural changes in 1949 and 1950 welded all journalism teacher and administrator groups into one organization. The American Association of Teachers of Journalism in 1949 adopted a new constitution and voted to change its name to the Association for Education in Journalism. In 1950 AASDJ and ASJSA agreed to become coordinate bodies within AEJ. The educator group serving on ACEJ was reconstituted to consist of two (later four) representatives from AEJ, three from AASDJ and two from ASJSA. The merger of the several organizations into AEJ was hailed as an action giving greater recognition to the individual teacher and uniting schools, administrators, and teachers of journalism into one cooperative group. AEJ in 1972 had a membership of 1108 teachers and administrators. The organization was expanded in 1972 to include secondary school teachers as well as those in higher education.

In 1965 AEJ, already the publisher of *Journalism Quarterly,* began *Journalism Monographs* as a serial, nonperiodic scholarly publication.

Two separate organizations for education in specialized fields are the American Academy of Advertising, publisher of the *Journal of Advertising,* and the Association for Professional Broadcasting Education, sponsored by the National Association of Broadcasters, with the *Journal of Broadcasting* as its publication.

### INDUSTRY ATTITUDES AND COOPERATION

Journalism as an educational discipline has engaged in a half-century struggle toward full acceptance and recognition. Many hard-bitten newspaper executives who had learned their craft the difficult way, without benefit of higher education, would have none of "those college-educated fellows." In the first few decades of the twentieth century, journalism teachers were forced to demonstrate their ability to duplicate actual newspaper conditions on the campus and to produce graduates who could report and edit well soon after joining a newspaper staff.

The pendulum then swung the other way, and the cry went up: "Give us men and women with a strong liberal arts background; we'll teach them the techniques." The educational world responded by emphasizing what it already had learned: that every valid journalism education program had to permit its students to take at least two-thirds—and preferably three-fourths—of their work in liberal arts areas, with the remaining journalism courses enabling students to bring those materials and insights into sharp focus as effective communicators of news and opinion. A 3–1 ratio between nonjournalism and journalism subjects now is considered by most media executives and educators to provide the best preparation for careers in mass communications, and it is the stated goal of the American Council on Education for Journalism.

Today a college education is the minimum requirement for most newspaper editorial positions, particularly those on large newspapers. The majority of newspaper editors definitely prefer journalism graduates. Some papers, however, find that men and women who have majored in history, political science, English, or some other field are equally acceptable as, if not more desirable than, journalism graduates. The crux of the matter appears to be the individual; if he demonstrates maturity, ability, and industry he may find a place for himself in mass communications regardless of his college major field of study. By far the greatest supply of newsroom talent, however, is issuing from journalism schools and departments because young people who seriously contemplate careers in mass communications almost invariably are drawn to journalism training programs.

Although a few broadcast executives urge that radio-television instruction be made more practical and that students learn techniques so as to be immediately useful in their job assignments, most station managers recommend that students be given a broad general background and that any high degree of specialization be left for development on the job. Polls have indicated that most station managers regard the liberal education courses in the broadcast curriculum to be of indispensable value to the student. One such executive declared: "Training beyond the fundamentals is not as important as a liberal education. We promote from within, which means that we are looking at the potential man, not the technician." Another stated: "A liberal arts background is something we look for. If the applicant knows only TV, speech, and allied subjects, he doesn't have the depth of background to continue day-by-day doing a creative job. He should know art, music, languages—and, incidentally, TV."

Broadcast executives usually search out speech, general radio-television, and drama graduates for their performing and production positions. For news jobs, they tend to employ journalism graduates.

Some of the reasons why newspaper executives generally prefer journalism graduates to nonjournalism applicants were advanced in a poll. One managing editor declared that the journalism graduate "had a better foundation on which to build." Another cited his "greater ability to recognize the newsworthiness of a situation." Other comments: "Possesses wide fundamental knowledge of newspaper craft and requires less training to acquire skill." "J-school grads move up much faster if they show they can out-produce non-J-school grads, which they usually do." "General preference based on the fact that his choice of journalism indicates a more avid interest in newspaper work." "Usually better equipped to tackle major assignments, more worldly wise, aims at jobs requiring more education, such as editorial writing, business editing, etc."

Although the legal, medical, and dentistry professions support their schools more fully than journalism schools are backed by the media, journalism educators and media personnel have developed a multiplicity of programs of mutual support; and cooperation by the industry is improving steadily. After the media for the most part failed to assume the responsibility of providing recruits for employment, the schools took on this function. The media have accepted virtually all these young men and women, and have wanted more. Educators needed new or modernized buildings and better equipment; in many states the media both individually and through their associations have given money and other support for these undertakings. A number of schools and some media groups wanted to raise the standards of journalism education; the American Council on Education for Journalism was established, with media associations underwriting most of the expense of operation. Educators saw the value of summer internship programs both for themselves and for their students; such plans to provide realistic training with newspapers, magazines, radio-television units, and other media groups have been operating in some areas for several decades.

Some schools have felt a need to employ nearby practitioners of journalism as part-time teachers; the media almost invariably have cooperated. Educators asked that the number of scholarships, fellowships, and loan funds be increased; in a number of states media groups have responded wholeheartedly. Educators in some states wanted to establish foundations to aid journalism education; in North Carolina tax-deductible funds thus contributed by newspapers by 1972 exceeded $500,000, and the School of Journalism at the University of North Carolina at Chapel Hill had received more than $225,000 in income from the School of Journalism Foundation of North Carolina, Inc.

Many schools regularly conduct seminars, conferences, and other such gatherings so that professional men and women may exchange ideas and learn of new advances in their fields; these meetings almost always are well attended by personnel from the newspaper, press association, magazine, radio-television, advertising, public relations, and related fields. Virtually every institution calls on practitioners in mass communications to speak for classes, convocations, and other student gatherings; numerous organizations have established national bureaus to provide speakers, audiovisual materials, and printed literature for college students, and local and regional media personnel are always available for campus appearances.

The Association of Advertising Men and Women and the Advertising Club of New York established in 1950 a program known as "Inside Advertising Week." Its purpose was to show the nation's leading advertising students, enrolled in colleges and universities, a glimpse of the advertising business, its aims and ideals, in an attempt to explain the why and wherefore of the industry. Each year advertising and marketing seniors have participated in a five-day program of activities in New York City. The Chicago Advertising Club sponsors a similar annual event, the Midwest Advertising Conference.

Other advertising groups have provided guest speakers and films for college career days and clinics, arranged scholarships and loans, donated advertising libraries, invited students to professional meetings, arranged tours, helped place graduates in jobs, sent agency executives on "task force" visits to campuses, and provided summer work opportunities for both the students and their teachers. One advertising agency has had as many as 15 students with it in a single summer. Various councils of the American Association of Advertising Agencies sponsor scholarships, as do at least 16 agencies that are Four A members.

Summer internships for teachers with general magazines and with radio and television stations have been provided by the Magazine Publishers Association and the National Association of Broadcasters. Daily newspapers also have accepted teachers for summer intern spots.

The National Association of Broadcasters provides the Harold E. Fellows Memorial Scholarship for students of broadcasting in member schools of the Association for Professional Broadcasting Education. Named for the NAB's president and chairman from 1951 to 1960, the fund provides two annual scholarships in the amount of $1100 each.

## A COMMUNICATIONS EDUCATION NEVER ENDS

It's a truism, of course, to point out that a college diploma, or its equivalent in individual attainment, is only the beginning of a lifetime of education. For no other group does this fact hold greater validity than for those who embark on careers in mass communications. Every aspect of human experience and emotion can become their concern; the world changes and so must their ability to understand and interpret those changes.

The man or woman who wants to develop his fullest potential in the field of mass communications cannot neglect his reading, both fiction and nonfiction. Aside from sheer enjoyment and enrichment of the inner self, books and magazines of high quality provide information and insights that surely will improve his performance as a mass communicator. The reading of trade and professional publications is essential to this process of continuous educational development. Just as the physician peruses similar periodicals to keep abreast of advances of knowledge in medicine, so the journalist must examine on a systematic, continuing basis such research journals as *Journalism Quarterly, Public Opinion Quarterly,* and *Journal of Marketing;* newspaper trade journals such as *Editor & Publisher* and *Publishers' Auxiliary;* other trade journals such as *Broadcasting, Advertising Age,* and *Public Relations Journal;* and general interest professional journals such as *Nieman Reports, Quill,* and *Columbia Journalism Review;* and critical periodicals such as the *Chicago Journalism Review* and [*MORE*].

In the trade and professional periodicals he finds the latest developments in many areas of continuing concern for which there are no fixed answers: What is the social justification for printing or refusing to publish the names of juveniles involved in crimes? How far should government supervise the conduct of television and radio stations? What advertising procedures are unethical? What is the meaning of the latest research developments in communication? No journalist can be truly professional and remain ignorant of changing attitudes and legal actions that affect any of the mass media.

The journalist also can remain well informed of developments in communication through maintaining active membership in organizations that are engaged in programs of self-study. According to his particular field or position, he may find highly stimulating the conferences and literature of such organizations as the American Society of Newspaper Editors, the National Conference of Editorial Writers, state press associations, the Associated Press and United Press International, the Association for Education in Journalism, the American Association of Advertising Agencies, Sigma Delta Chi, Theta Sigma Phi, and the National Association of Broadcasters.

With society becoming increasingly complex and new knowledge appearing in almost every sector, many media people have returned to college for regular courses as well as for such adult education activities as residential workshops, summer laboratories, short courses, educational camps, community development projects, seminars, forum series, and televised discussions. For example, in addition to the programs described in Chapter 8, Columbia University has initiated a study program for science writers; Northwestern University has sponsored periodic seminars for crime news reporters; Pennsylvania State University has provided forums bringing together newspaper and broadcast men, public officials, and community leaders and opinion makers for a critical examination of key communication issues. Other universities are offering similar refresher experiences for communicators.

Dow Jones and Company's Newspaper Fund, Inc., has sent more than 5900 high school and junior college journalism teachers back to college for special summer training. Sigma Delta Chi has cosponsored seminars for such specialized groups as business news writers from over the nation, and the professional journalism society's eleven annual regional conferences are planned as forums for the exploration of pressing news problems.

Several hundred newspapermen have been selected by the Nieman Foundation for a year of study at Harvard University under a million dollar endowment left in 1936 by the widow of Lucius W. Nieman, founder of the Milwaukee *Journal*. A dozen highly qualified newspapermen are selected annually as Nieman Fellows; they spend the year pursuing any course of study they desire. Louis M. Lyons, emeritus curator of the foundation, established a quarterly magazine, *Nieman Reports,* in 1947.

Another opportunity for intensive study and discussion of problems is provided through the American Press Institute seminars conducted at Columbia University in New York for managing editors, city editors, circulation managers, and similar identical-interest groups. Press associations in some states sponsor similar seminars.

## JOURNALISM TEACHING IN THE SECONDARY SCHOOL

There are more potential openings for teachers of journalism in the secondary schools of the United States than in any other field for which journalism training provides preparation. The best estimates are that approximately 45,000 senior and junior high school publications—newspapers, magazines, and yearbooks—are being issued regularly. More than 1,000,000 students work on these publications, which cost collectively around $40,000,000 a year. About 175,000 students are enrolled each year in journalism courses offered at approximately 5000 high schools.

Expert instruction should be provided for these undertakings and for the journalism classes that usually produce them, both for credit and as an extracurricular activity. So severe, however, is the shortage of qualified instructors that frequently a teacher of language arts, business education, or social studies—with no background whatever in journalism—is assigned to provide a measure of guidance. This happens, too, when a principal fails to realize the importance of providing qualified instruction in the high school journalism field.

The first known high school paper, the *Literary Journal,* appeared in the Boston Latin Grammar School in 1829. Other publications were founded by New England high schools in the 1850's and 1860's. It was not until 1912, however, that the first known class in high school journalism was started in Salina, Kansas. The movement became widespread in the 1920's, apparently in an effort to motivate students in English composition and to broaden the curriculum beyond the traditional classical subjects. A number of local, state, and national organizations were founded in the mid-1920's. Among them were three of the current national organizations: Quill and Scroll, the honorary society of high school journalists, now housed at the State University of Iowa; the Columbia Scholastic Press Association at Columbia University; and the National Scholastic Press Association, with headquarters at the University of Minnesota. Their national magazines, begun at this time, are *Quill and Scroll, School Press Review,* and *Scholastic Editor,* respectively.

The Catholic School Press Association, founded at Marquette University in 1931, publishes *Catholic School Editor.*

High school journalism matured during the 1930's and 1940's as school boards, superintendents, and principals noted its educational value. The objectives outlined for the Baltimore, Maryland, secondary school course in journalism exemplify those elsewhere: To teach the functions of a school paper; to foster an understanding of the role of the newspaper in a democracy; to encourage the development of qualities essential to a competent school journalist; to develop a working knowledge of newspaper ethics; to promote the critical selection and reading of newspapers and periodicals; to develop skill in accurate, clear, and forceful journalistic writing; to provide experiences in the technical processes in producing a school newspaper; and to give practice in the use of the correct mechanics of English.

Those who have taught high school journalism over the years speak with genuine enthusiasm about the satisfactions they have found in handling journalism classes and advising school publications. For one thing, they enjoy having many of their school's most brilliant students on their publications staffs; frequently the highest ranking group of students in the English placement tests is assigned to the teacher producing the school paper. These imaginative and creative youngsters are stimulated by actually writing for print. Many of them go on to other fields of study at the universities, but some become the prize students of journalism or communications schools and eventually take their places in professional work. Many an editor or reporter can trace his interest in journalism back to a high school journalism teacher or publications adviser who transmitted some of the enthusiasm of the craft to his or her students. The school paper and the annual are major activities at the high school level; this gives their adviser additional prestige as a teacher. He or she also is brought into close contact with school administrators, and quite a number of able journalism teachers have moved into administrative work.

The most substantial support accorded to high school journalism teachers has come from the Newspaper Fund. More than $1,400,000 has been invested in the development of high school journalism teachers by the Fund. Many teachers needed training in journalistic writing and production of student newspapers because of a lack of prior education in the field. These studies also increased the teachers' enthusiasm for high school journalism as a socially important academic field which would be the starting block for students interested in newspaper work and other communications fields. In addition, the national grants were credited with improving the prestige of teachers of journalism.

Men and women entering journalism teaching at the junior and senior high school levels also have the support of such organizations as the National Scholastic Press Association and the Columbia Scholastic Press Association, which issue publications and guidebooks for teachers and students and conduct critical services providing professional evaluation and ratings of school newspapers, annuals, and magazines. The National School Yearbook Association and its affiliated National Newspaper Service, both of Memphis, Tennessee, offer critical services for both high school and college yearbooks and newspapers and publish a monthly magazine, *Photolith*. There are also regional associations, like the Southern Interscholastic Press Association, with headquarters at the University of South Carolina, and the Mid-America Association for Secondary Journalism, established at the University of Missouri. The associations and many schools and departments of journalism hold conventions for high school journalists. The teachers themselves are organized as the Journalism Education Association, affiliated with the NSPA. Newsmen and educators also cooperate in organizing high school chapters of the Future Journalists of America, founded at the University of Oklahoma.

The educational preparation necessary to teach secondary school journalism varies widely from state to state. A study reported in the Fall 1971 issue of *Communication: Journalism Education Today* showed that about 30 percent of the states have no specific journalism certification requirements, about 30 percent grant journalism certification for completing fewer than 15 semester hours of college journalism course work, and about 40 percent require the equivalent of a minor in journalism. Only two states required a major in journalism. An apparent trend against further certification of any kind hampered efforts to add journalism certification in some states.

Less than a year after the National Council of Teachers of English recognized journalism as "necessary in the experience of learning to communicate effectively," the California Board of Education reclassified journalism as an academic subject, including it as one of the humanities subjects in the curriculum.

Some prospective teachers major in journalism and minor in an area such as English or the social sciences, meanwhile acquiring sufficient hours in education courses to qualify for certificates. Others major in education and take first and second minors in journalism and some other field. Still others major in English or language arts and take as many journalism courses as they can work into a four-year program that often is crowded because of the double professional preparation required. All realize that they likely will be teaching only one or two courses in journalism, with the balance of their instructional load in another subject.

Salary levels, which also vary widely throughout the country, have risen considerably in recent years because of the shortage of teachers and increased public awareness of the necessity for better supporting the schools. Many teachers, after acquiring some experience in the classrooms, return to seek a master's degree both for increased proficiency and for higher pay. Summer work on newspapers and other media can provide both additional pay and professional experience that makes a teacher better qualified to teach journalism. With the dearth of adequately prepared teachers in the field, those who take at least a substantial minor in journalism or who return for graduate work are sought after by those school systems which place some real emphasis on high school journalism and publications work.

## JOURNALISM TEACHING IN THE JUNIOR COLLEGE

Hundreds of opportunities for teaching journalism are available in junior colleges throughout the United States, which are growing steadily in enrollment and importance as the population increases.

Fifty-nine percent of the 936 junior colleges which responded to a survey conducted by Dr. Frank Deaver in 1971–72 offer some courses in journalism. Most often these courses include introduction to mass communications, beginning newswriting and reporting, news editing, and photography. Two-thirds of the courses serve as laboratories for student publications—newspaper, magazine, or yearbook. In most of these two-year colleges the journalism program is designed to encourage these student publications and to give basic preparation for students planning to major in journalism or communications at four-year colleges and universities. A number of junior college educators state that their primary purpose is to acquaint students with the mass media and to teach them to become discerning "consumers" of news and opinion so they will be better able to discharge their responsibilities as citizens. In some junior colleges enough advanced instruction is given to prepare graduates to take jobs with the media, but the high degree of specialization required and the inadequacy of faculty staffing present problems which most junior college educators prefer not to face.

Junior college educators are organized as the Junior College Journalism Association, an affiliate of the Association for Education in Journalism. The Newspaper Fund worked with the educators to develop their organization, through annual seminars at the University of Texas. In California, more than 60 junior and city colleges belong to the Journalism Association of Junior Colleges. The typical degree of the two-year college educators is the M.A., earned by 75 percent, with 20 percent holding the B.A. in addition to media experience and 5 percent the Ph.D. Many junior college educators serve as advisers to student publications or as publicity directors for the college administration. A substantial number are women.

## THE COLLEGE AND UNIVERSITY LEVEL

Journalism and communications faculty members at the university or college level are engaged in three major activities: teaching, research, and service. They have one or more specialties in the journalistic techniques, acquired through their own professional experience with the mass media: reporting, news editing, magazine writing, radio and television news, typography and graphic arts processes, advertising, public relations, news photography, critical writing, broadcast programing and production, and editorial writing are among these technique fields. The young teacher usually starts at this techniques level, but he is well advised to be equipped for teaching and research in one or more of the scholarly fields of interest: history of journalism, literary journalism, the press and society, economics of mass communications, legal aspects of communications, international communications and foreign journalism, public opinion and propaganda, mass communication theory, and the advanced fields of advertising research. He should be interested, too, in performing services for the mass media with which the school or department is in close contact and in spending long hours offering advice and counsel to students who turn to him for guidance and stimulation.

Those who aspire to the top ranks of university or college teaching in journalism and mass communications usually seek master's degrees in the field. They then undertake study toward the Ph.D. degree in the graduate school of a college or university which offers either a major or a minor in the subject and which has a journalism and communications faculty of graduate school caliber. Some prefer to minor in journalism or communications and to do their major doctoral work in political science, history, psychology, sociology, economics, speech, American studies, or another related field; others enter universities which award Ph.D. degrees in journalism or in communications. In either case, there is a blending of study and research in journalism or communications with study and research in the social sciences, behavioral sciences, or the humanities. One major school of journalism and mass communications, for example, has on its staff 13 men with Ph.D. degrees: five in mass communications, two each in psychology and political science, and one each in sociology, speech, history, and American studies. Six other staff members hold M.A. degrees, two in journalism, and one each in marketing, economics, fine arts, and English.

Not all college journalism or communications faculty members need undertake doctoral work; some with sound professional experience and specialized abilities in such fields as graphic arts, news photography, weekly journalism, or radio and television writing, production, and programing find their services amply rewarded at the M.A. level. There have been shortages of qualified teachers in the advertising and broadcast media fields, particularly. As the size of the institution or of the journalism or communications teaching staff decreases, there is additional emphasis upon the teaching function and the all-around ability of faculty members to handle technical work. The amount of emphasis placed upon the research function, for which the discipline of doctoral study is highly important, varies from campus to campus.

Opportunities for research and publication in the mass communications field are almost unlimited. Many aspects of the history of communications remain to be explored, despite the fact that this area traditionally has been a favorite one for journalism professors. Biographies and histories of individual newspapers, broadcast facilities, and magazines remain to be written in virtually every section of the country; for example, there are no really good and recent biographies of such newspaper greats as James Gordon Bennett and Adolph Ochs, let alone many other capable editors and publishers of regional importance. Nor are there adequate histories of more than a score of the country's many newspapers, broadcast stations, and magazines. The literary aspects of journalism constitute another little-plowed field. Important studies of the relationships between the press and society, and of the conflicts between press and government, await future scholars. Only a start has been made on penetrating studies of the economics of the mass media. Advertising offers wide opportunities for advanced study and research projects of both basic and applied character. As explained in Chapter 18, the fields of mass communications theory and research, of public opinion and propaganda, and of other studies allied to the behavioral sciences have barely been opened by scholars. Particularly, there is a need for interpretative analysis of scientific findings and quantitative data by men who can relate what the researchers have found to the everyday problems of the mass media. The processes of international communications and the study of foreign journalism have become more important in recent years, also, with few faculty members qualified to do advanced teaching and research in the field.

Many teachers serve as advisers to college newspapers. After compiling the *Directory of the College Student Press in America,* Dr. Dario Politella, associate professor of journalism at the University of Massachusetts, estimated that there are at least 2600 student newspapers in U.S. colleges and universities, with press runs of 8,000,000 issues. In addition, he reported, students publish 4,500,000 copies of yearbooks and 3,200,-000 copies of magazines of various types.

At the level of the 500 or more institutions offering nondegree study in journalism, there are at least 150 colleges which offer more than 18 semester hours (or 27 quarter hours) in journalism, including 30 or more which offer a journalism minor. Another 75 offer up to 12 semester hours; the remainder provide one or two courses, usually connected with the college student publications. About three-fourths of these institutions house their journalism instruction within the English department; the others list it separately. Men and women with M.A. degrees, at least, in journalism can find beginning teaching positions in these colleges, and sometimes they are able to carve out satisfying professional careers in them; this is true particularly of those who also are interested in the teaching of English and writing. They may become publications and broadcast advisers, as well, and sometimes also serve in the college's public relations and publicity offices.

Offering assistance to the publications adviser at the junior college and college level are the Associated Collegiate Press, companion organization of the National Scholastic Press Association, the National Council of College Publications Advisers, and the National School Yearbook Association and its affiliated National Newspaper Service. The ACP, NSYA, and NNS issue guidebooks and other publications for college publications staffs and maintain critical services for newspapers, annuals, and magazines.

Salaries for communications teachers in colleges and universities run somewhat above the averages for other disciplines, because of the competitive bidding from the mass media for the services of those who are preparing for teaching careers. University and college salaries have improved substantially in recent years, and those who reach professorial status can look forward to nine-month salaries running from $15,000 to as high as $30,000 a year. There also are opportunities for additional income from summer teaching, summer "refresher" work in the media, consultantships to advertising agencies and other groups, research projects, and book publication and other writing.

# BIBLIOGRAPHY

This is a selected, annotated bibliography of books dealing with mass communications and journalism. It is organized to correspond with the four principal sections and 19 chapters of this book.

It is the authors' aim to introduce the reader to some of the basic books which, if he has the time and interest to explore them, will take him beyond the necessarily limited syntheses of an introductory survey of mass communications. If a student reader has the interest and opportunity to elect further studies in the field, he will meet many of these books again in advanced courses; if he goes no further, this bibliography will give him a personal reading list for more detailed examination of various facets of the field. It is in no sense an all-inclusive bibliography; for that purpose the reader is referred to Warren C. Price's *The Literature of Journalism: An Annotated Bibliography* (Minneapolis: University of Minnesota Press, 1959), and a ten-year supplement to it compiled by Price and Calder M. Pickett, *An Annotated Journalism Bibliography* (1970). Another excellent aid is Eleanor Blum's *Basic Books in the Mass Media* (Urbana: University of Illinois Press, 1972). A general source book is the annual Directory issue of *Journalism Educator*, published by the American Society of Journalism School Administrators.

This bibliography also lists the principal journals and trade publications with which students of mass communications should be familiar, and in a few instances makes references to articles in them. In cases where books have gone through revised editions, the date given is for the most recent revision. In subsequent listings of a book, place and date of publication are not repeated.

# Periodicals, Annual Publications, and Directories

## GENERAL RESEARCH JOURNALS

*Journalism Quarterly*—published by the Association for Education in Journalism, devoted to research articles in journalism and mass communications. Contains extensive book reviews, bibliographies of articles in American and foreign journals, news of journalism education.

*Public Opinion Quarterly*—emphasizes political and psychological phases of communication. Book reviews and summaries of public opinion polls. Published by the American Association for Public Opinion Research.

*Gazette*—international journal, published in Amsterdam, devoted to research in mass communications. Book reviews and bibliographies.

*AV Communication Review*—reports on research activities and findings in the communication area. Published quarterly by the Department of Audiovisual Instruction of the NEA.

*Journal of Communication*—research quarterly focusing on methodology; interests in speech and interpersonal communication areas. Book reviews. Published by International Communication Association.

*Journal of Typographic Research*—research quarterly of the graphic arts area, published by the Cleveland Museum of Modern Art.

*Journalism Monographs*—published serially by the Association for Education in Journalism, beginning in 1966, for research findings falling between article and book lengths.

## GENERAL PROFESSIONAL JOURNALS

Professional journals with general interest articles on press problems: *Nieman Reports,* published by the Nieman Foundation; *Columbia Journalism Review* (Columbia University Graduate School of Journalism); *Quill* (Sigma Delta Chi); *Matrix* (Theta Sigma Phi); *Journalism Educator* (American Society of Journalism School Administrators); *Communication: Journalism Education Today* (Journalism Education Association); *IPI Report* (International Press Institute).

## NEWSPAPER AREA

Professional journals: *ASNE Bulletin* (American Society of Newspaper Editors); *Masthead* (National Conference of Editorial Writers); *Chicago Journalism Review; National Press Photographer* (National Press Photographers Association).

Trade journals: *Editor & Publisher,* whose focus is on the daily newspaper and general industry problems, but which reports on advertising, marketing, and public relations areas; *Publishers' Auxiliary* and *American Press* (National Newspaper Association), both primarily covering weeklies and small dailies, with the first named being the widest in scope; *Guild Reporter* (American Newspaper Guild); *Circulation Management; Inland Printer,* for the printing industry.

Annual publications: *APME Red Book,* containing the record of the annual meeting and the reports of the Continuing Studies Committee of the Associated Press Managing Editors Association; *Problems of Journalism,* covering the annual meeting of the American Society of Newspaper Editors.

Directories: *Editor & Publisher International Year Book,* source for statistics and information about dailies; N. W. Ayer and Son, *Directory of Newspapers and Periodicals,* covering all newspapers and magazines.

### TELEVISION, RADIO, AND FILM

Research journals: *Journal of Broadcasting* (Association for Professional Broadcasting Education); *Television Quarterly* (National Academy of Television Arts and Sciences); *Educational Broadcasting Review* (National Association of Educational Broadcasters). All carry articles, book reviews, notes.

Professional journals: *RTNDA Bulletin* (Radio-Television News Directors Association); *Film Quarterly Communication Arts* (photography, television); *TV Communications* (cable television).

Trade journals: *Broadcasting,* the spokesman for that industry; *Television/Radio Age; Variety,* voice of the entertainment world; *Billboard.*

Directories: *Broadcasting Yearbook,* source for statistics and information about radio and television; *Television Factbook.*

### MAGAZINES AND BOOK PUBLISHING

Trade journals: *Publishers' Weekly,* for the book publishing industry, whose focus is largely on general and children's books with limited attention to textbooks, technical books, and reference works; *The Retail Bookseller; Bookbinding and Book Production; Author and Journalist, Writer,* and *Writer's Digest,* for free-lance magazine writers; *Reporting* (International Association of Business Communicators), for people in organizational communications.

Directories: *Literary Market Place,* for book publishing; N. W. Ayer and Son, *Directory of Newspapers and Periodicals,* for magazine statistics and information; *Writer's Market* and *Writer's Year Book,* guides for magazine article writers; Gebbie Press, *House Magazine Directory.*

## ADVERTISING AND PUBLIC RELATIONS

Research journals: *Journal of Marketing* (American Marketing Association), articles and book reviews; *Journal of Marketing Research* (Advertising Research Foundation); *Journal of Advertising* (American Academy of Advertising).

Professional journals: *Public Relations Journal* (Public Relations Society of America); *Public Relations News* (newsletter).

Trade journals: *Advertising Age,* the major spokesman for the advertising industry; *Advertising Agency; Advertising Requirements; Sponsor,* for buyers of broadcast advertising; *Industrial Marketing; Sales Management; Direct Marketing.*

Directories: Standard Rate and Data Service, *Consumer Markets; Editor & Publisher Market Guide; Broadcasting Marketbook.*

### Part I

## The Role of Mass Communications

Perhaps no book better illustrates the importance which society attaches to the mass communicator and the mass media than the brief *A Free and Responsible Press* (Chicago: University of Chicago Press, 1947). It summarizes the opinions of the 13 scholars who comprised the Commission on Freedom of the Press regarding the duties and the shortcomings of the mass media. Commission chairman was Dr. Robert M. Hutchins of the University of Chicago.

William L. Rivers and Wilbur Schramm's *Responsibility in Mass Communication* (New York: Harper & Row, 1969) is the best treatment of communication ethics. It discusses the role of the mass communicator in developing the political, social, and economic fabrics of a democratic society, and the development of modern mass communications. A survey of similar vein is William L. Rivers, Theodore Peterson, and Jay Jensen, *The Mass Media and Modern Society* (San Francisco: Rinehart Press, 1971). Examining advertising's role in the economy and its social contribution are Jules Backman, *Advertising and Competition* (New York: New York University Press, 1967), and Charles H. Sandage and Vernon Fryburger, *The Role of Advertising, A Book of Readings* (Homewood, Ill.: Irwin, 1960).

Several books of readings deal with the role of mass communications in society. Listed in order according to the increasing complexity of their materials they are: *The Press and Society,* edited by George L. Bird and Frederic E. Merwin (New York: Prentice-Hall, 1951), organized for historical use; *Interpretations of Journalism,* edited by Frank Luther Mott and Ralph D. Casey (New York: Crofts, 1937), a collection of 64 of the "chief utterances of the past 300 years on the subject of newspapers and the press"; *Communications in Modern Society,* edited by Wilbur Schramm (Urbana: University of Illinois Press, 1948), 15 essays on communications problems and research trends; *Mass Communications,* edited by Wilbur Schramm (Urbana: University of Illinois Press, 1960), selected readings on mass communications "through the windows of the social sciences"; *Reader in Public Opinion and Communication,* edited by Bernard Berelson and Morris Janowitz (New York: Free Press of Glencoe, 1966), dealing with public opinion theory, media content, audiences, and effects; *People, Society, and Mass Communication,* edited by Lewis A. Dexter and David M. White (New York: Free Press of Glencoe, 1964), dealing with communication research with a sociological emphasis; and *Dimensions of Communication,* edited by Lee Richardson (New York: Appleton-Century-Crofts, 1969), focusing on problems of communication and persuasion at both personal and media levels.

Melvin L. DeFleur's *Theories of Mass Communication* (New York: David McKay, 1970) is a readable, useful survey of contemporary theory. Provocative discussions are found in Marshall McLuhan's *Understanding Media: The Extensions of Man* (New York: McGraw-Hill, 1964), his earlier *The Gutenberg Galaxy: The Making of Typographic Man* (Toronto: University of Toronto Press, 1962), and his 1967 attention-getter, *The Medium Is the Massage* (Bantam Books). More difficult books in the theory area are William Stephenson, *The Play Theory of Mass Communication* (Chicago: University of Chicago Press, 1967); Alfred G. Smith, *Communication and Culture: Readings* (New York: Holt, Rinehart and Winston, 1966); and Charles E. Osgood, George Suci, and Percy H. Tannenbaum, *The Measurement of Meaning* (Urbana: University of Illinois Press, 1957).

The effects of the mass media on the social fabric are discussed in various articles in *Mass Culture: The Popular Arts in America,* edited by Bernard Rosenberg and David M. White (New York: Free Press of Glencoe, 1957). There are sections on the mass literature, motion pictures, radio, and television. An updated version by the same authors is *Mass Culture Revisited* (New York: Van Nostrand Reinhold, 1971). A briefer survey is John C. Merrill and Ralph L. Lowenstein, *Media, Messages, and Men* (New York: David McKay, 1971).

More complex studies of effects are Joseph T. Klapper's *The Effects of Mass Communication* (Glencoe, Ill.: The Free Press, 1960), and *The Process and Effects of Mass Communication,* edited by Wilbur Schramm and Donald F. Roberts (Urbana: University of Illinois Press, 1971).

Essays on communication research are offered by Schramm in *The Science of Human Communication* (New York: Basic Books, 1963), which contains articles by Leon Festinger, Charles E. Osgood, Klapper, Elihu Katz, Paul Lazarsfeld, Ithiel de Sola Pool, and others, on subjects ranging from cognitive dissonance to voting behavior. Lee Thayer's *Communication and Communication Systems* (Homewood, Ill.: Irwin, 1968) is a readable synthesis ranging through a difficult field, aimed at practitioners in organizations, management, and interpersonal relations.

The communication process is analyzed most completely in David K. Berlo's *The Process of Communication* (New York: Holt, 1960), and most simply by Chilton R. Bush in the first chapter of *The Art of News Communication* (New York: Appleton-Century-Crofts, 1954). Wilbur Schramm describes "How Communication Works" in the opening chapter of *The Process and Effects of Mass Communication*. Harold D. Lasswell's "The Structure and Function of Communication in Society" (in which he posed the question "Who, says what, in which channel, to whom, with what effect?") appears both in Schramm's *Mass Communications* reader and in *The Communication of Ideas,* edited by Lyman Bryson (New York: Harper, 1948).

Among the leading books on public opinion are William Albig, *Modern Public Opinion* (New York: McGraw-Hill, 1956); V. O. Key Jr., *Public Opinion and American Democracy* (New York: Knopf, 1961); Erwin P. Bettinghaus, *Persuasive Communication* (New York: Holt, Rinehart and Winston, 1968); Robert E. Lane and David O. Sears, *Public Opinion* (Englewood Cliffs, N.J.: Prentice-Hall, 1967), focusing on voting; Norman Powell, *Anatomy of Public Opinion* (New York: Prentice-Hall, 1951), which treats the mass media more extensively than most books on public opinion; and Curtis D. MacDougall, *Understanding Public Opinion: A Guide for Newspapermen and Newspaper Readers* (Dubuque, Iowa: Wm. C. Brown, 1966), with a focus as indicated in the subtitle.

The impact of public opinion and the mass media upon politics is analyzed by Walter Lippmann in his classic *Public Opinion* (New York: Harcourt, Brace, 1922); by Douglass Cater in *The Fourth Branch of Government* (Boston: Houghton Mifflin, 1959), a study of the key role of the Washington press corps; by Bernard C. Cohen in *The Press and Foreign Policy* (Princeton, N.J.: Princeton University Press, 1963), a study of Washington diplomatic reporting; by James Reston in another study of press influence on foreign policy, *The Artillery of the Press* (New York: Harper & Row, 1967); by Elmer Cornwell Jr. in *Presidential Leadership of Public Opinion* (Bloomington: Indiana University Press, 1965); and by William L. Rivers in his *The Opinionmakers* (Boston: Beacon Press, 1965), a study of leading Washington newsmen, and his *The Adversaries* (Boston: Beacon Press, 1970), a study of press manipulation by public officials.

Books dealing with the mass media and the voting process include Angus Campbell and others, *The American Voter* (New York: Wiley, 1960); Bernard Berelson, Hazel Gaudet, and Paul F. Lazarsfeld, *The People's Choice* (New York: Duell, Sloan and Pearce, 1944), analyzing 1940 presidential voting in Erie county, Ohio; and Bernard Berelson, Paul F. Lazarsfeld, and William N. McPhee, *Voting: A Study of Opinion Formation in a Presidential Campaign* (Chicago: University of Chicago Press, 1954), case analyses of 1948 presidential election voters in Elmira, New York. Elihu Katz and Paul Lazarsfeld, *Personal Influence: The Part Played by People in the Flow of Mass Communications* (Glencoe, Ill.: The Free Press, 1955), develops a new aspect of the problem.

International communication research and theory are reported upon in Lucian W. Pye, *Communications and Political Development* (Princeton, N.J.: Princeton University Press, 1963); Wilbur Schramm, *Mass Media and National Development* (Stanford, Calif.: Stanford University Press, 1964); Wilson P. Dizard, *Television: A World View* (Syracuse, N.Y.: Syracuse University Press, 1966); and Daniel Lerner and Wilbur Schramm, *Communication and Change in the Developing Countries* (Honolulu: East-West Center, 1967).

**Part II**

## The Historical Perspective

The most widely ranging of the histories of American journalism is Edwin Emery's *The Press and America: An Interpretative History of the Mass Media* (Englewood Cliffs, N.J.: Prentice-Hall, 1972). It correlates the narrative of journalism history with social, political, and economic trends and is especially comprehensive in its treatment of Twentieth Century journalism—newspapers, magazines, radio and television, press associations, and the relationship of the mass media to government and society.

Frank Luther Mott's *American Journalism: A History, 1690–1960* (New York: Macmillan, 1962) is designed for both classroom and reference shelf, contains much rich detail in its comprehensive treatment of newspapers, but puts little emphasis on other media. Alfred McClung Lee's *The Daily Newspaper in America* (New York: Macmillan, 1937) offers a sociological approach and much valuable data in its topical treatment of such subjects as newsprint, printing presses, labor, ownership and management, news, advertising, and circulation. Willard G.

Bleyer's *Main Currents in the History of American Journalism* (Boston: Houghton Mifflin, 1927) remains an excellent account of American journalism until the early twentieth century, with emphasis upon leading editors. Kenneth Stewart and John Tebbel, in *Makers of Modern Journalism* (New York: Prentice-Hall, 1952), sketch early American journalism history and concentrate on twentieth century journalistic personalities. Tebbel, in his *Compact History of the American Newspaper* (New York: Hawthorn, 1969), does the reverse, sketching twentieth century journalism in only the broadest terms. Sidney Kobre adds details about many regional papers in his sociologically-based *Development of American Journalism* (Dubuque, Iowa: Wm. C. Brown, 1969).

Reproductions of full front pages of newspapers on an extensive, planned scale are found in Edwin Emery's *The Story of America as Reported by Its Newspapers 1690–1965* (New York: Simon and Schuster, 1965) and in *America's Front Page News 1690–1970,* edited by Michael C. Emery, R. Smith Schuneman, and Edwin Emery (Minneapolis: Vis-Com and 3M Co., 1970). Will Irwin's 1911 study of *The American Newspaper* for *Collier's* is reproduced, with comments, by Clifford F. Weigle and David G. Clark (Ames: Iowa State University Press, 1969).

Articles about Twentieth Century journalists first published in the *Saturday Evening Post* are found in *Post Biographies of Famous Journalists,* edited by John E. Drewry (Athens: University of Georgia Press, 1942), and its sequel, *More Post Biographies* (1947). A collection of the best magazine articles about leading American newspaper editors and publishers of all periods is found in *Highlights in the History of the American Press,* edited by Edwin H. Ford and Edwin Emery (Minneapolis: University of Minnesota Press, 1954).

The best historical accounts of specific areas of mass communications are found in the following:

Radio and television: Erik Barnouw's three-volume history of U.S. broadcasting, *A Tower in Babel, The Golden Web,* and *The Image Empire* (New York: Oxford, 1966, 1968, 1970); Sydney W. Head, *Broadcasting in America* (Boston: Houghton Mifflin, 1972); Gleason L. Archer's classics, *History of Radio to 1926* (New York: American Historical Society, 1938) and *Big Business and Radio* (1939); and Llewellyn White *The American Radio* (Chicago: University of Chicago Press, 1947). For technical history, Orrin Dunlap, *Communications in Space* (New York: Harper & Row, 1970), and W. R. Maclaurin, *Invention and Innovation in the Radio Industry* (New York: Macmillan, 1949).

Magazines: Frank Luther Mott's monumental *A History of American Magazines,* in five volumes (Vol. 1, New York: Appleton, 1930 and

Vols. 2–5, Cambridge, Mass.: Harvard University Press, 1938–68); James Playsted Wood, *Magazines in the United States* (New York: Ronald, 1956); Theodore Peterson, *Magazines in the Twentieth Century* (Urbana: University of Illinois Press, 1964); John Tebbel, *The American Magazine: A Compact History* (New York: Hawthorn, 1969).

Book publishing: Hellmut Lehmann-Haupt and others, *The Book in America: History of the Making and Selling of Books in the United States* (New York: Bowker, 1951); Frank A. Mumby, *Publishing and Bookselling: A History from the Earliest Times to the Present* (London: Jonathan Cape, 1956).

Films: Paul Rotha and Richard Griffith, *The Film Till Now* (London: Spring Books, 1967), world cinema survey; Richard Griffith and Arthur Mayer, *The Movies* (New York: Simon and Schuster, 1970), American film history.

Photography: Beaumont Newhall, *The History of Photography from 1839 to the Present Day* (New York: Museum of Modern Art. 1964): Helmut and Alison Gernsheim, *The History of Photography* (London: Oxford, 1970) and *A Concise History of Photography* (1965).

Press associations and syndicates: Victor Rosewater, *History of Cooperative News-Gathering in the United States* (New York: Appleton, 1930); Elmo Scott Watson, *A History of Newspaper Syndicates in the United States, 1865–1935* (Chicago: Publishers' Auxiliary, 1936).

Advertising: Frank Presbrey, *The History and Development of Advertising* (New York: Doubleday, Doran, 1930), the standard account; James Playsted Wood, *The Story of Advertising* (New York: Ronald, 1958), more readable and up-to-date.

Graphics: Isaiah Thomas, *The History of Printing in America* (Albany, N.Y.: Joel Munsell, 1810 and 1874) is the earliest journalism history account; Daniel B. Updyke's two-volume *Printing Types: Their History, Forms and Use* (Cambridge, Mass.: Harvard University Press, 1937) is the standard work; S. H. Steinberg, *Five Hundred Years of Printing* (New York: Criterion, 1959) is a briefer survey.

Additional references, by chapter topic, follow:

*Chapter 3*
THEORIES AND REALITIES OF PRESS FREEDOM

Companion books trace the story of U.S. press freedom: Leonard W. Levy, *Freedom of the Press from Zenger to Jefferson,* and Harold L. Nelson, *Freedom of the Press from Hamilton to the Warren Court* (Indianapolis: Bobbs-Merrill, 1966). They are unexcelled surveys.

Lucy M. Salmon's *The Newspaper and Authority* (New York: Oxford,

1923) is an extensive historical survey of restrictions placed on news-papers. Important periods of the history of press freedom struggles are covered in Fred S. Siebert, *Freedom of the Press in England, 1472–1776* (Urbana: University of Illinois Press, 1952); Leonard W. Levy, *Legacy of Suppression: Freedom of Speech and Press in Early American History* (Cambridge, Mass.: Harvard University Press, 1960); Clyde A. Duni-way, *The Development of Freedom of the Press in Massachusetts* (New York: Longmans, Green, 1906); John C. Miller, *Crisis in Freedom: The Alien and Sedition Acts* (Boston: Little, Brown, 1951) and Frank Luther Mott, *Jefferson and the Press* (Baton Rouge: Louisiana State University Press, 1943); and Zechariah Chafee Jr., *Free Speech in the United States* (Cambridge, Mass.: Harvard University Press, 1941), a study emphasizing the effects of modern wartime conditions. James E. Pollard, *The Presidents and the Press* (New York: Macmillan, 1947), covers presidential press relations from Washington to Truman, and has been supplemented by his *The Presidents and the Press: Truman to Johnson* (Washington: Public Affairs Press, 1964).

Excellent discussions by newspaper editors of current problems in protecting freedom of information and access to news are found in James Russell Wiggins, *Freedom or Secrecy* (New York: Oxford, 1964), and Herbert Brucker, *Freedom of Information* (New York: Macmillan, 1949). More detailed studies are Harold L. Cross, *The People's Right to Know* (New York: Columbia University Press, 1953), and Zechariah Chafee Jr.'s two-volume *Government and Mass Communications* (Chicago: University of Chicago Press, 1947).

Supreme Court trends are traced in William A. Hachten's *The Supreme Court on Freedom of the Press* (Ames: Iowa State University Press, 1968) and also in Kenneth S. Devol's *Mass Media and the Supreme Court* (New York: Hastings House, 1971). J. Edward Gerald's *The Press and the Constitution* (Minneapolis: University of Minnesota Press, 1948) analyzes constitutional law cases involving press freedom from 1931 to 1947. David L. Grey reports on court coverage in *The Supreme Court and the News Media* (Evanston, Ill.: Northwestern University Press, 1968). Donald M. Gillmor analyzes a major conflict in *Free Press and Fair Trial* (Washington: Public Affairs Press, 1966). E. R. Hutchi-son's *Tropic of Cancer on Trial* (New York: Grove Press, 1968) is a case study of censorship.

The two major general works on press law are Harold L. Nelson and Dwight L. Teeter Jr., *Law of Mass Communications: Freedom and Control of Print and Broadcast Media* (Mineola, N.Y.: Foundation Press, 1969), a continuation of the classic *Legal Control of the Press* by Frank Thayer, with substantial historical base; and Donald M. Gillmor and Jerome A. Barron, *Mass Communication Law: Cases and Comment* (St. Paul: West Publishing, 1969), designed for both journalism and law schools and case-oriented, with sizable attention to broadcasting.

Philosophical problems of press freedom are analyzed by the Commission on Freedom of the Press in *A Free and Responsible Press,* by William E. Hocking in *Freedom of the Press: A Framework of Principle* (Chicago: University of Chicago Press, 1947), and by Fred S. Siebert, Theodore Peterson, and Wilbur Schramm in *Four Theories of the Press* (Urbana: University of Illinois Press, 1956). Among discussions of press freedom by newsmen are Walter Lippmann, *Liberty and the News* (New York: Harcourt, Brace, 1920); Elmer Davis, *But We Were Born Free* (New York: Bobbs-Merrill, 1954); and Alan Barth, *The Loyalty of Free Men* (New York: Viking, 1951).

The film area is covered by Ira H. Carmen, *Movies, Censorship and the Law* (Ann Arbor: University of Michigan Press, 1966), and by Richard S. Randall, *Censorship of the Movies* (Madison: University of Wisconsin Press, 1968); books by Richard McKeon, Robert K. Merton, and Walter Gellhorn, *The Freedom to Read: Perspective and Program* (New York: Bowker, 1957); and radio and television by Sydney W. Head, *Broadcasting in America,* and Walter B. Emery, *Broadcasting and Government* (East Lansing: Michigan State University Press, 1971). Movie and television censorship is decried in Murray Schumach's *The Face on the Cutting Room Floor* (New York: Morrow, 1964).

*Chapter 4*
GROWTH OF THE PRINT MEDIA

The best book-length discussion of the news function is Frank Luther Mott's *The News in America* (Cambridge, Mass.: Harvard University Press, 1952), a survey of the concepts, forms, and problems of news, with historical backgrounds. No one interested in newspapers should miss reading it.

The best books on the opinion function and editorial page writing are A. Gayle Waldrop's *Editor and Editorial Writer* (Dubuque, Iowa: Wm. C. Brown, 1967) and Hillier Krieghbaum's *Facts in Perspective* (New York: Prentice-Hall, 1956). Jim A. Hart traces the history of the editorial, 1500–1800, in *Views on the News* (Carbondale: Southern Illinois University Press, 1971), and Allan Nevins continues in the introductions for sections in his collection of editorials, *American Press Opinion: Washington to Coolidge* (New York: Heath, 1928).

Arthur M. Schlesinger, *Prelude to Independence: The Newspaper War on Britain, 1764–1776* (New York: Knopf, 1958), analyzes one period of major press influence. Nevins, *American Press Opinion,* has an excellent section on the partisan journalism of the 1790's. C. C. Regier, *The Era of the Muckrakers* (Chapel Hill: University of North Carolina Press, 1932), examines magazines during the Progressive era; Louis Filler, *Crusaders for American Liberalism* (New York: Harcourt, Brace, 1939), also covers newspapermen. So does Jonathan Daniels in *They Will Be Heard: America's Crusading Newspaper Editors* (New York: McGraw-Hill, 1965), a 200-year survey. Writings of the muckrakers are edited by Arthur and Lila Weinberg in *The Muckrakers* (New York: Simon and Schuster, 1961).

The best anthology of news stories is *A Treasury of Great Reporting,* edited by Louis L. Snyder and Richard B. Morris (New York: Simon and Schuster, 1962), covering stories written under pressure since the sixteenth century. Current collections are Bryce W. Rucker's *Twentieth Century Reporting at Its Best* (Ames: Iowa State University Press, 1964) and John Hohenberg's *The Pulitzer Prize Story* (New York: Columbia University Press, 1959).

Biographical essays about leading journalistic figures from Benjamin Franklin to Robert R. McCormick are found in Ford and Emery, *Highlights in the History of the American Press.* Twentieth century figures are subjects of articles in Drewry, *Post Biographies* and *More Post Biographies.* Charles Fisher, *The Columnists* (New York: Howell, Soskin, 1944), has sketches of 20 columnists of the period; *Molders of Opinion,* edited by David Bulman (Milwaukee: Bruce, 1945) offers biographies of 14 newspaper and radio commentators. William L. Rivers up-dates in his 1965 *The Opinionmakers.* The histories of journalism and the *Dictionary of American Biography* are other sources.

Top-flight biographies of key figures in the development of the news function include: Carl Van Doren, *Benjamin Franklin* (New York: Viking, 1938); Oliver Carlson, *The Man Who Made News: James Gordon Bennett* (New York: Duell, Sloan and Pearce, 1942); Francis Brown, *Raymond of the Times* (New York: Norton, 1951); Fayette Copeland, *Kendall of the Picayune* (Norman: University of Oklahoma Press, 1943); Candace Stone, *Dana and the Sun* (New York: Dodd, Mead, 1938); Raymond B. Nixon, *Henry W. Grady: Spokesman of the New South* (New York: Knopf, 1943); Don C. Seitz, *Joseph Pulitzer* (New York: Simon and Schuster, 1924); W. A. Swanberg, *Pulitzer* (New York: Scribner's, 1967); Julian Rammelkamp, *Pulitzer's Post-Dispatch 1878–1883* (Princeton, N.J.: Princeton University Press, 1966); George Juergens, *Joseph Pulitzer and the New York World 1883–1887* (Princeton, N.J.: Princeton University Press, 1966); Oliver

Knight, *I Protest: Selected Disquisitions of E. W. Scripps* (Madison: University of Wisconsin Press, 1966), both a biography and collection of Scripps' writings; W. A. Swanberg, *Citizen Hearst* (New York: Scribner's, 1961); John Tebbel, *The Life and Good Times of William Randolph Hearst* (New York: Dutton, 1952); Gerald W. Johnson, *An Honorable Titan: A Biographical Study of Adolph S. Ochs* (New York: Harper, 1946); James W. Markham, *Bovard of the Post-Dispatch* (Baton Rouge: Louisiana State University Press, 1954); and Homer W. King, *Pulitzer's Prize Editor: A Biography of John A. Cockerill* (Durham, N.C.: Duke University Press, 1965).

Leading biographies of opinion makers include John C. Miller, *Sam Adams: Pioneer in Propaganda* (Boston: Little, Brown, 1936); Mary A. Best, *Thomas Paine* (New York: Harcourt, Brace, 1927); Glyndon G. Van Deusen, *Horace Greeley: Nineteenth Century Crusader* (Philadelphia: University of Pennsylvania Press, 1953); George S. Merriam, *The Life and Times of Samuel Bowles* (New York: Century, 1885); Joseph F. Wall, *Henry Watterson* (New York: Oxford, 1956); and Joseph L. Morrison, *Josephus Daniels Says* (Chapel Hill: University of North Carolina Press, 1963). William Cullen Bryant and Edwin Lawrence Godkin are most easily read about in Allan Nevins, *The Evening Post: A Century of Journalism* (New York: Boni and Liveright, 1922). The McCormick and Patterson families and their Chicago *Tribune* and New York *Daily News* are analyzed by John Tebbel in *An American Dynasty* (New York: Doubleday, 1947).

The best autobiographies are Benjamin Franklin, *Autobiography* (New York: Putnam, 1909); *The Autobiography of William Allen White* (New York: Macmillan, 1946); *The Autobiography of Lincoln Steffens* (New York: Harcourt, Brace, 1931); Horace Greeley, *Recollections of a Busy Life* (New York: Ford, 1868); Fremont Older, *My Own Story* (New York: Macmillan, 1926), the memoirs of a crusading San Francisco editor; Josephus Daniels, *Tar Heel Editor* (Chapel Hill: University of North Carolina Press, 1939), volume one of a five-volume series; and E. W. Howe, *Plain People* (New York: Dodd, Mead, 1929), the story of a Kansas editor and his readers, also told in Calder M. Pickett, *Ed Howe: Country Town Philosopher* (Lawrence: University Press of Kansas, 1969).

Excellent reminiscences of newsmen include Melville E. Stone, *Fifty Years a Journalist* (New York: Doubleday, Page, 1921); Will Irwin, *The Making of a Reporter* (New York: Putnam, 1942); Webb Miller, *I Found No Peace* (New York: Simon and Schuster, 1936); and Vincent Sheean, *Personal History* (Boston: Houghton Mifflin, 1969 reissue). The best of a great writer's news work is found in William White's *By*

*Line: Ernest Hemingway* (New York: Scribner's, 1967); the biography in Carlos Baker's *Ernest Hemingway* (New York: Scribner's, 1969). Lee G. Miller, *The Story of Ernie Pyle* (New York: Viking, 1950), is very readable. Ishbel Ross, *Ladies of the Press* (New York: Harper, 1936), tells the story of dozens of women journalists.

Among important histories of individual newspapers are Frank M. O'Brien's *The Story of the Sun* (New York: Appleton, 1928), covering the New York *Sun* from 1833 to 1928; Gerald W. Johnson and others, *The Sun-papers of Baltimore, 1837–1937* (New York: Knopf, 1937); Meyer Berger, *The Story of the New York Times* (New York: Simon and Schuster, 1951); Gay Talese, *The Kingdom and the Power* (New York: World, 1969), analyzing recent New York *Times* history and personalities; Erwin D. Canham, *Commitment to Freedom: The Story of the Christian Science Monitor* (Boston: Houghton Mifflin, 1958); Will C. Conrad, Kathleen F. Wilson, and Dale Wilson, *The Milwaukee Journal: The First Eighty Years* (Madison: University of Wisconsin Press, 1964); and Jim A. Hart, *A History of the St. Louis Globe-Democrat* (Columbia: University of Missouri Press, 1961).

Two basic historical studies of the black press are Frederick G. Detweiler, *The Negro Press in the United States* (Chicago: University of Chicago Press, 1922) and Vishnu V. Oak, *The Negro Press* (Yellow Springs, Ohio: Antioch Press, 1948). A comprehensive survey is *The Black Press, U.S.A.* by Roland E. Wolseley (Ames: Iowa State University Press, 1971). Three books on the protest press are Michael L. Johnson, *The New Journalism* (Lawrence: University Press of Kansas, 1971), Everette E. Dennis, *The Magic Writing Machine* (Eugene: University of Oregon, 1971), and Robert J. Glessing, *The Underground Press in America* (Bloomington: Indiana University Press, 1971).

Magazine editors and publishers are the subjects of books by Oswald Garrison Villard, *Fighting Years* (New York: Harcourt, Brace, 1939), the memoirs of the editor of the *Nation;* Peter Lyon, *Success Story: The Life and Times of S. S. McClure* (New York: Scribner's, 1963); S. S. McClure, *My Autobiography* (New York: Stokes, 1914); John Tebbel, *George Horace Lorimer and the Saturday Evening Post* (New York: Doubleday, 1949); Edward W. Bok, *The Americanization of Edward Bok* (New York: Scribner's, 1921), autobiography of the *Ladies' Home Journal* editor; George Britt, *Forty Years—Forty Millions: The Career of Frank A. Munsey* (New York: Farrar and Rinehart, 1935); James Thurber, *The Years with Ross* (Boston: Little, Brown, 1957), the story of editor Harold Ross and the *New Yorker;* Norman Cousins, *Present Tense* (New York: McGraw-Hill, 1967), by the former *Saturday Review* editor; John Kobler, *Luce: His Time, Life and Fortune* (Garden City, N.Y.: Doubleday, 1968); and Robert T. Elson, *Time Inc.* (New York: Atheneum, 1968), first of two volumes, covering 1923–41 formative years.

News magazines are discussed in James Playsted Wood, *Magazines in the United States;* Theodore Peterson, *Magazines in the Twentieth Century;* and Stewart and Tebbel, *Makers of Modern Journalism.* Victor Rosewater's *History of Co-operative News-Gathering in the United States* is supplemented by two histories sponsored by the press associations: Oliver Gramling, *AP: The Story of News* (New York: Farrar and Rinehart, 1940), and Joe Alex Morris, *Deadline Every Minute: The Story of the United Press* (New York: Doubleday, 1957).

*Chapter 5*
GROWTH OF RADIO, TELEVISION, AND FILM

The best historical accounts are found in Erik Barnouw's *A Tower in Babel* and *The Golden Web,* Sydney W. Head's *Broadcasting in America,* and Llewellyn White's *The American Radio.* Chapter 1 of Mitchell V. Charnley's *News by Radio* (New York: Macmillan, 1948) traces the history of radio news. Francis Chase Jr., *Sound and Fury* (New York: Harper, 1942), is an informal history of radio.

Biographies include Alexander Kendrick, *Prime Time: The Life of Edward R. Murrow* (Boston: Little, Brown, 1969); Eugene Lyons, *David Sarnoff* (New York: Harper & Row, 1966); John Tebbel, *Putting Electrons to Work: David Sarnoff* (New York: Encyclopaedia Britannica Press, 1963); Roger Burlingame, *Don't Let Them Scare You: The Life and Times of Elmer Davis* (Philadelphia: Lippincott, 1961); and chapters on H. V. Kaltenborn, Gabriel Heatter, Fulton Lewis Jr., and Raymond Gram Swing in David Bulman's *Molders of Opinion* (Milwaukee: Bruce, 1945). Autobiographies are *Father of Radio: The Autobiography of Lee De Forest* (Chicago: Wilcox & Follett, 1950); and H. V. Kaltenborn, *Fifty Fabulous Years, 1900–1950: A Personal Review* (New York: Putnam's, 1950). Two collections of writings are *In Search of Light: The Broadcasts of Edward R. Murrow 1938–1961* (New York: Knopf, 1967) and *Looking Ahead: The Papers of David Sarnoff* (New York: McGraw-Hill, 1968).

Relationships with government are analyzed in Walter B. Emery, *Broadcasting and Government* (East Lansing: Michigan State University Press, 1971), the best source; John E. Coons, editor, *Freedom and Responsibility in Broadcasting* (Evanston, Ill.: Northwestern University

Press, 1962); Harvey J. Levin, *Broadcast Regulation and Joint Ownership of Media* (New York: New York University Press, 1960); and by Head and White. For sources, see Frank J. Kahn, *Documents of American Broadcasting* (New York: Appleton-Century-Crofts, 1972).

Educational uses of television are examined in Wilbur Schramm, editor, *The Impact of Educational Television* (Urbana: University of Illinois Press, 1960); Wilbur Schramm, Jack Lyle, and Ithiel de Sola Pool, *The People Look at Educational Television* (Stanford, Calif.: Stanford University Press, 1963); Charles A. Siepmann, *TV and Our School Crisis* (New York: Dodd, Mead, 1958), a report on uses of television as a teaching instrument; Paul Saettler, *A History of Instructional Technology* (New York: McGraw-Hill, 1968), covering broadcasting and film; Allen Koenig and Ruane B. Hill, *The Farther Vision: Educational Television Today* (Madison: University of Wisconsin, 1967), and the 1967 Carnegie Commission report, *Public Television.*

Motion pictures: *Film: An Anthology,* edited by Daniel Talbot (New York: Simon and Schuster, 1959), contains readings on aesthetics, social commentary, and analysis; theory and technique of film making; and history and personal reminiscences. Rotha and Griffith, *The Film Till Now,* and Griffith and Mayer, *The Movies,* are the leading historical surveys.

The history of documentary films is told by Paul Rotha, Sinclair Road, and Richard Griffith in *Documentary Film* (London: Faber and Faber, 1966) and by A. William Bluem in *Documentary in American Television* (New York: Hastings House, 1965). Newsreels are covered in Raymond Fielding's *The American Newsreel, 1911–1967* (Norman: University of Oklahoma Press, 1972).

## Current Problems and Criticisms

An excellent basis for any discussion of the duties and the performance record of the mass media is the summary report of the Commission on Freedom of the Press, *A Free and Responsible Press* (see bibliographical note for Part I). The commission sponsored publication of four studies already cited, Chafee's *Government and Mass Communications,* Hocking's *Freedom of the Press,* White's *The American Radio,* and Ruth Inglis' *Freedom of the Movies,* as well as *Peoples Speaking to Peoples,* by Llewellyn White and Robert D. Leigh (Chicago: University of Chicago Press, 1946), an analysis of international news channels.

Rivers and Schramm's *Responsibility in Mass Communication* is the best general study of media ethics. J. Edward Gerald's *The Social*

*Responsibility of the Press* (Minneapolis: University of Minnesota Press, 1963) examines the press as a commercial as well as a professional agency and argues for a higher degree of professionalization. John Hohenberg is "a journalist looking at his profession" in *The News Media* (New York: Holt, Rinehart and Winston, 1968). Bryce W. Rucker presents a comprehensive survey of media dilemmas in his renewal of Morris Ernst's 1946 study by the same title, *The First Freedom* (Carbondale, Ill.: Southern Illinois University Press, 1968).

The problems of violence and sensationalism are covered in Otto N. Larsen, editor, *Violence and the Mass Media* (New York: Harper & Row, 1968); Helen M. Hughes, *News and the Human Interest Story* (Chicago: University of Chicago Press, 1940), a sociological study; and Simon M. Bessie, *Jazz Journalism: The Story of the Tabloid Newspapers* (New York: Dutton, 1938). For details on studies of violence, see *Report of the National Advisory Commission on Civil Disorders* (Kerner Report), 1968, chapter 15, "The News Media and the Disorders," and *Rights in Conflict,* the Walker Report to the National Commission on the Causes and Prevention of Violence, 1968, pages 287–327, "The Police and the Press."

Two books edited by Warren K. Agee provide extensive criticisms of the media: *The Press and the Public Interest* (Washington: Public Affairs Press, 1968) contains the annual William Allen White Lectures delivered by 18 of America's leading reporters, editors, and publishers; in *Mass Media in a Free Society* (Lawrence: University Press of Kansas, 1969) six media spokesmen discuss challenges and problems confronting newspapers, television, motion pictures, and magazines. Other criticisms of press performance are found in *The Press in Perspective,* edited by Ralph D. Casey (Baton Rouge: Louisiana State University Press, 1963), a series of 17 lectures by leading journalists at University of Minnesota over 16 years; *Social Responsibility of the Newspress* (Milwaukee: Marquette University Press, 1962), a group of talks by leading newsmen and educators; Hillier Krieghbaum's *Pressures on the Press* (New York: Crowell, 1972); John L. Hulteng and Roy Paul Nelson, *The Fourth Estate* (New York: Harper & Row, 1971); A. Kent MacDougall's collection of *Wall Street Journal* articles, *The Press: A Critical Look from the Inside* (New York: Dow Jones, 1972); and a book of 55 articles edited by Michael C. Emery and Ted Curtis Smythe, *Readings in Mass Communication: Concepts and Issues in the Mass Media* (Dubuque, Iowa: Wm. C. Brown, 1972), examining current debates and changes in all fields.

Additional references by chapter topic, follow:

**Chapter 6**
CRITICISMS AND CHALLENGES: TELEVISION, RADIO, AND FILM

Two recently edited comprehensive collections of readings are David Manning White and Richard Averson, *Sight, Sound, and Society: Motion Pictures and Television in America* (Boston: Beacon Press, 1968) and Harry J. Skornia and Jack W. Kitson, *Problems and Controversies in Television and Radio* (Palo Alto, Calif.: Pacific Books, 1968). William Wood's readings in *Electronic Journalism* (New York: Columbia University Press, 1967) offer a defense of television news. Rosenberg and White, in *Mass Culture* and *Mass Culture Revisited,* cover broadcasting and film. Barry Cole edited 77 articles from *TV Guide* on all aspects of TV in *Television* (New York: The Free Press, 1970).

Critical appraisals by the Alfred I. duPont-Columbia University Awards committee were begun with *Survey of Broadcast Journalism 1968–1969,* edited by Marvin Barrett (New York: Grosset & Dunlap, 1969). Harry J. Skornia contributed *Television and the News: A Critical Appraisal* (Palo Alto, Calif.: Pacific Books, 1968) and *Television and Society* (New York: McGraw-Hill, 1965), with an "agenda for improvement." Robert E. and Harrison B. Summers wrote *Broadcasting and the Public* (Belmont, Calif.: Wadsworth, 1966), revised in 1972.

A first-hand criticism of network policy affecting CBS News appears in Fred W. Friendly, *Due to Circumstances Beyond Our Control . . .* (New York: Random House, 1967). The 1969 speeches of Vice-President Spiro T. Agnew attacking the fairness of television commentators and other media news are collected in Spiro T. Agnew, *Frankly Speaking* (Washington: Public Affairs Press, 1970). Television news crises are covered in William Small, *To Kill a Messenger* (New York: Hastings House, 1970), summing up the 1960's. Gary Steiner, *The People Look at Television: A Study of Audience Attitudes* (New York: Knopf, 1963), is based on extensive research. Leo Bogart, *The Age of Television* (New York: Frederick Ungar, 1958), objectively analyzes scores of research studies seeking to determine the impact of television on American society. Robert Lewis Shayon, *Open to Criticism* (Boston: Beacon Press, 1971), Charles A. Siepmann, *Radio, Television and Society* (New York: Oxford, 1950), and Sydney Head, *Broadcasting in America,* also offer criticism of the two media.

**Chapter 7**
CRITICISMS AND CHALLENGES: THE PRINT MEDIA

Selections from the files of the *Nieman Reports* make a comprehensive survey of news problems and trends in Louis Lyons, *Reporting the News*

(Cambridge, Mass.: Harvard University Press, 1965). Hillier Krieghbaum treats one problem in *Science and the Mass Media* (New York: New York University Press, 1967). Curtis D. MacDougall, *The Press and Its Problems* (Dubuque, Iowa: Wm. C. Brown, 1964) is an up-dated version of his *Newsroom Problems and Policies*. Lucy M. Salmon's *The Newspaper and the Historian* (New York: Oxford, 1923) is a classical historical study which analyzes the position of editors, critics, and advertisers, and the authenticity and authoritativeness of the press.

Two interesting studies of press performance during political campaigns are Nathan B. Blumberg's *One Party Press?* (Lincoln: University of Nebraska Press, 1954), a report on how 35 metropolitan dailies covered 1952 presidential campaign news, and Arthur E. Rowse's *Slanted News: A Case Study of the Nixon and Stevenson Fund Stories* (Boston: Beacon Press, 1957), an analysis of how 31 metropolitan dailies reported an episode in the 1956 campaign. News coverage of the 1960 election is analyzed by Wayne A. Danielson and John B. Adams in "Completeness of Press Coverage of the 1960 Campaign," Autumn 1961 *Journalism Quarterly,* and by Guido H. Stempel III in "The Prestige Press Covers the 1960 Presidential Campaign," Spring 1961 *Journalism Quarterly.* The shift in editorial page support in the 1964 election is reported in Edwin Emery, "Press Support for Johnson and Goldwater," Autumn 1964 *Journalism Quarterly,* together with a historical summary. Stempel re-examines "The Prestige Press" in the 1964 and 1968 campaigns in the Winter 1965 and Winter 1969 issues of *Journalism Quarterly.*

Among professionals' criticisms, Herbert Brucker's *Freedom of Information* is an enlightened defense and analysis of the newspaper press. By contrast Carl E. Lindstrom uses for the title of his book *The Fading American Newspaper* (New York: Doubleday, 1960). Stanley Walker explains the problems facing editors in *City Editor* (New York: Stokes, 1934); he held that post on the New York *Herald Tribune.* A. J. Liebling brought together his satirical articles on press shortcomings, written for the *New Yorker,* in *The Press* (New York: Ballantine, 1964) and in *The Wayward Pressman* (New York: Doubleday, 1948), devoted heavily to New York papers. Silas Bent, *Ballyhoo* (New York: Liveright, 1927) is strongly critical of the newspaper press of its day, as are Upton Sinclair's *The Brass Check* (Pasadena, Calif.: Published by the author, 1920) and George Seldes' *Freedom of the Press* (Indianapolis, Ind.: Bobbs-Merrill, 1935). Oswald Garrison Villard, *The Disappearing Daily* (New York: Knopf, 1944), and Morris L. Ernst, *The First Freedom* (New York: Macmillan, 1946), exhibit a critical concern over newspaper ownership concentration trends but are not statistically accurate.

Helen M. Hughes, *News and the Human Interest Story,* is the best analysis of the entertainment role of news. Two recent histories of the comics, George Perry and Alan Aldridge, *The Penguin Book of Comics* (London: Penguin, 1967), and Pierre Couperie and Maurice C. Horn, *A History of the Comic Strip* (New York: Crown, 1968), update Coulton Waugh's excellent *The Comics* (New York: Macmillan, 1947). Stephen Becker, *Comic Art in America* (New York: Simon and Schuster, 1959), surveys comic strips, political cartoons, magazine humor, and animated cartoons. David M. White and Robert H. Abel, *The Funnies: An American Idiom* (New York: Free Press of Glencoe, 1963), reports on a major research project.

*Chapter 8*
CRITICISMS AND CHALLENGES: INTER-MEDIA

Marshall McLuhan's major books have been *The Gutenberg Galaxy* (1962) and *Understanding Media* (1964) although his *The Medium Is the Massage* (1967) created the most public attention. Ben H. Bagdikian's *The Information Machines* (New York: Harper & Row, 1971), projects the impact of technological change and offers a wealth of research data based on findings of RAND corporation research teams. All are available in paperback.

Ownership of media: Bryce Rucker, *The First Freedom* (Carbondale: Southern Illinois University Press, 1968), has a wealth of statistics and analysis. John Tebbel, *Open Letter to Newspaper Readers* (New York: Heineman, 1968) is a brief paperback explanation of newspapers' economic plight and a defense of their worthiness. Historical trends in concentration of newspaper ownership are reported in chapters 22 and 27 of Emery, *The Press and America,* and by Raymond B. Nixon in *Gazette* (*1968, No. 3*) and in the Winter 1961 *Journalism Quarterly.*

Audience: *The Continuing Study of Newspaper Reading,* sponsored by the American Newspaper Publishers Association and the Advertising Research Foundation from 1939 to 1952 and covering readership studies of 142 newspapers, offers evidence of readership trends. The results were analyzed by Charles E. Swanson in "What They Read in 130 Daily Newspapers," Fall 1955 *Journalism Quarterly.* Gary A. Steiner, *The People Look at Television* (New York: Knopf, 1963) is a voluminous study of viewing habits and attitudes of the American people by sex, education, income, religion, etc.

Advertising: Jules Backman, *Advertising and Competition,* and Charles H. Sandage and Vernon Fryburger, *The Role of Advertising,* show its importance to the economy. Raymond A. Bauer and Stephen

A. Greyser's 1969 study for the American Association of Advertising Agencies, *Advertising in America: The Consumer View,* found essential public support. Otis Pease, *The Responsibilities of American Advertising* (New Haven, Conn.: Yale University Press, 1958) emphasizes national advertising. Neil H. Borden, *The Economic Effects of Advertising* (Chicago: Irwin, 1942) is a lengthy study of the role advertising plays in the national economy; a portion is reprinted in Wilbur Schramm, *Mass Communications.* E. S. Turner, *The Shocking History of Advertising* (New York: Dutton, 1953), is constructively critical; so is Martin Mayer, *Madison Avenue, U.S.A.* (New York: Harper, 1958), primarily a study of advertising agencies. Vance Packard assigned almost unlimited powers to advertising men in *The Hidden Persuaders* (New York: McKay, 1957). Both the Mayer and Packard books are available in pocket book editions.

The only book-length critical study of a newspaper trade association or organization is Edwin Emery's *History of the American Newspaper Publishers Association* (Minneapolis: University of Minnesota Press, 1950). Discussions involving press criticism are to be found in the American Society of Newspaper Editors' *Bulletin* and *Problems of Journalism* series, in the Associated Press Managing Editors Association's *APME Red Book* series, and in the periodicals *Journalism Quarterly, Columbia Journalism Review, Nieman Reports, Masthead, Guild Reporter, Quill, Editor & Publisher, Broadcasting, Journal of Broadcasting, RTNDA Bulletin,* and *Advertising Age.*

## Part IV
### *The Mass Communications Industries and Professions*

The listings in this section are confined to books dealing with the operations of the mass communications industries and professions, and books describing professional techniques and qualifications. For histories of the various media see the bibliography for Part II; for books dealing with the role of the mass media in society and with media performance see the bibliographies for Part I and Part III. Research journals, professional journals, trade publications, and directories for the various fields of mass communications are listed at the opening of the bibliography.

*Chapter 9*
NEWSPAPERS

Textbooks on reporting and newswriting: Curtis D. MacDougall, *Interpretative Reporting* (New York: Macmillan, 1972), and Carl N.

Warren, *Modern News Reporting* (New York: Harper & Row, 1959), have been widely used since they first appeared in the early 1930's. Other current leading texts are Mitchell V. Charnley, *Reporting* (New York: Holt, Rinehart and Winston, 1966); John Hohenberg, *The Professional Journalist* (New York: Holt, Rinehart and Winston, 1969); Julian Harriss and Stanley Johnson, *The Complete Reporter* (New York: Macmillan, 1965); and Laurence R. Campbell and Roland E. Wolseley, *How to Report and Write the News* (Englewood Cliffs, N.J.: Prentice-Hall, 1961). In addition: Phillip H. Ault and Edwin Emery, *Reporting the News* (New York: Dodd, Mead, 1959), with emphasis on reporting techniques; Charles H. Brown, *Informing the People* (New York: Holt, 1957); Chilton R. Bush, *The Art of News Communication* (New York: Appleton-Century-Crofts, 1964), restricted to the area of newswriting; Charles C. Clayton, *Newspaper Reporting Today* (New York: Odyssey, 1947); Grant M. Hyde, *Newspaper Reporting* (Ne⁻ ⸱ York: Prentice-Hall, 1952); and John Paul Jones, *The Modern Reporter's Handbook* (New York: Rinehart, 1949). A valuable adjunct to the reporting texts is E. L. Callihan, *Grammar for Journalists* (New York: Ronald, 1969).

Two books combine coverage of reporting, writing, and editing for print and broadcast media with mass media introductory material: Verne E. Edwards Jr., *Journalism in a Free Society* (Dubuque, Iowa: Wm. C. Brown, 1970), and William L. Rivers, *The Mass Media: Reporting, Writing, Editing* (New York: Harper & Row, 1964). Both are newspaper-oriented.

Special fields of reporting and writing: Neal Copple, *Depth Reporting* (Englewood Cliffs, N.J.: Prentice-Hall, 1964); Robert D. Murphy, *Reporting Public Problems* (Philadelphia: Chilton, 1960); Chilton R. Bush, *Newswriting and Reporting of Public Affairs* (Philadelphia: Chilton, 1971); Victor J. Danilov, *Public Affairs Reporting* (New York: Macmillan, 1955); Curtis D. MacDougall, *Covering the Courts* (New York: Prentice-Hall, 1946); Louis I. Gelfand and Harry E. Heath Jr., *Modern Sports Writing* (Ames: Iowa State University Press, 1968); Rodney Fox, *Agricultural and Technical Journalism* (New York: Prentice-Hall, 1952); Roland E. Wolseley, *Critical Writing for the Journalist* (Philadelphia: Chilton, 1959).

News editing and copyreading: Bruce Westley, *News Editing* (Boston: Houghton Mifflin, 1972); Alfred A. Crowell, *Creative News Editing* (Dubuque, Iowa: Wm. C. Brown, 1969); Gene Gilmore and Robert Root, *Modern Newspaper Editing* (Berkeley, Calif.: Glendessary Press,

1970); Floyd K. Baskette and Jack Z. Sissors, *The Art of Editing,* successor volume to Bastian and Case (New York: Macmillan, 1971); Charles H. Brown, *News Editing and Display* (New York: Harper, 1952); Robert E. Garst and Theodore M. Bernstein, *Headlines and Deadlines* (New York: Columbia University Press, 1961).

Community journalism: John Cameron Sim, *The Grass Roots Press: America's Community Newspapers* (Ames: Iowa State University Press, 1969); Morris Janowitz, *The Community Press in an Urban Setting* (New York: Free Press of Glencoe, 1967); Kenneth R. Byerly, *Community Journalism* (Philadelphia: Chilton, 1961); and three books by Thomas F. Barnhart: *Weekly Newspaper Writing and Editing* (New York: Dryden, 1949), *Weekly Newspaper Makeup and Typography* (Minneapolis: University of Minnesota Press, 1949), and *Weekly Newspaper Management* (New York: Appleton-Century-Crofts, 1952).

Graphics and production: Edmund C. Arnold, *Modern Newspaper Design* (New York: Harper & Row, 1969), and *Ink on Paper* (Harper & Row, 1963); Arthur T. Turnbull and Russell N. Baird, *The Graphics of Communication: Typography, Layout and Design* (New York: Holt, Rinehart and Winston, 1968); Ruori McLean, *Magazine Design* (London: Oxford University Press, 1969); Allan Woods, *Modern Newspaper Production* (New York: Harper & Row, 1963); Roy Paul Nelson, *Publication Design* (Dubuque, Iowa: Wm. C. Brown, 1972).

Advertising and management: Frank W. Rucker and Herbert Lee Williams, *Newspaper Organization and Management* (Ames: Iowa State University Press, 1969); Leslie W. McClure and Paul C. Fulton, *Advertising in the Printed Media* (New York: Macmillan, 1964); Charles M. Edwards and Russell A. Brown, *Retail Advertising and Sales Promotion* (Englewood Cliffs, N.J.: Prentice-Hall, 1959); Paul S. Hirt, *Designing Retail Ads for Profit* (New York: International Newspaper Promotion Association, 1968); Frank W. Rucker and Bert Stolpe, *Tested Newspaper Promotion* (Ames: Iowa State University Press, 1960); Frank W. Rucker, *Newspaper Circulation* (Ames: Iowa State University Press, 1958); Frank Thayer, *Newspaper Business Management* (Englewood Cliffs, N.J.: Prentice-Hall, 1954).

*Chapter 10*
TELEVISION AND RADIO

Introductory books for the broadcasting field include Giraud Chester, Garnet R. Garrison, and Edgar Willis, *Television and Radio* (New York: Appleton-Century-Crofts, 1971); Robert L. Hilliard, editor, *Understanding Television: An Introduction to Broadcasting* (New York: Hastings House, 1964), and *Radio Broadcasting* (Hastings House,

1967); A. William Bluem and Roger Manvell, *Television: The Creative Experience* (New York: Hastings House, 1967), a collection of 37 articles by leading U.S. and British television professionals which originally appeared in *Television Quarterly* and the *Journal* of the British Society of Film and Television Arts; Waldo Abbot and Richard L. Rider, *Handbook of Broadcasting* (New York: McGraw-Hill, 1957).

Books which deal with television news are Irving E. Fang, *Television News* (New York: Hastings House, 1972); Jim Atkins Jr. and Leo Willette, *Filming TV News and Documentaries* (New York: Amphoto, 1965); Bob Siller, Ted White, and Hal Terkel, *Television and Radio News* (New York: Macmillan, 1960); *Television News Reporting* (New York: McGraw-Hill, 1958), an excellent survey by the CBS News Staff; and Edward Bliss, Jr. and John M. Patterson, *Writing News for Broadcast* (New York: Columbia University Press, 1971).

Books dealing only with radio news include William F. Brooks, *Radio News Writing* (New York: McGraw-Hill, 1948); Mitchell V. Charnley, *News by Radio* (New York: Macmillan, 1948); Baskett Mosse, *Radio News Handbook* (Evanston, Ill.: Medill School of Journalism, Northwestern University, 1947); Carl N. Warren, *Radio News Writing and Editing* (New York: Harper, 1947); and Paul W. White, *News on the Air* (New York: Harcourt, Brace, 1947).

Books treating various types of writing are Edgar E. Willis, *Writing Television and Radio Programs* (New York: Holt, Rinehart and Winston, 1967); Robert L. Hilliard, *Writing for Television and Radio* (New York: Hastings House, 1967); and Norton S. Parker, *Audiovisual Script Writing* (New Brunswick, N.J.: Rutgers University Press, 1968).

Management: Yale Roe, editor, *Television Station Management* (New York: Hastings House, 1964); Howard W. Coleman, editor, *Color Television: The Business of Colorcasting* (New York: Hastings House, 1968); Edd Routt, *The Business of Radio Broadcasting* (Blue Ridge Summit, Pa.: TAB Books, 1972), one of a series issued by that publisher.

Production and graphics: Gerald Millerson, *The Technique of Television Production* (New York: Hastings House, 1969); Herbert Zettl, *Television Production Handbook* (Belmont, Calif.: Wadsworth, 1968); Rudy Bretz, *The Techniques of Television Production* (New York: McGraw-Hill, 1962); and for a key book in radio sound, Robert Oringel's *Audio Control Handbook* (New York: Hastings House, 1968). Arthur L. Gaskill and David A. Englander cover newsfilm production in *How to Shoot a Movie Story* (New York: Morgan and Morgan, 1959). Two books on graphics are Walter Herdeg, *Film and TV Graphics* (New York: Hastings House, 1967), and Roy Laughton, *TV Graphics* (New York: Reinhold, 1966). A reference work for the technologies of film and television: *The Focal Encyclopedia of Film and Television: Techniques* (New York: Hastings House, 1969).

The advertising area is described in Eugene F. Seehafer and Jack W. Laemmar, *Successful Television and Radio Advertising* (New York: McGraw-Hill, 1959); Clark M. Agnew and Neil O'Brien, *Television Advertising* (New York: McGraw-Hill, 1958); Harry W. McMahan, *The Television Commercial* (New York: Hastings House, 1957); and Charles A. Wainright, *The Television Copywriter* (New York: Hastings House, 1966).

## Chapter 11
### PRESS ASSOCIATIONS

There is no one book describing the press associations. Frank Luther Mott paints a picture of the Associated Press operation in a chapter of *The News in America.* Ault and Emery discuss reporting for press associations in a chapter of *Reporting the News;* Emery traces their history in *The Press and America;* and Ault tells youthful readers how big stories are covered in *News Around the Clock* (New York: Dodd, Mead, 1960).

Oliver Gramling, *AP: The Story of News,* and Joe Alex Morris, *Deadline Every Minute: The Story of the United Press,* capture a good deal of the reportorial excitement of the press associations. Hugh Baillie, *High Tension* (New York: Harper, 1959), is the readable autobiography of a former president of UP. *Kent Cooper and the Associated Press* (New York: Random House, 1959) is the second personal account by the most famous general manager of AP; the first, *Barriers Down* (New York: Farrar and Rinehart, 1942), is Cooper's story of his effort to break up international news monopolies. Melville E. Stone, *Fifty Years a Journalist,* is the autobiography of the first AP general manager.

A UNESCO publication, *News Agencies: Their Structure and Operation* (New York: Columbia University Press, 1953), gives summary accounts of AP, UP, and INS and analyzes other world news agencies. John C. Merrill, Carter R. Bryan, and Marvin Alisky, *The Foreign Press* (Baton Rouge: Louisiana State University Press, 1970), includes world news agencies in its over-all picture. UNESCO's *World Communications: Press, Radio, Television, Film* (New York: UNESCO, 1964) is a reference work for international communications. John Hohenberg covers foreign correspondents generally in *Foreign Correspondence—The Great Reporters and Their Times* (New York: Columbia University Press, 1964).

Other books describing the international media the press associations serve include John C. Merrill, *The Elite Press* (New York: Pitman, 1969), a study of a selected worldwide group of papers; Kenneth E. Olson, *The History Makers* (Baton Rouge: Louisiana State University Press, 1966), a survey of European press history; Graham Storey, *Reuters* (New York: Crown, 1951), and Theodore E. Kruglak, *The Two Faces of Tass* (Minneapolis: University of Minnesota Press, 1962), two press association histories; James W. Markham, *Voices of the Red Giants* (Ames: Iowa State University Press, 1967), a study of the Soviet and Chinese mass media systems; Burton Paulu, *Radio and Television Broadcasting on the European Continent* (Minneapolis: University of Minnesota Press, 1967); and Walter B. Emery, *National and International Systems of Broadcasting* (East Lansing: Michigan State University Press, 1969).

A good picture of the variety of the feature syndicates can be obtained by scanning the annual *Syndicate Directory* issued by *Editor & Publisher* as a supplement to a July issue.

## Chapter 12
### PHOTOGRAPHIC COMMUNICATION

History and development: Beaumont Newhall, *The History of Photography from 1839 to the Present Day* (New York: Museum of Modern Art, 1964); Helmut and Alison Gernsheim, *History of Photography* (London: Oxford Press, 1970); Peter Pollack, *Picture History of Photography* (New York: Abrams, 1969); Nathan Lyons, *Photographers on Photography* (Englewood Cliffs, N.J.: Prentice-Hall, 1966); R. Smith Schuneman, *Photographic Communication: Principles, Problems and Challenges of Photojournalism* (New York: Hastings House, 1972); A. William Bluem, *Documentary in American Television* (New York: Hastings House, 1965); Paul Rotha, Sinclair Road, and Richard Griffith, *Documentary Film* (London: Faber and Faber, 1966).

Techniques: Robert B. Rhode and Floyd H. McCall, *Introduction to Photography* (New York: Macmillan, 1971), and *Press Photography* (Macmillan, 1961); Arnold Rothstein, *Photojournalism: Pictures for Magazines and Newspapers* (New York: Amphoto, 1965); Andreas Feininger, *The Complete Photographer* (Englewood Cliffs, N.J.: Prentice-Hall, 1965); Rodney Fox and Robert Kerns, *Creative News Photography* (Ames: Iowa State University Press, 1961); Wilson Hicks, *Words and Pictures* (New York: Harper, 1952); Roy Pinney, *Advertising Photography* (New York: Hastings House, 1962).

Biographical: James Horan, *Mathew Brady: Historian with a Camera* (New York: Crown, 1955), and *Timothy O'Sullivan: America's For-*

*gotten Photographer* (New York: Crown, 1966); Judith Gutman, *Lewis W. Hine and the American Social Conscience* (New York: Walker, 1967); Richard Griffith, *The World of Robert Flaherty* (New York: Duell, Sloan and Pearce, 1953); Margaret Bourke-White, *Portrait of Myself* (New York: Simon and Schuster, 1963); David Douglas Duncan, *Yankee Nomad* (New York: Holt, Rinehart and Winston, 1966); Carl Mydans, *More Than Meets the Eye* (New York: Harper, 1959); Gordon Parks, *A Choice of Weapons* (New York: Harper & Row, 1966); Edward Steichen, *A Life in Photography* (Garden City, N.Y.: Doubleday, 1963).

Picture books: Alfred Eisenstadt, *Witness to Our Times* (New York: Viking, 1966); David Douglas Duncan, *War Without Heroes* (New York: Harper & Row, 1970); John Szarkowski, *The Photographer's Eye* (New York: Museum of Modern Art, 1966); Leonard Freed, *Black in White America* (New York: Grossman, n.d.); Cornell Capa, editor, *The Concerned Photographer* (New York: Grossman, 1969), 200 photos of protest by six leading photographers; Charles Harbutt and Lee Jones, *America in Crisis* (New York: Holt, Rinehart and Winston, 1969).

*Chapter 13*
THE FILM

Gerald Mast's *A Short History of the Movies* (New York: Bobbs-Merrill, 1971) offers detailed, highly readable descriptions and analyses, primarily of U.S. and European films. To the major film histories, Rotha and Griffith's *The Film Till Now* and Griffith and Mayer's *The Movies,* may be added Arthur Knight, *The Liveliest Art* (New York: Macmillan, 1957, also Mentor paperback), particularly good for years 1895–1930.

Kenneth Macgowan, *Behind the Screen* (New York: Delacorte Press, 1965, also Delta paperback), discusses the American industry and the introduction of sound. New are Lewis Jacobs, *The Documentary Tradition: From Nanook to Woodstock* (New York: Hopkinson and Blake, 1971) and Alan Rosenthal, *The New Documentary in Action: A Casebook in Film Making* (Berkeley: University of California Press, 1971). The standard work on the history, principles, and technique of the documentary motion picture is Paul Rotha, Sinclair Road, and Richard Griffith, *The Documentary Film* (London: Faber and Faber, 1966).

Lewis Jacobs, *The Emergence of Film Art* (New York: Hopkinson and Blake, 1969) offers carefully selected essays to illustrate the evolution of the motion picture as an art, from 1900 to the present. Roger Manvell, in *New Cinema in Europe* (New York: Dutton, 1966), gives brief descriptions of movements, film-makers and films in post-war feature film-making in Europe. Gregory Battcock's *The New American Cinema* (New York: Dutton, 1967) is a stimulating collection of essays covering theory and practice of contemporary experimental film-makers.

Louis Giannetti, *Understanding Movies* (New York: Prentice-Hall, 1972) explains basic techniques film directors use to convey meanings. Personalities from the silent film era are interviewed in Kevin Brownlow, *The Parade's Gone By* (New York: Alfred Knopf, 1968). Also of note are Andrew Sarris, *The American Cinema: Directors and Directions 1929–1968* (New York: Dutton, 1968) and Bosley Crowther, *The Great Films: Fifty Golden Years of Motion Pictures* (New York: G. P. Putnam's Sons, 1967).

David C. Stewart, editor, *Film Study in Higher Education* (Washington: American Council on Education, 1966), contains an appraisal of the state of film study in America's colleges and universities.

*Chapter 14*
MAGAZINES

An overview of the magazine field is provided by Roland E. Wolseley's *Understanding Magazines* (Ames: Iowa State University Press, 1969), which treats editorial and business operations of consumer, business, and specialized publications. John Tebbel's *The American Magazine: A Compact History* (New York: Hawthorn, 1969), emphasizes a current industry wide survey. Robert Root, *Modern Magazine Editing* (Dubuque, Iowa: Wm. C. Brown, 1966) gives a general introduction; Russell N. Baird and Arthur T. Turnbull, *Industrial and Business Journalism* (Philadelphia: Chilton, 1961), covers the business press area in detail. James L. C. Ford, *Magazines for Millions* (Carbondale, Ill.: Southern Illinois University Press, 1970), tells the story of specialized publications in such fields as business, religion, labor, homemaking.

Views of specialized magazine work can be obtained from Rowena Ferguson, *Editing the Small Magazine* (New York: Columbia University Press, 1958, paperback 1963); DeWitt C. Reddick and Alfred A. Crowell, *Industrial Editing: Creative Communication through Company Publications* (New York: Bender, 1962); Bernard Smith, *Industrial Editing* (New York: Pitman, 1961); William C. Halley, *Employee Publications* (Philadelphia: Chilton, 1959); Garth Bentley, *Editing the Company Publication* (New York: Harper, 1953); Julien Elfenbein, *Business Journalism* (New York: Harper, 1960); James McCloskey, *Industrial Journalism Today* (New York: Harper, 1959); and Delbert McGuire, *Technical and Industrial Journalism* (Harrisburg, Pa.: Stackpole, 1956).

Textbooks on magazine and feature writing include George L. Bird, *Modern Article Writing* (Dubuque, Iowa: Wm. C. Brown, 1967); Stewart Harral, *The Feature Writer's Handbook* (Norman: University of Oklahoma Press, 1963); Clarence A. Schoenfeld, *Effective Feature Writing* (New York: Harper, 1960); Helen M. Patterson, *Writing and Selling Feature Articles* (New York: Prentice-Hall, 1956); DeWitt C. Reddick, *Modern Feature Writing* (New York: Harper, 1949). Richard Gehman, *How to Write and Sell Magazine Articles* (New York: Harper, 1959), tells the story of a successful free lancer.

*Chapter 15*
BOOK PUBLISHING

Charles G. Madison's *Book Publishing in America* (New York: McGraw-Hill, 1967) is the definitive survey of the book publishing industry by a former editor and publisher. There are many useful insights into the art of publishing and the history of the major companies. A well-rounded picture of the trade or general side of the book publishing industry is given by a score of specialists in *What Happens in Book Publishing,* edited by Chandler B. Grannis (New York: Columbia University Press, 1967).

Sir Stanley Unwin, *The Truth About Publishing* (New York: Bowker, 1960), is basic, brief, and highly readable. Julie Eidesheim, *Editor at Work* (New York: Rinehart, 1939), describes what book editing really is like. William Jovanovich, *Now, Barabbas* (New York: Harper, 1964) presents thoughtful essays on his field by a publishing executive.

Roger Smith, editor, *The American Reading Public: A Symposium* (New York: Bowker, 1964), is a particularly succinct and useful collection of authoritative essays by a number of publishing executives.

*Chapter 16*
ADVERTISING

Among the general text and reference books on advertising are Charles H. Sandage and Vernon Fryburger, *Advertising Theory and Practice* (Homewood, Ill.: Irwin, 1967); S. Watson Dunn, *Advertising: Its Role in Modern Marketing* (New York: Holt, 1969); John S. Wright, Daniel S. Warner, and Willis L. Winter, Jr., *Advertising* (New York: McGraw-Hill, 1971); Maurice I. Mandell, *Advertising* (Englewood Cliffs, N.J.: Prentice-Hall, 1968); John W. Crawford, *Advertising: Communications for Management* (New York: Allyn and Bacon, 1965); Otto Kleppner, *Advertising Procedure* (Englewood Cliffs, N.J.: Prentice-Hall, 1966);

C. A. Kirkpatrick, *Advertising* (Boston: Houghton Mifflin, 1964); Charles J. Dirksen and Arthur Kroeger, *Advertising Principles and Problems* (Homewood, Ill.: Irwin, 1968); Albert W. Frey, *Advertising* (New York: Ronald, 1970); Julian L. Simon, *The Management of Advertising* (Englewood Cliffs, N.J.: Prentice-Hall, 1971).

Four collections of readings are Wright and Warner, *Speaking of Advertising* (New York: McGraw-Hill, 1963); Sandage and Fryburger, *The Role of Advertising;* Arnold M. Barban and C. H. Sandage, *Readings in Advertising and Promotion Strategy* (Homewood, Ill.: Irwin, 1968); and S. Watson Dunn, *International Handbook of Advertising* (New York: McGraw-Hill, 1964), a guide to advertising abroad.

Media is the topic of Roger Barton, *Media in Advertising* (New York: McGraw-Hill, 1964); Leo Bogart, *Strategy in Advertising* (New York: Harcourt, Brace & World, 1967) and *Psychology in Media Strategy* (Chicago: American Marketing Association, 1966); and Leslie McClure and Paul Fulton, *Advertising in the Printed Media* (New York: Macmillan, 1964).

Copy writing is described by Aesop Glim (George Laflin Miller) in *Copy—The Core of Advertising* (New York: Dover, 1963) and *How Advertising Is Written—and Why* (1961); Hanley Norins, *The Compleat Copywriter* (New York: McGraw-Hill, 1966); Philip Ward Burton and G. Bowman Kreer, *Advertising Copywriting* (Englewood Cliffs, N.J.: Prentice-Hall, 1962); Clyde Bedell, *How to Write Advertising That Sells* (New York: McGraw-Hill, 1952), and S. Watson Dunn, *Advertising Copy and Communication* (New York: McGraw-Hill, 1956). Advertising production is explained in Thomas B. Stanley, *The Technique of Advertising Production* (New York: Prentice-Hall, 1954), and David Hymes, *Production in Advertising and the Graphic Arts* (New York: Holt, 1958). Both fields are covered in Hugh G. Wales, Dwight L. Gentry, and Max Wales, *Advertising Copy, Layout and Typography* (New York: Ronald, 1958).

Graphics and design: Arthur T. Turnbull and Russell N. Baird, *The Graphics of Communication: Typography, Layout, Design* (New York: Holt, Rinehart and Winston, 1968); Roy Paul Nelson, *The Design of Advertising* (Dubuque, Iowa: Wm. C. Brown, 1967); Edmund C. Arnold, *Ink on Paper* (New York: Harper & Row, 1963); Stephen Baker, *Advertising Layout and Art Direction* (New York: McGraw-Hill, 1959); Peter Croy, *Graphic Design and Reproduction Techniques* (New York: Hastings House, 1968); Carl Dair, *Design with Type* (Toronto: University of Toronto Press, 1967).

Advertising agencies: Roger Barton, *Advertising Agency Operations and Management* (New York: McGraw-Hill, 1955), is a practical guide.

Kenneth Groesbeck, *The Advertising Agency Business* (Chicago: Advertising Publications, 1964), is a compendium from the author's column in *Advertising Age,* covering all facets. Martin Mayer, *Madison Avenue, U.S.A.,* provides a good picture of advertising agencies. Ralph M. Hower, *The History of an Advertising Agency: N. W. Ayer & Son at Work, 1869–1939* (Cambridge, Mass.: Harvard University Press, 1939), is a documented history of one. David Ogilvy tells a fascinating story about life in an agency in *Confessions of an Advertising Man* (New York: Atheneum, 1963; paperback, Dell, 1964). The story of the pioneering Albert Lasker is told by John Gunther in *Taken at the Flood* (New York: Harper, 1960).

For books about newspaper advertising and television and radio advertising, see the bibliographies for chapters 9 and 10, respectively. The industrial advertising field is described in Fred R. Messner, *Industrial Advertising* (New York: McGraw-Hill, 1963); Roland B. Smith, *Advertising to Business* (Homewood, Ill.: Irwin, 1957); and Warren R. Dix, *Industrial Advertising for Profit and Prestige* (Pleasantville, N.Y.: Printers' Ink Books, 1956). Basic principles of direct mail are given in Edward N. Mayer Jr., *How to Make More Money with Your Direct Mail* (New York: Marketing Communications, 1961), and 300 examples of design techniques are presented in Raymond A. Ballinger, *Direct Mail Design* (New York: Reinhold, 1963).

*Chapter 17*
PUBLIC RELATIONS AND INFORMATION WRITING

The best book to read in exploring the public relations field is Scott M. Cutlip and Allen H. Center, *Effective Public Relations* (Englewood Cliffs, N.J.: Prentice-Hall, 1972).

Other general books include Bertrand R. Canfield and Frazier Moore, *Public Relations: Principles, Cases, and Problems* (Homewood, Ill.: Irwin, 1973); John Marston, *The Nature of Public Relations* (New York: McGraw-Hill, 1963); Gene Harlan and Alan Scott, *Contemporary Public Relations: Principles and Cases* (New York: Prentice-Hall, 1955); Roy L. Blumenthal, *The Practice of Public Relations* (New York: Macmillan, 1972); Charles S. Steinberg, *The Mass Communicators: Public Relations, Public Opinion, and Mass Media* (New York: Harper, 1958); J. Handly Wright and Byron H. Christian, *Public Relations in Management* (New York: McGraw-Hill, 1949); Louis B. Lundborg, *Public Relations in the Local Community* (New York: Harper, 1950); and Allen H. Center, *Public Relations Ideas in Action* (New

York: McGraw-Hill, 1957), which describes some 50 successful public relations projects. Otto Lerbinger and Albert J. Sullivan edited *Information, Influence & Communication: A Reader in Public Relations* (New York: Basic Books, 1965), focusing on research and theory.

Groups of public relations professionals contributed chapters for *Public Relations Handbook,* edited by Philip Lesly (Englewood Cliffs, N.J.: Prentice-Hall, 1967), and *Handbook of Public Relations,* edited by Howard Stephenson (Englewood Cliffs, N.J.: Prentice-Hall, 1960). A leading counselor, John W. Hill, tells his story in *The Making of a Public Relations Man* (New York: McKay, 1963). New York's practitioners are described by Irwin Ross in *The Image Merchants* (New York: Doubleday, 1959). Edward L. Bernays, in *Public Relations* (Norman: University of Oklahoma Press, 1952), presents a case-history type of discussion by a longtime practitioner. His memoirs are in *Biography of an Idea* (New York: Simon and Schuster, 1965). Ray E. Hiebert contributed the biography of another pioneer in his *Courtier to the Crowd: The Life Story of Ivy Lee* (Ames: Iowa State University Press, 1966). Alan R. Raucher traced early PR history in *Public Relations and Business 1900–1929* (Baltimore: The Johns Hopkins Press, 1968).

Publicity practices are described in James W. Schwartz, editor, *The Publicity Process* (Ames: Iowa State University Press, 1966); Clarence A. Schoenfeld, *Publicity Media and Methods* (New York: Macmillan, 1963); Stewart Harral, *Patterns of Publicity Copy* (Norman: University of Oklahoma Press, 1950); Herbert M. Baus, *Publicity in Action* (New York: Harper, 1954); and Howard Stephenson and Wesley F. Pratzner, *Publicity for Prestige and Profit* (New York: McGraw-Hill, 1953).

Among books on specialized subjects are Ray E. Hiebert and Carlton Spitzer, editors, *The Voice of Government* (New York: Wiley, 1968), with two dozen Washington information men discussing their work; James L. McCamy, *Government Publicity* (Chicago: University of Chicago Press, 1939); Benjamin Fine, *Educational Publicity* (New York: Harper, 1951); and Harold P. Levy, *Public Relations for Social Agencies* (New York: Harper, 1956). References for other areas may be found in Scott M. Cutlip, *A Public Relations Bibliography* (Madison: University of Wisconsin Press, 1965).

*Chapter 18*
MASS COMMUNICATIONS RESEARCH

The reader interested in this field can gain an impression of its scope and methods by examining *Introduction to Mass Communications Re-*

*search,* edited by Ralph O. Nafziger and David M. White (Baton Rouge: Louisiana State University Press, 1963). It has eight chapters by leading research specialists in journalism and mass communications.

A book which describes more varied types of journalism research is *An Introduction to Journalism Research,* edited by Ralph O. Nafziger and Marcus M. Wilkerson (Baton Rouge: Louisiana State University Press, 1949). Wilbur Schramm surveyed "Twenty Years of Journalism Research" in the Spring 1957 *Public Opinion Quarterly* while Allan Nevins discussed "American Journalism and Its Historical Treatment" in the Fall 1959 *Journalism Quarterly.*

Four books which introduce the reader to research methods are David M. White and Seymour Levine, *Elementary Statistics for Journalists* (New York: Macmillan, 1954); Charles H. Backstrom and Gerald D. Hursh, *Survey Research* (Evanston, Ill.: Northwestern University Press, 1963); at a more sophisticated level, Richard W. Budd, Robert K. Thorp, and Lewis Donohew, *Content Analysis of Communication* (New York: Macmillan, 1967), and Julian Simon, *Basic Research Methods in Social Science* (New York: Random House, 1969).

Advertising research methods are outlined in Daniel Starch, *Measuring Advertising Readership and Results* (New York: McGraw-Hill, 1966), and in Darrell Blaine Lucas and Steuart Henderson Britt, *Measuring Advertising Effectiveness* (New York: McGraw-Hill, 1963). A discussion of research opportunities in the newspaper area is found in Jack B. Haskins and Barry M. Feinberg, *Newspaper Publishers Look at Research* (Syracuse, N.Y.: Newhouse Communications Center, 1968).

Examples of mass communications research studies involving the media, which illustrate the range of the field, can be found in the *Journalism Quarterly* as follows: Gary C. Lawrence and David L. Grey, "Subjective Inaccuracies in Local News Reporting," Winter 1969; David E. Carter, "The Changing Face of *Life*'s Advertisements," Spring 1969; Donald L. Shaw, "News Bias and the Telegraph: A Study of Historical Change," Spring 1967; Christopher H. Sterling, "Decade of Development: FM Radio in the 1960s," Summer 1971; Peter Clarke, "Does Teen News Attract Boys to Newspapers?", Spring 1968; Lewis Donohew, "Communication and Readiness for Change in Appalachia," Winter 1967; Thomas H. Allen, "Mass Media Use Patterns in a Negro Ghetto," Autumn 1968; Guido H. Stempel III, "The Prestige Press Meets the Third Party Challenge," Winter 1969; Don R. Pember, "The 'Pentagon Papers' Decision," Autumn 1971; Bradley S. Greenberg and Hideya Kumata, "National Sample Predictors of Mass Media Use," Winter 1968; Robert N. Pierce, "Public Opinion and Press Opinion in Four Latin-

American Cities," Spring 1969; Leo Bogart, "Negro and White Media Exposure," Spring 1972.

Many of the references listed for Part I of this bibliography also are pertinent to this chapter, especially those dealing with effects, the communication process, and public opinion.

*Chapter 19*
MASS COMMUNICATIONS EDUCATION

The growth of journalism education is reviewed in Albert A. Sutton, *Education for Journalism in the United States from Its Beginning to 1940* (Evanston, Ill.: Northwestern University, 1945). *The Training of Journalists* (Paris: UNESCO, 1958) is a world-wide survey on the training of personnel for the mass media. Three American journalism educators wrote chapters: Norval Neil Luxon on recent curricular trends, Burton W. Marvin on education for journalism in the United States, and Harry Heath on radio and television journalism education.

Books about career opportunities include Herbert Brucker, *Journalist: Eyewitness to History* (New York: Macmillan, 1962); Edward W. Barrett, editor, *Journalists in Action* (New York: Channel Press, 1963), stories of 63 Columbia University journalism graduates; Leonard E. Ryan and Bernard Ryan Jr., *So You Want to Go into Journalism* (New York: Harper & Row, 1963); M. L. Stein, *Your Career in Journalism* (New York: Messner, 1965); George Johnson, *Your Career in Advertising* (New York: Messner, 1966).

Available in paperback are Arville Schaleben's *Your Future in Journalism,* Edward L. Bernays' *Your Future in Public Relations,* and *Your Future in Advertising* (New York: Popular Library, Inc., 355 Lexington Avenue, New York 10017; price 50 cents each).

Career information is available from the office of the Executive Secretary, Association for Education in Journalism, 425 Henry Mall, University of Wisconsin, Madison 53706. *Programs in Journalism* is available from the American Council on Education for Journalism, School of Journalism, University of Missouri, Columbia 65201.

Other pamphlets available are *Your Future in Daily Newspapers* (American Newspaper Publishers Association), *Broadcasting the News, Careers in Television,* and *Careers in Radio* (National Association of Broadcasters), *Magazines in the U.S.A.* (Magazine Publishers Association), *Careers in the Business Press* (American Business Press, Inc.), *Occupational Guide to Public Relations* (Public Relations Society of America), and *Careers Unlimited* (Theta Sigma Phi).

Quill & Scroll, University of Iowa, publishes annually *Careers in Journalism,* in magazine form. The Newspaper Fund, Inc., issues a *Journalism Scholarship Guide* annually.

Catalogues describing the curricular offerings of individual schools and departments of journalism are available upon request to the school or department concerned or to the registrar of the institution.

# INDEX